Witness
to a Century

Also by George Seldes

The Great Quotations

The Great Thoughts

Witness
to a
Century

Encounters With the Noted, the Notorious,
and the Three SOBs

George Seldes

Ballantine Books / New York

Grateful acknowledgment is made to the following for permission to print previously unpublished material:
Sigmund Freud Copyrights: a letter from Sigmund Freud to the author dated June 29, 1924. Used by permission of Sigmund Freud Copyrights.
Society of Authors: a postcard from George Bernard Shaw to the author. Copyright © 1987 The Trustees of the British Museum, the Governors and Guardians of the National Gallery of Ireland and Royal Academy of Dramatic Art. Used by permission of The Society of Authors on behalf of the George Bernard Shaw estate.

Grateful acknowledgment is made to the following for permission to reprint previously published material:
Franklin Roosevelt, Jr., Trustee: a letter from Eleanor Roosevelt to the author.
The Estate of Gilbert Seldes: selections from "E.E. & O (Excuses, Errors and Omissions)" by Gilbert Seldes.

Library of Congress Cataloging-in-Publication Data
Seldes, George, 1890–
Witness to a century
Includes index.
1. History, Modern—20th century—Miscellanea.
2. Interviews. 3. Biography—20th century. I. Title.
D412.S35   1987   909.82   86-47804
ISBN: 0-345-33181-8

Photo Research by Flavia Rando

Manufactured in the United States of America

First Edition: May 1987

10   9   8   7   6   5   4   3   2   1

To my Vermont neighbors
and other friends who have made
living alone possible.

Contents

〜〜〜〜

Part IV
Tribune Decade: Berlin to Baghdad

Part V
Trotsky, Lenin, Lenin's America

Part VI
Rome, Mussolini, and Fascism

Part VII
Damascus and Mexico via Chicago

Contents

Part XII
Through the Iron Curtain

Part XIII
In Our Time

Part XIV
And in Conclusion . . .

List of Photographs

~~~~~~~~~~~~~~~~~~~~~~~~~

After page 234.

After page 330.

An Unusual Disclaimer

In many states, notably New York, you cannot libel the dead.

In Congress, members can libel the living as well as the dead. These privileged persons fill the *Congressional Record* with libels, slanders, defamations (at times), and cannot be sued for libel.

In my view the States and Congress are both wrong. Telling the facts (or truth, if you wish) should be respected, for the departed as well as the living.

I do not subscribe to the cliché *de mortuis nil nisi bonum*. I favor the viewpoint of the great *Biographie Universelle de France*, whose motto is: "We owe respect to the living; to the dead nothing but truth." Truth, not libels.

An anecdote of a man is worth a volume of biography.

—Channing

Nor is it always in the most distinguished achievements that men's best virtues or vices may be best discovered; but very often an action of small note, a short saying, or a jest, shall distinguish a person's real character more than the greatest sieges, or the most important battles . . . .

—Plutarch

Introduction

"So Many Interesting People . . ."

I t is now nearly eighty years since the morning of February 9, 1909, when I was hired for $3.50 a week—apologetically called "lunch money"—as a cub reporter on the Pittsburgh *Leader*. Apprenticeship under City Editor Houston Eagle and his assistant, Harold Thirlkeld, prepared me for the journey to New York, considered by Americans if not all Europeans the capital of world journalism, then London, Paris, the press department of General Pershing's army, a decade with the *Chicago Tribune* Foreign News Service with Berlin to Baghdad as my field, and then five decades of writing books and publishing magazine articles and a weekly newsletter, all in whole or part a criticism of the press.

Nineteen hundred and nine probably marked the peak of the great muckraking era, which was dominated by Lincoln Steffens, Ida Tarbell, Ray Stannard Baker and Will Irwin. Irwin in 1911 published the first series of articles in America criticizing, even exposing, the newspapers of his time. In 1920, Upton

Sinclair, an outsider to journalism, wrote *The Brass Check,* the first book exposing the press. It was this book, plus a friendship with the author lasting many years, that influenced me and the books I wrote on the press, beginning in the 1930s.

The last years of that decade internationally witnessed one of the most outrageous newspaper campaigns of falsehood in modern history; it influenced the leaders of many governments, notably Britain, France and the United States, and it resulted in the destruction of the liberal, democratic Republic of Spain. Only one head of state of the time, Franklin Delano Roosevelt, had the courage, later, to admit his own error. For me that decade also witnessed the success of the major advertising agencies of Madison Avenue in destroying the integrity of the proposed first popular illustrated American weekly "one step left of center." It was to have had two press columns by me, one reporting suppressed news, one of press criticism; and it was to have supported liberal causes such as the Spanish Republic against Naziism and Fascism. But Madison Avenue said "No."

The failure of this magazine, of which I was the only "working" editor, was directly responsible for my starting the newsletter *In fact* in 1940, then totally boycotted by the media, now recognized as the first publication in America, probably in the world, devoted entirely to press criticism.

In 1950 *In fact* was red-baited to death by the McCarthyites, who rode top saddle in the nation's press in those days. The Senator had been exposed as a crook, but exposés by the Madison *Capital Times, In fact,* and liberal but small-circulation weeklies were ineffective. McCarthy, despite great press support, finally virtually defeated himself.

In the 1960s and notably in the 1970s, it seems to me, a change so gradual it escaped the notice of both its friends and critics at the time came over the great all-powerful American press, so that probably for the first time in the two-hundred-year history of the Republic it began to serve one of the Constitutional objectives for which the nation was founded—the general welfare of the American people. The name "Watergate" means many things to many people. For me it means not merely the work of two *Washington Post* investigative reporters in unearthing a scandal that destroyed (or should have destroyed) a crook who happened to be President, but the commitment of that paper as well as the influential *New York Times,* the Los Angeles *Times* and many others to the purpose for which all papers are supposedly dedicated, namely, to publish all the news.

Not that ideal utopian journalism has arrived. But we have come a long way from Will Irwin's 1910, ladies and gentlemen! Watergate is an imaginary pennant flying over an imaginary institution called "freedom of the press," a phrase that means, or should mean, not only the right of the owners to publish without government control or Moron Majority censorship, but the right of the buyer of a paper to read hitherto suppressed news, such as the Federal Trade Commission fraud orders against bad medicine, bad automobiles and cancer-causing cigarets.

"I am a firm believer in the people," said Mr. Lincoln; "if given the truth, they can be depended upon to meet any national crisis. The great point is to bring them the real facts."

This reporter believes that the time has come for him to conclude his job with a personal anecdotal-historical review of his past seventy-seven years—not another criticism of the press but the "human-interest story," sometimes the "inside" story, sometimes a correction of the falsifications of history-in-the-making as witnessed by the writer, sometimes just Mr. Lincoln's "real facts" about people who have made history, as well as the front page—the noted, the notorious and, unfortunately, encounters with at least three of the leading SOBs of our time.

George Seldes
Hartland-4-Corners, Vermont
Spring 1986

Part I

The Muckraking
Era

Chapter 1

First Encounter With the Press

My first encounter with the American press, more than eighty years ago, was unforgettable and probably determined me to be a newspaperman. My brother, Gilbert, and I were farm boys; in summer we hoed and dug potatoes and picked strawberries at one cent a quart—the selling price was eight or nine cents at nearby Wallabout Market in Philadelphia. In autumn we joyfully skipped school to pick grapes, which Grandfather sold to a man named Charlie Welch, the inventor of alcohol-free wine he called grape juice. This, our only crop, brought us three hundred dollars a year, which, plus the $16.66 we earned every month by keeping the fourth-class post office in the family, made us one of the more affluent families in Alliance, New Jersey.

Father, who had failed to turn the farm colony into a small Utopia, had gone to Philadelphia after Gilbert and I were born. He got a job in a drugstore, so he could add to the family income, and studied law at night. Eventually he was put into the drugstore business with the help of friendly doctors and a mortgage, but the post office remained in the hands first of my mother, who died when I was six, and then my aunt, Father's sister, a head nurse at a small Philadelphia hospital whom father persuaded to sacrifice her career and go to the farm.

In 1905 there was a revolutionary uprising in St. Petersburg, the first armed attempt to overthrow the Tsar of Russia. Father, who was a libertarian, an idealist, a freethinker, a Deist, a Utopian, a Single Taxer, and a worshipper of Thoreau and Emerson, was also a joiner of all noble causes, and one of them was called Friends of Russian Freedom, of which he was either one of the founders or the secretary.

By coincidence that year the annual summer week or fortnight vacation Gilbert and I got in Philadelphia took place during the days of the Russian uprising, and all Philadelphia newspapers rushed to father's drugstore to get "the local angle," as they called it. (How important the local angle is I learned years later when I read that a man named Bonfils, owner of a Denver newspaper, frequently said to his staff, "Remember that a dog fight on Champa Street is a bigger story for us than three thousand [or it may have been 300,000] Chinese drowned in a typhoon".)

We were having breakfast in the living room back of the laboratory when the press began to arrive, one on every streetcar. And they wasted no time. The uprising, they told Father, was a failure; it had been betrayed by its leader, a certain Father Gapon; the revolutionists had been dispersed, arrested, perhaps shot—so what did the Friends of Russian Freedom think of it and what were the Friends going to do now?

Shocked as Father was by the latest news, which had not yet appeared in print, he quite naturally told the reporters that the movement to overthrow the Tsar would go on and that the Friends of Russian Freedom would become more active than before. A conventional reply. But this is just what the reporters wanted to hear, it would make a good story, and they rushed to the telephones. To my great surprise I heard them quoting Father verbatim. A country boy of fifteen, I had imagined reporters creating masterpieces and brilliantly improving upon everything that came to their attention. And then I heard one reporter without stopping for breath shout over the telephone:

"Next item. There was a unique spectacular fire this morning all along Carpenter Street—more spectacular than dangerous—when washing that had been hung out and dried on one tenement house roof somehow caught fire, spread from line to line, then jumped to the clothes lines of the adjoining house, and then the next, and so on down the whole block, so that it seemed as if the whole street was on fire, and thousands of people came running from every direction, and everyone said he or she had never seen anything like that in their lives."

We waited anxiously for the evening papers, which I soon learned were published before noon, and sure enough I learned my first great lesson in news values: Carpenter Street Fire, with a photograph and headline, was on the front page, while the interview with father was a follow-up, or as I later learned to call it, a "shirt-tail," to the whole Russian revolution, now reduced to page three.

And just a year later, by another coincidence, Gilbert and I were again having our vacation in the city, when a taxi arrived with Maksim Gorki, his common-law wife or companion, Mme. Andreyeva, the greatest Russian actress of the time, and all their belongings. Gorki had come to America sponsored by a group of leading writers headed by Mark Twain. His purpose was to make a lecture tour on behalf of both the imprisoned and free leaders of the previous year's uprising, and to continue the movement to overthrow the Tsar. The American group had arranged for Gorki to stay at the best hotels, but it knew nothing about Mme. Andreyeva until the Russian Embassy or consulate issued a statement to the press denouncing the couple for living together without a marriage license. The famous Philadelphia hotel immediately threw the couple into the street, bag and baggage, and— as Father later told us, Gorki had said to him: "But why did they have to steal my watch?" Gorki fortunately had known of the organization Friends of Russian Freedom, had planned to visit them, knew Father's address, and so found refuge for a while. And Father was again in the newspapers, and Gilbert and I had to give up the guest room.

And, within a day or two, there was more news. This time it was a long-distance dispute between Father and Mark Twain, who, interviewed by a great news service, tried to make a joke of the whole affair, saying of the unmarried notable Russian writer, "Why, that man might just as well have appeared in public in his shirt-tail." (One paper said "galluses.") This statement outraged another leading sponsor of the Gorki trip, Edgar Lee Masters, who in the press chided Mr. Clemens for using this opportunity for a witticism and thus further helping to make Gorki's trip to America a failure.

I do not think Alla Nazimov and her friend and dramatic teacher Paul Orlenov stayed at Father's house, but they were there every day during their first months in America and I do remember my stepmother giving Alla Nazimov her first English lessons. I remember Orlenov coming to speak to Father long after Miss Nazimov stopped showing up, and I soon enough learned why. She had succeeded in landing a contract with the Schuberts to appear as Nora in *A Doll's House,* provided she master the English language in time for the season openings. The Schuberts found my stepmother's English instruction too slow; they got the actress a room in a nice hotel and hired a specialist who knew many tricks and guaranteed his work. And first of all the Schuberts changed the actress's name to Nazimova for reasons of euphony. (Father later explained to us that the Russian *ov* meant an unmarried woman; a married woman took her husband's name and added an *a* at the end—therefore unmarried Alla Nazimov could not possibly be Alla Nazimova, except on the Schubert Theatre marquee and in their playbills.) Nazimova's Nora was one of the historic theatre successes of the century.

When Aunt Bertha left her nursing job to come to Alliance, she shocked the entire community by blowing smoke through a cigaret. It looked to them as if she were smoking, and at that time none but street women and occupants of bordellos really smoked. And so the emancipated women, the votes-for-women advocates, took up the cigaret as a sign of emancipation.

Our grandparents also had a considerable part in our upbringing; Grandfather was one of the few really educated men in the colony, but Grandmother was illiterate. She could not read or even write her own name, but she was a brilliant storyteller and her fairy tales rivaled those of the Brothers Grimm—one that involved the royal peacocks which swallowed all the king's treasury of gold pieces I remember to this day. But in almost every one of Grandmother's tales there were wicked witches and wicked stepmothers, and in the course of the years all the witches were stepmothers and all the stepmothers witches, and my brother and I from our infancy hated the idea of ever living with one of them; and although father did not marry a second time until I was twelve and Gilbert nine and one-half, Gilbert never lived with our stepmother and I did for only a short time, probably less than two years while I was preparing to get a job so that I could leave home. Many years later when I was mature and objective enough, I realized that Father's second wife was a very fine woman, educated, cultured, a modernist, kind-hearted, and an excellent friend and companion for my father to whom we should have been grateful for making his life livable, and perhaps at times even happy.

Again, it was not until my brother and I grew up and began to think that we realized we had an extraordinary father. It is true we saw very little of him—he came to the farm one or two times a month, and we had only a week or two each year with him in the city—but I do remember how he guided our education, and many of the activities in which he engaged during his lifetime. (He died in 1931.)

First of all, Father insisted that we not waste our time reading Alger and Henty and rags-to-riches "boys' books" and popular novels, but read books of some value, frequently a little beyond our understanding. We were told to begin making a library as soon as we were able to buy books, or to suggest good books to relatives who sent birthday presents. Father would say, "Don't waste your time reading a book that you will never look at again. Read books that you will reread—and that you will never outgrow. When you are older you will not hesitate to underline lines, whole chapters, you believe to be the most important ideas or thoughts in these books—do not be afraid to write in the margins. All this world's civilization is to be found between the covers of books."

In all the hundred or more homes of the colonists at Alliance at this time I do not think there was a book in more than four or five. In Alliance there were perhaps three persons who had what might be called a library and one was our cousin, S. S. Bailey, the town "philosopher." I can still remember after, say, seventy-five years Farmer Bailey walking the road, pasturing his cow, which he led by a long cord in his left hand, while in his right he held up and read a book, either Kant or Spinoza. Kant and Spinoza! Gilbert and I knew at least their names many long years before we would be able to understand a word of their writings.

When we grew up, we realized that Father was a member of that rare minority anywhere in the world of educated, cultured and civilized human beings. He was a freethinker and resented being called a heretic or an agnostic and sometimes even an atheist. He frequently told us he believed in the last seven of the Ten Commandments—he did not believe in a jealous god who visited the sins of the fathers upon generations of children—and he believed in the Sermon on the Mount. "That is all that is necessary to rule the world," he once said.

He was not always successful in what he believed were good ideas. He opposed the inculcation of religion in children too young to understand it. When they were grown up enough to begin thinking for themselves they could study all the great religions and make a choice: some might prefer to be Buddhists, rather than Protestants, Catholics or Jews. And so Gilbert and I, brought up without a formal religion, remained throughout our lifetimes just what Father was, freethinkers. And, likewise, doubters and dissenters and perhaps Utopians. Father's rule had been, "Question everything, take nothing for granted," and I never outlived it, and I would suggest it be made the motto of a world journalists' association.

In the matter of learning foreign languages I think Father's rule was right. He could read eleven, speak eight and write at least five correctly. He insisted that my brother and I speak no foreign language until we were in high school or even later because he maintained that a bilingual person never loses a foreign accent in either language, including that of his native land.

As for Utopia in Alliance, New Jersey, Father found he could get no followers except in community affairs, such as a wagon journey he organized to Salem, the county seat, where he told Congressman Wood that the colony needed roads and a schoolhouse capable of seating all its children: roads and a schoolhouse, or at least two hundred Republican votes would go to the Democratic Party candidate come next election. Father got roads and a two-story schoolhouse. He also got something he did not expect. Congressman Wood, having realized that the ignorant farmers had learned something about the power of the ballot, arrived with his henchmen just before the next election and distributed two one-dollar bills to every voter they could find, always at the same time reminding the takers that the Republican Party was the friend of the farmer.

When Father heard of this in Philadelphia, he was very angry with his fellow Utopians. He came to Alliance, called a meeting, told them never to touch political money again, and begged that each man turn over his two dollars to his proposed public library. But two dollars was a powerful sum of money in those days, no library was built, and the Baileys and Seldeses remained two of the four or five families that had a book.

Not only was Father unable to establish Utopia, but he could not get the farmers to cooperate in buying some of the new and marvelous machines that were taking the misery and drudgery out of farm life. It was not until Father was free even of his drugstore that he was able to help found or join in one after another of the Utopian colonies that sprang up in the eastern states after the turn of the century. There were Mohegan Colony, and Stelton, and Mt. Airy in which he lived for a time; they were in New York State and in New Jersey. The fourth Utopia was named Belle Terre by Father, but I do not think he ever succeeded in establishing it; I do know that he wrote a charter, its main point, if I remember rightly, aimed at preventing the Communists from ganging up and taking control and ruining the colony as father said they had done in all colonies to which he had ever belonged.

So far as I remember, Karl Marx—the man who more than any other changed the course of twentieth-century history—was never mentioned or worshipped by Father and his closest friend, Harry Kelly, and his fellow Utopians. Thoreau and Emerson and Wendell Phillips were their teachers—and idols. They believed with Thoreau that "that government is best which governs least," and least government was the subject of Father's correspondence with both Count Tolstoy and Prince Kropotkin. Naturally enough these followers of Thoreau were labeled anarchists not only by outsiders but by most of their fellow Utopians at Mohegan, Mt. Airy and Stelton.

One of my earliest memories was Father asking me, on one of his weekend trips to Alliance, to help him go through the tons of papers, the records that post offices were required to keep for a number of years, of every transaction made during the year, in a search for the Tolstoy and Kropotkin letters he had received, which were to guide him and his friends in the various colonies. I was to give Father all letters with foreign stamps on them, and certain letters in foreign languages I could not understand. We collected a score or more of Tolstoy's and of Kropotkin's.

What eventually happened to these priceless documents? Many years later, during the late 1907–February 1909 period in which I lived in my father's house in Pittsburgh, the immigrant girl my stepmother employed for at least one day a week was preparing as usual to boil the laundry. When she found a leak in the wash boiler, she looked around and spotted another large metal container that would do temporarily. She got rid of all the papers it contained by throwing them into the stove to hasten the water's boiling. And that was the end of many immortal words written by two of the great men of Father's time. All Father could do was to try to say in his own words what he remembered—for example, on the subject of mutual aid, he quoted Kropotkin writing on the management of a colony with "a theory of life and conduct under which society is conceived without government—harmony in such a society being obtained not by submission to law, or obedience to any authority, but by free agreements, freely constituted for the sake of production and consumption, as also for the infinite variety of needs and aspirations of a civilized being." (Kropotkin repeated parts of what he had written to Father in his contribution entitled "Anarchism" in the eleventh edition of the *Britannica*. This article set the Tsarist police after him and he fled to Switzerland.) Tolstoy, Father said, in several of his letters pleaded for "the revival of the pure and ideal philosophy of primitive Christianity."

My Pittsburgh years in Father's house were based on his view, probably incorrect, that his sons would never be able to enter a college with a diploma from a small-town high school such as Vineland's. He wanted us to have our senior year in a big city. Gilbert left almost immediately after our arrival, went to Philadelphia, rejoined Aunt Bertha, went to Central High, got a scholarship to Harvard and a grant of five hundred dollars and eventually graduated with honors. But I, not being a very bright boy, was asked to retake the junior year at the Pittsburgh high school, so I rebelled and went to work in the drugstore. I became an excellent soda jerk and eventually a qualified assistant pharmacist; I could fill prescriptions, but I was not allowed to touch the cabinet containing the "dangerous" drugs.

Incidentally, Father told me he had bought the drugstore at 1812 Center Avenue, corner of Roberts Street, from an honest Connecticut Yankee named Harley who assured him he would easily make fifty dollars a day clear profit—a fortune in those days—and if he did not, he, Harley, would buy back the store.

On the first day when Father opened the doors at 6:00 A.M., he was surprised to find a lineup of thirty or more shabbily dressed men who came crowding into the store, each one banging a silver dollar or half dollar on the counter and pointing to a drawer behind it marked SOD. Bicarb. Father opened the innocent drawer and there found two neat rows of powders prepared by Mr. Harley, the left row marked "Heroin 50¢ " and the right "Cocaine $1." Father was shocked. He drove the mob out of the store and told its members never to come again.

And then nothing happened. No one came to the drugstore. No one came to have a prescription filled, no one came to buy five cents' worth of castor oil. Apparently this drugstore was known far and wide as a dope joint, and the neighborhood shunned it. Instead of making a fortune, Father did not make a cent.

In desperation he called on the doctors of nearby Passavant Hospital and on the many doctors with offices on Center Avenue to explain the situation. Rather hesitatingly they began to send patients to him, and by the time Gilbert and I arrived the laboratory and the living room behind it had become an intellectual center, a meeting place of the best doctors, an oasis of civilization in what was then known as "the Hill District" of Pittsburgh.

Chapter 2

~~~~~~~~~~~~~~

Bryan, Theodore Roosevelt, Andrew Mellon

I
t is now more than three quarters of a century since that
morning of February 9, 1909, when I walked into the editorial
office of the Pittsburgh *Leader* and said I wanted to be a reporter.
There was no vacancy, I was told, but if I would care to stay on
awhile and learn, they would give me $3.50 a week for lunch
money. I stayed on.

The long stay in my father's house had not cured me of my
childhood hatred of witches and stepmothers, and besides, newspaper adventures still appealed to my farm-boy mind as the
greatest of all callings.

And then in 1909 and 1910 it all came true: imagine it, a
country boy, with not even a high school diploma, just turned
twenty, being sent to interview William Jennings Bryan; to be
for a whole day with the greatest man of the time, Theodore
Roosevelt; and to report the divorce case of the richest man in
town, one of the billionaires of the world, Andrew W. Mellon.
On each of these occasions I thought I had reached the zenith,

the perihelion of journalism; it could not then enter my mind that in two cases the press—and that meant all public opinion—considered my heroes as more or less has-beens, and in the third instance there was no intention ever to print my reports—but instead perhaps to use them for financial, or blackmailing, purposes.

My First Hero: Bryan

In his three campaigns for the Presidency Bryan had become known as "the silver-tongued orator," "the Tiberius Gracchus of the West," who "spoke for the wage-laborer, the country lawyer, the cross-roads merchant, the farmer and the miner." He was a populist, and he had become famous when, in a speech at a Democratic national convention in which he had intended to nominate someone for President, he had concluded with the words that still echo in American history: "You shall not press down upon the brow of labor the crown of thorns. You shall not crucify mankind upon a cross of gold."

But "great" as Mr. Bryan may have appeared to a large part of the world—a "great man," said Disraeli, was "one who affects his generation"—to my city editor in 1910 he was merely a politician who got licked three times. "Ask him if he is going to run for President again," said Mr. Eagle, and he laughed and named the hotel.

There was no difficulty getting to see my first hero. The surprise was that at about 11:00 A.M.—our first "evening" edition already on the streets—Bryan was still in bed. Not being a trained reporter, knowing nothing about the diplomacy of interviewing, I began by naming my paper, the Pittsburgh *Leader,* and doing exactly what I had been instructed to do.

"Mr. Bryan," I said, "do-you-intend-to-run-for-President-a-fourth-time?"

Even before I had finished my question William Jennings Bryan, clad in a one-piece Yeager suit of yellowish-gray spotty woolly underwear, neck to wrists to ankles, flap in front and back, heaved from his bed and shouted, "Out! Out! You impudent cub!"

He seemed to rush at me. I fled.

Now, one of the first good newspaper stories a cub hears is about the stupid reporter who came back from his assignment and said, "No story. There was no ascension. Balloon blew up. Everyone killed." And yet, I acted just as stupidly.

"He didn't answer," I told Mr. Eagle. "Just got out of bed and threw me out."

"Did he hit you?" asked my city editor eagerly.

"No. Just shoved me through the door." I described the scene.

"Great," said Mr. Eagle. "Write it. Don't forget the one-piece woolen underwear. Don't forget the flap in front and the flap in back. And the edgings at the neck, wrists and ankles."

I wrote it. Our main edition, the night edition, came out at 3:00 P.M. It was the first time I had ever made the front page. But there it was, unsigned but somewhat enlarged by Mr. Eagle, with a four-column headline:

BRYAN ASSAULTS LEADER REPORTER

A Day With T.R.

Sometime later that same year I got my greatest assignment; I was to travel for one day with a man whose "greatness" was never questioned by friend or enemy. I do not now remember what front-page news Theodore Roosevelt made in Pittsburgh in 1910 but I was already journalistically wise enough to know why a big newspaper—one of the very few supporting a third party, and the only one in Pittsburgh—could afford to send a half-trained reporter (me) to cover so great an event. The speech was made in the evening—hours after our night edition was on the streets—and this meant extra work, and needless to say no extra pay, and all the old-timers hated these assignments. Moreover, as I learned the next morning, the city editor had the speech in advance, as well as the morning papers to copy, and all I had to do was write what was known in the trade as "local color."

However, there was an unforeseen complication: T.R. spoke from one of several large balconies of the Monongahela House, facing a vast open space leading to the river, now crowded with tens of thousands of uproarious citizens. The reporters were with T.R. But the camera crews with their explosive flashlight powder were on the next balcony, and it so happened that being the youngest, I was pushed away from the center by the other newspapermen. When the photographs were developed, the person nearest the camera (me, not T.R.) came out biggest of all. As I could not be scissored out, the pictures appeared in all seven papers, morning and evening, with a large figure in the foreground, retouched, bearded, an unidentified old man. Even my own newspaper disowned me.

The notes, which I had written frantically, trying to keep up with T.R.—no newspaperman in those years used shorthand—were thrown into the wastebasket, but my report on the lights, the crowds, the words most enthusiastically applauded did appear in print. Mr. Roosevelt was not yet officially a candidate on the Bull Moose or Progressive Party ticket, but no one who heard him doubted that he would run or that he was actually running. He was as usual denouncing the trusts (without of course naming them) and advocating better laws favoring the working man, and more democracy—everything that made him then a dangerous radical in the Republican Party press. He also favored a graduated income tax, which was the idea and almost the exact words of two real radicals I did not hear of until I became Berlin correspondent of the *Chicago Tribune* in the 1920s—Karl Marx and Friedrich Engels in their Communist Manifesto of 1848.

Moreover, in Pittsburgh the day I spoiled the photographs, and the next day when I was permitted to accompany T.R. on the first of his three-day swing in our tri-state territory (the Pittsburgh corner of Pennsylvania, a part of West Virginia and a part of Ohio), the great trust-buster and the alleged hero of San Juan Hill became also my hero.

How heroic a figure Theodore Roosevelt was then, and how corrupt the age, can hardly be imagined now. T.R., Bryan the populist, Senator Robert La Follette of the Progressive Party and Eugene Debs the Socialist rose to national leadership almost simultaneously with the great movement that revolutionized American journalism (although in its time, the early years of the century, it was the magazine medium and not the daily newspaper that dared to investigate and expose the almost universal corruption).

Muckraking is given only one decade, 1902 to 1912, by various later historians, dating from three articles in the January 1903 issue of *McClure's*. The rival claimants to the title "first muckraker" were Ida M. Tarbell and Lincoln Steffens. Both began their investigations years earlier, Miss Tarbell in 1897 on Standard Oil, "the mother of trusts," and Steffens on boss rule in the major cities—"Tweed Days in St. Louis" was the first of his series—in 1902.

The muckrakers not only exposed the "vested interests," the "money power" and the "ruling families" but named them. T.R. did not. The other radicals—Bryan, La Follette and Debs— failed to win the Presidency, and Mark Hanna thought he had disposed forever of the fourth radical, T.R., by burying him in the Vice Presidency. The "bullet coming from the west," which had been predicted in a Hearst editorial, made T.R. President in 1901, and Mark Hanna called him publicly "that damned cowboy in the White House." In 1904 T.R. seemed to have no difficulty being nominated and elected, and two years later, for reasons then unknown and unprobed, he made a famous speech that turned Bunyan's good word "muckraking" into one of the most pejorative words in the English language.

The Mellon Divorce Hearing

Late in 1910, the year I graduated from my teens in September, I was assigned to report the Mellon divorce case, which was soon to become one of the great newspaper sensations of the era—but not in Pittsburgh, where it was totally suppressed in the Republican, Democratic and self-styled independent newspapers, and even the generally accepted liberal weeklies. Whether this news was used for blackmail, I cannot truthfully say, but surely it was not a mere coincidence that the *Dispatch,* the most respectable of the morning journals, shortly afterwards blossomed with page advertisements for not only the Mellon bank but other Mellon enterprises.

The son of the owner of one of the largest department stores believed that, like medieval lords who had "the right of the first night" with the bride of every one of his serfs, he had the right to rape every pretty salesgirl. When I reported his court hearing, my city editor for the first time in my life gave me a sheet of carbon paper and said to make a copy. I made it. It was sent immediately to the business department. It was not printed. However, within a few days the *Leader,* along with all other papers, printed double that department store's advertising every Sunday. The price per page, so we were told, had also gone up. Not one Pittsburgh newspaper ever mentioned this rape story.

How rich Andrew Mellon was the day I saw him in court I do not know, but with the bank, Alcoa, Koppers, and even a nationally known whiskey called Old Grandad, he was rated in the hundreds of millions. Today the Mellon family is said to be the richest in the country, its wealth estimated at five billion dollars.

My first surprise in the divorce courtroom was to find myself the only reporter present. (Why waste a reporter's time when there was no intention to have him write anything or to publish anything?) My next was to see the leading lawyer of Pittsburgh, Rody P. Marshall, in friendly conversation with his rival, William Blakely, formerly known as "the fearless prosecuting attorney of Allegheny County." Mellon had hired not only these two stars, but also the former governor of Pennsylvania, a man named Stone, and a half dozen others of almost equal prominence—in other words Mellon, who had a monopoly on aluminum and other commodities, now had a monopoly on legal talent in Pittsburgh, and his wife, Nora Mullen Mellon, had to find a noted Philadelphia lawyer, Paul Ache, to represent her.

Although present-day book writers credit Ache with breaking the so-called conspiracy of silence about the most sensational divorce trial of the century, I am certain that the Philadelphia *North American* got its tip and its first story from the Pittsburgh News Bureau, a one-man outfit flourishing on the sale abroad of the almost daily suppressed Pittsburgh news. The News Bureau was John Goldstrom, a colleague and friend of mine to whom I, and other reporters young enough in the profession still to feel shame about its lack of ethics, gave the news gratis and enjoyed seeing the items published elsewhere.

Although the Mellon divorce case was headlined in New York and other cities, only the *North American* had the enterprise to ship in bundles of hundreds of copies for sale in our fair city— but the moment the Mellon forces heard about it, they created another sensational news item: they sent the Pittsburgh police into the streets by the dozens, the papers were grabbed, the newsboys clubbed, their property destroyed. The next day's bundles were bought up at the railroad station. All copies that escaped confiscation changed hands easily at one dollar each.

Nor was clubbing of newsboys the only illegal action sponsored by the Mellons. When the *North American* reporter arrived, I gave him my notes and he wrote a thousand-word story, which he sent press-rate collect, as usual. It was suppressed by Western Union. He tried the rival company, Postal Telegraph, and again he could not get through. Both great national services deliberately violated the law at Mellon insistence. But even the Mellon hundred-million-dollar fortune could not stop telephonic communication, and this is how the *North American* got through.

The third Mellon illegality was having a law passed by the State of Pennsylvania legislature ending the right of jury trial in divorce cases. Divorces became secret; they could be held in a judge's chambers or before a referee. The vote in favor was 168 to 0—the name of the bill's sponsor was Rep. John Scott. It was signed immediately by Governor Tener.

Said the *North American* editorially: "This act robs a wife of her constitutional right of a jury trial. Friends of Mrs. Mellon . . . fear the new law is a demonstration of Mellon's skill in noiseless, effective methods in all his undertakings."

There was a secret hearing. Mellon won his divorce. The Scott law was then declared unconstitutional. But whenever anyone called at the prothonotary's office, lawyer or reporter, to examine the legal papers on file, he was told they were out, they had been mislaid, they were somehow unavailable. They may have been destroyed.

In July 1911, three months after the passage of the Scott law, six months after Mellon began his suit, Will Irwin, one of the original muckrakers, in his series "The American Newspaper," in *Collier's*, then rightly known as "the national weekly," published his chapter on Cincinnati and Pittsburgh. He told all of us who worked for the seven dailies how ignorant we were of their ownership and control, he showed us that all our papers were corrupt, he stated categorically that, in Pittsburgh at least, "freedom of the press" was nonexistent.

Of our seven dailies the public may or may not have known that two were actually owned by a bank—Mr. Mellon's chief rival, the Farmers National—and two others belonged to Senator George T. Oliver. All four followed the fortunes and decisions of the Republican Party and the biggest of Big Business.

T. Hart Given's Farmers National actually sent a vice president named Arthur Braun, whom I hated the several years I worked for the *Post*, to censor all the news in that paper and the evening *Sun*. The sacred cows and golden calves of the two Given and two Oliver papers were money, power, business, the G.O.P.

But Irwin's revelations about the three self-styled "independent" dailies were the real shock to their editorial employees. The *Dispatch*, which we thought the best of the seven, Irwin disclosed as secretly in the clutches of the Mellon banks, the Frick interests and the Pennsylvania Railroad.

As for the *Press*, the supposedly "liberal" paper, its owner, Colonel Oliver P. Hershmann, wrote Irwin, was a friend of the two city bosses, Flynn and Magee. "Gang-established, gang-favored," Irwin concluded, "the *Press* was of no use for the purposes of reform."

The Pittsburgh *Leader*. My paper. When John Nevin owned

it, Irwin wrote, "it fought for a better Pittsburgh. When Nevin died, his descendants sold it to Alexander Pollock Moore, who was backed by William Flynn, the old joint boss with Christopher Magee, a contractor . . . grown rich on city jobs. Moore had always been associated with the gang. . . . " This was a reference to the great national scandal known as "The Pittsburgh Graft Cases."

Many years later, in Berlin for the *Chicago Tribune,* I read the final revelations in the case of the now deceased Pittsburgh *Leader.* In the list of holders of bonds worth a total of $503,000, the two most important were:

> Union Trust Company (Mellon) . . . $188,000
> Union Savings Bank (Mellon) . . . $172,000

Chapter 3

~~~~~~~~

"The Divine Sarah,"
"Red Emma," and Others

The best of all possible worlds for a beginner reporter in my time and probably at all times, was and is the small city. In a metropolis chances were small; in a country town there may be notable experiences. Looking backward, I think my Pittsburgh apprenticeship, 1909–1916, was ideal, years bulging with great names, noteworthy events.

The explanation for my getting the opening-night tickets for the "last" or "final" or "positively last final" farewell appearance of the actress universally known as the "greatest in the world," Sarah Bernhardt, is quite simple. No one wanted them. In those journalistic days everything damned by the word "highbrow" was the subject of laughter in the city rooms of all seven papers, the word "culture" was pejorative, the word "art"—in a city that held an international exhibit every two years—joined four-letter unprintable words. Not one evening paper in my time ever mentioned a book. If there was a college graduate among my hundred or more fellow reporters, he kept his sin a secret.

22

And so every Monday Mr. Eagle would hand out the theatre
tickets, Pittsburgh and visiting orchestra tickets, tickets for
famous lecturers and for recitals by, among others, Rubinstein,
Ysaye, Nordica, Melba and Schumann-Heinck, and I would get
them all. What the rest of the staff fought for were the baseball
tickets, the tickets for the fights, for all sporting events, and the
Gayety and the Grand—the one showing burlesque, the other
vaudeville. At the two legitimate theaters, the Nixon and the
Alvin, I remember seeing Richard Mansfield, at least three
Barrymores, Forbes-Robertson in *Romeo and Juliet,* Richard Bennett
in *Damaged Goods,* and even James O'Neill, the ham-actor father
of the great playwright Eugene O'Neill; and best of all, the
Divine Sarah.

"Talk to the theatre manager—not to her," Mr. Eagle
instructed me, "and find out if she has her coffin with her—or if
it's only a press agent yarn."

Opening night tickets were for *L'Aiglon.* I wanted to see all
seven Bernhardt performances, but evening newspapers did not
rate more than two tickets for opening night, gallery prices had
gone sky-high, and although my pay was now eight dollars a
week, I could not afford it. Fortunately the Nixon needed more
ushers, and I had a friend who made extra money ushering, so
he got me one of the two jobs. I gave my tickets to my father
and ushered all week for Sarah Bernhardt.

It was an opening night to remember forever. The curtain
went up to disclose an almost empty stage that the program said
represented the battlefield of a famous Napoleonic victory. The
Divine Sarah, dressed in a Napoleonic uniform, the youthful son
of the great soldier—she was now well into her sixties and
always opened with *L'Aiglon* to prove her youthfulness—walked
across the wasteland and filled it with her sublime voice, uttering—yes, "uttering"—the one word, twice: "Wagram! Wagram!"

I can hear it now. The word "Wagram" seemed to penetrate the minds and bodies of everyone in the audience—a sort
of shock wave—and the great Bernhardt, apparently aware of its
effect, said nothing more for a long time; she neither spoke nor
moved until the spell was broken.

It was a wonderful week for me. I was present every night and for every matinée, and although my high school French was of little help, I understood the plots. I recall vividly the climactic scene in *La Dame aux Camélias* in which my heroine tore up many hundred-franc, or perhaps thousand-franc, notes and threw the pieces in the face of her lover whom, even in my innocence, I suspected of betraying her, or discarding her; and again, although I did not understand the words, I still remember that at the time I thought every word, every gesture was sublime and that the world would never see her like again.

Years, decades, more than half a century passed, and then one day a few years ago my niece Marian Seldes, who has starred in several plays on Broadway and won many awards, and who is noted for the beauty of her voice, was given the lead in a play in which she portrayed Sarah Bernhardt. Marian asked me to repeat to her all I remembered of my week as an usher in the Pittsburgh theatre.

I remembered the divine voice. I remembered the word "Wagram" spoken twice, and thinking it over I concluded that if the Divine Sarah were to appear in New York today in *L'Aiglon,* every critic in the metropolis would describe her as a "ham actress," or at best "a very old-fashioned actress."

Was I wrong in 1910? Am I wrong now? Fortunately a friend has recently sent me as a gift a cassette called "Voices of the 20th Century," a remarkable achievement that begins with the voice of Florence Nightingale and ends with that of Helen Keller, narrated by Henry Fonda. And for a moment I was thrilled to hear the voice I remembered—Sarah Bernhardt in the emotional climax of a French play—and immediately I realized that what was divine in 1910 *is* "ham" in 1980. The divinity of the earliest decade of the century is shouting, ranting, emoting, in the ninth decade.

As for the rosewood satin-lined coffin in which La Bernhardt was supposed to sleep at times—to accustom herself to the inevitable, as some said—and which was supposed to accompany her on her American tour, neither the ushers nor the theatre workers could find a trace of it. Its existence was not admitted, and Mr. Eagle had to do without a good story. On closing night, however, the Divine Sarah called everyone connected with the theatre, from the manager to the ushers, and the extras for mob scenes, and thanked us in a beautiful-sounding little speech, blending the most beautiful voice with the most beautiful language, which no person present fully understood. We felt well paid for the week.

Lillian Russell

So far as my paper was concerned—and probably so far as America cared—the visits of Lillian Russell were more newsworthy than any one of the final appearances of Sarah Bernhardt, or any other foreigner, for that matter.

Russell was not only a heavenly star. She was for many years a local celebrity, first as the special friend of "Diamond Jim" Brady, the salesman who sold engines and rolling stock for the Pressed Steel Car Company and made millions, and later, as the wife of Alexander Pollock Moore, the editor and presumed millionaire owner of the Pittsburgh *Leader*.

Mr. Moore told everyone he had "a great interest in the theatre," which for several years before the advent of Lillian Russell meant exclusively young and beautiful and usually very blonde young ladies, many from the chorus, but destined, Mr. Moore said, to become stars. He also assured them that newspaper publicity was the ladder to heaven. He himself was too big a man to engage in public relations jobs, so he sat his young ladies on his office couch and called in one of the hired hands to do the interviewing and writing.

In my second or third year on the *Leader,* when Mr. Moore heard that I was doing what passed for "dramatic criticism"— which meant rewriting the Tuesday morning papers or the Monday press agent handouts—and also that I had become the stringer for *Variety,* he called me frequently to the front office to write up his weekly discoveries, giggling girls who would, Mr. Moore would say in their presence, "play Shakespeare—Juliet, you know—or that new man Isben."

"Nora, in *A Doll's House,*" I would interpolate, unable to restrain myself from adding, "by Ibsen."

Mr. Moore would nod and say, "Yes, that's the guy."

A one-column story, two-column picture.

But things were different when Lillian Russell arrived—this time without Mr. Brady. The famous American beauty, still handsome in the robust style of the times but past her prime, magnificently sparkling with jewels, was interviewed not by me but by William Barr, the editorial writer, the newspaper man who according to a sinister rumor was a college graduate.

Mr. Barr was in a glow. He wrote glowingly of Miss Russell. Two-column picture, two-column interview, this time on the front page. Miss Russell awarded Mr. Barr the book she was carrying, the *Meditations* of Marcus Aurelius in limp leather, the noble thoughts of Plato's ideal ruler, the king-philosopher or philosopher-king of a future age, with paragraphs underlined by Miss Russell to constitute, she said, "my own philosophy of life." Mr. Barr read aloud for us many of the underlined thoughts. I was so impressed I remembered something about "living every day as if it were your last" for at least sixty years, since it was one of the first "great quotations" I looked for when I was compiling my book. Here are the several quotations I remembered:

> Live every day as if it were your last.
>
> No man is happy who does not think himself so.
>
> Whatever happens to thee, it was prepared for thee from all eternity.
>
> The happiness of your life depends upon the quality of your thoughts, therefore guard accordingly; and take care that you entertain no actions unsuitable to virtue and reasonable nature.

I do not remember the date of the marriage of Lillian Russell and Mr. Moore, but it was surely before the July 1911 Will Irwin exposé that revealed the *Leader* editor as a figurehead for Bill Flynn, the real owner, political boss, city contractor. Mr.

Moore was merely a glorified reporter, making perhaps twice the regular top pay of twenty-five dollars a week. Miss Russell was broke at the time. She may have thought the "owner" of a city paper worth a million, at least half a million, and everyone, including Mr. Moore, thought the actress sparkling with Jim Brady's diamonds worth at least as much. And so they were married.

But the marriage did not last very long, and the gossip columnists out of respect for a fellow journalist did not speculate on the financial surprises that followed. There was a separation— and in our office it was said vulgarly what the French say in a civilized manner: it was a *mariage blanc.*

As for the alleged owner of my first newspaper, I actually met him on the streets of Paris one day in the late 1920s, and he immediately invited me to join his party for dinner at Ciro's. Now he actually was rich. The rumors were that this former liberal Pittsburgh editor, friend of labor, backer of Theodore Roosevelt, of the Progressive Party and Bob La Follete had switched his allegiance, or Boss Flynn had switched it for him: the *Leader* had supported Warren Gamaliel Harding, and the Ohio Gang had shown its appreciation by giving Mr. Moore permits to import from Canada whiskey "for medicinal purposes," carloads of it, and eventually Mr. Moore had become so rich he could afford to retire and buy himself an embassy. He was our ambassador to Spain.

Emma Goldman

*T*he most noted—the press called her "the most notorious"— woman I met in Pittsburgh, and later in Paris and other capitals of Europe, was Emma Goldman. Even the few American newspapers that refrained from labeling her "Red Emma" never treated her as a normal human being worthy of the title "miss," but referred to her as "the Goldman woman," just as they referred later to Ruth Snyder, when she was tried and hanged for murder, as "the Snyder woman."

Although today Emma Goldman is honored throughout the world where women are making progress or have already achieved equality, along with Susan B. Anthony, Emmeline Pankhurst and Elizabeth Cady Stanton, and men and women can buy T-shirts with her face on them, in my time she was actually hounded from city to city, arrested "on suspicion" and for "disturbing the peace," jailed in every town in which a President of the United States ever appeared for a speech, and once charged with inspiring a mentally defective young man to assassinate President McKinley. (In truth and in fact, the assassin was influenced by editorials in Hearst Sr.'s New York *Journal*—and the only man in public life courageous enough to say so was Theodore Roosevelt.)

Wherever she went most of her public life Emma Goldman was refused a room in a hotel, and she rarely was able to rent a big hall for one of her lectures or speeches. Naturally enough, as with Gorki in Philadelphia and other notable Russians after him, when she came to Pittsburgh Emma Goldman would find refuge in the guest room over my father's drugstore.

On one occasion my city editor said to me, "She's staying at your house; you go and report her meeting tonight." So that night in 1910 or 1911 I went to a German Turnverein meeting place that Emma had been able to rent and found it crowded to the doors with about one hundred men and women.

Waiting for Emma to appear, I began to notice familiar faces in the small audience; they puzzled me at first, for they were not my father's friends. Then I recognized a man I knew well, and the mystery was solved: he was the chief of detectives at Central Police Station where I had served a part of my apprenticeship, and the other thirty-nine familiar faces were those of detectives or plainclothesmen from the same institution. But what were they doing here?

The lecture was entitled "The Emancipation of Women," or something very like that, and quoted largely from modern playwrights on the equality of the sexes, notably Ibsen's Nora in *A Doll's House* and *Hedda Gabler,* and Sudermann's play *Heimat,* which in English is entitled *Magda.*

Imagine the boredom of forty Pittsburgh police agents sitting through almost two hours of modern drama, listening to a plea for the liberation of women, votes for women, equality of the sexes.

Then Emma said, "In conclusion I want all of you to remember that Ibsen is one of the greatest revolutionary writers of our time." At the word "revolutionary" all forty members of the Pittsburgh police force, strategically placed in various parts of the hall, half rose in their seats, and I saw those nearest me reach into their jackets for their hidden guns. But Emma disappointed them. She threw no bombs.

On another occasion, I do not now remember where or when, I heard her lecture on anarchism. She began with her definition. "It is the philosophy of a new social order based on unrestricted liberty and the theory that all government rests on violence and is therefore wrong, harmful and unnecessary." The police present considered an arrest. She concluded that she was opposed to all violence, and especially to individual violence. Did that include the shooting of the steel tycoon Frick by her lover, Alexander Berkman? It did. The rest of the anarchism lecture was devoted to Prince Kropotkin, Tolstoy, Ferrer's Modern School, Proudhon's "Property is theft" and Thoreau's "Duty of Civil Disobedience." Another treat for the police forces.

But one day I found that "red" Emma was human, all too human. We were at breakfast, and the morning papers were on the table. There was a large illustrated feature story of a new fad sweeping the country: Irene Castle had introduced bobbed hair for women, boyish bobbed hair. Emma read and shook her head sadly.

"I introduced bobbed hair for women," she said. "Years ago. And I can prove it."

How could she prove it?

"All my Rogue's Gallery photographs in every city of the United States, in every police station—there I am in 1900 and ever after, with bobbed hair."

Ray Sprigle and Joe Hill

When my friend Ray Sprigle became city editor of the *Pittsburgh Post* in 1912, he offered me a job at twenty dollars a week. We were both considered radicals because we were friendly to all the labor leaders and especially to John L. Lewis. We declared ourselves for unionization, and we fraternized with the Typographical Union leaders and members in our own shop.

One day, during a strike, an unscheduled parade of several thousand men up Penn Avenue halted at the *Post* building. We heard men shouting, "We want Sprigle. We want Sprigle." But Ray could not very well make a speech to striking workmen from the balcony of one of Banker Given's buildings, so he walked down the two flights of stairs and promised the leaders he would address them elsewhere his next free day. (Sprigle, to our surprise, was not fired. He was the best city editor in town, frequently quit his desk and went out on a story himself. Years later he won the Pulitzer Prize for a series of articles and later a book about his life, disguised as a Black, in the still uncivilized South.)

When Bill Haywood came to the coal and iron capital of America, Sprigle and I went to his headquarters, not for news stories, which we knew would never be published, but out of interest in the new labor movement, the IWW, Industrial Workers of the World. And so by chance along with its new leaders we met the ballad-maker of the IWW, Joe Hill.

Joel Hägglund, born in 1879 in Sweden, on arrival at Ellis Island Americanized his name to Joe Hillstrom, and many years later on joining the IWW shortened it to Joe Hill. When Sprigle and I met him, he was in his early thirties, already famous for his union song, in which all of us joined at every meeting:

> You will eat, bye and bye,
> In that glorious land above the sky;
> Work and pray, live on hay,
> You'll get pie in the sky when you die.

At this conclusion everyone in the hall burst into a great shout of "And that's a lie," and cheered madly.

Joe Hill was a man of great enthusiasm and such easy friendship that in the week or ten days in which we knew him the three of us and another of his friends pledged a lifetime of loyalty to one another. But it was only a few months later that the last member of our foursome, whose name I have forgotten, sent me a photograph of Joe Hill sitting upright in his coffin with five bullet holes in his left chest. The State of Utah had accused him—and another man whom it made no effort to find—of holding up a grocery and killing the owner for a few dollars, a charge outrageous as it was laughable, had it not ended in a tragedy that shook the world—at least the liberal, labor world.

The Swedish government protested the arrest, then the sentence, then the execution; the President of the United States, Woodrow Wilson, intervened on Joe Hill's behalf, but nothing could stop the governor of Utah, William Spry, from knowingly, and with malice, committing the murder of Joe Hill.

Although for many years the ballad-maker had been called by the law enforcers, the union-busters, and the newspaper press, an "anarchist" and a "Communist," it was the Socialist Party in all the great nations of Europe that denounced not only Utah but the American war on labor unionization in the early years of the century.

Joe Hill's last words were "Don't mourn for me. Organize."

On the sixty-third anniversary of the execution, the State of Utah took a tentative step to pardon Joe Hill (for a crime he did not commit). The Utah legislature was told "that Joe Hill had been framed by powerful mining forces that feared his agitation on behalf of the IWW."*

The Reverend "Billy" Sunday

*W*hen the Reverend "Billy" Sunday, the great revival preacher of the time, came to Pittsburgh in 1912, American editorial writers agreed this was to be the major test of his "crusade." He

---

The New York Times, January 15, 1977.

had been converting hicks and hillbillies by the tens of thousands, but now, for the first time, he faced a sophisticated metropolitan audience.

As star reporter of the *Post* I was assigned the big story of the day. I was instructed to write the story exactly as it happened because this was a religious subject and might cause trouble.

I described the revival as a three-ring circus—parades, singing, hysteria, the sawdust trail. The Reverend Billy went through his theatrical exhibitions: he pitched curve balls and struck out the Devil, he boxed and knocked out the Devil, he wrestled and pinned the Devil to the mat amidst universal applause and shouted hysteria. I cannot remember if he played tennis with the Devil, but it was all on a sports basis, and Billy always the winner.

In between victories the Reverend denounced the "bastard theory of evolution" of that arch-villain and enemy of Christianity, Charles Darwin, and predicted that "the streets of America will run with blood" if the Bible were ever taken out of the public schools and school prayers were ever stopped. (Tremendous applause.)

These first paragraphs might not have gotten me into trouble, but I also reported what happened when, hysteria having reached a crescendo, the Reverend shouted for the sinners to come forward and repent. They rose immediately in all parts of the audience and began walking to the confessional benches. I noticed faces I knew. I investigated. My report said that almost all the first hundred "sinners" to come forward were frauds. They were stooges. They were what circus men called "shills"— hired men, the first to come forward when the fakers make their spiel and offer tuberculosis cures and similar frauds for a dollar a bottle. Someone has to start buying or none would be sold. The shills are the first to buy.

The scores who first appeared as repentant sinners at all the Billy Sunday revivals were good church members trained previously to lead the way. They were officers of the YMCA, members of the Epworth League and similar church societies. But there was not one real sinner or one real convert among the first hundred. They were acting a part.

It was only after the Reverend had created a great excitement over these sinners and a mob was shouting "Hallelujah! Hallelujah!" and he called for more repenters to join the "saved" that here and there in the vast audience men stood up and began moving forward. No one could escape the fact that there was a good proportion of drunks among them, and this being obvious, I so reported.

It was not muckraking; though it may have read like an exposé, it was merely a true account of what really happens at great revival meetings—but the facts apparently had never before been told. Sprigle liked my story; he led the paper with it, a two-column head, right, and the rare, perhaps once-in-a-year name of the writer.

Next morning I was fired—as a reporter, but not from the *Post*. Mr. Braun, the bank vice president who sat in the only closed office on the editorial floor, ordered Sprigle not only to shift me from the revival story, but never to let me report news again. I was made a copy reader, and soon enough head of the copy desk; I sat in the "slot" and wrote the world's headlines.

No one knew in those days that before Billy Sunday ever agreed to revive a town or city, his business representatives arrived along with his publicity staff. Conferences were held with the leading citizens—needless to say, leading businessmen—who did not need much urging to advance money to save souls and fatten the accounts in savings banks. The pitch was simple: every sinner, every drunkard, every bum or tramp or wastrel converted back to normal society put money in the bank, opened savings accounts, bought more at department stores, increased the flow of money. Did the fact that the Farmers National owned my paper have anything to do with my demotion? Mr. Braun lived to be one hundred years old and no one asked him.

Part II

Four Strange Interludes

Chapter 4

≈≈≈≈≈≈

Harvard: Professor Copeland, Jack Reed

Very soon after joining the Pittsburgh *Post,* a respected morning newspaper, I had received some of the best assignments, become perhaps "the" star reporter, and earned the highest wages of the time, twenty-four dollars a week.

But my Harvard brother kept writing me letters saying I would be an ignoramus all my life unless I went to college. In most of my replies I told him that he could learn more about human beings, more about the "world," more about all human life, in fact, in three weeks in Magistrate John J. Kirby's Central Police Station courtroom. There every morning the riffraff of the city, mostly prostitutes, drunks, derelicts, and a few muggers, appeared and heard the usual charges made by policemen, and "Judge" Kirby's sentence: "ten or ten" for first offenders, meaning a ten-dollar fine or ten days in the workhouse, or "thirty or thirty" for habitual offenders.

The result was a compromise: I got Gilbert a job on the *Sun,* our evening paper, for the entire summer, and having now saved the enormous sum of $676, in the autumn of 1912 I took the train to Cambridge and enrolled at Harvard. I was able to get a year's leave of absence from the *Post* because my pal, Ray Sprigle, was city editor.

Harvard accepted me as a "special student," a category that permits anyone to take any courses he chooses, so long as he does not seek a degree. I took exactly five courses, junior year, Gilbert's five.

The day I arrived in Cambridge Gilbert told me that those who wanted to enroll in English 12, taught by the famous Charles Townsend Copeland, who was the chief reason for my going to school, had to submit to him an original piece of work. At least a hundred, perhaps two hundred, students would apply and only twenty-five or thirty would be chosen. Gilbert submitted what we newspaper people called a "highbrow" piece, and I thought I had to do the same, so I wrote a fancy piece about something I knew nothing about, which I believe I entitled "Nature Catching Up with Art." Nevertheless, to my surprise, one morning when we went to the place students got their mail, we found two postal cards, all blank except for one word in the largest lettering possible, "IN," and three little letters, "C.T.C."

As I soon learned, Copey was that rarest of all birds, a professor of books. Emerson had said in one of his essays that colleges provided libraries but no professors of books, "and I think a chair is so much needed." Without using that term, Copey had planted himself in that chair—for at least a generation.

If it had not been for Copeland, that great Polish-born British writer Joseph Conrad (né Korzeniowski) might never have been known in America—or been "discovered" a century later. *Youth, The Heart of Darkness, The End of the Tether* were required reading, along with one or two novels. The three short-story masterpieces had been published in 1903; we were the tenth or eleventh class to whom Copey preached Conrad.

One of his favorite native writers was Mary E. Wilkins Freeman, whose short story, "The Revolt of Mother," Copey considered a masterpiece. He introduced us not only to Joseph Conrad but to a still unheralded writer, Arthur Machen, and he forced everyone in his class to buy a popular magazine to read a story by one of his former pupils, Henry Milner Rideout.

Repeatedly Copey told his class to "write what you know," so I wrote about my newspaper office and events I had reported. One story I called "The Black Cossacks," the epithet we used in Pittsburgh for the black-uniformed coal-and-iron police owned by the two major western Pennsylvania industries. It was an illegal force that nevertheless ruled several counties, broke strikes and heads, sometimes killed strikers. Its members rarely if ever were arrested for their crimes. In later years they would be called forerunners to Mussolini's Blackshirts.

"The Black Cossacks" was based on a news event full of blood and violence. But Copey liked it. He liked it so much that one day, after talking to his class about "Harvard esthetes who take three bites to a cherry," he read one of their contributions, an ecstasy over a sunset, and then "The Black Cossacks." He then spoke of realism, truth, real writing, contrasting the two, dismissing the first with a gentle sneer, praising my story.

Although my brother was not an esthete, he belonged to the top literary group. He was an editor of the *Harvard Monthly* in its great days. One afternoon, for some reason, Copey leaned toward him over his desk and, pointing a finger, said in a tense voice: "I do *not* like you, Mr. Gilbert *Vivian* Seldes, I like your brother, George Henry Seldes." I do not know for whom Gilbert was named—it was probably for one of Mother's romantic book heroes—but Gilbert never again in his lifetime used his middle name. Nor was he offended by being singled out by Copeland. We had all been warned by seniors, and we got what we expected from Copey: severe criticism, ironic remarks, and perhaps even a little rudeness. We had been told that Copey was a "character," and we found he lived up to his reputation.

But he was a great teacher, and moreover, many of his graduates, so looked down upon by the vast number of "self-made" successful great men of the time, actually became successful in the writing world; they appeared in diverse magazines, they wrote books, they lectured, they were nationally applauded.

Of all the advice Copeland gave his twenty-five or thirty students of each class, the most important, as I remember it, was this: "Read what you have written out loud to yourself. Read every word, every sentence, the whole day's output just as soon as you have written it. Out loud. Do not be self-conscious. Listen to the words. Make corrections and then read it all again. Out loud. It will make all the difference in your writing."

At the end of my Harvard year I found that Copeland had given me an A, although the returned manuscripts had usually been marked A−. It was the only A I got. But it made me eligible for the annual book of honor students.

George Pierce Baker

Professor Baker not only taught drama at Harvard, he created successful Broadway dramatists, thereby for many years giving a living answer to millions who sneered at a college education.

In my year Professor Baker also delivered a series of lectures in Boston, free to the public. He invited our class to attend. One evening his subject was the Elizabethan dramatist John Ford (1586–1639?). Eventually Baker had to name Ford's best-known play. The title was *'Tis Pity She's a Whore.*

In the dark, dark ages of this century that last word in the title hit the Boston audience like a bomb. There was a collective gasp, everyone shuddered, there were strange throat noises and a universal shuffling in the seats, followed by a terrible silence.

Baker described the love of Giovanni and Annabella, brother and sister. He could tell that story without ever having to use the forbidden word "incest."

But never again did he give the full title of the Ford play. "Now, in the second act of *'Tis Pity,*" he would say, or, "In the third act of *'Tis Pity.*"

Nevertheless Harvard voted him one of the bravest men of the year.

The Widow Nolan

There were beer festivals in the editorial offices of the *Harvard Monthly;* its semi-literary rival, the *Advocate; the Lampoon;* and finally a new "popular" magazine plainly called the *Harvard Illustrated Monthly.* The literary publications were beyond me, and I could not make Lampy. But on presenting my credentials— reporter on a city newspaper, 1909–1912—I was hailed and made an editor of the *Illustrated* immediately. In fact, I was given the contributions of others to whip into shape. Most of the offerings were very high-schoolish—I remember one with this opening sentence: "Oh, have you seen the glass flowers at the museum?"

I did very well for several months, until, being after all still a reporter, I got onto the story of the "Widow" Nolan and the Football Heroes, and wrote it. It was a simple, not a severe, exposé of the tutorial system at Harvard, similar I am sure to those of other Ivy League schools, perhaps of all colleges and universities. I do not know if times have changed, but in 1912–1913 football players were football players, they had no time for classes, they did no studying, they just played football and for millions of people were the ornament of the institutions with famous names.

Dr. or Professor Nolan—I remember nothing about him but his name and a meeting at which he defended his system— was known as "the Widow," I forget why, but he should have been called "the Midwife." Just as revolutions are the midwives of history, so Nolan was the midwife of the Harvard football team, nursing the members through the years, and finally delivering to each one a sacred diploma.

The Nolan system was largely mnemonics. And tricks. He supplied nursery verses, sentences, words made up of letters each of which stood for a word or name that might be asked for in an examination. Everything from mathematics to philosophy. Just as there is in Britain a long "poem" in which every king is named in proper order, so the Widow supplied Harvard heroes with verses naming the Presidents—or the decisive battles of the world, or of the Revolution, or the Civil War. And if you were asked which German words take the ablative, the Widow had a key for them also. He had everything. He was capable of miracles.

Was my story good investigative journalism, or was it muckraking? Neither. According to the chief editor of the *Harvard Illustrated Monthly,* a Mr. Gill, it was "plain, outright treason."

The manuscript was not handed back to me, it was thrown at me. I never went back to the offices, so I do not know if I was fired by Mr. Gill. I do remember one day going to Boston and taking the story to the magazine editor of the *Transcript*—I think his name was Burton Kline—and he was not only grateful, he sent me a check for fifty dollars along with a letter of thanks. Fifty dollars was two weeks' pay for the star reporters of the papers at home, and it was also one-third my Harvard tuition cost. Later on I sold the *Transcript* one or two more Harvard stories, but nothing raised such a sensation in the Yard as this report on the tutoring of football heroes by the nationally famous Widow Nolan.

But the only result of my exposé, outside of its helping pay my year's tuition, was exactly nothing. Harvard did nothing. The Widow Nolan continued, until he retired years later, to instruct the football players and get them their college degrees.

Jack Reed

*M*any Copeland graduates on their way to fame and fortune, who no doubt believed he was largely responsible for their success, made their way back year after year to the Copeland sweet-cider-and-cookie sessions he held once a week. The two I remember best are John Reed and Walter Lippmann. Lippmann was the founder of the Harvard Socialist Club, and in the 1912 election I remember vividly the uproarious cheers that greeted the club's arrival in the hall in which Presidential candidate Debs was to speak. Harvard's crimson banners were especially welcome.

The first time I met Jack Reed at Copey's he told me his father was the sheriff or a policeman in Portland, Oregon, but I afterward learned that Reed Sr. was such a distinguished citizen that President T.R. had had him appointed honorary marshal—whatever that may be. At Harvard Reed earned such a great reputation as a playboy, jokesmith, and writer of what were then, and perhaps even now, called "dirty" songs, they were remembered and sung not only in my day but long afterward. Incidentally, when the Warren Beatty crew came here to interview me for their film glorifying Reed and his wife Louise Bryant—they questioned me for five hours, made seven reels of film, and used two five-second statements with picture but no identification in the final product—they were delighted to hear about the ribald songs. "Sing them for us," they said. I said, "But they're dirty." They said, "There are no more dirty words; all the women's magazines use all the forbidden words now." So I sang one chorus I remember well:

> *Down in the sewer, digging up manure.*
> *Sure we do get buggered now and then;*
> *But our chiefest delight*
> *Is to hurl up the shite,*
> *For we're Tom and Jerry, the night soil men*

The Harvard singing sessions were always headed by Professor Robert Edmund Jones, who taught art, and who later went to New York and painted the scenery for several great successful plays. According to Jones, he and Jack Reed also once made an expedition through the mountains of snow in the Cambridge midwinter, during which they challenged each other first to write their names by urinating on the snow, and then to draw pictures on snow in a like manner. The result was a Reed ballad on how they painted the Libyan Venus, and that masterpiece had several really forbidden words in it. "Sing it again," said one of the Beatty editors. "We want it on another reel, just in case it doesn't come out clear on the first; we will surely use this." So I sang it again.

How this ribald Harvard minnesinger became a committed political and social revolutionary I could never understand. Reed, I knew, grew out of his playboy and prankster stage almost immediately after he left college, became a foreign correspondent, and attached himself to one of the rebel forces in Mexico—Villa's or Zapata's—and wrote for a liberal magazine called *The Metropolitan*. But then, and in later life, he never lost the sense of humor, either the common, the Homeric or the Meredithian; and as far as I could learn in the years I followed him in Berlin or Paris or Moscow Jack Reed remained in character even to the point of arguing the real meaning of Marxism with Zinoviev and other notables of the 1917 Revolution—and on one occasion I heard it said that he had an ideological confrontation with Lenin himself.

I do know from my own meetings with him when I was a Berlin correspondent of the *Chicago Tribune*—and spent all the time I could in Paris—that Reed once, on his way from Moscow to America and as usual joining the newspaper crowd in Berlin or Paris in whatever barroom hangout they then had, told us of having been appointed consul by the Soviet Russian Government in New York.

He said: "I now have the right to marry people. First thing I'll do is simplify the marriage ceremony. I'll tell all the Russian couples who come to my office in New York on the announced days several times a year, to hold hands, and while they're holding hands I'll say to the brides and grooms, 'Workers of the world, unite,' nothing more. And they'll be married for life."

Reed died of typhus in Moscow in 1920. (That part of the film *Reds* which shows Louise Bryant racing across hundreds of miles of snow from Helsinki, Finland, to Moscow to be with her husband is pure nonsense. All true Communists and fellow travelers had no difficulty at any time in getting a visa and a train ride to Moscow.) We non-Communist journalists never got into Russia until the Hoover-Litvinov "treaty" by which the Russians permitted the United States to feed and save the lives of six million children. That was in August 1922, and the first day after I settled into a room in the Hotel Savoy, I walked to the Kremlin wall to see the plaque behind which Jack's ashes were kept. Burial in the wall was the greatest honor the regime could pay a foreigner. Lenin had his mausoleum outside the wall, and the other several founders of the R.S.F.S.R. had statues nearby, whereas Reed, and later Bill Haywood and notables from many other countries, had places in the brick wall itself.

When I returned more or less secretly to Russia in 1964, I went to look for the Reed plaque in the Kremlin wall and found it had been removed. Bill Haywood's and those of lesser notables were still there, but not Jack's. I turned to our ever-present ever-vigilant Intourist guide and asked her why and when the Reed plaque had been removed. She looked at me angrily and, pointing to a black marble slab nearby, said: "Djon Rid never in Kremlin Wall. Djon Rid buried 'ere."

Each of these black marble slabs, which run alongside the Kremlin Wall, is inscribed with the names of three persons, not one of them known to the American people.

What had happened?

Stalin had suppressed and censored everything in print that did not make him a hero. Naturally enough, he suppressed Reed's masterpiece, *Ten Days That Shook the World,* which is true history and gives credit to both Trotsky and Lenin. After some years Stalin had the Russian edition of the book rewritten, making himself one of the heroic founders and eliminating most of Trotsky; and meanwhile he had ordered the Reed plaque removed, and the Reed ashes given a fourth-class burial place.*

---

*Stalin also forged what Soviet Russians called *The Great Soviet Encyclopedia,* again making himself the hero of the November Revolution, eliminating Trotsky. In *Ten Days That Shook the World* there are several tiny references to Stalin. Once he appears among signers of a document, and in another instance Reed says, "Stalin also spoke." On my 1964 trip a fellow member of the Committee for a Sane Nuclear Policy (SANE) was Dr. Milton Kissin of New York City, who as a medical school graduate in 1930 had visited Moscow. He confirmed my statement that Reed had been buried in the wall, not outside it. "Even the gods cannot change history," Aristotle wrote. But dictators can.

Chapter 5

~~~~~~~~~~~~~~

Greenwich Village in 1916

Although I am under oath never to write an autobiography—"All autobiographies are lies," said Bernard Shaw—I must devote a page or two of this and the next chapter to my personal history and incidentally to a woman who drove me out of Pittsburgh, and eventually out of the United States, and in this strange way was responsible for a large part of my life history after 1916. I now find it ironic that what I thought was a "romantic" episode could have such strange results. Were it not for Peggy Keith I would probably have remained in Pittsburgh the rest of my life and not had most of the adventures that make up this book.

In the early decades of this century in addition to "legitimate" theatres presenting audiences with actors and actresses still regarded as among the greatest in history—Bernhardt, Duse, numerous Barrymores, for examples—there were also second- and third-class traveling companies, the lowest of which were

known as "ten-twenty-thirties," which meant they played theatres or halls at these three prices per seat—in cents.

One day at the *Post* office we heard that the manager of one
of these groups had decamped with its money, the actors and
actresses were stranded, the cheap hotels they frequented had
seized their trunks with all their belongings and were threatening to put them in the streets. There was some sort of a hearing
in Central Police Station. It seemed a colorful story, so I was sent
to find out. Almost immediately I was struck by the innocent
beauty of the "soubrette"—there was only one in each company,
just as there was one villain with long moustaches to twirl. She
told me her stage name was Peggy Keith, that she had already
been thrown out of her hotel, that she owed ten dollars, which
was a considerable sum of money, her trunk had been seized, she
had nothing to wear, nothing to eat, no place to sleep.

Ten dollars was almost half my week's pay, but I gallantly
presented it to her, she got her trunk, and we took a taxi to my
lodgings. Within a day or two we found an apartment in a
suburb, Carrick, which I could afford, and we were living as
husband and wife. I was in love with her, and proposed marriage.
Unfortunately, she said, she had a husband somewhere in Ro-
chester, New York, and was hoping to hear from him that he
had divorced her.

When I went from star reporter to night editor—with a
raise of a magnificent four dollars a week—I went to work about
5:00 P.M. and put the last edition to bed at 4:30 A.M., but as the
Carrick streetcars ran only on the hour, I did not get home until
six in the morning, and this made our life together a topsy-turvy
affair. But I naïvely thought it was truly romantic. Imagine how
shocked I was two or three months later when, opening a drawer
somewhere in the kitchen, I found it stuffed with dollar and
two-dollar bills, and a score of silver dollars. What did this mean?
Naïve as I then was, I nevertheless suspected that Peggy, alone
in the house from 5:00 P.M. to 6:00 A.M. when I got home, had
not spent all her time cooking and cleaning and doing other
womanly chores but had also engaged in the first and oldest
profession; and when I accused her, she confessed.

Next day I withdrew my savings bank account of about two hundred dollars, gave Peggy half, gave her half my pay for the fortnight, went by streetcar to the railroad station, and bought a ticket to New York, where I knew my cousin Bill Randorf, a newspaperman, had a room. I cannot say he was overwhelmed with joy at seeing me, but he promised to take me to see a friend at the New York *World* office, and tell me all he knew about freelancing in the metropolis.

On my very first day in bohemia, and thereafter almost daily, I heard the older inhabitants sing their dirge, "The Village isn't what it used to be," "The great days are gone." Everyone blamed the disaster on newspaper publicity, the influx of out-landers, the daily procession of tourists from the hinterland, sightseers from uptown, snoopers, all secretly looking for some-thing immoral or at least unconventional, to retail elsewhere. What and when the great days had been I never learned.

But it was amusing sixty years later to read in *The New Yorker* Richard Harris's report that "a decade ago (1966) Green-wich Village was Greenwich Village. It was a relatively small area, and it was a polyglot community, to be sure, with artists and intellectuals. . . . The new Village is a realtor's concoc-tion. . . . " The Harris report also mentioned the "antique dealers, the homosexuals, the derelicts in Washington Park, the addicts and pushers of drugs and muggers who hang about ominously," the "Bowery bums sleeping in doorways, Polack and Puerto Rican whores wearing boots and hot pants, addicts looking for a fix or a hit. . . . " and "restaurants which charge fourteen dollars for *tournedos en chemise poivre*" and sixteen dollars for a trout. Each generation, each age, mourns the preceding one, apparently.

Bill introduced me to everyone in the real bohemia, the hundreds among the thousands of writers, artists, novelists, and poets he knew. I made many friends. But I was never invited to the magnificent salon of the millionairess Mabel Dodge, whom the newspapers persisted (wrongly) in calling the Queen of Greenwich Village. Neither Bill nor I was ever asked to call, but in my New York interval I did get to 23 Fifth Avenue twice, dragged along by persons who were usually invited. On these two occasions I met several persons already notable, Jack Reed again and Carl Van Vechten, Hutchins Hapgood (a sort of kindly philosophical anarchist), Emma Goldman, Elizabeth Gurley Flynn, known as the young and beautiful Joan of Arc of the Patterson silk-workers strike, and Max Eastman. Walter Lippman was there, too. I sold him a feature story for the Sunday edition of the New York *World,* of which he was the editor. He was of course by then no longer a Socialist. I do remember Mabel Dodge saying to her guests one night when I was there and Lippmann left early: "That man will never lose an eye fighting on the barricades." No truer summation in so few words was ever made of any man's character.

Freud had been discovered in America, in Greenwich Village naturally, the year before I arrived, and in 1916 the great Freudian wave was already receding from the shores of bohemia, and Freudianism had become so commonplace it was now the subject of good-natured humor. Susan Glaspell had used all the Freudian jargon in her play, *Suppressed Desires,* and the newspaper press loved it.

The real "queen" of Greenwich Village, to use a city newspaper term, was not Mabel Dodge but Renée La Coste. And the real center of Village events now for those "notables" who were not in Provincetown or Paris was Polly Holiday's restaurant, and the Village minnesinger was Bobby Edwards. His famous song, which I never forgot, could be heard almost every night:

> *Way down South in Greenwich Village,*
> *Where we get the Uptown swillage,*
> *Where the girls are unconventional,*
> *And the men are unintentional—*
> *Way down South,*
> IN WASHINGTON SQUARE.

(A photographic postcard of the interior of Polly's, featuring these lines and Mike the waiter in the center, substituted "spillage" for "swillage," for fear of offending the tourists.)

It was only a few weeks after my arrival that an unusual and scandalous event occurred that changed things considerably for me in Greenwich Village. I had been living in a hall bedroom, on half my savings and two weeks' newspaper pay, and freelancing along with many others. The *World* paid me ten dollars for an exclusive about Canadian officers recruiting a Yank regiment to fight the Huns, and sometimes I got five dollars for stories of a less sensational content. Then one morning, while I was still in bed, my cousin Bill burst into my room shouting, "Pack your things, I've got a millionaire's apartment for you. Free!" My "things" filled one small imitation-leather suitcase.

This is how I came to live in the best house on Washington Square. It was either Number 60 or Number 62, I forget; one was known as "the House of Genius" because scores of writers who had become famous had at one time lived in one of its tiny rooms; the other was a magnificent apartment house—and Bill had the keys.

The owner, or occupant, a Mr. T., let us say, had fled to Canada. The young woman with whom he lived had gone somewhere a day earlier for an abortion, and abortions in ancient times were not only illegal, they were crimes comparable to murder—and the murderer was not the doctor or the malpractitioner, but the man who paid the bill. On her way home Mr. T.'s friend had fainted in the street, and while being helped by a policeman, told him the truth.

Mr. T. left not only his toothbrushes and razors but his postage stamps and unanswered letters and his gray-green silk crêpe shirts, and word to feel at home. Within a week or two my apartment at 60 (or was it 62?) Washington Square became one of the centers of Village life. It was not regarded as *my* apartment but as Mr. T.'s (temporary) gift to the Village, and especially to the many true bohemians who had not acquired the fame or notoriety that gave them entrée to Mabel Dodge's salon and those of her successors.

Scores of persons came frequently to the apartment and used it as their own. Those who could afford it brought a bottle of unlabeled wine. Beautiful Renée La Coste seemed to preside.

The poet Charles Divine came with her. And if the elusive Edna St. Vincent Millay chose to adorn the Brevoort set, Mr. T.'s apartment frequently welcomed her more beautiful sister, Norma Millay. A noted artist, commissioned to draw a war poster showing "humanity crucified by the Huns," posed one of our visitors topless in my apartment.

Greenwich Village in 1916 was not merely a place of salons, drinking parties, cafés, adultery and decadence. It was a truly bohemian oasis of young people striving and hoping and working. Freud, radical causes, the war, art and poetry, the theater—especially the theatre—little magazines, occupied all levels of Village life. Although the "great days" were deplored as gone and never to be equaled, it was a wonderful world to live in.

Chapter 6

Wartime London: A Traitor, a Hero

The same eternal feminine that had driven me out of Pittsburgh now drove me out of New York. It seems that the fame of my Washington Square, Greenwich Village apartment as the center of bohemia had spread throughout the land, and so one day I was not too surprised by the arrival at my door of my former friend Peggy Keith.

Could I, would I forgive her? She began to cry. She would be a good woman, she would keep house for me, she would be my servant, if only I would forgive her and give her another chance. Please, and tears. A beautiful woman. I told her to unpack.

For most of the summer all went well—except that all that "center of Greenwich Village" partying, drinking and dancing and even reciting new poetry several nights a week made it almost impossible for me to do my own work. Had it not been for Cousin Bill's getting me assignments from the New York *World,* I would have starved. As it was I did not live in luxury.

And then one August day one of the bohemian crowd, a rather well-off writer, said to Peggy—in my presence, "I am going to Lake Saranac on a two-week vacation; how'd you like to come along?" and without hesitation Peggy went to pack her suitcase.

In wartime, visas to Allied countries were almost unobtainable, except for newspapermen and diplomats. If I were able to get to London it would probably be the only place Peggy could not follow me. I went to the British consulate—they demanded a birth certificate and questioned me about any German ancestors—and a few days later I was on a ship bound for Liverpool.

To my surprise, getting a job in wartime London was no problem at all: a man named Louis H. Moore, who had an incoming cable from New York at the United Press offices in Bouverie Street, off Fleet, paid me one pound sterling, then $4.86, for one hour's work every night expanding three hundred words of cablese into one thousand, which he sold to the leading newspapers in Great Britain and Ireland that did not have their own correspondents in America. Shortly afterward Ed Keen, UP chief, paid me a like amount, five pounds a week, to condense the World War and minor happenings in Europe into one thousand words, which he cabled to the greatest newspaper in Buenos Aires. I was very soon better off than I had ever been at home.

Jane Anderson, Traitor

My brother, Gilbert, had preceded me to London where he made a living writing on the arts, literature, the theatre in wartime. He had already become friends with one of Copeland's heroes, Arthur Machen, whose works I also knew although none had ever been published in America. But apparently he had never tried to find Copeland's "greatest living author," Joseph Conrad, whom a generation of Copeland students had succeeded in time in making known to America.

It was my reporter's luck not only to interview him but to

steal at least a glance at his "protégée," the beautiful and talented Jane Anderson, who was within a year or so to write at least one chapter in my brother's life—and perhaps a whole chapter in the American history of treason in wartime.

Veterans of the Second World War may remember when she was broadcasting for Hitler from Berlin, telling them to rebel or desert and come over to the Nazi side. She was then the Marquesa de Cienfuegos, "the Marquise of a Thousand Fires," the wife of a supposedly Spanish nobleman—in Madrid the title is discounted as Mexican—but she still used her maiden name, Jane Anderson, and still talked with a delightful Georgia accent.

In 1917, when Germany was about to launch its "sink without trace" war on British shipping, Lowell Mellett, second in command at UP, having heard me mention Conrad one day, sent me to his country place to get his views on the effectiveness of submarine warfare. I could hardly concentrate on the answers the great writer was giving me, I was so dazzled by the fleeting apparition of his "ward."

In July 1917 the U.S. Embassy invited Americans to volunteer for war service, and my brother and I were there when the door opened. My registration card had the number 8. We were never called. By the end of the year I went to Paris to work for the *Chicago Tribune* and Gilbert sailed for home. On the boat he met the stunning beauty Jane Anderson. (He eventually became a machine gunner, refused jobs in intelligence, lectured the officers on what the war was really like and was on a ship bound for France Armistice Day.)

In 1919, shortly after I returned home, a cousin who was a member of the 166th Infantry, Rainbow Division, gave a sort of engagement party for Gilbert and Jane. It was "sort of" because although we knew they had pledged themselves, Miss Anderson's divorce from the noted composer and music critic Deems Taylor was still not final. But, they said, it was only a matter of months, and everyone was happy and everyone believed it was a beautiful match, two brilliant minds, a beautiful woman, a writer destined soon to be known as one of the three great critics of his time. (The other two were Edmund Wilson and Walter Lippmann.)

What happened afterward I did not know and would not ask. Moreover, it so happened that my brother and I, ever since 1906 when Father had taken us to the cities to complete our high school education, were never together except for short periods, the year in London being the longest. The next time I saw Jane Anderson's name in print it was not over a brilliant magazine or newspaper story but in the society columns: the Southern beauty, the dazzling Jane Anderson of Atlanta, Georgia, was to marry a Spanish aristocrat, the Marques de Cienfuegos; she was now in Spain, or preparing to go there. When, in July 1936, the Spanish generals and colonels betrayed their oath to the Republic, and, with the aid of the bankers, landowners and Hitler and Mussolini, began the rebellion (falsely called a civil war), the Republic rounded up a number of traitors who could not escape from Madrid, and among them were the Marques de Cienfuegos and his American-born wife.

Although Jane Anderson had given up her U.S. citizenship, the outcry was great—it was led by Monsignor Fulton J. Sheen, who used his national radio hook-up to call the recent convert to his church "one of the living martyrs"; and the entire Hearst press, for which Miss Anderson usually wrote. Pressure was brought on the President, the State Department, on members of Congress. The Spanish Republic then freed the Marquesa despite the evidence that she was a Nazi agent.

The Marquesa immediately repaid the Republic by writing a series of falsifications for Mr. Hearst Sr.'s press, and a little later volunteered her services to Hitler in World War II. In 1942 *Collier's* editors obtained four pages of the British Monitoring Service, which it would not publish, dealing with persons the Nazis employed or reprinted. One of this magazine's editors (Kyle Crichton, now deceased, or I would not disclose his name) permitted me to copy them. Page 4 read:

NAZI RADIO
Summary   February 12, 1942
Jane Anderson—talk in English—"Truth will prevail;" 8.18
P.M. The only remarkable point of this talk was the reference to (and reverence for) the International News Service

55

which the speaker said had "always maintained the highest standard for reporting."

Recently, in searching for my brother's papers, I found several broadsides and little pamphlets that he wrote and published for private circulation. In one, entitled, "E.E. & O" (Excuses Errors and Omissions), he makes the following references to the Jane Anderson affair:

On June 25, 1960, *The New York Times* carried the report of the death, at the age of 70, of Joseph ("Boris") Hieronymus Retinger, described as a patriotic Pole, author of a book on Conrad, and best known for parachuting (at the age of 50 or so) into Poland, then in German hands, to lead a Polish underground.

I met Retinger right after the end of World War I, through Jane Anderson (later the divorced wife of Deems Taylor), who was then engaged to be married to at least one of us. . . .

She was born in Georgia, a redhead of spectacular beauty rather in the Gibson-girl style. . . .

She was so successful a reporter in London that the *Daily Mail* ran a front-page story protesting that British women in newspapers were not given the facilities granted to her, such as flying over London. I do not know whether this was before or after meeting Northcliffe. He came to see her in New York in his postwar visit. Her maid, answering the phone, said, "The Lord is here."

She was a close friend of the Conrads. He started a letter to her, "Fifth Pig, come home!" The letter also said, "I don't see why my last mistress should not be Boris's first. . . ."

John Balderston, who was in England during the war, told me, long afterwards, that Jane had been the mistress of someone very important in the Foreign Office, and, at the same time of Berthelot (I think) at the Quai d'Orsay. He implied that the British had grown suspicious of her and that eventually the French had, too. Hence her return to the United States early in 1917. . . .

His (Retinger's) life was international politics. He was anti-Bolshevist. For several months he was plotting the

assassination of Lenin—in which he was to participate—
and Jane insisted that the plan was simple and workable. . . .

By the time Jane got involved in American politics, we
both were aware of having drifted apart. . . .

During World War II an intelligence officer came to me
and played a recording of a broadcast from Berlin. I was
asked to identify the voice. It was Jane's. She was speaking
about Conrad. On another record I think she was violently
anti-Semitic. (The broadcasts were to our troops like those
of Tokyo Rose.)

She then married the Marques de Cienfuegos (Spanish). I
never found out what happened to her.

(However, I did. In the last days of World War II the
Soviets attempted to raze Berlin with gunfire and air bombs, in
retaliation for Hitler's destruction of scores of cities and a prob-
able twenty million dead. Thousands of human beings were hit
many times and turned into small pieces of bone and flesh. Not
one of these thousands was ever identified. Although no trace of
Jane Anderson was found, a romantic rumor persists in Berlin
that she, somehow, escaped.)

Floyd Gibbons

*T*he hero of our time in London was Floyd Gibbons. Whether
or not his eyewitness account of the sinking of the liner *Laconia*
brought the United States into World War I, as he insisted, is
disputed by historians who believe our entry was inevitable, but
no one who was there ever denied that the arrival of Floyd
Gibbons in London in February 1917 was a journalistic event,
more exciting now than a Zeppelin raid.

He was already famous for his invasion of Mexico with
General Pershing—as Floyd told it, but never published it, Villa
the "bandit" was on a hilltop while the U.S. Army was looking
for him, and as each detachment, infantry and artillery, passed
by, he "reviewed" it, raising his hand in a mock salute—not to
his forehead, but to his nose.

Gibbons told us he chose the *Laconia* rather than a ship
carrying German diplomats and considered safe because he was

sure it would be torpedoed, so sure he bought an extra life preserver, concentrated food, a flashlight. The liner was sunk without warning February 25, 1917, and the *Chicago Tribune* syndicated or sold the story throughout the non-German world, demanding a U.S. declaration of war.

President Wilson had said he would join the Allies if and when an overt act was committed by German submarines. But between the first of these declarations and the eyewitness account of a passenger ship sunk without warning, four ships had been sunk with loss of life—and nothing was done.

Gibbons arrived in London the day after filing his dispatch from Queenstown and immediately became the idol and center of American journalistic life. Many of us who worked in Fleet Street met at the bar of the Wellington Hotel—not the Savoy, the favorite place after the Armistice. From the day of his arrival Gibbons began his campaign to force Wilson—and the U.S. Senate—to declare war on Germany.

"This is the fifth 'overt' act," he told us,

but the first witnessed by a newspaperman. There were also survivors in the other four but their evidence was disregarded. We had seventy-three passengers on the *Laconia*. We were asleep. We were sunk without warning. Six of us were Americans. Two were from Chicago. Mr. and Mrs. Hoy. I saw them swept from their lifeboat and drowned. So we have Americans dead in the war.

When we were picked up by British ships and safely landed in Queenstown we were told this torpedoing would probably be passed over by the American President as had the other four, each a legitimate act of war but not considered by Woodrow Wilson as the "overt" act. When I heard this, I said, "over my dead body."

Actually the Gibbons story, headlined with streamers in every newspaper in the States, was accompanied by a minor one-column item saying President Wilson that very day in an address to a joint session of Congress had stated that as the Germans had previously announced they would begin unrestrained submarine warfare as of the first of February, no overt act requiring American action had yet occurred.

But the next day the pro-Allied interventionist press and a major part of the press of the civilized world repeated Floyd Gibbons's eyewitness story of an overt act and called for American entry into the war. Weeks later, on April 2, the President, described as "visibly pale and deeply affected," asked Congress to take action, and it did so after a few hours of debate.

Shortly afterward Gibbons went to Paris where he became a member of the press section of Pershing's army. He also telegraphed me at the United Press, London, where I had been slaving with the daily report for *La Nacion* (or it could have been its rival, *La Prensa*), Buenos Aires, offering me a job on the Army Edition of the *Chicago Tribune*.

Chapter 7

~~~~~~~~~~~~

Paris: Editor,
ChiTrib *Army Edition*

Next to Harry's Bar on the Rue Daunou, the office of the *Chicago Tribune* Army Edition, two flights above Maxim's, Rue Royale, was the best-known meeting place for Americans after July 4, 1917. The first invaders were the volunteer ambulance men of the Morgan-Harjes service, now ordered out and looking for new adventures. Congressmen, governors, diplomats, Chicagoans came every day.

I was the entire reportorial staff. My job was writing or stealing and pasting up fourteen columns of news daily and fooling the censors. But within a few weeks of my arrival the strange genius who had founded the paper—Joe Pierson, to whom Colonel McCormick said in mid-June 1917, "Go to Paris and have the first paper out on the Fourth of July"—came into the editorial office and said that the managing editor had "eloped with a French countess, the *Tribune* auto, and the *Tribune* payroll"; I was now managing editor as well as staff and my pay would be raised three dollars a week.

My most notable visitors were Ring Lardner, Ruth Hale, Heywood Broun, and George Carpentier, the prizefighter. George, I am sure, came because the *poules de luxe* from Maxim's were always in our office (I can't imagine why, since no *Tribune* journalist earned enough in a week to even take one of them to dinner), but Carpentier said it was for the American secretaries, and he wanted to learn English.

Ring Lardner told one and all that "the Colonel sent me to France to write the comic side of the World War." Ring was ironic. But we did our best: we introduced him to a young man who was a true Lardner character, a hanger-on named Jed Kiley, an adventurer whose style of talk and type of adventures we later found in the famous Lardner fictions. I remember Jed telling Lardner of once placing small advertisements in certain American religious weeklies offering to mail a small bottle of genuine "holy water" from the River Jordan for one dollar, postpaid. To his surprise he received thousands of orders almost by return mail. It took only five days for letters by boat in those days compared to eight or eleven by airmail today. Jed, who insisted he was an honest entrepreneur, had to telegraph his man in Palestine to increase shipments to Paris, but it was late one autumn before he got his first five thousand bottles, each with a facsimile of a certificate, into the post office, and began bottling thousands more. For a while Jed dreamed of becoming a rich man, perhaps a millionaire. But there was an early cold wave in America that year, and every bottle shipped north of Florida and Phoenix froze and then burst, holy water ruined thousands of letters, the U.S. Post Office got very angry at Jed Kiley, and he lost a lot of money. He then started an American ice cream factory in Paris, and tried to induce French children to go through the streets licking ice cream cones, and another disaster followed. But for Ring Lardner, Jed Kiley was a fascination.

One day two already noted newspaper writers, Heywood Broun and Ruth Hale, his wife—a member and, I believe, one of the founders of the Lucy Stone League—came to my office at the Army Edition. Heywood was the great iconoclast of American journalism of the time. Not even the landing of the first

U.S. soldiers in France brought him to his knees. The concluding lines of the first paragraph of his news story chronicling this historic event has a G.I. looking at the port of landing (name secret) and shouting, "Say, do they serve enlisted men in this town?"

Ruth Hale interested me more than her famous husband. She was not only a women's rights leader of the time, she was interested in my experiences with unions in a newspaper office.

I told them about the brothers Sterling, foreman of the composing room and makeup boss of the Pittsburgh *Post*. Both men had laughed at me and my salary—which had risen to twenty-eight dollars a week when I became night editor. My predecessor, named managing editor, was now paid fifty dollars. Every one of a dozen men in the composing room, the Sterlings assured me, was getting more money than the best reporters on the floor below, more than the city editor, more than the drama critic, more than the aristocratic lady who consented to be our society editor. All the men on the third floor belonged to the Typographical Union. None worked more than eight hours a day—we reporters and editors usually worked ten hours, sometimes twelve, and in times of disasters day and night, twenty-four hours, without an extra cent in pay.

When I told the brothers Sterling I would like to join their union, they said, form your own; and at this point in my story Ruth Hale said decisively, "That is just what we should do." But at this time, 1918, Heywood Broun was not interested.

In 1934 Heywood Brown organized the American Newspaper Guild as a unit of the CIO. Today he is honored in every branch of journalism. But no one seems to know that it was Ruth Hale who year after year talked union to her husband. Heywood Broun admitted it all to us one night when we were his guests at the fifth-anniversary celebration of the American Newspaper Guild. (But why hasn't the guild or one of the big journalism magazines looked into this bit of history and, if my suspicion is confirmed, honored Ruth Hale as the liberator of American journalists?)

Edward Marshall

One of the most interesting men I met in London, one who was to play an important part in my later history, was Edward Marshall, who operated his newspaper syndicate out of the offices of the *Chicago Tribune*. Marshall had been a correspondent in the Spanish-American War. He had been at Colonel Theodore Roosevelt's side at San Juan Hill and at Las Guayamas, where he was shot and lost a leg.

Long before there was any muckraking in world journalism or even investigative reporting, Marshall had tried to do his best to set the historic record straight. Marshall was an admirer of Theodore Roosevelt; nevertheless he was an honest enough journalist to tell us that the famous "charge up San Juan Hill," which eventually put T.R. in the White House, never took place. Marshall told me: "Theodore Roosevelt did not 'charge' up San Juan Hill. Nobody 'charged.' How can you 'charge' if you have no horses? Our regiment of cavalry had no horses at that time, the horses were still on the mainland, in Florida. We walked. It is true there was still some firing."

At Las Guayamas fellow war correspondents Stephen Crane, Richard Harding Davis and James Creelman carried Marshall from the battlefield to a dressing station where a doctor, then unknown—the doctor who later made the building of the Panama Canal possible by clearing it of yellow fever and malaria—probed for the bullet by candlelight. He was Dr. Gorgas.

Marshall was in a delirium most of the time, and when coming to he sang this verse of a popular tune that Crane and other war correspondents mentioned in dispatches repeated around the world:

> *Oh, the moonlight's fair tonight along the Wabash,*
> *From the fields there comes the breath of new-mown hay;*
> *Through the sycamores the candle lights are gleaming,*
> *On the banks of the Wabash, far away.*

Crane and others reported it was the smell of ether that Marshall mistook for new-mown hay, but "The Banks of the

Wabash" became the state song of Indiana, and its author, Paul Dresser, became famous. (Many years later Paul's brother, Theodore Dreiser, who had retained the original German family name, told me that it was he who had written the words for this one verse of the song, at Paul's request.)

Marshall frequently told me stories or asked questions I found amazing. "Did you know," he once said, "that Hearst had his own warship in the Spanish-American War?" Hearst also had his yacht standing by, and it was this ship that took Marshall to a hospital back home. Once Marshall asked me, "Do you know who greeted Roosevelt when we reached the top of San Juan Hill—walking? A company of Negro cavalrymen—dismounted of course. They had got there first. But no one ever gave Negroes any credit in those days."

Next to his Spanish-American War stories the most interesting subject Marshall spoke about was the friendship and annual excursions of a famous group of which he was a member—the only journalist—and he had never written a word on this subject. The three other regulars were Thomas A. Edison, John Burroughs and Henry Ford. Harvey Firestone, another member, did not go every year, but the meetings continued as long as the majority was alive.

What did they talk about?

We talked about only the forbidden subjects—politics and religion, what else is there? Sex? Money? Remember, these were mid-Victorian times.

Generally we agreed on one subject: religion. All of us were more or less freethinkers—do not confuse that with agnostics. We were agnostic in the sense that we did not know, but knew there was no way of knowing. None of our group was an atheist, although Edison was very nearly one: he did not believe in the Bible, the Creation in seven days or seven million days, he did not believe in a heaven and he did not believe in a hell, he did not believe in immortality. He may have had some idea of God—but not a personal God.

As for Burroughs, he was a very old man, and the first to die—he was born, I think, in the early 1830s. He had the greatest influence on all of us. He had no theological beliefs whatever, his only God was science, he worshipped science; he once told us science had done more good for the world than all the religions from the time of the Pharaohs, and that included Christianity.

Burroughs, I think, had the clearest mind of any man I ever knew, certainly the clearest in our group, although the oldest.

The Edward Marshall Syndicate consisted of some thirty of the leading newspapers in the United States—but not the richest. Not one of them then could have afforded to have its own man in London or in Pershing's press section—G-2D—and of the thirty, the following contributed the funds for putting me and keeping me in that outfit: The Atlanta *Constitution,* Boston *Post,* Cleveland *Leader,* Detroit *Free Press,* Pittsburgh *Dispatch,* St. Louis *Globe-Democrat,* Philadelphia *Press,* and Akron *Beacon-Journal.*

According to the U.S. Army records, I became a member of G-2D on May 8, 1918. By that time a number of the most prominent journalists, editors and newspaper owners who had constituted the first group had already gone back to America. The argument as to whether we were to accept full army captaincies and wear the entire Sam Browne belt still persisted. In the British and French armies every war correspondent attached to headquarters was a captain. Most of the American group, however, told General Pershing that although they did not object to saluting everyone from a major up, we did not want the poor doughboys, the fighting men, a number of whom would certainly lose their lives in a few days or weeks, to be saluting us, journalists, men who did not know one end of a rifle from another and could not fire even a revolver.

A few, notably Mr. James of *The New York Times,* wanted to be real captains. But Pershing, a very strict military man, sided with us, and so we remained throughout the war in officers' uniforms but without any sign of rank. And some of us wore only the bottom half of the Sam Browne belt.

Part III

The War to End All Wars

Chapter 8

Great Correspondents

Every newspaperman in the civilized world, I believe, would have given most of his fortune and several years of his life, if that was possible, to be a member of Pershing's Army Press Section, which the press-hating general had limited to twenty-one. (It is true that the record shows more than a hundred men—and one woman, Peggy Hull—who could claim membership, from a week to a year; although we had one fatality and one severely wounded, we had replacements almost every week.)

The original members, almost without exception, were already famous when they left America, and the replacements were star reporters—with one exception, the present writer of these adventures. Again, it was luck or accident that placed me in the company of such men as Irvin S. Cobb, Damon Runyon, William Allen White, Heywood Broun and Floyd Gibbons, and such lesser stars as George Patullo and William Slavens McNutt, who wrote for the million-circulation weekly magazines.

Cobb was probably the best-known and highest-paid member of G-2D, A. E. F. in France, famous for his Negro stories. It was a time when ethnic jokes flourished and the word "racist" was found only in dictionaries. The two best Cobb stories I remember concern Black soldiers in our army. In our time all Black units were commanded by white officers, and if Cobb had said so, one story at least would have lost its racist sting. But as Cobb told it:

"There was this terrible bombardment"—he mentioned the sector—"and these two companies got most of it, and they broke. I stopped one of the men on the road and said, 'Why didn't you sit it out in the dugout?'

" 'Boss,' he replied, 'where I was there was no dugout.'

" 'Well,' I said, 'you could at least have climbed a tree.'

" 'Boss,' he replied, 'there wasn't enough trees for our officers!' "

The other story concerned a walking wounded.

"I was coming up the road by the X . . . Division," said Cobb, "when I saw this Negro soldier"—he did not say "Negro"—"and I noticed he was wounded.

" 'I see you've really been in the war,' I said. 'I see you've been up front, you've been in a battle, you've been wounded. I'm proud of you.'

" 'Boss,' he replied, 'I don't know what you talkin' about. I was walkin' along with my buddies in those there woods up yonder, the captain he says, go there, and I goes there, and captain he says, go here, and I goes here, and then a perfectly strange gentleman come up and shot me.' "

(The vast majority of our men did not know what the Great War was about and why they were in France.)

When Damon Runyon died, the obituaries united in praising him. His date of birth was given, his career told. There was not one hint that in his youth he had been a radical reporter and poet.

In the year Pershing's press corps was stationed in Coblenz, Germany, we knew Damon as a straight Hearst man—with a sense of humor. In fact, on December 13, 1918, when our troops marched into town and across the bridge to the fortress on the other side of the Rhine, Runyon's story featured the First Division's dog, name Vesle in honor of a river in France and an American victory. Damon described Vesle leading the American army and "doing his duty" on the bridge pillar on the opposite side.

The press corps was quartered in a fine hotel. Our club had for its motto "Let us tell the truth." Damon renamed it the Raspberry Club: "We will give the whole world the raspberry."

Damon was the only war correspondent who did not touch a drop of whiskey, beer or wine. He said he was a reformed drinker. That is about all we knew of his past.

Floyd Gibbons

*I*n June 1918, when the Germans again broke through the French lines at the Chemin des Dames, Foch, and Pershing threw in more than a score of divisions to stop them. The entire press corps of the U.S. Army was in the wheatfields that day. We were free to choose our divisions and many, myself included, chose the Second because half of its infantry were the two marine regiments, noted for their bravery. But unlike all the rest of us, who were back of them, Floyd Gibbons was ahead of the marines, and when he stood up in the wheatfield a German sniper in a tree shot out his left eye. "I caught it in my hands," Gibbons said later.

I helped carry Floyd back to a road used by our ambulance service. Someone recognized a driver—Patterson McNutt, son of a member of our press section—and persuaded him to drive Gibbons all the way to the American Hospital at Neuilly, outside Paris, rather than dump him with thousands of wounded at a field hospital. Gibbons's dictated story, headlined "With the help of God and a few Marines," not only added to his *Laconia* fame but certified the great marine myth. Not that the marines were not indeed the best fighting brigade in our army, but whether they had the help of God is doubtful, and the impression that they won the battle, every battle, and won the war all by themselves, is somewhat exaggerated.

Foch had sent in twenty-three trained divisions, Pershing sent in the Second and Third. The marine brigade did better than any other. How bloody this battle was is evident from the casualty figures: before Château Thierry–Belleau Woods was over we had six thousand dead. (It was on the first day, when we were in the wheatfield, that a marine sergeant named Daniel Daly yelled to his men—at Lucy-en-Bocage—the immortal words, "Come on, you sons of bitches; do you want to live forever?")

A great part of the marine fame was the result of censorship. No more, no less stupid than all censors, our officers told us to be careful never to identify our units: you could say army, navy, artillery, infantry, marines, they warned us, but no more identification. We told the facts. But editors back home saw the word "marines," they knew all about the two regiments and the Second Division, they knew all about public interest in this outfit, and they knew that "marines" meant a thrilling story, and that "infantry" meant nothing to most readers.

When Floyd came out of the hospital, he wore a white patch over his left eye. This was not a romantic affectation; the German sniper's bullet had also destroyed his lower eyelid, so he could not use an artificial eye. But his arm was in a black sling and the French had pinned the Croix de Guerre and another fancy colored ribbon and medal on it, and Floyd left us and went lecturing through the United States to boost morale and do a "public relations" job long before that term was introduced.

When he came back to G-2D, Floyd told us stories of his experiences as a lecturer, and of the "bull sessions" of the wounded men in hospital in which all seven prohibited words were in daily use and no conventional respect for anything under heaven and on earth was ever shown.

"One day," Floyd once said, "the session was devoted to what are we going to do when we get home. They were full of grudges. They were going to change everything." (It is a fact, rarely mentioned, that the officer-bankers who first organized the American Legion in 1919 did so to quell the unrest among the veterans who saw actual service.)

"Most everyone, I think," continued Floyd, "was going to take up where he left off, but then strike out in a new direction. But one doughboy shook his head and said, 'I'm going back to my home town in Ohio. We still have the same old small-town post office and grocery store there, and the stove, and the cracker barrel, and we still sit around and talk and waste our time. I'm going to join these old-timers, I'm going to put my hand in the cracker barrel, and I'm going to talk, and by God, *I'm going to outlie the G.A.R.*' "

Chapter 9

Rickenbacker, Guthrie, MacArthur, Pershing, Patton, Woollcott

I
t was generally said that modern warfare, except for members of the air forces gave little opportunity for great individual acts of heroism—and every war needs heroes for morale purposes. For four years of trench warfare, four years of stalemate, the daily communiqués on both sides repeated the weary phrase, *"In Westen Nichts Neues,"* no news from the Western front: it was four years of staying in trenches and dugouts, sometimes advancing a few yards; it was nothing but life—and death.

With the arrival of the U.S. Army at the front everything, of course, changed. Millions of men came, young, fresh from the fields, mines, factories, and business offices of America, a few of them trained just well enough to attack and break the Hindenburg Line and end the war—and incidentally create new heroes, and also give the press section something to write home about.

In fact, in our eagerness to please our readers we frequently helped create new heroes whose clay feet showed notoriously later on, and we created myths that live, and will continue to live in history despite all the revisionist historians. However, although four of us from G-2D took an oath on the battlefield Armistice Day to tell the truth from then on, and although I once wrote "We all lied about the war," I did not mean to say that war correspondents were the liars. In all wars truth is the first casualty. The villain is not the war correspondent in most cases—it is the War Department, the propaganda department which may style itself "office of information," it is the paid propagandists and super-patriots, and only exeptionally the eye-witness, the reporter on the field of battle.

Eddie Rickenbacker

*B*ecause the newspapers that printed my mail stories were published from Boston to California, I found that next to the units in the Rainbow (42nd) Division, representing twenty-six or twenty-seven states, the newly arrived air squadrons were the best sources for my "mailers" because each would deal with officers or men in several cities and states—not only "human interest" but "local interest" would please my editors.

The first American airfield in France was commanded by Major Hartley, and the first man to become famous was Eddie Rickenbacker, the fighting airman who already had a reputation as an automobile racer. He became our first ace, and eventually the best friend I had in the U.S. armed forces.

In reporting the exploits of our airmen we, the members of the U.S. Army press section, had to force ourselves not to become friends with the pilots of the fighting squadrons, notably the 95th and the 94th—the "Hat-in-the-Ring" squadron, commanded by Captain Eddie. The chances of these aviators getting killed were the highest of all branches of the forces. You were bound to suffer.

One day Rick said to me, "Want to spend a week or two with the Ninety-fourth? I've got a cot for you."

To my obvious but unasked question he replied: "Lieutenant Coolidge was killed this morning." He and Rick had been flying side by side. Suddenly, without a sound he could distinguish, there was no Coolidge plane there. "The only explanation," said Rick, "is that a shell from a Big Bertha aimed at Paris completely annihilated Coolidge and his plane—our ground forces report not a trace of man or machine on the ground."

While I shared the tent with Rickenbacker he became the American ace of aces. During that year, 1918, he was wounded, and had to stay in the hospital a long time. Frank Luke beat him for the title for a few weeks. When Rick came back, he resumed his place as our best fighter and wound up ace of aces with twenty-six "kills." On Armistice Day I was his guest again, and he asked me to write his biography, but I was not free to do so.

A quarter of a century later, February 8, 1943, to be exact, I had to publish in my weekly *In fact* a small item headlined "Rickenbacker's Labor Record." It accused my former friend of repeating the greatest anti-labor falsehood of World War II, the report published throughout the United States that the labor unions sabotaged the war effort by refusing to unload war materials at Guadalcanal.

It became known—at least in the liberal and labor press— as "the Guadalcanal Lie." It originated in the Akron *Beacon-Journal,* the writer admitting it was a rumor, there was no evidence; but it was headlined everywhere, and when the U.S. Navy issued an official denial the newspapers that had given the fraud headlines and indignant editorials published one six- or eight-line paragraph of the fact. *In fact* said:

> Rickenbacker repeated his unfounded and unwarranted libels against labor at a meeting of the Society of Automotive Engineers, Detroit, Jan. 22. Previously it had been thought Rickenbacker got his perverted views from Peglerites . . . and other voices of the National Association of Manufacturers. . . . Now it appears the poison was in Rickenbacker's system ever since his own workingmen asked him for living wages, years ago, when he was a manufacturer . . . one of the worst records in a democracy as head of an auto firm bearing his name. . . .

On March 1 of the same year it was reported that the Ku

Klux Klan had endorsed Rickenbacker for his crusade against the labor unions.

You will find none of these facts about the later career of the ace of aces turned automaker and labor-union fighter in the Hollywood film *Captain Eddie* which I have seen several times on television, the last on November 21, 1976. Nor any mention that in the 1950s Captain Eddie said that Joe McCarthy was so great an American that the people would one day erect a statue to him in Washington.

Lieutenant Ramon Guthrie

*I*n the two observation squadrons on Major Hartley's famous field I can remember the name of only one hero, and his story was spectacular. These two observation squadrons flew De Havilland 4s, known as "the flying coffins." As Lieutenant Ramon Guthrie of the 11th Observation Squadron explained, the gasoline tanks were situated between pilot and observer and, when hit, were sure to explode and kill both men. Even a heavy landing might dislodge the tanks and cause an explosion. By the time our American squadrons were in the field, the British had replaced the 4s with De Havilland 9s.

This is Guthrie's story—he himself frequently denied many of the details, being a modest man:

A general was visiting the field. Guthrie's major wanted to show off. He told the 11th to go up.

"There are only six planes that can take off," Guthrie told the major; "the others are no good, and of the six only one has had its guns tested."

"Test them on the Germans," replied the major.

"What about a fighter escort?"

None was available.

"It is almost certain death," said Guthrie.

The major said, "Look here; America is lousy with aviators. We've got more than we can use if this war lasts ten years."

The six planes of the 11th went up, unguarded. No sooner were they near the German lines than they were attacked by at least thirty German fighters, probably a Richthofen squadron known to be in this neighborhood.

One by one Guthrie's five companions were shot down.

Guthrie's gun worked. He opened fire.

"It wasn't necessary to aim at anything," he told me on my next visit to his field; "there were so many Huns over me that all I had to do was fire without looking, and I hit one, two, three, four."

When all his companions had been killed, Guthrie returned to the base at Toul. As he taxied to a hangar Guthrie saw his major. He opened fire on him. The commanding officer ran into the woods.

Attempting to kill a superior officer is a major crime. Guthrie was held for court-martial. But the news was out, and a French officer arrived demanding a public ceremony in which he intended to pin the Croix de Guerre with four palms—one for every German plane shot down—on Guthrie's uniform. Citation from Marshal Foch.

(If Guthrie had shot down a fifth plane he would have been an ace—the only observer-ace in history, I was told.)

What was the outcome? A compromise. No court-martial. But no Croix de Guerre either.

In World War II Guthrie, by then a college professor, volunteered and became a member of Donovan's OSS. He was dropped behind the lines in France, fought with the Resistance, got the Distinguished Service Medal, the silver star for gallantry and other awards.

When the protests against President Johnson's war in Vietnam swept the campuses, Professor Guthrie returned all his medals.

He concluded his life teaching Proust at Dartmouth.

Douglas MacArthur

The first already well-known and eventually famous officer I met was Colonel (or Lieutenant Colonel) Douglas MacArthur.

He was on headquarters staff of the 42nd, the Rainbow

Division, which was his creation and which he named. It actually had units from a majority of the states—he had planned to have all forty-eight; and because my employer wanted me to get "local color" and "human interest" stories of men from all the States in which he had clients, I attached myself either to the Rainbow or the air force.

The Rainbow Division got its training in the quiet Luneville-Baccarat sector of France, facing a German division at rest or one of Ludendorff's reserves, the elderly men who later became Hindenburg's last resource. Captain Kindler and Lieutenant Meesie, L Company, 166th Infantry, the "Ohios," invited me to share their dugout the first two weeks I was in the trenches. The very first night I heard a German shell hit the dugout on our left, burying and killing six men of the Iowa infantry.

Two or three nights later we put over a box barrage, isolating in a square of heavy artillery fire a small part of a German trench, so that we could make a raid and bring back a prisoner who would tell us, or from whose uniform we could learn, if the old Landwehr still faced us, or a fresh German division, which would indicate that an attack was being planned against us.

It was usual for our colonel, Ben Hough of Columbus, Ohio, to send a lieutenant with three or four men on this mission. But this night, to everyone's surprise, a real live colonel from headquarters came into our trenches, asked for a few volunteers, and led the raid himself. This officer had a great reputation in the Rainbow and was soon to become famous.

When he and his men came back, MacArthur was leading in the German prisoner, an elderly man, by an ear. A sight to remember. Something for history, perhaps.

In no time at all this incident leaped the trenches of the Rainbow and became known throughout the American army.

Although I spent more time with the Rainbow than any other division, I never saw MacArthur again except at reviews and other events when the war ended. Many Rainbow officers worshipped MacArthur, but some were skeptical.

In 1932 MacArthur gassed the Bonus Army encamped in

Washington, causing a national sensation and angry debate. Some said there was a case to be made out in his favor; others, who like myself never "worshipped" military heroes, were shocked. Then in 1938, toward the end of my freelance decade in America, I had my own war with the general.

Three years earlier MacArthur, by then chief of staff of the U.S. Army, had published a pamphlet, "Military Aid in Civil Disturbances," which had become the guidebook for not only the army but also the National Guard and various vigilante outfits everywhere suppressing strikes and disturbances during the Great Depression.

It is true that General MacArthur did not mention the destruction of labor unions or even labor unrest as the real goal of his rules for suppression. He gives five illustrations, such as "domestic disturbances," "a mob determined upon lynching" and "a riot in a penal institution," but eventually he comes to the use of gas against strikers, and says:

> In conclusion, wish to state that all efforts should be made when the use of gas is contemplated to supply plenty of it.

Then, on page 18, appears his "Shoot to Kill" suggestion:

> Blank cartridges should never be used against a mob, nor should a volley be fired over the heads of the mob even if there is little danger of hurting persons in the rear. Such things will be regarded as an admission of weakness, or an attempt to bluff, and may do much more harm than good.

Again, on pages 13 and 14 of his little book MacArthur recommends that "airplanes may be used for the purpose of keeping rioters off roofs by means of machine-gun fire," "armored cars will be especially valuable in riot duty," coast artillery use "would depend upon the equipment"; he recommends cavalry because "armed men on horseback" have a great effect on morale; the hand grenades he recommends are "especially those filled with chemicals," machine guns, tanks, three-inch mortars can be used on occasions, but of course "infantry should and will invariably constitute the major part of any command employed in suppressing domestic disorders."

And so, for at least three years, the "Shoot to Kill" War Department manual justified every army, National Guard, militia, state and city police attack with gas and rifles and machine guns at factories, mines and workshops across the country where a great new force, known as the CIO, had begun organizing labor throughout the United States—all sorts of labor, from the lowest grade always ignored by the aristocratic AFL, to newspapermen.

In gathering the documentation for my article I found numerous parallels between the MacArthur War Department writings and fascist publications in Europe, notably Mussolini's Italy. For example *Basic Field Manual,* Vol. VII, Part 3, "Domestic Disturbances" (then available to anyone for ten cents) stated on page 22:*

> b. Troops will be disposed with the object of . . . . (2) Driving the mob into or through the district of the city where looting is the least profitable and where destruction of property incident to military operation will be reduced to a minimum and preferably fall on the rioters or the class of people composing the rioters. . . .

It has always been known that all Nazi and fascist movements were subsidized, if not originated, by special interests—although neither the Nazis nor the Fascisti ever admitted the Marxist theory of class warfare as apparently MacArthur did when he suggested that a certain class of people should be saved, while the "class of people composing the rioters" should be exposed to the looting.

Again, *Army Training Manual* No. 2000–25, used for training our forces from 1928 to 1932, attacks American democracy with harsher terms than Hitler or any European dictator ever did. Here is the U.S. War Department definition:

---

*All documents mentioned here are fully quoted in my 1938 book, *You Can't Do That,* written with the help of the American Civil Liberties Union. See pp. 194–203.

> Democracy: A government of the masses. Authority derived
> through mass meetings or any other form of direct expres-
> sion. Results in mobocracy. Attitude towards property is
> communistic—negating property rights. Attitude towards
> law is that the will of the majority shall regulate. . . . Result
> is demagogism, license, agitation, discontent, anarchy.

No sooner was this item, including the MacArthur "Shoot
to Kill" order and the War Department attack on American
Democracy published than the New York *Post* and the *World-
Telegram,* both then great liberal democratic dailies, took it up, as
well as, of course, the great standbys of liberalism in America,
The Nation and *The New Republic* (unfortunately, each able to
find only some 25,000 subscribers in all the forty-eight states).
The *Post* sent its Washington correspondent to confront the War
Department and the chief of staff.

So, early in the next year, without any public announcement, the U.S. government stopped selling the works of General
MacArthur for ten cents a copy. Several of my readers who tried
to order that part of the field manual and got their dimes back
with a printed form saying simply "B.F.M., Vol. VII, Pt. 3 has
been withdrawn." The then Hearst White House correspondent—whose name I have never divulged—sent me the following document, issued by the War Department:

Confidential
Headquarters First Army Corps. . . .
Subject: Return of Basic Field Manual.
1. The War Department has advised this headquarters that
the above publication is withdrawn from circulation and
use. . . .

Harvey W. Miller, Col. A.G. D.
Adjutant General.

But, some time later, writing the history of the foregoing
episode, with the aid of the American Civil Liberties Union, I
was also forced to add that investigations in several states by my
readers in the course of several years following the official withdrawal showed that the National Guard, state and city police

forces, and vigilante outfits that spring up every time a strike is called, or when crowds march for a great public reform, continued to use the Basic Field and Army Training Manuals, and where the booklets were no longer obtainable, they continued to use the suggestions they contained for dealing with "domestic disturbances." The spirit of General MacArthur survived.

Pershing and Saint-Mihiel

MacArthur in the Great War may or may not quite have equaled Alexander, Hannibal and Napoleon, but of this there is no doubt: he was a man made for Hollywood and television. Pershing, so far as the mass media is concerned, was just the opposite. Floyd Gibbons, who had been with him in Mexico, said he never saw the general smile, and neither did the press corps in France—with one exception.

That once was at the plank bridge over the Meuse River at Saint-Mihiel when I asked him to stop for a fraction of a second so I could take his picture. It was, and is still considered, a memorable event. The world had been told that morning that the American Army had "stormed" Saint-Mihiel, that this was our first great victory, and that General Pershing was the hero of heroes. Unfortunately, on their way to Saint-Mihiel the U.S. Signal Corps, Premier Clemenceau, the "Tiger" of France, and all the war correspondents of all the Allied countries except me got lost or were stopped by tank traps and mined and blown-up roads prepared by the Germans during their four-year occupation of the Saint-Mihiel salient. Pershing and his group were the only lucky ones besides me who found roads without tank traps. The secret of my and my artist guests' safe arrival in the town hours before Pershing was the brilliant thinking of my Cadillac driver, Sergeant Jack Corper, who went southwest and then far north of the town, trying to enter it from the west side of the Meuse, from Chouvroncourt. Here, as everywhere else, there was a tank trap, from house to house, across every road and every street. But from Chouvroncourt it was only a five-minute walk to Saint-Mihiel.

"Please, General Pershing," I said, "please stop for just a second." The general showed no surprise at seeing either French colonial troops building the plank bridge or a member of G-2D (and my two guests, two members of the six-man-strong U.S. art department, Wallace Morgan and Ernest Peixotto, each in a captain's uniform) confronting him. Perhaps he was psychologically incapable of accepting the fact that here he was making his first (and only) "triumphal entry" into a captured city, only to find that hundreds of French soldiers and at least three Americans had been there long before his arrival.

Pershing smiled.

There are no movies of the event. There is nothing in the War Department records except a duplicate set of my pictures—for which General Pershing later sent me a most gracious thank-you letter. Nevertheless, to this very day no historian, no journalist, no researcher, has ever asked or answered obvious questions. Historians, repeating the great falsehoods that appeared in the American press, are capable, for example, of such statements as " . . . the American First Army, 550,000 strong, took the offensive and wiped the Germans from Saint-Mihiel" (William Miller, *A New American History*), and "A force of more than 500,000 Americans wiped out the St. Mihiel salient near Verdun" (Professor Walter C. Langsam, Columbia University History Department, in *The World Since 1914*). And year after year the famous Hollywood film, *The Yanks Are Coming* is revived on television, fictionized and falsifying history. At the climax voices mention the "battle" and "capture" of Saint-Mihiel, "the first great all-American victory," and the beginning of the liberation of France after an occupation of four years.

Both the truth and the facts are clear: there was no "storming" of Saint-Mihiel, no "wiping out" of the Saint-Mihiel sector—and therefore no "triumphal entry" by General Pershing.

Pershing's headquarters and G-2D both knew early in September 1918 that the Germans were withdrawing from Saint-Mihiel rather than risking the salient being cut off and all their soldiers and guns and impedimenta captured. (In my first year as Berlin correspondent, when I tried to interview every prominent

German officer, I came upon a General Ledebour who told me it was he who had issued the order for withdrawal a fortnight before Pershing's entry, that Saint-Mihiel was stripped of everything of military value and every soldier gone at least a week before the French colonials entered.)

All the historic accounts, which are total falsifications, are based on the United Press—and perhaps other—news stories passed by the U.S. censor, both the writers and the censors innocent of intentionally planning what should now be called one of the greatest hoaxes of all time.

On the evening of September 12, 1918, Pershing sent his intelligence chief, General Denis Nolan, and his chief of operations, General Fox Connor, to brief the press corps on the Friday the 13th battle. The briefing began with a description of the great barrage planned for 4:30 A.M. and proceeded minute by minute, with the occupation of the enemy trenches, and finally the arrival of Pershing in the captured town. Fred Ferguson of the UP, and perhaps others, before leaving for the front that night wrote out the entire briefing, changing only the tenses: where Fox Connor said "we will," the war correspondent or correspondents wrote "we have." Captain Gerald Morgan was our censor, although the head of our press censorship section was Major Bozeman Bulger, a former magazine writer of national reputation. The arrangement was simple and legitimate and even ethical. The story was written in "takes," or on sheets, each with a paragraph or two. Each take recorded the "attack" by the quarter or half hour. While the war correspondents were in the trenches or advancing with the troops, the censor was to release each take the moment Pershing's headquarters announced the battle going according to plan.

As all went well as predicted and described by Connor and Nolan, the censor released the great news story take by take. There was only one error: the entire Battle of Saint-Mihiel was fought by the American army, 500,000 or 550,000 men strong, against empty air—against nothing. There were no Germans opposed to us. There was no artillery fire against us. No rifle fire. No airplanes. There was nothing. We had made the greatest attack of the war against an enemy that had departed at least seven days earlier.

Ferguson was congratulated by the United Press for one of the "greatest scoops in modern history." And history will no doubt continue to record the "triumphal entry of General Pershing into Saint-Mihiel."*

One of the famous members of the A.E.F. was Father Duffy, chaplain of the 165th Infantry, which had been the New York "Fighting 69th." Father Duffy was a great favorite with the war correspondents, who found the coincidence of a priest, an Irishman (naturally with a sense of humor), a famous regiment and New York irresistible.

The day after the Saint-Mihiel salient "attack" in which the Rainbow took part, Francis Patrick Duffy, caked with mud, unshaven, dead-tired, was brought in his car to our hotel in Meaux. He was barely able to whisper a request for a good shot of whiskey. By dinnertime that night he had recovered. He told us this story:

"The day before the attack one of the boys came to me and said, 'Father, you know I am going into my first attack tomorrow?'

"I said I knew. He went on: 'Father, I'm scared. I was brought up without religion. Father, I want to be converted, right now.'

---

*I have tried to set the historical record straight in a book called *Even the Gods Cannot Change History*—the phrase is Aristotle's (*Ethics,* V, vi.)—but only three newspapers reviewed this book; 297 other leading dailies in America, including *The New York Times* and *The New York Times Book Review* refused to mention it.

Two postscripts: but what about the capture of several divisions of German troops with artillery and full equipment at Saint-Mihiel? The facts are: with usual military headquarters stupidity and blundering, the Germans weeks earlier had ordered reinforcements sent and forgot to recall the troop trains; the Germans arrived days after the "capture" and were surrounded.

In another instance of Ferguson's journalistic trick, Henry Wales of the *Chicago Tribune* in 1927 wrote the whole story of the arrival of Lindbergh at Le Bourget hours before he went there by auto to greet the flier. He could not communicate from the flying field. When the French announced Lindbergh's landing, the Paris office released the story, detailed and imagined, nevertheless a world scoop—of sorts.

"I said, 'That's fine, my boy, but I can't do it in a minute. It takes time. I'll have to give you a lot of Bible instruction first.'

" 'Oh, that's all right,' the soldier replied, 'I believe in the whole goddamn business.' "

Every war correspondent loved a priest who could talk that way.

(In New York City there is a well-deserved monument in Father Duffy's honor.)

Patton

*A*mong the scores of "historic" reports on Saint-Mihiel, all of them wrong, there is one that the 304th Tank Brigade participated in the capture.

No American, or any other tank, ever got near Saint-Mihiel. There was no possible road or way to Saint-Mihiel that had not been mined or that did not have tank traps. Subsequently at tank headquarters, Paris, I was told that the corps was commanded by someone they called "Rockenback," but that was the only time I heard that name. I did hear from cable correspondents that we at last did have a tank corps, so for a feature story I went looking for it and a certain major or lieutenant colonel named George Patton, Jr., who could always be distinguished from all other officers by his two pearl-handled revolvers.

I found him. I also found that he had been able to collect a total of six little Renault tanks, and in the hope of some day having a full deck of fifty-two, had begun painting playing cards on the turrets. On four he painted the 10s, and his command tank had on it the ten of diamonds. His next choice was queens—he had two, but whether they were hearts, spades, diamonds or clubs I no longer remember.

Patton had been in battle. But not at Saint-Mihiel. He told me all about it because, he said, I was the first war correspondent to visit his outfit, and he hoped I would write a story telling America how small his tank corps was and how important it was to build American tanks and send vast numbers of them against the enemy.

Patton, in 1918, was a most unassuming man. He let me get into his ten of diamonds, told me where to stand behind him, and drove it around. When I said I would like to duplicate battlefield conditions, he obligingly drove the tank into a huge shell hole nearby and rolled around and out of it, knocking me about considerably, but making a good Sunday feature story back home.*

Alexander Woollcott

My last adventure in World War I was joining the editors of the army's *Stars and Stripes* in a search for the "Lost Battalion." On October 2, a few weeks before the Armistice, one of the most dramatic episodes of the war had occurred: in the advance of the entire American army in the field amidst unparalleled confusion, this New York unit—2nd Battalion, 308th Infantry, 77th Division—was reported missing. What had happened was simply this: it had, along with other battalions, regiments and divisions, advanced rapidly and victoriously—but then it came to an almost perpendicular cliff, hundreds of feet high, and hundreds of feet long, not shown on any map; and so this company just stopped there because it could not advance another step.

The Germans immediately closed in behind it. But it was never lost, although history books then and now refer to it as "the lost battalion." The United Press had had a world scoop: "Major Whittlesey with provisional battalion 77th Division cut off north Charlevaux Valley. Only contact pigeons." This story made page one in New York five days in succession—a great human interest story, everyone said.

One day—it was early in October and I happened to be in Paris—as I came out of the Place de la Concorde station of the

---

*In World War II Patton captured Saint-Lô. He marched or rolled from Chartres to Czechoslovakia. In Sicily in August 1943, according to war correspondent Noel Monks—one of the few journalists who witnessed the Nazi Condor Legion destroy Guernica in Spain for the Spanish Führer Franco and told the facts—Patton had called a soldier suffering from shell shock a "yellow bastard," had slapped the man—the wrong man, incidentally—and had shouted, "There is no shell shock. It's an invention of the Jews."

Metro I was surrounded by three GIs whom I did not know and who did not know me, but I knew the insignia of the *Stars and Stripes* and they knew the red C on the green brassard signifying Pershing's press corps. They identified themselves as Sergeant Alexander Woollcott, Private Harold Ross (later a founder-editor of *The New Yorker*) and Private Hudson Hawley of *Stars and Stripes,* the official U.S. Army weekly. There had always been rivalry and dirty words, perhaps even enmity, between the war correspondents in the two camps. The *Stars and Stripes* men accused us of staying at headquarters, shunning the shellfire at the front. (In historic fact, it was later shown that our casualties were proportionately larger than theirs.)

"We are going to look for the lost battalion," said Woollcott; "we dare you to come along."

The highlight of the ensuing adventure was the volunteer work of Sergeant Woollcott the second night, when near the front we stopped at a provisional hospital in a roofless church. A number of blankets had been rigged as a tent so as to hide the light from the German aviators, and here our surgeons were working nights as well as days, trying to save the lives of wounded men. Woollcott, who had come over with an ambulance service, not only volunteered, but after a whole day's driving worked all night carrying stretchers soaked with blood or aiding the surgeons until they dropped to the floor exhausted. Ross and I were amazed by Woollcott's heroic work.

Next morning we came to Charlevaux Valley, just after 194 men had marched out alive, on their own feet. But we found buried or half-buried, many with hands or feet sticking out of the earth, the bodies of 107 men. The rest of Whittlesey's 679 men had been evacuated on stretchers.

We also learned that in the five days, October 2 to 7, in which the battalion had been surrounded, a body of myth, fiction and false reporting had come to life, the most popular item of which was Major Whittlesey's supposed reply to the German demand that he surrender. He is supposed to have said, "Go to hell." (In those days the last word was a forbidden one in most of the media.)

It is true that an American soldier, a prisoner, was sent by the Germans with a note requesting surrender. Whittlesey did not reply. He did, however, order two white airplane panels lying in the battalion area, which might have been mistaken for the equivalent of a white flag, hidden or destroyed. Knowing that his silence would provoke a German attack, he gave this order: "Fix bayonets and set yourselves." The Germans attacked. They were withstood. Altogether those heroic five days constituted one of the greatest ordeals experienced by any unit in World War I.

The "Lost Battalion" story was made for American journalism. It "made" the front page day after day. But soon we had the news that shook the world: Mr. Roy Howard's false armistice on November 8, and the real, November 11th, Armistice at eleven o'clock European time.

Chapter 10

~~~~~~~~~~

Armistice Day, 1918

Historians, notably those who know the despair, the hopelessness that the British, the Belgians, the French—and the Germans, too—suffered toward the end of four years of trench warfare—the fear it would last a lifetime, that everyone would be killed or wounded or die of starvation and disease—sometimes describe what happened at 11 A.M. on the eleventh day of the eleventh month of 1918 in words such as these:

> In that hour there fell a silence so overmastering, so unearthly, after the monstrous salvos of mighty siege pieces, the hideous rattle of murderous machine guns, which had shaken the souls of men and women over all the globe with their brutal reverberations, that the soldiers of both sides were held trance-like, gazing at each other with wide eyes of unbelief. It was too heavenly a thing to realize at first; too tremendous a truth, too solemn for acclaim. . . .

Not on our front. Not with the Rainbow Division.

At eight that morning, for reasons unexplained and never questioned, American artillery put down a tremendous barrage on all parts of our front as if to indicate a new great massed infantry attack, which, despite dugouts and helmets and withdrawals, undoubtedly added hundreds of dead and thousands of wounded to the twenty million or more casualties of World War I—thirty-four million if you include starvation victims in your statistics.

The bewildered enemy was forced to reply, and so the killing continued, and did not stop on our front at the magical hour of eleven. I can bear witness. Individual gunners and individualists among the infantrymen continued to fire indiscriminately, hoping no doubt to gain eternal glory by describing themselves later as the guys that fired the last shot in the war.*

At 10:59 the great rumble from afar, heard in Paris, heard in the towns and villages where the war correspondents lived, which had sounded like millions of men and women drowning in the seven seas, did diminish. For most continental Europeans it had never been artillery shells exploding, machine guns clattering, individual shots heard. For almost five years the sound of war had been this rumbling, drowning-gurgling sound, day and night, titanic but low, universal. The silence that came finally, when all the heroes had finished prolonging the war on a miniature scale, nevertheless was impressive—so impressive indeed it felt like a warning of death to millions of old soldiers—boys who had grown old in two or three years in the trenches.

A Man Could Stand Up, a soldier-novelist wrote, capturing in this one phrase out of the torment of his own experience the whole great story of the Armistice. Ford Madox Ford wrote this title several years later. His onetime pupil Joseph Conrad called it a stroke of genius, and some of us who had been in the trenches four weeks and not four years could imagine if not share the feeling. Millions of men had kept their heads down four years;

*In World War I 215 U.S. soldiers were killed and 1,114 wounded on Armistice Day. In World War II on V.E. day in Europe, one was killed, 12 wounded. (*Time,* May 28, 1945.)

no one could stand up without fear of the bullet bearing his name.

Men stood up. From the English Channel to the mountains of Switzerland men stood up and shouted. The British shouted, "We have come through." The French shouted, "We are alive." There was no shout of victory from Britain to Switzerland. It was a shout of joy, a shout in praise of life itself. (It was the civilians back home who shouted victory).

From our line I saw helmeted heads of German soldiers slowly appearing over the parapets. The Germans came into no-man's-land shyly, awkwardly, still frightened, but the Americans, followed by the French, rushed into the field and extended their hands in welcome. The Americans gave away food and cigarets. A large part of Armistice Day at the front was spent in swapping souvenirs. (The French had a saying, "The Germans fight for the Kaiser, the French for Glory, the Americans for Souvenirs.") For a five-cent chocolate bar you could get a Luger pistol. Strangest of all was the sudden revival of the German language by many American soldiers of German parentage.

On some sectors of the front there was a drizzly London fog, which may have made some British soldiers feel at home. Tommy Atkins did not go mad with victory. Most of the French veterans I saw permitted themselves to fraternize with men they had called "*sales Boches*" the day before, but their manner was restrained. The Americans, who had had the least warfare, were the wildest in celebration of peace.

Many Germans were also enthusiastic. They rushed into no-man's-land shouting "*Nie wieder Krieg*"; the French replied with "*Jamais plus la guerre,*" and the Americans who understood said nothing.

The terror had even gone out of the landscape. Every tree, every bush, every little rise in the ground, every little gulley, everything in nature had been evil in the days and nights of four years of trench warfare, and now sometimes a brave little bird might come over and perhaps even sing.

The very next day, November 12, commanding generals on both sides of the armistice line, frightened by all this "*Nie wieder*

Krieg" and "*Jamais plus la guerre*" stuff, and all this "brotherhood of man" nonsense, gave orders on all fronts for soldiers to remain resting on their arms, so to speak; the Armistice was not peace, it was an "arrangement"—and, besides, "discipline must never be relaxed in the armed forces."

Pershing came to Paris. He and Marshal Foch embraced, kissing each other on both cheeks. For once it seemed Black Jack actually betrayed an emotion, but he quickly pulled himself up and said a few words as he pinned the Distinguished Service Medal on his colleague.

Foch was overcome. His lips quivered. But the Generals Pétain, Gouraud, Weygand and Mangin—"Mangin the Butcher"—never betrayed human feelings. They were men of blood and iron. The official proclamation posted throughout Paris, said: "Blood ceases to flow. Our dead can sleep in peace. *Le jour de gloire est arrivé. Vive la France.*"

It was possible only for members of G-2D, the press department of the intelligence service of Pershing's army; I am sure that even a major general could not do this, but I did it. That great morning I was in no-man's-land watching the soldiers and officers of the Rainbow fraternize with the men they had been trying to kill the day before; and shortly afterward I was with the Rickenbacker 94th Squadron having a drink and celebrating, and then after a long drive to Paris I was there for the Pershing-Foch meeting. Toward evening I had to spend about two hours pushing my way through the crowds—I thought there were at least one million Parisians on the streets and in the public squares, but I finally got to the Café de la Paix and joined in the ribald singing of the American officers and war correspondents present.

G-2D took orders from no one but General Pershing himself, and so far as I remember he never gave us any. We wore officers' uniforms but had no duties. We were paid by great American press organizations, not the U.S. Army. Each of us, by contract with the army, was assigned a Cadillac and a sergeant or corporal to drive it. Nothing we ordered from any U.S. Army depot for the car cost us money. We had been assigned a mess officer by Pershing, and three meals a day cost us nothing. We were assigned a hotel wherever army headquarters went in France and Germany. Only in such adventures as trips to Paris did we spend our own money. (We were, however, each under a $5,000 cash-deposit bond to behave ourselves, and only one member of the corps was ever expelled—and we were never told why. His name was Westbrook Pegler.)

In return for all this, we did our best to be the daily historians of what we thought was the greatest war in all history, Wilson's "war to end war."

Chapter 11

~~~~~~~~~~~~~~

Hindenburg Confesses: U.S. Won the War

This was the biggest story of the war, certainly the most important news story of my journalistic three-quarters of a century, an important paragraph in the history not only of the United States, but of the world, and so far as I know it has never been published by anyone but me and appears in no historical work.

It all began Armistice Day in an accidental conversation among four of the twenty-one members of the press corps who happened to be in one group watching developments: Herbert Corey, who like myself wrote feature stories and sent them by mail to a syndicate, Lincoln Eyre of the New York *World,* St. Louis Post *Dispatch* and affiliated papers, Cal Lyon of the United Press, and I.

From the wild behavior of millions of human beings, soldiers and civilians that day, it was apparent that few, if any, thought of the millions of dead, the hundreds of thousands of men blown to pieces, the many more millions wounded, the pain and the suffering on a scale previously unknown in history. I do not remember which one of us—it was not I—suddenly said: "This must not happen again," and there walking in no-man's-land we stopped and solemnly shook hands and pledged each other to devote the remainder of our lives to writing the truth about this war—as a warning to the world that it must never again be repeated. In the story I later wrote for the Marshall Syndicate I concluded that "if the angel of the Lord had appeared before us on that battlefield and said to each one, 'Would you give your life to prevent another such war?' all four of us would gladly have gone out and died."

We four also decided that day that military discipline no longer applied to newspaper correspondents, and that we could break the Armistice regulations, drive into Germany, see for ourselves what really was going on there, and attempt to interview Field Marshal Hindenburg.

Success or failure, it turned out to be the greatest adventure of our lives.

It all began quite peacefully. We took our two Cadillacs—although we were technically entitled to one car each, the army never had enough to supply more than ten or eleven for us. Pershing had a Locomobil, the only one in France, and brigadier generals got Dodges. We drove from Luxembourg through a large part of France the Germans had held since 1914. One town, St. Menehold, was intact, and every store ready for business except that there was nothing inside, and no one outside to buy—not a human being, not even a dog. Deserted in 1914, it was too far from the trenches for even a stray shell to damage it. It was ghostly, even frightening. The roads were excellent; we drove fast and soon came upon the entire German Army in retreat.

At the sight of American uniforms there was a moment of surprise or fright among the soldiers. Then a high officer—we figured him to be at least a colonel—came over to see what the commotion was all about and gave a brisk order: "Take them into the woods and shoot them."

While Eyre was trying to explain, shouting now, that we

were not fighting soldiers but journalists, a sailor with a red armband arrived; everyone seemed respectful to him, and he asked a few questions. Eyre explained. The sailor became a friend: he suggested we go to headquarters in Frankfurt, find the sailor he named who was running that city, and ask for transportation to Kassell, where Hindenburg was now stationed. And, to Eyre's question, he pointed to the armband, which read Arbeiter und Soldatenrat, Workers and Soldiers' Council. He, and all the sailors running a vast part of Germany, were from Kiel; they had mutinied in the last days of the war and were now ruling the country.

We went to Frankfurt. The authorities there, headed by another sailor with an armband, told us to send our Cadillacs back to the American army. He found a car for us—it had no rubber tires, but something, perhaps rope, on the rims—and we traveled so slowly we might just as well have walked. But we somehow got to Kassel and put up at the best hotel—magnificent, but totally foodless. The sailor in charge listened to our request, and the next morning, after Hindenburg had refused to see us, telephoned to someone at headquarters to send Hindenburg's personal auto for us, and to order Hindenburg to talk to us.

The Hindenburg car had rubber tires. The officers at headquarters gave us a formal if not too friendly reception. We began diplomatically, each in turn asking a question: was it starvation that forced the end of the war? was the first. My colleague was diplomatic enough not to say "surrender." Another asked if the demobilization was continuing successfully. Then it was my turn.

I could not rudely ask "Who" or "What won the war?" but I did manage, thanks to a diplomatic interpreter, to ask what ended the four-year stalemate. As I noted it immediately after we left the room, Hindenburg made this historically important answer:

I will reply with the same frankness: the American infantry

in the Argonne won the war. I say this as a soldier, and soldiers will understand me best. . . .

Germany could not have won the war—that is, after 1917. We might have won on land. We might have taken Paris. But after the failure of the world food crops of 1916, the British food blockade reached its effectiveness in 1917. So I must really say that the British food blockade and the American attack decided the war for the Allies. . . .

The Argonne Battle was slow and difficult. But it was strategic. . . . The Americans are splendid soldiers. But when I replaced a division it was weak in numbers and unrested, while each American division came in fresh and fit and on the offensive.

The day came when the American command sent new divisions into the battle and when I had not even one broken division to plug up the gaps. There was nothing left to do but ask for terms. . . .

From a military point of view the Argonne Battle as conceived and carried out by the American command was the climax of the war and its deciding factor. The American attack continued from day to day with increasing power but when two opposing divisions had broken each other, yours were replaced with ten thousand eager men, ours with decimated, ill-equipped, ill-fed men suffering from contact with a gloomy and despairing civilian population.

I do not mean to discredit your fighting power. I repeat: without the American blow in the Argonne we could have made a satisfactory peace at the end of a long stalemate or at least held our last positions on our own frontier indefinitely—undefeated. The American attack won the war.

Then Hindenburg said, "*Mein armes Vaterland, mein armes Vaterland,*" and sobbed and bent his head, and wept.

I saw Hindenburg crying.

What makes this interview historic news of world importance, and not merely an American story, is the admission that the war was won fairly in the field—no excuses, no blaming starvation (the British blockade), or betrayal at home (the Ludendorff myth). Naziism was founded on a total (or totalitarian) lie: that Germany did not lose the war on the battlefield, but because of the *Dolchstoss,* or stab-in-the-back, "by civilians," "by the Socialists," "by the Communists," and "by the Jews." Ludendorff originated the *Dolchstosslegende,* as it was soon known, and Hitler armed it.

One man could have stopped this falsehood, but he did not speak out again. The man who had declared forthrightly that the war was a stalemate that neither side could have won, that the American divisions broke the balance and won the war, now kept silent. The last hero of the German war became finally a coward. Hindenburg betrayed not only himself, he betrayed the German people, he betrayed history.

If the Hindenburg confession had been passed by Pershing's (stupid) censors at that time, it would have been headlined in every country civilized enough to have newspapers, and undoubtedly would have made a lasting impression on millions of people and become an important page in history; and I believe it would have destroyed the main planks of the platform on which Hitler rose to power, it would have prevented World War II, the greatest and worst war in all history, and it would have changed the future of all mankind. Of course few could realize its importance until more than a decade later when Hitler became *Der Führer.* We in G-2D did not think it worthwhile to give up our number-one positions in journalism in order to be free to publish.

Almost equally to blame with General Pershing and his advisers, notably General Nolan, chief of intelligence, was a minority group in the press corps whose spokesman was the superegotistic but nevertheless brilliant journalist Edwin L. James of the *New York Times* news service. Led by Mr. James, these colleagues, who without doubt would be blamed by all their editors for being scooped on the biggest story of the war next to the Armistice, demanded of Pershing that he fire the four adventurers and forbid us to publish a word of the Hindenburg confession. The U.S. Army bowed to *The New York Times.* It compromised somewhat by permitting us to remain in the corps but only on condition that we never write or publish the story. (Years later, when it had lost all its significance except as a page in history, the story appeared either in liberal weeklies or in histories and reminiscences.)

An entire book has been written about our press section and the most important chapters, in my opinion, are Emmet Crozier's revelations of how close the five who violated the Armistice and notably the four who interviewed Hindenburg, came to being court-martialed and shot. We did of course hear, as did everyone in intelligence, that it had been proposed by someone that we be court-martialed and pay the consequences, but it is Crozier in *The American Reporters on the Western Front* who emphasizes the insistence of the French premier, Clemenceau, "*Le Tigre,*" on having us publicly executed by a firing squad so as to warn every American in uniform not to attempt to go into Germany.

I do remember that when we knew we were in trouble Lincoln Eyre of the *World,* who was a close friend of Colonel House (Wilson's gray eminence), to whom he had sent weekly confidential letters to be disclosed to the President, either went to Paris to see House or wrote him in detail; and House immediately warned Wilson that the Clemenceau plan would shock the world and would be considered in history as an atrocity. Wilson agreed. Our lives were spared. But the James clique in the press section won one point: our Hindenburg interview was never published.*

---

*Documentation: A completely researched account of the Armistice violation is given by Emmet Crozier in *American Reporters on the Western Front* (Oxford University Press, 1959), dedicated to "The Five Runaway Correspondents." (The fifth was F. A. Smith, who flew to Berlin and did not see Hindenburg.) See pp. 273–79.

Chapter 12

~~~~~~~~~~

Peace Journey With Woodrow Wilson

Although I kept my room at the Riesenfürstenhof in Coblenz, where the army stationed us—and which was supplied us free—I went frequently with Eyre to Paris to see what the peace conference at Versailles was up to. Eyre and I were in Paris to greet "the new Messiah," as Woodrow Wilson was actually and seriously called in what is known as "cold" print in the Allied press in Europe and America. The American press at the time of the announcement of Wilson's Fourteen Points editorially said our President was "an instrument in the hands of God," and Paris papers welcomed him as "the King of Humanity."

(Very few nations and individuals were not swept along in this emotional deluge. Journalists and professional politicians, notorious dissenters, alone withstood this tidal wave. Among the correspondents, the best Wilson story, and this one vouched for as true, concerned the voyage to France, the U.S. delegation on one ocean liner, the newspapermen filling another. As Wilson's ship was passing the S.S. *Orizaba,* with its hundreds of press representatives, James J. Montague remarked: "There goes Woodrow Wilson, on the S.S. *George Washington,* making twenty-one-may-I-knots an hour.")

The reception in Paris over, the President crossed the Channel on a British destroyer. Eyre and I were the only men in U.S. uniform, except for the President's bodyguard, to accompany him. We were escorted by two more destroyers, right and left, which at times dashed out ahead of us, then fell back, making gigantic patterns in the water, like fleurs-de-lys.

Wilson tried to avoid meeting the press. However, he had been receiving lectures from Colonel House and other close friends who could speak to him on the value of good publicity in the treaty making; on how to be more outgoing, or friendly, more of a human being, and so he tried to do his painful best. He stood at the rail of the stern deck surrounded by his diplomats, and the press corps filled all vacant space available. It immediately became evident that he was addressing us either as semi-intelligent beings or as schoolchildren. He talked down to us. He was too ill at ease to be friendly. He tried to use common language, he tried too hard to be ungrammatical.

"The Italians ain't goin' to pull no wool over my eyes," he said.

("Ain't" from the former president of Princeton!)

Colonel House once said, "Woodrow Wilson loves humanity but he does not like people." The people he seemed to like least were the several hundred newspapermen who came to tell the world of his plans to bring about eternal peace on earth, goodwill to men.

Wilson, of course, had never been what we called "a man of the people." But neither had Lenin—also a schoolteacher—nor Trotsky, a journalist, nor most of the other heads of state. Unlike others, he was not a demagogue. He certainly was not a hypocrite. Although I had not yet heard of Colonel House's remark, I wrote in my 1918 daybook:

Demagogues always embrace the people, but Wilson is neither a demagogue nor a hypocrite; he may not have loved the common man as Lincoln did, but he had as much faith in him, because he too was an idealist. He believed in people, he believed people were intelligent and would listen to his reasoning, he felt he could win them over if he had the chance to speak to all of them. But he could not bring himself to be one of the people.

Vociferous, but British and therefore never mad, was the welcome two million Londoners gave President Wilson when he rode in the state carriage with the King and Queen and the Duke of Connaught, surrounded by the glistening Household Cavalry. In the distance cannon sounded. "A welcome unprecedented in history," the evening papers called it, perhaps surprised at their own headlines.

King George V, Buckingham Palace

Some two hundred of us journalists were put up at the Savoy and the Cecil. The next afternoon we were taken into the main courtyard at Buckingham Palace and left shivering near the steps, awaiting King George and his guest. The American camera crews behaved as they did at home. They owned the place. But they either did not know or had not counted on the British custom of driving on the left, and they had set up their cameras in the wrong corner.

As the King's auto approached, the American cameramen realized they would miss the arrival pictures if they tried to walk around the solid bloc of Guardsmen that filled the court. So, with cameras on tripods over their shoulders they began a diagonal rush through the ranks of the Royal Guards, shoving and pushing and in a few instances knocking them over. It was a mad scene that should have been immortalized on film.

King George took his place on the palace steps, and the visitors were herded together on his right. Four or five were formed into a line out of this herd and accompanied by chamberlains to the steps. We each gave our name to a chamberlain, who passed it on, until it finally reached the King. Just ahead of me was Montague Glass, whose play, *Potash and Perlmutter,* was a wartime hit in New York and London. How he had managed to get into the press section I do not know.

"Your name?" said the chamberlain.

"Montague Glass."

"Mr. Montague Glahss," said the chamberlain.

"Your Majesty, Mr. Montague Glahss," said the second chamberlain to the king.

King George, who had automatically spoken names and automatically shaken hands, hesitated.

"Mr. Glahss," he said, "I know the name; I think I have seen a play of yahrs."

Mr. Glass was delighted.

"How did you like my stuff, King?" he stammered.

His Majesty did not reply. The line moved on and he was now letting me have a very limp hand.

That night King George invited the Wilson party to dine at Buckingham Palace and Sir George (later, Lord) Riddell invited visiting journalists to dine with him at the Savoy. In addition to oysters, lobster and turkey *farci à l'Anglaise,* et cetera, we were given cocktails, French wine (Graves supérieur) and two brands of 1911 champagne, followed by a choice of liqueurs and as many other drinks as we wanted.

Sir George spoke for Anglo-American friendship, then invited others to speak. At my table of five, one was the editor and publisher and I believe the owner of the Norfolk, Virginia *Pilot* (may his ashes rest in peace), who had never before, so he said, sampled Benedictine or Grand Marnier and such other nice sweet drinks. He drank them from wine glasses. Then, at a break in the speechmaking he half-rose to his feet and said:

"Gennelmen, before the war I used to think the British were a lot of goddam sonsabitches, but now I want to say. . . . " No one will ever know what he wanted to say. We jumped him, the waiters carried him out of the great Savoy, and he was never heard from again.

The Prince of Peace

Although President Wilson's December journey to Great Britain was probably his greatest achievement in uniting the two English-speaking nations, the continuation of his triumphal journal into Italy, which began almost immediately afterward, produced some of the most extraordinary scenes of modern times.

On January 1, 1919, Mr. Wilson entrained for Rome, accompanied by his usual entourage, and fewer correspondents than had made the London journey. The President immediately caused controversy by insisting on meeting and speaking to common working people, not merely rulers and politicians and "notables," as he had done in France and Britain. Among themselves the politicos whispered that Wilson was going crazy, although it is true that several of them suspected he, although an American, was more Machiavellian than they were.

Wilson found Italy in a state of national hysteria. Everywhere in the industrial north surging mobs of peasants and industrial workers and city people of all classes filled the streets from house to house, ending all traffic, shouting, even weeping, and—where there was a little space—both men and women knelt not only on the sidewalks but in the dirty streets, and sang and prayed out loud.

Wilson was hailed as the prince of peace; he was worshipped by many as a man sent from heaven to help the poor, the dispossessed, the homeless, the jobless, the miserable of the earth. Some even believed the prediction of the Second Coming of the Messiah was being fulfilled.

The Italian monarchy and the premier, Orlando, were alarmed by the praying peasantry and the outburst of socialist rhetoric among the working people. They actually canceled the major Wilson oration "not only to the Romans but to all Mankind," which had been publicly announced. The Italian govern-

1 *Above:* Grandmother and Grandfather Seldes on the porch at Alliance, Summer 1899.

2 *Left:* Seldes's parents, George Sergius and Anna Verna (née Saphro) Seldes about the time of their marriage.

3 Seldes's father in front of the Carpenter Street drugstore in Philadelphia—the home of "the local angle" on world events.

4 Two young farm boys of Alliance, New Jersey—George standing, brother Gilbert seated.

5 Aunt Bertha, cigaretless, one of the early influences in Seldes's life.

6 *Left:* Seldes in 1914 during the Pittsburgh apprenticeship days — "years bulging with great names, noteworthy events."

7 *Below:* T.R. on the speech trail, without Seldes in the picture.

8 *Right:* Lillian Russell, "handsome in the robust style of the times."

9 *Above:* The Divine Sarah—"every word, every gesture was sublime."

10 *Right:* "Red" Emma Goldman, one of several political figures who stayed in the Seldes's guest room over the drugstore.

11   Seldes in the Paris *ChiTrib* days searching the wartime skies with American relief workers.

12   Paris during the World War I years—women on the food store front.

13 *Above:* G-2D, Pershing's Army Press Corps—Seldes stands to the far right, Edwin L. James of *The New York Times* beside him.

14 *Right:* General Pershing as the press corps knew him—without the smile.

15 Floyd Gibbons with eyepatch and sling after Chemin des Dames.

16 A German movie ticket—souvenir of the "glorious" capture of Saint-Mihiel.

17 "Every day above the news, no matter how important."

18 The front, November 11, 1918: *Jamais plus la guerre!*

19 *Right:* Hindenburg at the height of power in World War I—the moving confession at Kassel was yet to come.

20 *Below:* London heartily greets Woodrow Wilson, the acclaimed Prince of Peace.

ment sent regiments of armed soldiers to disperse the hundred thousand in Rome who nevertheless came shouting for Wilson. (Ironically, the President had been scheduled to make his great speech from the balcony of the Palazzo Venezia—one of the two balconies later made famous, or infamous, by the Fascist dictator of the country.)

So far as I know, not one of the hundreds of newsmen who accompanied Wilson reported two of the most important facts of the Peace Conference: that the main support for the President in Europe came from the working class, the Have-Nots, while the Haves of the middle class and ruling class laughed at all the idealism of this naïve American; and that socialists were beginning to lead the working class.

No one reported that Wilson landing at Brest was greeted by the city's mayor, a socialist; or that the delegation of workers calling on Wilson in Paris was led by Jean Longuet, the grandson of Karl Marx; or that the Albert Hall meeting in London that endorsed the entire Wilson program was organized by Ramsay MacDonald—the future prime minister—and Arthur Henderson and Philip Snowden, the future rulers of the British Empire, leftists, liberals, Laborites.

In Sweden the socialist premier Branting's socialist newspapers joined the Swiss *Journal de Genève* not only in supporting Wilson but also in hinting that Clemenceau, his semi-official *Le Temps* and the official Havas news agency were joined in an effort to destroy Wilson's idealism. When Wilson suggested that food rather than guns was the cure for the spread of Bolshevism in Europe, the reactionary British press, led by Northcliffe's *Times,* began a war against the President. The well-bribed Italian editor, B. Mussolini of the Milan *Popolo d'Italia,* who had quit the Socialist Party for money, now attacked Wilson as a "dangerous radical." The only noted American journalist (outside the liberal weeklies) who not only supported the President but also exposed the character of his enemies—labor and the socialists for him, the ruling classes and their reactionary press against him—was the owner and editor of the Emporia *Gazette,* William Allen

White. (But what could the small Kansas daily accomplish vis-à-vis the *Chicago Tribune* or even the Kansas City *Star*?) The vast American press laughed at Wilsonian idealism, sneered at Wilsonian politics; it turned into a wolf pack that snarled at him and eventually destroyed him.*

---

*The heads of the two great Allied nations were too diplomatic to utter any official criticism, but confidentially they told colleagues they trusted not to repeat their words that they thought the American President, as were all Americans, too naïve and too unworldly for international politics. When George Adam interviewed Clemenceau and mentioned Wilson's fourteen Points, the old "Tigre" interrupted with *"le bon Dieu n'avait que dix,"* "the good Lord had only ten." And after the Versailles conference Lloyd George said, "I think I did as well as might be expected, seated as I was between Jesus Christ [Wilson], and Napoleon [Clemenceau]."

Chapter 13

Foch Originates the Cold War

The few of us who were members of Pershing's press department and considered ourselves the elite, the "tops" of American journalism, had found ourselves not only overshadowed but actually treated as second-class citizens by the famous arrivals—Herbert Bayard Swope, editor of the New York *World,* for one—who accompanied Wilson. We were glad to be back at our headquarters in Coblenz.

We were crowded off the front page. Several members were called back to the States. In desperation we asked friendly generals to arrange for an interview with Marshal Foch, who was without question the greatest military man of the age. He had refused interviews not only throughout the war but ever since the Armistice. But we were electrified one day in mid-January when General Dickman called us to headquarters and told us Foch would arrive at Trier in the Armistice car with General Pershing on the seventeenth for the express purpose of talking to us. We were so thrilled with the news that no one then, or for a long time afterward, questioned whether Foch might have an ulterior purpose for this visit, simply this: to manipulate through us the minds of not only the American people, but also the people of all the Allied nations and any other anti-Russian nations, for the purpose of inaugurating what has now become known as "the cold war."

He began his talk by outlining a plan to keep the Allied forces permanently on the Rhine prepared at all times to march into Germany, cross Germany, and fight Bolshevism on the German-Russian border. If necessary, he said, the Allied armies should be prepared to march all the way to Moscow itself; he thought this was the only way to save Western civilization from the greatest evil in all known history!

In the question period that followed, someone asked Marshal Foch what would have happened if the Germans had not asked for the Armistice on November 11. Marshal Foch, not realizing that he was giving us such a sensational front-page story that would totally eclipse his "cold war" ploy, described in some detail what he called "The Battle of Lorraine." Scheduled to begin November 14, it would have been without question the greatest battle in the history of the world, with the entire armies of France and the United States engaged in a gigantic pincer movement that would eventually have ended with the capture of Berlin, and incidentally have given us about one million German soldier prisoners.

"The Battle of Lorraine." "Greatest Battle in World History Planned by Foch." We could see the headlines in America; we couldn't wait to end the Foch interview and rush to typewriters and telegraph offices. Every American without exception wrote this news story and every American without exception made no mention at all of Foch's proposed war on Russia, the cold war. (Bailey of Northcliffe's London *Daily Mail* and Hall of Reuters, the two British journalists attached to our press corps, not being under the spell known as "get the American angle," sent the cold-war story to London, but it was never reported in the United States.)

Foch himself, in his memoirs published in August 1927,

admits he was the father of the cold war—although he does not use that American term. "In February 1919," he writes, meaning a few weeks after his trip to Trier, "in the early days of Leninism I declared to the Ambassadors Conference meeting in Paris that if the states surrounding Russia were supplied with munitions and the sinews of war, I would undertake to stamp out the Bolshevik menace once and for all."

Foch was the gentlest general I ever met in my life. There was nothing military about him. He was the exact opposite of Pershing. The smile instead of the frown. One of the buttons of his tunic was unbuttoned—one can imagine Pershing's shock at seeing this. He was a friendly man, the Father of Victory, and the would-be father of the cold war.

The Associated Press, the leading American news service, never sent the cold-war story over its wires, which reached most of the world. When I queried its director decades later, he maintained the usual attitude: if the Associated Press did not report it, it never happened.

During about half of 1919 the Army of Occupation in the Rhineland and the press section saw little of General Pershing— he came only for great occasions, such as a review of the troops at which his guests were the King and the Queen of the Belgians. But early in the year, after Foch's great cold-war gun had misfired, Pershing instructed his chief intelligence officer in Coblenz, Colonel Bagley, to round up the war correspondents for a most important meeting.

By this time Floyd Gibbons had quit the press section and was bossing the Army Edition of the *Chicago Tribune,* and every day above all the news, no matter how important, he published this headline: COME ON YOU YANKS—TOOT SWEET!! For once Gibbons and McCormick agreed. Both were now isolationists, and both thought the occupation of Germany a useless and expensive gesture. Both were in favor of quitting all of Europe without a second to lose, or a second thought.

Whoever it was who ran Pershing's public relations was a very clever man—Foch probably had none, or he would not have made such a major faux pas at the Trier meeting. Now Bagley and his intelligence staff (under General Dickman) came up with a story, to which the name and voice of General Pershing was to be given within a few days, almost as *kolossal* as Goebbels's Reichstag fire was to be in 1933: nothing less than their discovery of a vast German-Bolshevik plot to seize the Rhineland, kill every American soldier and officer, and raise the red flag over Dickman's hotel, the Coblenzerhof.

Pershing arrived. We, what was left of us, no longer the full twenty-one members, came to headquarters. Pershing spoke:

"The American army of the Rhineland must hold the frontiers of civilization against Bolshevism.

"There must be no let-up in discipline.

"There is a Bolshevik-inspired German uprising planned against the American Army of Occupation.

"There will be no fraternization with Germans."

It wasn't much of an oration, but it sent the cable boys flying to their typewriters, while we, the leisurely mail-copy minority, sat and wondered if a German population that liked the Yanks and liked everything they could get from us, from food to soap to candy, unarmed people who were truly grateful we were so lenient in our rule, would under orders from that mysterious "central committee" arise some night and slit the throats of all of us sleeping blissfully in our hotel—and barracks—beds.

But the news was official. Pershing said so. No one questioned it, everyone believed it—in America at least, where it was published. The European press had better sense. It is even quite likely that Colonel Bagley and General Pershing himself did not know then, or ever, that they were just being pushed around, the pawns, in the great cold war that Foch had planned and continued to plan during his whole remaining lifetime.

As for "no fraternization," it was explained to us that no man in American uniform was to speak, let alone have other relations, with any German, man or woman. By coincidence, again, it was at this time that a Colonel Jenner of Milwaukee, who ran one of the big "soap and chocolate" hospitals, took me through the wards. He explained first that the natives had had no soap or chocolate for almost four years, and many German girls could be "had" for as little as one bar of either. Unfortunately, too many of our men had brought v.d. with them from France, and now the v.d. wards, despite no fraternization, were overcrowded.

Part IV

Tribune Decade: Berlin to Baghdad

Chapter 14

〜〜〜〜〜

Colonel McCormick,
Captain Patterson

B y mid-summer 1919 nothing at all seemed to be happening in the occupied part of Germany, and the American people seemed to have forgotten everything about the Great War except Gibbons's daily demand to get the men home *toute de suite.* The first great fighting unit to be sent home was the Rainbow, and I applied for membership in it. General Harboard sent me all the official papers, and I joined my favorite regiment, the Ohios. I sailed on the *Leviathan* along with an estimated 11,999 others.

Fortunately for me the ruling made at the time our group was formed that we were to be given the rank of captain, as were all the British and French war correspondents, and which most of us disdained or ignored, helped me now. I had a cabin along with three regular officers, and fairly decent meals—if army mess food can be called even that. All the enlisted men had to wait in line for their food, and inasmuch as the *Leviathan* kitchens had been prepared to feed two thousand and there were almost six times that number on board, many veterans had to spend three or four hours—in other words the whole day—in line for their meals.

This caused great grumbling but little more. What struck the great Rainbow Division an unforgettable blow was the reception—or rather the lack of a reception—it got on arrival in New York. It seems that all the jubilation over peace had been spent by the American people on the first arrivals, men from the training camps who had seen no service, engineering outfits that had spent the war digging latrines for the men at the front and never got into a battle, and the like—men in fighting men's uniforms who had not fired a shot. The sorriest, angriest ten or twelve thousand men I ever saw were my companions of the Rainbow at the New Jersey camp where we were sent for discharge.

I came back to New York and looked up old friends. My pal from the old days, Ferdinand Reyher, invited me to his parents' house in Belmar, New Jersey, to see what I could do writing articles for magazines or newspapers. He had already had two books published and was at work on a third. I went to Belmar and spent the rest of the summer and part of autumn writing short stories, mailing them and getting them back by return mail.

Then one day in mid-September my brother, who fortunately was in the New York City telephone book, forwarded me a cable from Floyd Gibbons in Paris offering me one of the main posts in a foreign news service that Colonel McCormick had ordered established immediately. The Colonel, envious of the *Times,* the *World,* the *Herald,* and the *Tribune* in New York, and the *Daily News* in Chicago, had decided suddenly he too must have a foreign service. His order to Gibbons was almost equivalent to the one he gave Joe Pierson in June 1917: "Go to Paris, establish the Army Edition of the *Tribune,* and give it free to every man in uniform on July 4." Gibbons, in desperation, offered jobs to every journalist in Harry's Bar ("Sank Roo Dounoo") then wrote, telephoned or telegraphed every member of Pershing's press section whose address he could find. He got seven takers. I was one.*

In the ten years I worked for him as a reporter for and editor of the Army Edition, in Paris, and as Berlin correspondent for the *Chicago Tribune* Foreign News Service, I met the colonel many times but never knew him at all. Gibbons, who began his career as a young newsboy selling the *Tribune* on the streets of Milwaukee, and who grew from cub reporter to the boss's star, assured me it was impossible to know him. He was a strange man and remained a stranger. In three days I spent with his brother, Senator Medill McCormick, we arrived at understandable human terms. In twenty or thirty meetings the great press lord remained the same iceberg: cold, frozen, even the seventh part above water remaining a mystery.

One key to many of his actions was undoubtedly his xenophobia. He was a man who cared nothing about anything foreign—from people to paintings—except German guns; in fact, according to colleagues in the home office, to whom I talked every day during my great "re-Americanization" visit in 1927, the Colonel hated New York, a foreign city, and had little liking

---

* I had met Colonel Robert Rutherford McCormick twice, once when he was commanding an artillery outfit in the First Division, the second time in the Hotel Crillon, press headquarters during the Versailles Peace Conference. The Paris *ChiTrib* had tried to make a hero of him after the so-called battle of Cantigny. In the early days of the war, when Pershing, rightly, refused Foch's suggestion that American troops be brigaded with the French and insisted on not fighting until he had prepared our troops for victory, French morale was low, and the French begged Pershing to do something. It was decided to put on a "show"—the Americans would attack and win a big victory without risking anything, the French press would announce it with *élan* and *éclat*. It was decided to capture Cantigny, on whose trenches McCormick's guns were aimed, after a bombardment which today we would call "over-kill." That the doughty colonel, before getting the range, shelled our own lines, killing several infantrymen, was a rumor that circulated during the war, but in 1972 Waverly Root, a *Tribune* alumnus, published in his memoirs in the present *International Herald-Tribune* the story of the sports writer who, at a staff dinner the Colonel gave in Paris, "blurted out 'And the worst thing, Colonel, the very worst thing that happened in our army was when our artillery shelled its own infantry at Cantigny.'" Root alleges that this reporter was not fired, and this hushed up the incident.

for almost all the world outside "Chicagoland"—and his Cantigny farm.

He did want the red ribbon of the Legion of Honor despite the fact that it was French—he felt he had been slighted because most of his officers were wearing it. How this secret—perhaps not so secret—desire became known to not one but each of the leaders of two rival factions in the Paris office was never told. But inasmuch as the decoration has to be applied for, the Paris business manager, J. H. Hummel (known also as "Black Jack Hummel" and "Give-'Em-Half Hummel" for his work on expense accounts), and the *Tribune*'s general factotum, a Dutchman named Windblad (the Mr. Fix-It, the man without whom an American company could not get along in France), both applied at Legion headquarters at about the same time, and waited.

There came the day of rejoicing—and catastrophe. The magnificent bureaucracy that ran the Legion read the petition of Jack Hummel on behalf of the deserving officer, and awarded the ribbon of the Legion of Honor. The same board but probably another section of it heard the request of M. Windblad on behalf of the deserving Colonel, and awarded the ribbon of the Legion of Honor.

No one remembers which of the two men announced it first to the admiring staff, but in no time at all there was an uproar. It was heard eventually at the offices of the Legion, and to resolve a now impossible situation the directors withdrew both citations and made nasty remarks to both Mr. Hummel and Mr. Windblad about such outrageous behavior.

Although the colonel was innocent in Chicago, he became quite angry and ordered his Paris man, Wales, to write a piece "exposing" the red ribbon as a cheap thing, usually obtained by bribery and corruption, a fraud, utterly beneath the contempt of any decent American—despite the fact that so many of his fellow citizens were sporting not only the ribbon but the rosette of a "commander" in their buttonholes. Wales was ordered to cable a complete list of these un-American Americans.

He soon found that they numbered not only thousands but perhaps tens of thousands, and he figured it out that if he gave full names, street and city and state addresses—this was long before the zip code was known—it would mean tens of thousands of words costing thousands of dollars; he so notified the Colonel. The list of these reprehensible wearers of a foreign decoration was sent by mail; whether it was ever published I do not know.

I do know that in later years when leading citizens—ambassadors and generals included—were exposed for accepting decorations from Mussolini and Franco, the *Tribune* refrained from naming them.

At times I found the Colonel either eccentric or paradoxical. Everyone knew his politics—rightist, Republican up to and including a form of American fascism. When in 1923 I was thrown out of Soviet Russia (for writing news stories that were entirely factual), the Colonel told me to write a long series of articles exposing the Communist system. This was understandable: the majority of the press lords were anti-Communist and the editorial and news columns were fitted accordingly. But in 1925, when I was thrown out of Rome (for writing news stories that were entirely factual), the Colonel told me to write a long series of articles exposing Fascism.

Again, when a successor to Floyd Gibbons as roving world correspondent (the best journalistic job ever) was needed, McCormick called us to a conference in Paris and questioned each—how long have you lived in Europe, how many foreign languages do you speak, et cetera. Then the Colonel announced the appointment of Larry Rue, a newcomer. In answer to the asked, or unasked question, he explained: "Larry has been here only a short time and he doesn't speak any foreign languages. I do not want my fine American boys ruined by these damned foreigners."

In one of my first years in the Berlin office, and one of the terrible years of German inflation, Colonel McCormick ordered me to write a detailed story of the failure of government ownership of the railroad system. (A like cable had been sent to his men in other countries). When I reported government ownership a great success, the cable was suppressed. In 1925 the doughty Colonel sent an ultimatum to Soviet Minister of Foreign Affairs Chicherin, telling him to end press censorship or face a world boycott of Russia that he would organize.

One of the great advantages of working for McCormick in Europe was that we were left free most of the time; the Colonel hated everything foreign so much he was not interested in European affairs. The CTFNS was merely a prestige service; he was keeping up with the Ochses.

Nothing angered Colonel McCormick so much as a resignation. He fired men—he fired the foremost correspondent of the time, Floyd Gibbons—but he never forgave a resignation. I resigned when I had a book contract late in 1928. Immediately afterward the Colonel cabled John Steele in London to have my name chiseled out of the bronze plaque honor roll in the *Tribune*'s office. In the famous Tribune Tower in Chicago there were two stones in the entrance hall, one from St. Peter's, the other from the Colosseum, that I had supplied. My name was chiseled out from these stones.

Twenty years later the *Tribune* announced it was sending a correspondent to Moscow "for the first time in its history." Floyd Gibbons, in 1922, had reported the Russian famine. Although he stayed only a short time, I was appointed correspondent in 1922 and worked in Russia in 1922 and 1923. Now both Floyd Gibbons and I had become, so far as the *Tribune* was concerned, non-persons.

Joseph Medill Patterson

In mid-September 1919, when Gibbons hired me for the Foreign News Service, he directed me to apply at Captain Patterson's offices in New York for credentials, money, and a steamship ticket. Patterson's newspaper was then known as the New York *Illustrated Daily News*—the first American tabloid. Patterson, of course, did not remember me from our Rainbow Division days in France, but when I mentioned them he became very friendly.

He told me that early in 1919 he had gone to London to call on Lord Northcliffe to discuss journalism and human nature. Both agreed human nature was the same the whole world over. Northcliffe urged Patterson to copy the British in starting a tabloid and Patterson urged Northcliffe to change *The Times* of London by putting headlines rather than want ads and an agony column on its entire front page.

"I took Northcliffe's advice, but he didn't take mine," Patterson told me. Lord Beaverbrook did—his *Daily Express,* with an American-style sensational front page, became the biggest success in British journalism. Patterson's *Daily News* eventually became the largest-circulating newspaper in America.

When I asked Patterson about his policy—the paper was only a few months old then—he replied:

"We can't miss. You remember the IQ tests the army used—they revealed that 47¾ percent of the population of the United States have the mentality of children of twelve.

"Well, I always knew that Hollywood aimed the movies at the mentality of eleven.

"I am publishing a picture paper—aimed at the ten-year-old mentality. It is sure to be a great success."

When he built the *Daily News* skyscraper he had inscribed on it " 'God must have loved the common people, he made so many of them.'—Lincoln." (This is one of hundreds of imprecise Lincoln quotations, but it will probably never be corrected.)

Years later, when I looked for biographical material on Joseph Medill Patterson I found in the New York Public Library three versions of his first writing, a pamphlet called "Confessions of a Drone," published while he was still a student at Yale and had become a dues-paying card-carrying member of the Socialist Party of America.

"I am talking about myself, the type of idle, rich young man," "Confessions" begins. "He has an annual income of between ten and twenty thousand, he does nothing, his chief dividends come from U.S. Steel, the Pennsylvania Railroad, and

American Tobacco Company, plus real estate holdings." Patterson then denounces "the Capitalist System" which permits him to live in idleness while millions of common people slave. "Socialism," he concludes, "urges the underpaid to unite and insist on receiving the full amount of the wealth they produce."

Apparently the author was attacked in the press for his criticism of capitalism, for in the final edition he answers his critics with even stronger language:

"As long as the working class is satisfied with its present arrangement of poverty, obedience and laboriousness, the present arrangement will continue. But whenever the working class wants to discontinue the present arrangement it can do so. It has the great majority."

(Luckily for the author there was no Dies or McCarthy Un-American Activities Committee in his Yale days to charge him with advocating overthrow of the government.)

After graduation Patterson wrote a novel, *The Little Brother of the Rich,* and a play, *The Fourth Estate,* each with a socialist point of view. But there was not a socialist, radical or even a liberal trace left in the man I interviewed in 1919. The "common people" remained cut into the stone of his office building, but his *Daily News* had no more use for its readers than to sell them merchandise, reactionary ideas and eventually Fascism.

By the time Mussolini had suppressed the common people of Italy and made one international tourist express run on time—but no other trains—the *Daily News* was one of the first American newspapers to praise the Fascist dictator editorially. A decade later, when the Spanish Republic appealed for help, the Patterson daily smeared the Loyalists with the word "reds." The paper favored Joe McCarthy and McCarthyism. Millions of readers, the common people, the working people with their IQ of ten-year-olds to whom Patterson catered, accepted everything. On November 25, 1937, Patterson's editorial writer said enthusiastically that China was "licked" and advocated that the United States do business with Japan, "all the business we can, regardless of disapproval of the way the land"—i.e., parts of China occupied by Japan—"was acquired."

JMP, as he liked to be called, treated his own workers better than other press lords treated theirs. He was indeed one of the few owners friendly to the organization of a union of reporters; he alone welcomed the Newspaper Guild. That was perhaps the last flicker of the old liberal, radical, socialist Yale days.

Chapter 15

~~~~~~~~

Lady Astor, Irish Rebels, D'Annunzio

Although the Berlin office had been promised me, I received orders from Gibbons to proceed to London, where new instructions would be given me by John S. Steele, who was generally regarded as next in command of Colonel McCormick's forces. Steele was born in Dublin, a Protestant Irishman who became an American citizen, never lost his sense of humor, and was without doubt the fairest-minded man in the *Tribune* service. He told me I would have to stay in London until Gibbons could replace the present Berlin man without firing him or causing a scandal.

My first assignment was to report on the campaign for a seat in the House of Commons that an American-born woman, married to a British lord, was waging in Plymouth. Her maiden name was Nancy Langhorne; she was now Lady Astor. She was beautiful, witty and rich—and moreover, she treated the press, notably the American contingent of about twenty among the total of about a hundred, in a most friendly manner. The campaign exceeded everyone's dreams, expectations; she made fools of her hecklers, she had empathy, she had charm, and she was powerful—she could use all the old adjectives, polish all the old clichés. Everything Lady Astor said was reported by every one of us who were in her entourage for a week or more.

Her opponent was named Foote. She would storm into a Foote meeting, break it up with shouts and applause. "Save your cheers for Mr. Foote," Lady Astor would say, "and save your votes for me."

Quick-witted repartee like this set the crowds crazy.

The uproar I remember best, one that turned a crowd of thousands in her favor, occurred the last day of the campaign. There were many hecklers. Many nasty things were shouted. The leader of the hecklers was a big, heavy-voiced man who seemed to us strangers to have a decided accent:

> *Heckler:* Go back to the country you came from. You're imported.
> *Lady Astor:* (imitating Irish brogue): You'rre imporrted yirrself."
> *Heckler:* I'm not. I was born right here in Plymouth.
> *Lady Astor:* Then you're drunk.
> *Heckler:* Indeed, I haven't had a drop today.
> *Lady Astor:* Then go and buy yourself a drink. It might sweeten your disposition.

There was a great uproar in favor of Lady Astor. She defeated both the Labor and the Liberal parties.

In several speeches she declared: "One section of the Labor Party, the young intellectuals, are red-hot Bolshevik cranks. Half of them never fought in the war."

This was how the campaign went. The Tory press thought Lady Astor was simply brilliant. She never discussed an issue. She made emotional appeals, she answered hecklers cleverly, and she red-baited the Liberals and the Laborites. What we, the American reporters with her every day, did not know was that Lady Astor was spending a lot of money and handing out a lot of food along with her demagoguery. Nor did the British mention it.

Some days after she was elected the press came again for the official announcement at the Plymouth Guildhall. At the conclusion Lady Astor invited the "pressmen" to her home for a celebration. A beautiful house, a beautiful hostess, the best whiskey and food. But I had to file a telegram first. When I returned alone and rang the bell a butler answered.

"Who are *you*?" he asked.

"One of the journalists," I replied.

"Tradesmen's entrance," the butler said, closing the door.

I returned to London.

Headlines throughout the world read "First Woman Ever Elected to Parliament." The first woman ever elected was the Countess Markiewicz of Dublin—an Irishwoman married to a Polish count. Irish rebel. A veteran of the 1916 uprising. An Irish heroine. The Sinn Fein elected her with some seventy others. That they never came to London and took their seats is a technicality. Only history books published in Ireland tell the public this fact.

(Lady Astor never devoted herself to any cause in all the time she sat in the House of Commons—until Hitler arrived in Berlin. She then opened her country house at Cliveden, which became the center for pro-Hitler, pro-Mussolini, and pro-Franco intrigue. The "Cliveden Set" became part of British history.)

The Irish Peace

*A*lthough Lady Astor was the first titled person I ever encountered, I never saw her except for the Plymouth campaign; but the second titled person, Sir Philip Kerr (later Lord Lothian), was a frequent visitor to the *Tribune* office, Henrietta Street, Covent Garden, and by a strange coincidence, many years later, one of the leading members of the Cliveden Set of which Lady Astor was the reigning head.

Sir Philip was then secretary to the Prime Minister, David Lloyd George, and therefore the best of all news sources the *Tribune* chief, John Scott Steele, could have. But what I did not at first realize was that a truly great news event was being created in our own office, nothing less than the making of a peace treaty to end six hundred years of warfare between Ireland and England.

All I knew in early autumn 1919 was that mysterious meetings were being held in our back room, and that Mr. George's secretary was a participant. Today the world—or at least many world historians—knows that Arthur Griffith, eventually known as the first president of Ireland, and other Irish Republican leaders, along with Sir Philip and John Steele, first discussed peace somewhere and that eventually peace was made. Eamon De Valera was still in America at the time, and Steele kept him informed by cable. I am quite sure that John Steele, the go-between of Ireland and England, is still unknown to historians.

When De Valera became prime minister of Ireland, he wrote me saying he had read in one of my books about the 1919 and 1920 days. He asked me to send him every detail I could remember because, he said, there was very little documentation on that period and he was trying to complete the Irish Republic's archives. The lengthy report I sent him may be summarized as follows:

On my first assignment to Dublin I was to deliver a message to the first president of the unrecognized Republic, a "president on the run" as he was called, Arthur Griffith. It was not a coded message, but it was secret; it merely named a time and place. I was to bring back a similar message from Griffith to the *Tribune* chief correspondent, Steele, who in turn would relay it to Sir Philip, who would give it to David Lloyd George.

There was nothing of international intrigue, the secret agent, about these months of my Irish trips, and perhaps years of John Steele's activities; their sole aim was to get representatives of two people who had fought each other for almost seven centuries to sit at a table in the back room of a newspaper office and plan peace. Steele was an American citizen, born in Protestant Belfast, and he was the originator of the idea of an Irish settlement. His closest friend in British politics was Sir Philip Kerr and his closest friend in Catholic Ireland was Pat Moylett, who behind the shelves of his ordinary grocery store had a whole arsenal of guns, machine guns and munitions for Michael Collins, the commander of the illegal Irish Republican Army.

Thanks to Steele I got to know them all—not only Griffith but the Countess Markiewicz (née Gore-Booth), who during the 1916 Easter Rebellion, revolver in hand, had led 120 troops into St. Stephens Green and occupied the Royal College of Surgeons and held it for three days; and Michael Collins, who was "on the run" but could be seen at a certain pub in Watertown (name revealed to me by Griffith); and Jim Larkin, the American who organized the Irish Transport Workers; and the writers, notably AE, and the poets, and everyone in the Abbey Theatre. All doors were opened to me (including 32 Harcourt Street, which was the IRA's chief arsenal) thanks to Steele's letter to Griffith.

Within a year there were many meetings in our London office. Griffith, Countess Markiewicz, Pat Moylett and Sir Philip attended, and sometimes Steele and I would be questioned. When later I asked Steele why he was the only journalist trusted by both sides, he said his friendship with Kerr had been a long one; as for Griffith, the president of Ireland told Steele one day that every American he had asked replied that, sure, Ireland could get complete independence. Steele was the only one who had said independence was possible, but only under dominion status. Griffith then said, "All the rest told me what they think I want to hear; all of them fibbed; you are the only man honest enough to tell me the truth to my face, so I trust you."

On December 6, 1921, about two years after the time I carried the messages arranging a meeting in our office, Griffith went to 10 Downing Street and said, "It is peace," to Lloyd George, and they signed a treaty.

On January 8, 1922, Ireland became a member of the British Commonwealth.

On December 21, 1948, Ireland withdrew from the Commonwealth and at last became an independent Republic.

Mr. Griffith also suggested that I interview the (secret) minister of finance, the poet Darrel Figgis; the (secret) minister of agriculture, one of the great literary figures of the time,

George Russell (AE); and other (secret) members of his cabinet, and I did so.

No one talked of finances or agriculture; all the notables I met talked about the renaissance of Irish literature, of Irish poetry, Irish drama, the Abbey Players.

My appointment with AE was at ten. He lived in Count Plunkett's house, facing a park—I think it was Bethnal Green. Every room I saw was frescoed with Irish myths and legends, the work of AE and his helpers. We talked Irish literature until it was time for lunch; and we talked Irish literature until it was time for tea; and again we talked Irish literature until it was time for supper—I think it was close to midnight before I was back in my room at the Shelburne.

AE had known them all, the great of his age, William Butler Yeats, Padraic Colum, James Stephens, and, as he said in a letter to Yeats, "a young fellow named Joyce whom I wrote to Lady Gregory about half jestingly." He was in fact the publisher of the first things James Joyce ever wrote.

"I sent Synge, I sent them all, to the Aran Islands," AE told me. "I told them they must live in the west of Ireland to know Ireland." He mentioned especially the influence the Aran Islanders had had on Synge. He even advised me to go to the islands, telling me how to get there. He knew just what day and hour the boat left from Galway, and for a while I was determined to give up making a living and go there.

D'Annunzio, My Number-One SOB

Gibbons, an Irishman who had never been to Ireland, liked my Irish reporting so much that he cut my London visit short, made me a roving correspondent, the very best job in all Europe. He telegraphed me in the late autumn of 1919: PROCEED FIUME INTERVIEW DANNUNZIO. I proceeded.

One of the great myths of our time, destined probably to live for generations, credits (or discredits) Mussolini with originating Fascism. The fact is that the novelist with the romantic and poetic mind, Gabriele D'Annunzio, organized the Dalmatian

Legion, designed its uniforms, introduced black shirts, revived the Roman salute and invented all of Fascism except its terrorism and its bloodshed. (When the first Fascio was formed in Milan, Mussolini was not one of the founders: his party card was number 7.)

With his black-shirted Dalmatian Legion D'Annunzio "captured" a Yugoslav town already occupied by regular Italian Army troops. The "capture" consisted of a conversation with a general named Pittaluga, who saluted and went home. The League of Nations threatened to bombard D'Annunzio—with a navy it did not have—and the European world read the newspapers and laughed.

By the year 1919 this once-beautiful young man, this youth with flowing hair and romantic dress, this self-proclaimed great lover, this boasting genius D'Annunzio had become a baldheaded, obscenely dirty old man, although dressed in the magnificent uniform of a field marshal, strutting about like a splay-footed Napoleon. He put himself on exhibit almost daily, reviewing his troops. He introduced the balcony to the political world.

Thanks to an inevitable meeting in the foyer of the only hotel in Fiume at this time—there were no tourists and there was almost no food—I soon became friendly with a man who called himself Lieutenant Henry Furst, a native of Summit Avenue, Newark, New Jersey, now the volunteer secretary to D'Annunzio. He told me the story of the "capture" and arranged for an interview.

D'Annunzio received me in the governor's palace, in a room overwhelmed with purple draperies, second-rate statues, third-rate paintings, purple hangings, too many chairs, an enormous couch with too many pillows.

The first question I asked was, what will you do if President Wilson and the League of Nations send a fleet against you? I spoke bad French; he answered in what I think are dactylic hexameters:

All the rebels of all races of mankind will gather under our banners

And the weaponless shall be armed,
And violence will oppose violence.
There shall be a new crusade of all the poor and impoverished
   nations, of all poor men and all free men
Against the nations which usurp power and accumulate riches
Against predatory nations,
Against the caste of usurers which yesterday made the profits of
   the war and today profit by the peace.
And we shall reestablish the true justice which a cold and foolish
   man with a hammer borrowed from a former German
   chancellor, crucified with Fourteen Nails. . . .

The Fourteen Nails was a reference to Wilson's Fourteen Points.

But there was no waste. The foregoing lines and almost all those preceding and following them appeared shortly afterward in a slim volume of D'Annunzio's poetry, published in Fiume.

As I was leaving the poet, he suggested I interview the so-called president of Fiume, who would assure me that the Yugoslavs as well as the Italians favored him. Dr. Grossich was a very old man and probably did not know the meaning of what he was saying. When I asked about the plebiscite that elected him and endorsed D'Annunzio, he replied:

"It was fair and honestly conducted. All the good citizens were allowed to vote—we cleared out all the undesirable elements, all the socialists, the workingmen who were trouble-makers—we deported some five thousand of them."

The plebiscite that endorsed the Italian commandante D'Annunzio had a majority of a few more than one hundred. All the five thousand who had been deported before the voting were Yugoslavs.

When this strange little story appeared in the Paris edition of the *Chicago Tribune*—I had smuggled the text of the interviews out three days earlier—the hotel owner warned me to leave by the next train or "D'Annunzio will have you shot."

At Abbazia, halfway to Trieste, three members of the Dalmatian Legion entered my compartment and ordered me back to Fiume. I refused to go. The three then punched me several times, seized my arms and legs, and carried me into the station. I insisted on telegraphing the American consul in Trieste and told my captors that the consul would send an American warship to free me. They did not send my telegram, but they believed what I said about an American warship. I was permitted to take the next train.

Eventually D'Annunzio was defeated. He was starved out. When he had organized his Blackshirts and captured Fiume, he had appointed the editor of the Milan *Popolo d'Italia,* a friend, to collect money and send him food and supplies. This friend, the journalist B. Mussolini, collected twenty-five to fifty thousand dollars, mostly from Italian-Americans. He sent D'Annunzio nothing. When Mussolini was put on trial before the Association of Lombardy Journalists for stealing this money, he denied "stealing" but admitted he had "diverted" it, but for the same purpose, the outfitting of black-shirted illegal troops with the name "Fascisti" substituted for Dalmatian Legion.

Italian-Americans became, in this left-handed way, the original subsidizers of Fascism. With the fifty thousand American dollars he stole from D'Annunzio Mussolini was able to make the Milan Fascio into a national Blackshirt army—which eventually took over the country.

D'Annunzio was perhaps a great writer. Two of his books have been called masterpieces by many whose judgment I trust. Frances Winwar in her *Wings of Fire* praises D'Annunzio and also informs her readers that *Il Fuoco (The Flame)* is "the child of himself and Duse, just as *Trionfo della morte (The Triumph of Death)* had been the offspring of his love for Barbara Leoni."

Apparently this genius needed a new love for each great book, just as Hemingway did (so F. Scott Fitzgerald once told Morley Callaghan). But although Hemingway married four times and wrote a great book after each marriage, he neither degraded nor betrayed the inspirations of his literary achievements—he merely abandoned them. D'Annunzio, however, used his loves for literary advancement and, having done so, he threw them away. In the instance of Eleonora Duse he committed the unforgivable crime of selling the "child" of their love for money.

Moreover, long before *Il Fuoco* was published, Duse had been told it was not only their love story but also a book devoted largely to their lovemaking, sex so explicit it was later to shock the literary world not only of Italy but of England and the United States. She hurried to see him.

D'Annunzio assured her that the heroine, Foscarina, was not the actress and what he had written was not degrading or shocking, as Duse had been told. As proof, he would read her several pages; which he did, and Duse departed.

Although I have been unable to find documentary proof for the story which follows, I report it here as told me and vouched for by persons I trust.

Duse came to see D'Annunzio a second time. She told him he had lied to her. D'Annunzio shrugged and said he was broke, dead broke, he needed the money.

Duse asked how much.

D'Annunzio said his publisher in Milan had promised him $25,000.

Duse asked her former lover to wait a little while. Hurriedly she arranged for another "farewell" tour of America, she played to great audiences, many critics wrote she was greater than Sarah Bernhardt had ever been, and she returned to Italy with $25,000 in her hands and gave the money to D'Annunzio. He gave her the manuscript.

In her own apartment, before the fireplace, Duse read *Il Fuoco*. It was a beautiful book, probably a masterpiece. But as a *roman à clef* it needed no key. Foscarina was only too obviously herself; and in his most beautiful poetic prose D'Annunzio devoted chapter after chapter to every detail of their love affair, not even forgetting the blue veins of his mistress's loins or her pubic hair.

Page by page Duse threw the manuscript into the fireplace.

About three months later the book appeared in all the bookshops in Milan. It was set in type from the carbon copy—something Duse knew nothing about—and D'Annunzio collected a second $25,000.

(Treason is treason, to a person as well as to a state. Many traitors have betrayed their country for what they believed in, a noble cause. This man merely doubled his money. I think he is entitled to head my unholy trinity of SOBs.)

On regaining Trieste, after escaping D'Annunzio's bullyboys, I found a letter from Gibbons saying he had not completed arrangements for my taking over the Berlin office; also a telegram to proceed to Turin immediately because there was a "revolution" in progress there. In Trieste the Italian papers spoke of a strike. In Paris the headlines read:

WORKERS' REVOLUTION IN ITALY; AUTO PLANTS OCCUPIED. SIGNOR FIAT MURDERED

Because photographs never, never lie, you can find proof of at least the first two-thirds of this headline in the 1919 newspapers: the occupied factories, the words *Viva Lenin* painted on the walls of the FIAT factory and behind the barricades the autoworkers "brandishing" guns and swords and bayonets and even little pocketknives.

All these pictures, the only evidence of a "red" revolution, had been staged by the Hearst International Newsreel photographer, Ariel Vargas, an old friend of mine, who had preceded me to Turin. He confided to me that he had found nothing, but he had orders from New York. So he paid a man to paint *Viva Lenin* on the FIAT walls, and after buying up every old gun and sword and even a few Mohammedan scimitars, he "armed" the strikers and ordered them not to laugh while he took stills and movies. He had to justify the American headlines to make his living.

As for the murder of Signor Fiat, as reported in the foreign press, it was the work of the women, the wives of the strikers, "always more bloodthirsty than their husbands," the papers said. They captured the owner of the plant and threw his living breathing body into one of the great furnaces, shouting and rejoicing as they watched it consumed.

When I asked the man at the desk of the Excelsior Hotel about the horrible death of Signor Fiat, he was puzzled for a moment, then, laughing, he explained that the founder and still-living owner of the FIAT works was a Signor Agnelli, and if I so desired, he would telephone him and ask for an appointment for an interview by me. As for FIAT, didn't everyone know that these initials (then as now) stand for Factory-Italian-Automobiles-Torino?

It was, probably still is, one of the tricks of the trade: when an expensive assignment fails, find something nearby to make up for it—and justify your expense account. (If there was no story in Beirut, Damascus and Baghdad, you could always report the Kurds in revolt against their rulers.)

No revolution in Italy. Eyre of the *World* and I went to see a fellow journalist with whom we worked occasionally; his name was Mussolini and he had been thoroughly discredited for having taken money from a foreign country. He told us that "Italy needs a blood bath." There was a small earthquake near Fivizzano. I helped pull injured and dead from the frail wrecked homes. Then I got a tip that a group of Oriental rulers—kings, emirs, pashas, several temporarily between thrones—were holding a conference at the Villa d'Este on Lake Como.

Two of the men I met were notable: Prince Faud, who shortly afterward was proclaimed King of Egypt, and the deposed King of Syria, the Emir Feisul. The only non-Arab present was the Patriarch of Damascus, known in the Near East as the Pope of the Eastern Greek Catholic Church; he had come along to bear witness, the Emir Feisul told me.

"I accuse Great Britain," he said, "of failure to honor its secret treaty which gives me the throne of Syria. I accuse France of a reign of terror in Damascus. I accuse the rest of the Allied Powers and chiefly the United States of failure to keep the promise of the sovereignty of all Arab nations. Wilson promised us independence. Half the Arab world is ruled by the Allies."

With each "*j'accuse*" the Emir half-nodded to the Patriarch, and at each hesitation the Patriarch nodded solemnly in affirmation.

"I shall insist on a throne," concluded the Emir. "I am the ruler the people want. I will restore liberty. All peoples will live in harmony, Christian and Muslim alike. I, a Muslim, have with me the head of the Christian Church who will testify that the Christians especially trust me. Isn't that so?" (Another nudge.)

"Yes. Yes. Yes," replied the Patriarch.

I was invited to stay for lunch. Emir Feisul now presided as at a cabinet meeting, in the most princely of the princely Villa d'Este halls, wearing the uniform of a British officer of General Allenby's staff, on which the green and gold Muslim insignia glittered.

There were many courses and wine with each. One might say it was a feast fit for a king. But the Emir put each glass of wine to his lips, did not taste it, put it down. So did all the other kings and princes. Only the Patriarch and I drank a little of the three or four varieties, and I figured there was a good hundred dollars' worth of French wine wasted.

When the Emir rose, we all had to rise. Coffee was served in an adjoining hall. A number of bottles of French champagne were brought in, opened, poured, enjoyed by a minority of two, left sparkling in a score of glasses. A good news story, a good feature story.

Later that day, in the Villa d'Este gardens, a heavy, elderly man in a black stovepipe hat and a cassock came breathlessly fumbling after me. He held up his ikon as if to prove his claim that he was the Patriarch of the lunch table. He seized my arm and whispered:

"This man, this Emir Feisul, he told you I came to speak for the Christians. I came because if I had not come it would have been death or suffering for my people. He, this emir, is a terrible man. In his nice European clothes he is a civilized man. But in his native clothes, at home, when he puts on his headdress, and his sword, he is a barbarian—a slaughterer, an enemy of Christianity. We tremble. We fear him. If Lloyd George gives him back the throne, he may have to protect us Christians, and that is why I came with him to say we want him king again. Otherwise he will raise an Arab army and massacre us all.

"This is the truth. I cannot let you go away without telling you the truth."

This concluding part of my news story is one of the few in my seventy years of writing that I myself censored. The innocent Patriarch did not realize that if I had quoted the "truth" he had whispered to me, word for word, it would endanger not only his own life, but probably the whole Christian minority of Beirut, Damascus and Baghdad. I left the conclusion out entirely.

Chapter 16

Berlin: The Men Who Lost the War

T he wonderful year of wandering and blundering around Europe, the Lady Astor campaign, the Irish rebels, Emir Feisul at the Villa d'Este, D'Annunzio in Fiume and a hundred minor adventures unfortunately came to an end when I finally took over the Berlin office in the Hotel Adlon. Gibbons informed me that although this hotel, where the *Tribune* had a suite of three rooms, was to be my base, I was also to report Vienna and Budapest fully, and make at least one long trip annually to Belgrade, Sofia, Bucharest, Beirut, Damascus and Baghdad.

Fortunately for me I inherited the *Tribune* interpreter, Sigrid Schultz, who, despite her German family name, was the daughter of a noted Norwegian painter, and a native-born Chicagoan. (Eventually, after I had trained her to be a journalist, she became my successor in Berlin.)

The first job I set for myself for the days when there was no "hot" front-page news was to interview the generals and admirals who lost the Great War. Having already heard Hindenburg's confession, I placed first on my list the name of Von Kluck: why had he not taken Paris in 1914? Next was Admiral Scheer who, the Germans said, had beaten the British Navy; and then Udet, Richthofen's successor, the living ace of aces; then Max Hoffmann—frequently called "Von Hoffmann" because of his high rank, the general who dictated the peace of Brest-Litovsk with Russia in 1917, one of the most disgraceful military-diplomatic actions in history—the direct and chief, if not the only cause for the destruction of the Kerensky government and the victory of the Lenin-Trotsky forces. We called Hoffmann the "godfather of Bolshevism."

My first sortie was a total failure—one of the many similar failures that journalists almost universally never report. Von Kluck had refused to meet the press for almost three years but now, probably due to the insistence and the logic of the appeals of my assistant, Miss Schultz, he agreed to see me in his home. It was Miss Schultz who told me about the Schlieffen plan which the Kaiser had made, both for the invasion of every country bordering Germany, friend or foe, and for the defense of Germany against one and all.

When war broke out in August 1914, Von Kluck was given the Schlieffen plan to lead his army to a point northwest of Paris, turn south, surround and occupy the capital—and it had worked perfectly. Up to a point—and that point was also my point: why had Von Kluck not turned south and taken Paris? Why?

I was received by a dignified elderly gentleman every inch a secretary of state—or a Protestant bishop—in striped trousers and a cutaway coat. The figure rose. We shook hands.

Eventually, having acquired a little reportorial diplomacy since my encounter with Mr. Bryan more than a decade earlier, I mentioned the Schlieffen plan and how brilliantly Von Kluck had carried it out across all of France. Neither Galliane's taxicabs nor Foch's attack had saved Paris from German occupation. Who was the villain—from the German viewpoint—of this failure to turn south, and not only capture Paris, from which the government had already fled, but perhaps win the war? Von Kluck refused to name anyone. No matter how I worded it, repeated it, the answer was always the same: "Great headquarters."

Whom was he protecting? Could it have been Ludendorff?

This I did find out—in the course of many years: that the head of the intelligence department of Supreme Headquarters, a Colonel von Hentsh, who was sent to Von Kluck on the very day he had reached all his straight-line objectives, told him to "proceed with caution." Von Kluck observed caution.

My failure with Von Kluck was followed by a success with Admiral Scheer; in fact, a world scoop—one of the several that should be credited more to Miss Schultz than to me.

It was also an important front-page news story. Historically it answered the question who won, or rather, who, Germany or Britain, had the better of the great encounter at sea called the greatest since the destruction of the Spanish Armada. Up to now the result had been disputed—even the name of the battle differed, the British calling it Jutland, the Germans Skagerrak.

The Allied world in the early 1920s was engaged in an arms race. The Congress of the United States was considering how many hundreds of millions of dollars would be spent on either dreadnaughts or submarines—the future of the nation seemed to depend on the question "big ships or little ships?" The answer, it was said in many countries, could be found in the secret report Admiral Scheer had made to Kaiser Wilhelm. Every correspondent in Berlin tried to get a copy. The Kaiser's, of course, had disappeared. The admirals who had copies were under obligation to Scheer to keep them secret. Had thirty-seven copies been printed, or seventy-five? This too was disputed. It was known that one copy went down with Admiral Hipper's flagship when the Germans sank their navy after surrendering it to the British (in accordance with the Versailles Treaty). Did British divers recover it—did Britain know and not tell her Allies? Mere rumors. In the 1920s Miss Schultz knew that there were four copies extant, three in private archives of German admirals and one in the library of the historian of the German Navy, himself a participant in the Battle of Skagerrak, Captain Otto Groos.

At first Groos would not let us even look at the document

from a distance. We argued that there was now no illegality or breach of ethics in disclosure, we told him that the British surely had the Hipper copy, and finally we flattered him by asking him to annotate his original work, write an introduction and a summary, for all of which he would be credited in the American press, and besides, given a check for, say, five hundred dollars by the *Tribune*—a fabulous sum in daily-falling German marks.

He brought the document to our office, we photographed it, we photographed him holding it, ourselves holding it. We copied paragraphs, notably those in which Scheer told the Kaiser that the day of the dreadnaughts was over, capital ships were useless, the submarine had changed naval warfare; the Kaiser would win the war by building nothing but submarines, sinking all food ships, starving Britain into submission. The concluding paragraph read: "A victorious end of the war is conceivable at this time only by crushing England's economic life, that is, by using submarines against British commerce. I urgently advise against using submarines moderately." (The action of Admiral Von Capelle canceling Scheer's plan was later called in the Reichstag "a crime . . . this failure led to our defeat.")

The *Tribune*'s publication of the Scheer report echoed around the world; it even reached the eyes and ears of the admiral, who was now in seclusion. I went to Weimar on January 12, 1921. I found the little house. The threshold had been holystoned, there were no traces of blood. Only a few days earlier the admiral's wife had answered a knock at the door. A stranger stood there. She asked him what he wanted and he stabbed her to death and fled. The mystery was never solved.

Admiral Scheer was sad but gracious. He thanked me for making his report public, for now the world would know that the Battle of the Skagerrak was not a British victory.

On the table he spread a map, and with the help of scores of old-fashioned sulphur matches he placed on it his twenty-seven capital ships and Jellicoe's and Beatty's forty-five and moved them through the entire battle, removing a match for each sunken vessel. Finally he went through his famous night maneuver. He said, "The British failure to attack was an error—there is no Nelson in England now."

The first report, in the London *Times,* which he showed me, that "the Grand Fleet suffered a severe reverse," was correct. It lost three battle cruisers, three armored cruisers, eight destroyers, 6,097 men killed, 177 taken prisoner. As for his losses, Scheer again quoted British sources: one battleship, one battle cruiser, four light cruisers, five destroyers, 2,545 men killed, no men taken prisoner.

Then Admiral Scheer told me a real news story. The British claim that regardless of their losses it was a victory, because the German fleet never put to sea again, was also untrue. Three months later, his fleet restored, Admiral Scheer, with twenty capital ships and his submarines on their flanks, steamed into the North Sea to challenge Britain again. The admiral then read me a report from the *Times* of Jellicoe's fleet caught in a "snarl of torpedoes" and retiring to harbor.

"Our fleet remained in possession of the North Sea that day," continued Scheer. "The 'snarl of torpedoes' came from our submarines. They taught the world a lesson that day. It is this: that a few submarines could make England uncertain of the value of the Grand Fleet. . . . The course of naval history was changed.

"Without historic tradition, without experience, we built a navy that came out victorious in the one great battle and wrote a gallant record of heroic exploits. The Allies robbed us of our fleet but British propaganda must not rob us of our glory."

Ludendorff and Hitler

Ludendorff in 1919, before my arrival, gave the American correspondents in Berlin an interview. He said, "We must abandon not only Jehovah but Christ and Christianity, which have reduced the once strong and powerful people to whimpering and humility. We must go back to worshipping Wotan."

However, in 1920 when I questioned him on the same subject—was it true he and his wife had built an altar in their home and were now worshipping Wotan?—Ludendorff telegraphed me: ALLES ERLOGEN UND ERSTUNKEN—LUDENDORFF. (Translated, "a pack of lies, and they stink.")

I immediately put the telegram in the *Tribune* office window, first to the right of the Hotel Adlon entrance, and crowds gathered.

Ludendorff was never as frank as Hindenburg in crediting the American army with breaking the stalemate, but he was once a halfway honest man, and in his *Memoirs,* Vol. II, 1919, he halfway admitted his defeat. He wrote: "August 8, 1918, was the black day of the German Army in the history of the war."

But no one, no one in power, no political party leader, no press lord throughout Hitler's rise to dictatorship, thanks to the stab-in-the-back legend, ever brought up this statement, which was almost a confession.

The first press mention abroad of a former German corporal organizing an armed force to march on the Bavarian capital, Munich, called him "Otto Hitler." One newspaper said Otto Hitler was leading three thousand men, another said he had a new flag, the old abandoned monarchist red, white and black, with a symbol from India, a swastika, reversed, in the center.

Count Hugo Lerchenfeld and his countess, the American-born Ethel Louise Wyman, were chosen to explain the new movement to the American people. (Another instance of good public relations: every foreign correspondent usually looked for "the American angle," and the countess was it.) She told the American press in 1923:

> The first and most important dogma in Hitler's creed from the very beginning has been anti-Semitism. Jewish influence is the root of all social and moral evil. Eliminate international Jewry from Capitalism and Capitalism will cease to be a menace to humanity. . . .
>
> Hitler looked upon Socialism and internationalism as purely Jewish inventions.
>
> The Nazi Party [National Socialist Labor Party] has increased from 5,000 last July [1922] to 50,000 . . . and is spreading like a forest fire. . . .

• • •

Again, when Hitler marched into Nuremberg—about the time the French occupied the Ruhr and the mark fell to fifty thousand to the dollar—he had by his side another American angle, another lady of title, the Baroness von Wrede, the former Ray Beveridge, daughter of a governor of Illinois, veteran of a stock-company production of *The College Widow,* the original of the popular statue "The American Venus," ex–war correspondent, passionate monarchist, passionate Hitlerite. Berlin paid little attention to the doings of the little man now correctly called Adolf but still regarded as harmless. But many of the British correspondents did go to Munich when that city's walls were plastered with posters announcing beer-hall meetings. These read:

NATIONAL SOCIALISTS!   ANTI-SEMITES!

14 Mass Meetings
on Thursday, the 27th of September, evenings, 8
o'clock in the following Munich halls will be held:

Bürgerbräu Cellar
Franziskaner Cellar
    (Hochstr.)
Löwenbräu Cellar

Thomasbräu
    (Kapuzinerpl.)
Hofbräuhaus Cellar
Salvator Cellar
    (Nockerberg)

and several others

Our Führer
ADOLF HITLER
will speak at all gatherings. . . .

These meetings of September 27 are now known as the famous Beer Hall Putsch, which we fully reported as an enormous farce.

Armed with revolvers, Hitler and two of his men entered the Bürgerbräu Cellar, were ignored, climbed onto tables and fired their guns into the ceiling—Hitler shouting that this was the Nazi Revolution: "Five years ago this Revolution was started. Tonight it is ended. A new government is taking Power."

Most of the beer drinkers still paid no attention. Hitler then fired his revolver again; this caused some commotion, and protest, and so he was thrown out of the beer hall.

With his faithful followers, three hundred strong, and his leading disciple, the former commander of the Germany armies, Ludendorff, Hitler marched on the Bavarian War Ministry. But now some fifty uniformed policemen stood in their way. "I order you to surrender to the Nationalist Army," shouted Hitler. The policemen then fired into the air.

At the first shot Hitler dropped his revolver and ran for his life. (Other reports had him crawling on the street, trying to get around a corner.) Ludendorff also ran—with his hands up— looking for someone to whom to surrender. Two policemen arrested him.

Thus ended the famous Nazi Beer Hall Putsch.

For Ludendorff, incidentally, this was not the first time he had taken flight. At the monarchist attempt to restore the Kaiser, the 1920 Kapp Putsch in Berlin when the unions finally destroyed the monarchy by declaring a general strike, General Ludendorff fled to Sweden, in dark glasses, disguised as "Eric Lindstrom." It was when he returned to Munich that he discovered Wotan and Hitler.

At his trial for treason, February 26, 1924, Hitler said: "There is no such thing as treason against the traitors of 1918."

In prison, Hitler dictated *Mein Kampf* to his cellmate, Rudolf Hess. Besides expounding the theory of the value of the Big Lie, it contains statements such as this: "Any nation whose purpose is not the intention to wage war is senseless and useless."

As for Hitler himself, before I mention our meeting, I feel I must say a kind word in explanation, or defense, of my Berlin-Vienna colleague, Dorothy Thompson of the *Ledger* Syndicate. The book reviewers, the press, the political world laughed and jeered at this brilliant journalist when Hitler took power while the book she had written, *I Saw Hitler,* was being set in type. Miss Thompson's first paragraph read: "When I walked into Adolf Hitler's salon in the Kaiserhof Hotel I was convinced I was meeting the future dictator of Germany. In something less than fifty seconds I was quite sure I was not. It took me just that time to measure the startling insignificance of this man who has set the whole world agog."

Miss Thompson's great error, it seems to me, was overestimating the masses of people who followed Hitler, not underestimating the leader himself. It is also a fact that in the early days the press did not know that the greatest industrialists and the biggest banks had put their future and their money on Hitler. Mencken once told his assistant editor, "No one ever went broke underestimating the intelligence of the American people"—he was referring to a possible success for *Reader's Digest* which, like the New York *Daily News,* catered to a low intelligence quotient. But however low the IQ of the American people may be, Mencken could not also accuse them of totally lacking a sense of humor. One can imagine Huey Long calling out his National Guard for his own purposes, but can one imagine a Huey Long running after such an episode as the Beer-Hall Putsch, the firing of revolvers into the ceiling, and the fleeing or crawling in the streets?

It was not until many years after World War II at an impromptu reunion of former Berlin correspondents, when I said I had seen Hitler many times at public gatherings but never met him, that Pierre Loving, now stationed in the Washington Hearst bureau, corrected me. "Don't you remember the big Wilhelmstrasse party given by Baron von Maltzan?" he asked. I said yes. "Then you must remember," continued Loving, "that one sour-faced party leader who sat by himself and talked to nobody, except for the '*Guten Abend*' with the handshake coming and going—the man with the Charlie Chaplin moustache. . . . "

Two or three hours with Hitler in 1925—almost totally forgotten. I knew why Dorothy Thompson's forty-eight seconds with Hitler had resulted in her phrase, "startling insignificance."

If it is true that Hitler in his first years after the ludicrous Beer Hall Putsch was overlooked, discounted and forgotten by the press, it is even truer that one of Germany's great men of the century, the co-inventor of the Haber-Bosch process for extracting nitrogen from the air, was never even mentioned, either at home or abroad, and remains unknown to the world today despite his receiving the Nobel Prize for chemistry in 1918 and being listed twice in the American Chemical Society's roll of honor of the past hundred years.

I came upon the almost incredible story of another unrecognized achievement of his. There had been an explosion at a plant at Oppeln where the Haber-Bosch nitrogen fixation process was in operation. Every human being and animal in the vicinity, more than six hundred men, women and children, had been killed and the factory and every house and every tree nearby destroyed. Everything had disappeared in one blast, in one second, or whatever the time was for the Hiroshima or Nagasaki bomb, but this was in 1922 or 1923, not 1945.

I went to interview Fritz Haber, who received me in his home in Berlin. Gracious and frank, he told me he was the co-inventor of the Haber-Bosch process, and nitrogen, 500,000 tons a year, could increase crop production and prevent starvation from becoming the chief weapon in a war. The Allies had known this and hastened their 1918 offensive, which won the war. The Allies had also heard rumors that Haber was experimenting with explosives "a hundred, perhaps a thousand times as deadly as any now known."

The first words Haber said to me were: "There has never before been an explosion in a nitrogen fixation plant. I do not know what caused this one. If we can discover the cause of the Oppeln blast we may find a new and most terrible force, hitherto unknown to man." (This statement was made some time before Einstein wrote out his atomic bomb formula.) If the Germans ever learned the secret of the Oppeln explosion, they told no one. Haber did not know it.

As I was leaving his office, I noticed a framed picture because it had writing over it and WILHELM R (R for Rex, or Kaiser) in enormous letters. It was a page from a wartime *Illustrated London News* showing the first gas attack—on the Canadians, at Ypres, in April 1915. Why had the Kaiser sent Professor Haber this autographed picture?

"Because," he replied, "I had invented the liquid, which is generally called gas, in 1914."

Then he told me how Kaiser Wilhelm, Ludendorff and the general staff refused to use it for various reasons and finally agreed on a small-scale experiment—instead of a great attack on several miles of front, breaking the stalemate and bringing victory.

"I would never have thought of 'gas' as a war weapon," Professor Haber continued, "if I had not read in the British and French press stories about a Frenchman named Turpin who said he would win the war with a new weapon 'which killed without touching, but left an odor.' This could mean only a liquid which vaporized, and killed." He went to work on it that very day.

When I tried to pin Professor Haber down to who was responsible for Germany's failure, he refused to be specific. The Kaiser, Ludendorff? He wouldn't say. But he insisted that the British had been just as stupid with their tanks. The British command did not believe in them. Used them on a small scale. Terrorized the Germans. Had they waited, built thousands, used them on a large front, they too could have won the war in one day.

"Every new weapon is capable of winning a war," said Haber.

In Ambassador Dodd's *Berlin Diary,* July 28, 1933, there is this entry:

"Dr. Fritz Haber, perhaps the foremost chemist in Germany, brought me a letter from Henry Morgenthau, Jr., of New York, and told me the saddest story of Jewish persecution I have ever heard. He is sixty-five years old, has serious heart trouble, and has been dismissed from his position without the pension to which he was entitled under the law prior to the Nazi regime."

Haber wanted to go to the United States.

Dodd cabled Washington for permission to give him a visa.

The U.S. State Department replied that the German quota was full.

Haber went to Spain and died.

Chapter 17

~~~~~~~~

Einstein, Freud, Isadora Duncan

In many of my Berlin years I received orders from Chicago—cables sometimes signed "McCormick," sometimes by the Paris bureau chief—ordering me to spend from $5,000 (Isadora Duncan's love letters) to $25,000 (for Freud to come to Chicago) and various sums in between. The most repeated cable of all, however, involved no dollars. It simply said "Ask Einstein what he thinks of . . . " or "interview Einstein about . . . " the most important subject of the day.

I do not remember how many times I talked to Einstein—at least three, perhaps five. I was surprised to find him always friendly, almost cordial, always willing—he never refused an inquiry. On one occasion he even offered to write a little article on the subject. But Einstein always concluded the telephone conversation with a simple little request: "Could the *Chicago Tribune* in consideration of an interview or an article donate a small sum, say twenty-five dollars, to a fund for establishing a homeland to save the Jews of Europe?"

151

This is why I never got to interview Einstein. The Colonel always replied he was "not buying news," he would not give Einstein twenty-five dollars for anything. Although the Einsteins were a non-religious family, and his earliest education had been in a Catholic school, and in later life he called himself a free-thinker, Einstein explained that it was not for political or religious reasons that he favored an independent nation for the Jews. "I favor a free state for any oppressed people," he said.

In 1954, when I began compiling *The Great Quotations,* I wrote Einstein, asking him if he would correct the selections I had made from his writings and public statements. To my great surprise I received a most cordial reply. Dr. Einstein wrote from Princeton, "I am gladly willing to review the quotations you intend sending me. Such a review is indeed necessary. For many things which go under my name are badly translated from the German or are invented by other people."

On October 24 he returned the manuscript with several corrections. Only one quotation had been eliminated: a ship reporter's statement that on his request for "a one-line definition of the theory of relativity," Dr. Einstein had replied, "There are no hitching posts in the universe."

Freud

*T*he year was 1924. Two rich, well-educated young men named Loeb and Leopold had murdered another rich young man named Frank. There seemed to be no reason for the crime—it was called a "thrill murder" and the Chicago press was so occupied with this story it cabled all its European correspondents to go easy on everything except another world war.

In June Colonel McCormick cabled me to invite Professor Freud to join the *Tribune* staff in reporting the Loeb-Leopold trial, but Freud refused. The Colonel's next cable to me read: OFFER FREUD $25,000 OR ANYTHING HE NAME PSYCHOANALYZE /LOEB-LEOPOLD/ RETURN MAIL.

Freud replied by letter (here "painfully" translated by my assistant, Sigrid Schultz):

Wien IX, Berggasse 19
29 VI. 24

Sehr geerter Herr:

Your telegram reached me belatedly because of the incorrect address. My reply is, that it cannot be my intention to deliver an expert opinion about persons and an action if I must rely on newspaper reports and have no opportunity for a personal examination. An invitation from the Hearst press to come to New York during the duration of the trial, I must reject for health considerations.

Hochachtungsvoll, Prof. freud.

Although I knew the letter was genuine, I thought the signature that of a secretary—why sign it "Prof." and why spell Freud with a small "f"? But I was assured by Freud's nephew, the noted New York public relations counsel Edward L. Bernays, that this was how Uncle Sigmund usually signed his letters.

Isadora Duncan

Isadora Duncan's one and only true autobiographical work—i.e., self-written, not ghostwritten, or written this side of idolatry— is the chapter she dictated to a secretary I engaged in 1924. At the time she had promised to sell me the story of her life plus copies of her love letters (from several noted men, including Gordon Craig and D'Annunzio) for $5,000.

The two or three thousand words she dictated show that Isadora could have written a good book; she expressed herself well. Isadora had come from Moscow to Paris for a reconciliation with her Russian-poet husband Essenin (or Yessenin, as he was called). She fought endlessly with him when he got drunk, which was daily. She had followed him to Berlin, but he again left her and returned to Moscow.

I found her in the Central Hotel, a third-class house near the Friedrichstrasse railroad station, my onetime goddess of the dance (Nixon Theatre, Pittsburgh, 1909) now fat, frowsy, all puffed out, and a prisoner in her room because she had no money to pay for anything. She may have been starving, too. But before I could do more than tell her why I had come, she asked if she could have a drink. When I called the waiter, she told him to bring a quart of gin. I paid, wondering how to disguise this item on my expense account.

The first paragraph of what was to be Isadora's biography indicates that she meant to go through with it. She dictated:

> I find it difficult to write this book. I find it hard to speak when I know that every word is being taken down. I want this book to be something worth while leaving behind. It will only be worth doing if it is a book which will help people to live. I want to tell the truth about my loves and my art because the whole world is absolutely brought up on lies. We begin with lies and end on nothing but lies. We begin with lies and half our lives at least we live with lies.

This is Isadora talking—I have not changed a word. Her first chapter rambled from subject to subject. She had made no outline. She went on to discuss love:

> I want to show mankind it does not know how to love. . . . In the flesh there is no love. I have had as much as anyone of that sort of thing which men dare call love—men foaming at the mouth—men crying they would kill themselves if I didn't return their love. Love—rot! . . . From all sides I was besieged by all sorts of men. What did they want? . . . They say to the bottle, "I'm thirsty. I want to drink you up. I want to possess all of you." To me they say the same things. "I'm hungry. I want you. I want to possess your body and soul." Oh, they usually add the soul when they plead for the body! Was that love? It was hysteria.

Isadora also had views that I doubt Colonel McCormick would have published in the world's greatest newspaper. She said:

> All that is necessary to make this world a better place to live in is to love—to love as Christ loved, as Buddha loved.
> That was the most marvelous thing about Lenin: *he* really loved mankind.
> Others love themselves, money, theories, power: Lenin loved his fellow men.

They say to me, "How can you be so enthusiastic about Lenin—he did not believe in God." I reply: "This is simply a phrase. Lenin was God, as Christ was God, because God is Love and Christ and Lenin were all Love."

Toward the conclusion of the dictated first chapter she turned to the subject of her art:

I am not a dancer. I never *danced* a step in my life. I hate all dancing. . . . What I am interested in doing is finding and expressing a new form of life. The Greeks lived. People do not live nowadays.

No second chapter of this book was ever written. The British secretary came to my office the next day with her transcript and asked to be paid off. She did not want to be associated with Isadora Duncan. She disapproved of both her morals and her politics.

Several days passed before I could find someone who could take English dictation. When I called again, Isadora put me off for some reason, said she would telephone me, and when there was no call I went again to her shabby hotel. I found Isadora sober and dressed in fine clothing and packing a new trunk with the aid of smiling (well-tipped) maids.

"I'm off to Spa," she said. "To take the cure. I've quit drinking. I'm too fat, but I'll reduce . . . I'm going to have a studio again. I'm going to Nice for the winter. . . . "

What had happened in the preceding three or four days? The only clue was Isadora's telling me that somehow stories had been appearing in the European—and probably American—newspapers saying she was selling her love letters for publication. She had received several telephone calls, and one or two important personal pleas, asking her not to do so. She would decide after consulting her friend in Paris—the gentleman who had promised the studio in Nice. She might write her autobiography—but *sell* love letters? Isadora was indignant on this subject. "I'll telephone you from Paris," she said, but of course she never did.

I did see her once again, in Nice, three years later. The studio was full of guests and Isadora "danced" for us. It was a mere nostalgic memory of the great artist I had seen in Pittsburgh in 1909.

In 1976 my niece, Marian Seldes, had the lead in a play called, for some reason, *Isadora Duncan Slept with the Russian Navy.* Marian asked me if I knew more about Isadora than I had already written—i.e., the episode of the love letters. I thought the time had now come, since Isadora Duncan is so great a name, that I could not harm her by following the dictum of the *Biographie Universelle de France,* that "to the dead we owe nothing but the truth." I replied:

Nov. 1, 1976

Dearest Marian:

Of course you know of my three encounters with her— my youthful infatuation with the dancer of Mendelssohn's Spring Song . . . and the 1924 adventure in Berlin. . . .

There is one episode I never wrote because I think it would be too cruel—but nevertheless, perhaps not cruel if played on the stage.

It so happened that in 1924 at the time Isadora was at the Central Hotel . . . deserted by everyone, that a German musical comedy company either imported a show call *Little Jesse James* or imported six chorus girls from that show to appear in a German musical comedy. They were the usual type, all six but perhaps only five blondes, beautiful in the magazine cover sense, and all but one available. Eyre of the *World* dated them all.

Someone, probably a rich German or American with a magnificent apartment, threw a big party for Isadora Duncan, inviting everyone who knew her, and the press, and the six *Little Jesse James* girls. By the time I arrived Isadora had had too much, as usual, and was stretched on a couch, fat and bloated. We, however, tried to cheer her up, and then followed the cruel scene I refer to. The six American chorus girls, who knew nothing of classic dancing to say nothing of ballet, improvised their own dance, an American musical comedy dance, around and around the couch where the half-drunken Isadora lay with glazed eyes—each chorus girl kicking up her legs and all singing some chorus from one of their latest American shows. It is a scene I'll never forget although it is one of the few things I have witnessed I have never before cared to write or even tell anyone.

Prince Yusupov

Shortly after my arrival at the *Chicago Tribune* office in the Hotel Adlon building in 1920, a man in his early thirties came to see me, said he was Prince Felix Yusupov and that he and his companions had killed Rasputin, the man who had had an evil influence not only on the Tsar and Tsarina of Russia, but on the whole country.

He said that they first poisoned the monk, and when that failed they stabbed him, and when that failed they shot him. The new news in the Yusupov story was this: to save each of the persons present from being accused of murder the revolver was passed around, and each nobleman fired a shot into Rasputin. No one would ever know who killed him.

Yusupov asked for a large sum of money. Chicago was not interested.

Some time that same year another man came into my office with a still more amazing tale. He gave the name Aron Simonovich, said he was the Tsarina's jeweler, and offered me the story free if I would put something in the paper that would help him find relatives in America.

"This monk, Rasputin," he said, "was in truth a German agent. Knowing that I received millions of dollars from Jewish philanthropists for the purpose of aiding Russian Jews to escape to Europe and America, Rasputin offered me a fortune, actually one million dollars, if I would use my influence with American Jews to support the German side instead of the Allies. This was before America got into the war."

Simonovich also alleged that it was Rasputin who informed the Germans that Lord Kitchener was coming to Russia on the battleship *Hampshire* via the northern route, thus permitting the Germans to lay a new minefield, which sank the ship carrying Britain's war leader.

When this betrayal became known in court circles, Simonovich told me, Prince Yusupov and other nobles intrigued to get rid of Rasputin. They invited him to the Yusupov palace and he came. At the banquet he was given poisoned wine, which he drank and enjoyed.

"The most interesting thing about the assassination of Rasputin," which followed, continued Simonovich, "was that the man who claims the credit for it is the only person present who had no hand in it.

"When the cyanide poison failed, one of the four officers in the Yusupov conspiracy fired his revolver at Rasputin. The monk fell to the floor but was only slightly wounded. The officer who shot him insisted that every man present have an equal share in the death and passed the revolver. The next officer shot the man lying down on the floor and passed the revolver. When it was placed in Prince Yusupov hand he trembled so that he missed the victim. Yusupov was the only man there whose bullet did not strike Rasputin."

A great many important persons and a great many important news stories just walked into the *Tribune* office, situated as it was in the news epicenter of Germany. Among the well-known persons I went to interview outside Berlin I consider Anton Lang one of the most noteworthy. I had cabled Christmas week 1921 that the Passion Play, postponed from 1920, would be revived in 1922 but owing to the German mark having already begun its cataclysmic fall—it went from only four to seventy-five to the dollar in early 1922, four hundred later, but eventually to quintillions to the dollar in 1924—the Passion Play producers could not afford to buy thirty pieces of silver. I suggested that *Chicago Tribune* readers contribute. By return mail I was overwhelmed. I had to send back perhaps as many as a thousand silver coins after sending Herr Lang thirty.

At Oberammergau, spring 1922, I stayed at a Lang *gasthaus.* Anton Lang had been the Christus of the 1910 Passion Play and was to resume the role in 1922. He thanked me for the silver, but added:

"I am not using the silver coins you gave me. The words 'American dollar' have taken on an evil meaning in Europe nowadays. However, it is due to the generosity of your readers in Chicago in sending me the dollars that I have been able to buy thirty pieces of silver of another country to use in this year's play. See, I have bought these with your dollars." He showed me the thirty pieces of silver. Each piece was German.

Lang talked to me about hatred still ruling the world and the Passion Play's mission of healing the war's wounds. "Do not you in America have a special mission, the mission to make the world better?" he asked. "We have a mission—to bring the nations together, promote brotherhood. We say in the prologue, 'This is the story that transformed the world and will yet transform it.' "

There was, however, the question of anti-Semitism. The original Passion Play of 1633 was totally anti-Semitic, but a Benedictine monk had rewritten it in 1750, making Lucifer rather than "the Jews" the villain. Nevertheless a lot of anti-Semitism remained in the Passion Play, and, moreover, the whole town without any doubt was one of the most anti-Semitic of all the towns in Germany.

Chapter 18

The Adlon: A World in Itself

Of all the grand hotels in the world the grandest was the Adlon in Berlin. People came, people went. Everything happened.

In March 1920 the first attempt to restore the monarchy—or perhaps initiate a fascist dictatorship—was led by Dr. Wolfgang Kapp, standing upright in his auto, followed by his illegal Ehrhardt Brigade, which was to appear many times later and eventually in Hitler's army, while crowds cheered and the American press corps, mostly residents of the Adlon, stood on its roof and watched. (I missed this one event and report this history as told me by my colleagues.)

The procession came from the Tiergarten, divided so as to enter Pariser Platz without going through the Brandenburg Gate, passed the Adlon, turned sharply right into Wilhelmstrasse, and began occupying the republican government's buildings. From the roof the reporters saw the last occupants fleeing in cars and on foot.

It was the big world news event of the time and, like all history in the making mixed with wild rumors and speculations. However, the first act of the Kapp regime was to send a man in uniform, probably an important officer, mounted on a horse, to the Hotel Adlon, to summon the press, mostly American, to read the Kapp Proclamation. The monarchy would be restored. He was merely the caretaker. The good old days would return. The proclamation was signed "Imperial Chancellor and Premier of Prussia" and also by a name no one had ever heard of before, Ignatz Trebitsch-Lincoln, who the next day became the censor and suppressed all the news.

It was not until many decades later, when the general American attitude toward foreign news changed (for the better, obviously), that I realized, in the Kapp Putsch, the Hitler beginnings, and even in the *Laconia* sinking, how immoral or amoral or irresponsible was the part played by American journalism in obeying the written or understood order: "Get the American angle."

Wolfgang Kapp was born in America. He had in fact been a Brooklyn boy at one time. This story did get through. His second in command, General von Lüttwitz, who a few years earlier had been denounced by Herbert Hoover, then saving Belgian lives, as a vicious murderer of women and children, now became a sort of American hero because his wife was Mary Curtis Cary of Cleveland, Ohio. Brooklyn and Cleveland thrilled—all America found the Kapp Putsch more interesting than "think pieces" and background pieces on the march of reaction in Germany, the possible return of the Kaiser. Here was the establishment of a regime with an "American angle."

But why had a revolutionary change in the government of one of the major nations of the world been announced at a hotel? The press representatives living in the Adlon did not ask, did not wonder; they knew that there were two Germanys after the Great War, and that the Hotel Adlon was one of them. There had probably in modern history never before nor after it been such an entire world as this hotel was then and would remain for many years. Whether or not the Kaiser was half-owner was unimportant. The fact that kings and queens stayed there does not distinguish it from half a dozen Ritzes. The Adlon was the epicenter of the journalistic world, the center of the cold-war conspiracy and other military adventures of a decade, the center of great industrial undertakings—Hugo Stinnes, called the richest industrialist in the world, lived there—a center for great political events, such as the conferences of the authors of the Dawes-Young Plan; and it was the center of the cultural life of Germany—the greatest dramatist of continental Europe, Gerhart Hauptmann, had his tea table and his coterie daily. If Hollywood can also be considered cultural, it too was there, from the owners of great film companies to almost every living star who ever sparkled anywhere or fulminated in America. Writers and publishers met in the Adlon bar. A foreign correspondent could spend all his time at the Adlon and find something to cable or write home about every day of the year.

Along with the kings and queens and princes and princesses of Europe who came to the Adlon almost every week of the several years I was there, the American film tsars began arriving from Hollywood, and almost immediately afterwards, the stars of the then silent film.

My first celebrity was Charlie Chaplin. But the Germans, who from 1914 on had been deprived of all American films and were now too poor to import the great stars, had not shown a Chaplin for at least six years, and so nobody turned out to greet him, except the newspaper mob—perhaps a dozen of us. Chaplin was plain and friendly—and one of the most astonished persons I ever saw in my life.

The Hollywood Blumenthal brothers did their best for Charlie. One of the European stars who came almost daily to the Adlon to see the film representatives was Pola Negri, blossoming in her early twenties. One of the Blumenthal brothers immediately introduced Miss Negri to Mr. Chaplin, and arranged a dinner lunch for them at Horscher's, the number-one restaurant of the country. Mr. Blumenthal also asked me and one or two other American correspondents to be his guests—obviously for publicity purposes.

Charlie was either smitten with Pola Negri or pretended to be. I heard him whisper to Blumenthal, "How do you say in German, 'You are the most beautiful woman I have ever seen'?"

Blumenthal whispered back, "*Du bist ekelhaft,*" which can be translated as "You are disgusting."

Charlie made a graceful bow and said adoringly, "Madam Negri, *Du bist ekelhaft.*"

Pola Negri either rose and then slapped Charlie Chaplin's face, or slapped him first, then arose—it happened so quickly I can't say which was first. I can say she disappeared from the room in about one minute—and we never saw her again at the Adlon as long as Charlie Chaplin was there.

In 1923, a year after the unknown Charlie Chaplin visited Berlin, Douglas Fairbanks arrived. By this time American films were again being shown, and Fairbanks got a good reception. I happened to be near the reception desk when Fairbanks arrived. As he looked to his left he saw the vast showroom the Adlon had rented to a new automobile manufacturer, and it was flashing its enormous initials day and night in hundreds of electric lights: E--G--O. Fairbanks turned and said, "Well, I see that Mr. Chaplin has been here before me."

Another year later, when the Coogan family arrived, there were crowds of thousands around the Adlon, on Unter den Linden and in Pariser Platz, all shouting they wanted to see "The Kid." We of the press surrounded the Coogans. "Too bad Jackie has grown so big," someone said. "Oh," the gallant elder Coogan replied, "there's a replacement under way." Mrs. Coogan blushed.

In my ten years in the Adlon I made many German friends, but my closest were Ernst Udet and Benvenuto Cellini Hauptmann, son of the famous Gerhart Hauptmann. Udet and Hauptmann were in fact the only two Germans who used the familiar pronoun *Du* instead of *Sie* in speaking to me.

Young Hauptmann took me one day to a theater—it was probably the Grosse Schauspielhaus—to watch Max Reinhardt, who had produced his father's plays, rehearse Bernard Shaw's *Saint Joan.* It was to be the first performance anywhere. Reinhardt had chosen a famous actor for every part except the title role, in which he cast a newcomer, a young and beautiful and extraordinarily gifted woman: Elizabeth Bergner.

Rehearsals obviously had been under way for several days because on this day Reinhardt announced that Miss Bergner would not have to go through her part. He used the word *mockiert,* which I took to mean that she would imitate or mime her part, which is what she did. But several times during this rehearsal Reinhardt lost his temper, and each time he did so he would shout, "Remember, you are not actors. *Sie sind nicht Künstler!*" (*"You are instead artists."*)

The rehearsal over, Miss Bergner came over to us and young Hauptmann introduced me. I mentioned incidentally that Shaw had indicated the character of Saint Joan in a lengthy preface to his play, which I had read. Miss Bergner had never heard of a preface by Shaw. Neither had Reinhardt. Both were intensely interested and both begged me to come the next day and bring the book along.

Young Hauptmann and I translated the preface. Reinhardt asked me where he could get a copy of the book—would I sell him mine and get another? Miss Bergner begged me to lend her the book for a few days—she wanted to study every word Shaw had written in the preface. It was a first edition, but I lent it to her. Miss Bergner sent me opening-night tickets.

When the play was reviewed in 1924 Miss Bergner was called "the greatest actress in the world." That was the year Duse died. I never got my first edition back. Reinhardt brought out in Bergner an illiterate girl of healthy robust ignorant peasant stock, religious, with vision, with her "voices—" everything Shaw said about her in his preface. Whether or not it was because he read the book I gave Bergner I do not know, but Bergner read or had read and translated to her many times every word of the preface.

Lunch With Arnold Bennett

*W*hen Lord Beaverbrook (the Canadian Max Aitken, founder of the London *Daily Express*) and his entourage came to the

Adlon in 1927, he met Sinclair Lewis at the bar one day, and invited him to come to a lunch party and bring a friend. He took me.

We were the only outsiders. His Lordship's group included Viscount Castlerosse, who was his gossip columnist; Lady Diana Manners, reputed to be the most beautiful woman in England, if not in the world, and the star of Reinhardt's production of *The Miracle,* and several others whose names were mumbled but each had a "Sir" before it.

Another guest was Arnold Bennett. Sinclair Lewis was awed by his presence. Mark Schorer, to whom I gave all the details of this day's encounter, seems to have gotten a few of them wrong (see page 491 of his biography of Lewis). It is correct that Lewis, after a few drinks, began calling Bennett "Maestro," bowing deeply every time and lifting his glass, but the episode at the Adlon bar which followed is entirely wrong; and since I was there I will recount it immediately.

The lunch was taken up mostly with Viscount Castlerosse telling nasty stories about noted people, two about a novelist who had the misfortune of being born in a small foreign country, its people frequently the butt of crude humor. Moreover, this foreigner had changed his name to one purely English and had made a fortune with several novels, one a best-seller. Castlerosse, after referring to certain ethnic groups as "gyps" and "wogs," said of this successful and popular novelist that he was "every-other-inch a gentleman." Everyone laughed. Then Castlerosse told the story of one hot London night when Lady Diana was dancing with this successful novelist, and he asked her: "Am I perspiring and disgusting?" to which Lady Diana replied, "You are not *perspiring.*" (Lady Diana said nothing.)

But the most interesting encounter was after lunch in the Adlon bar. After an additional drink or two I was bold enough to tell Arnold Bennett that his book *The Old Wives' Tale* was the main novel we studied in Copeland's English 12 at Harvard; that Copeland had us buy copies and write critiques because he considered it one of the great novels not only of the time but of a century. Bennett was delighted. He was then asked why he had never again written books equal to *The Old Wives' Tale.* Bennett replied frankly:

"Some years ago Lord Beaverbrook invited me to a cruise on his yacht, and it was a revelation to me. I had never been on a yacht before. I asked Lord Beaverbrook how much such a yacht might cost, and he replied, about twenty thousand pounds. I said, I can get that by writing a potboiler for a popular magazine, and so I did.

"I bought a yacht. But then I found that it would take about twenty thousand pounds a year to maintain and operate this yacht, and I have had to write another potboiler every year so I can enjoy my yacht. . . . "

Sinclair Lewis said nothing. He just looked sharply at me.

If you lived ten years at the Hotel Adlon, 1920–1930, you met almost everybody. One of the very few already famous, or on the way to fame, who was only rarely seen in the Adlon lobby, which every afternoon became a tearoom, was Maria Magdalena Dietrich, who belonged to a rival world center on the Kurfürstendamm, on the other side of the Tiergarten. Emil Jannings, with whom she appeared in 1923 in *Tragödie der Liebe,* and Lya de Putti, her colleague in 1926 in *Manon Lescaut,* were Adlon regulars. So was Josef von Sternberg, who in 1929 directed Marlene in *The Blue Angel,* which made her famous.

Marlene's picture first appeared in theatre programs in ads for Etam stockings—made of something new called rayon and advertised as "artificial silk." The stocking people looked for the prettiest girl with the most beautiful legs in the country, and chose Marlene. The ads showed her waving them, clad in rayon, years before that marvelous voice was heard in *The Blue Angel.*

One day the producers of *Der Letzter Mann*—called, I think, *The Last Laugh* in America—invited members of the press to visit the studio at Bebelsburg. The place was enclosed with a high fence. A porter, in a magnificent uniform, unlocked it and obsequiously waved us in. Half an hour later we were taken to watch the shooting of one of the last scenes, and there was our porter playing the lead—none other than Emil Jannings.

At the Adlon bar one day it would be Will Rogers, another

day Mayor Walker, or Udet, or one of the Maxim brothers. This Maxim, an inventor of what he called Maximite, would take from one of his pockets a small brown stick, half the length and triple the thickness of an ordinary pencil, and say, "There is enough force here to blow up a city block." Then he would light it with a match, and apply the burning explosive to the tip of his cigar. The explanation was beyond us.

Mr. Rogers was on his way home from Soviet Russia. We were standing at the bar, listening. "Why, there isn't a single bathing suit in all Russia," said Will Rogers. Albert Boni, the publisher, said, "Make that the title of a book, and I'll publish it," and he did.

Another day it was Colonel Pepys Cockrell of the British Army. What was he doing in Germany? "The Foreign Office," he explained, "asked me if I could speak Turkish. I could. Just the man they wanted, they said: there is trouble in Silesia. And so they dispatched me to the Polish-German border. There was, of course, always trouble between the Germans and the Poles over their borders and especially in Silesia, but what the devil was I doing there speaking Turkish? Eventually I found out. There was a sector somewhere along the Turkish border known as Cilicia, and that's where I should have been sent. Typical of the army brass, isn't it?"

However, being on the Polish border, he went to see what the trouble there was about. The British favored the Germans. The Poles were commanded by a patriot named Korfanty. During a skirmish the Poles captured Cockrell, accused him of fighting with the Germans, sentenced him to be shot.

"I was actually put up against the wall," he told us. "And then I said: 'Although invisible, the British Union Jack flies over me. Now, do what you damn please.'"

Korfanty heard about this incident. He not only freed Colonel Cockrell, "he invited me to lunch, and then to stay with him awhile as his guest."

One day at the Adlon our noted visitor was the newly elected mayor of New York. He was invited to address the American Club—a business outfit, no women, no journalists allowed. But today we were permitted to report what Jimmy Walker was saying. He began by addressing us as "fellow refugees of the Eighteenth Amendment. As Julius Caesar said to Cleopatra when he came into her tent at three o'clock in the morning, 'I did not come here to *talk.*' "

Tremendous applause. But in those days no one could print such a remark—it was considered "dirty."

Walker also said: "Mussolini I admire without reserve. Mussolini stands high above the political men of the whole world and I long to shake his hand."

I do not remember whether I met Ernst Udet at the Adlon bar or in the Adlon lobby. The notables who crowded the hotel every day belonged to groups that had nothing in common; it was probably the bar. He was a very lonely man. He appeared to the American correspondents the very opposite of what they had expected in the greatest living German aviator. He rarely mentioned the Richthofen Squadron. But he did tell me it was he who had shot down the American flier named Wanamaker, had landed as near as possible to Wanamaker's crashed plane, found the American alive, had taken him to Richthofen headquarters and treated him as a guest instead of an enemy, until forced to turn him over to authorities.

For a while I was Udet's only friend. He apparently had no relatives. When he decided to get married, he asked if he could use my suite at the Adlon, and the only persons present at the affair were my friends. It was rather a late marriage for Udet; the reason he had postponed it, he told me, was that he could not find a girl who would permit him to have birds, housebroken or not, flying around his apartment. Udet never stopped watching and studying birds in flight.

When Goering organized the Nazi air force, he made Udet commander of his old Richthofen Squadron.

When Udet, who was so skillful a flyer he could pick up a handkerchief from the ground with the tilted wing of his plane, suddenly crashed and was killed in December 1941, Goering announced it an accident. Friends who knew Udet said after the war it was a suicide. Udet knew almost nothing about the causes of war, nothing of politics, but he hated what he found going on in Goering's air force. For once he spoke out. Friends told me Udet had heard a rumor he would be purged. He outwitted Goering.

In the Adlon lobby group, the man I knew best—never a friend—was Max Hoffmann.

From the day the Bolsheviks defeated the Mensheviks for the control of Russia, General Hoffmann devoted himself to plotting a war to destroy that government. He lived for years at the Adlon, mingling with the diplomats of the world, international tycoons, rulers of nations, international plotters and American foreign correspondents.

In 1923, when I was expelled from Russia, I stopped at the Adlon on my way back home, having received an invitation to tell President Coolidge what I had seen and heard in Moscow. When General Hoffmann heard of this he buttonholed me one day in the Adlon lobby and said:

"When you see President Coolidge, I wish you would give him my ideas on this subject: Europe is in great danger from Bolshevism—and America too. There is something in this Bolshevism which sweeps over people.

"I know also that the American people are disgusted with the outcome of the war. The Americans would not go to war again under any circumstances. But we Germans would fight again. Right now. We would fight the Russians. . . .

"Good. You too want to get rid of Bolshevism—now—before it sweeps over all of Europe—and eventually America. Then finance us. American dollars. French cannon. British ships. And German soldiers—but the most important of all is American dollars.

"I will command the army. I will have a staff of the best of the old German army generals. We will march into Russia and succeed where Napoleon failed. It will be simple. With roads and with airplanes Moscow is no longer impossible. German infantry, American dollars. Tell President Coolidge I promise him an end of Bolshevism in a short time and with little loss."

It is perhaps important to say at this point that Hoffmann

was not unique among German generals who offered to lead an invasion of Russia to destroy Bolshevism either because they feared it or because they believed this was the only way by which Germany could immediately free herself from the strictures of the Versailles Treaty, and build a new army, navy, and a great air force. Ludendorff, Hitler, and Ehrhardt and other commanders of illegal regiments, all the Junkers and the nobility and the great steel, iron, coal and other industrialists of the right—all the future Nazis—promoted the same plans that General Hoffmann wanted me to propose to President Coolidge.

The tall, fat, wobbly, pasty-faced industrialist Arnold Rechberg received the "Potash King" title immediately after his brother died. However, from its very first days he was known as one of the financial backers of Naziism. He was also the sponsor of Alfred Rosenberg, a German Estonian, who had brought Berlin the notorious forgeries, originally published in Paris as "Dialogues of Machiavelli in Hell," since changed and retitled "The Protocols of Zion."

It was Rechberg who introduced Rosenberg to one of his friends, an anti–labor union spy and Reichswehr stool pigeon, an undistinguished former corporal named Hitler. Soon afterward Rechberg helped finance Hitler's newspaper, *Völkischer Beobachter,* and made Rosenberg editor. The main editorial theme of the *Beobachter* then became the Rechberg-Hoffmann plan to conquer Russia and thereby restore Germany.

Rechberg made no secret of his hope to set up a puppet government in Moscow once Hoffmann had seized the capital, and then exploit the vast treasures of gold, coal, oil and grain, giving equal parts to the nations supporting his adventure— England, France, the United States and Germany. He told me on one occasion of interviews with the German Crown Prince; Baron von Papen, who later became Hitler's chancellor; Ludendorff; and the Archbishop of Cologne, Cardinal Schulte. One day he boasted he had persuaded the Cardinal to transmit the plan to Monsignor Foch, brother of the French marshal.

Chapter 19

〰〰〰〰〰

The Greatest Inflation in History

A t the Adlon, and elsewhere, every foreigner with a dollar a day to spend became a millionaire, a billionaire, a trillionaire, during the inflation—which is still considered the greatest in history.

Being a millionaire or trillionaire was a mere technicality. Many people in many lands could joke about having millions— marks, kronor, pesos, whatnot. But we were rich. I mean, we could do what the rich did, or what we thought they did. For example, the Hearst man, Karl von Wiegand, wanted to own a castle. So he bought a castle. It was on Starnberg See, a beautiful lake in Bavaria, and no matter what fantastic sums in marks it cost him, it was only $10,000 in American money. His wife wanted a medieval suit of armor. He bought one. Had I wanted a yacht—as Mr. Arnold Bennett wanted one—I am sure I could have bought one.

Do the rich spend their money on wine, women and song? One of our press corps had a predilection for beautiful women, but he was perhaps a psychiatric case. (Until that certain day in Berlin when he found the only woman whom he had ever wanted after one night; he married her.) He had spent what in other lands would have been called a small fortune on restaurants, theaters, nightclubs and gifts—another woman every night of the year, year after inflation year. Our crowd, the poker-playing crowd, referred to him as Jim—or Harry, or whatever his name was—"the grim raper."

At the Adlon I lived better than Hugo Stinnes who in 1920 was on the road to becoming the richest man in the world. I had a better suite of rooms—the *Tribune* paid for them—and our taste in food differed. He preferred peasant food. Having had a taste of Paris, Lyon and Dijon, where once one could be a gourmet for a dollar, and having eaten caviar in Moscow for more than a year—at one dollar a pound—I ordered at the Adlon, so long as the old stock lasted and was sold in inflated money, the gray beluga "malossol" or "little-salt" Russian caviar, the best French champagne, sometimes a bottle of Chateauneuf du Pape, sometimes Chateau d'Yquem, or Liebfraumilch Pharrarhaus Hinterhaus Auslese, sometimes Berncastler Doktor, of which Peltzer in the Neue Wilhelmstrasse, nearby, had an unlimited cellar. On a dollar a day I lived the gourmet life of a rich man.

And once I bought an original Van Gogh for twenty-five cents. Not a painting, to be sure—but a signed lithograph. It was similar to a famous painting by the same artist; it shows a hussar sitting stiff and straight in a chair. I came upon it by accident. The great Berlin department store, Wertheim, was having a sale of old art catalogues, well illustrated, at a few billions of marks each, dated years before the war, and in one there was this lithograph listed at a mere four or five hundred marks—hard money, of course, say one hundred dollars. It had probably been a bargain then, and I said so to the salesgirl. "I'd gladly give a hundred dollars for it today," I said.

"I think we still have one left," she replied. "Before the war when we framed pictures to put them into an exhibition, or to use in our windows, we did not put them back in stock, but stored them for use again. I'll look for it."

In a few minutes she was back.

And there it was, an original Van Gogh.

The price?

"Wertheim," said its representative proudly, "never has and never will change prices, once an article is marked." She no doubt referred to rivals known in those inflation days to change prices not only every day, but sometimes twice a day.

"I can have this for four hundred marks?" I said.

"That is the price marked on the back. Yes," she said.

At the morning rate of exchange it was about twenty-five cents.

"However," continued the very intelligent salesgirl, "we have not yet marked the price on the frame, and that will be extra."

It was a nice frame, worth perhaps ten dollars.

"How much will that be?"

She gave me a fantastic price in marks, somewhere between a hundred and two hundred thousand marks, but just one hundred dollars in my money, and so my original Van Gogh, framed, cost me exactly $100.25.

Berlin rather than Paris or London was the center for Oriental art, books on Oriental art, and its study in the schools. I bought many great books, magnificently illustrated, for a few cents each. I became madly interested in Japanese prints and thanks to the inflation, which made foreigners millionaires while ruining millions of natives, I began a magnificent collection. I tried to find the entire thirty-five (or thirty-six) views of Fuji by the famous Hokusai and I was able to buy at least a hundred works by Hiroshige and some of the very great Utamaros.

One day, seeing some gold coins in a window display, I entered the shop to ask for some 1849 California one-dollar pieces. Herr Hall, the owner, said he had quite a number but was unable to sell any because the dollar was well on its way to four billion marks, and there were few persons alive who could afford to buy coins.

To my amazement Herr Hall then showed me something I did not know existed at all: little flat oblong California pieces with the words "Eureka, California. 1849" and "25 cents" on the tiny ones, "50 cents" on the bigger ones.

As a joke I then said, "I suppose you will now show me the Alexander four-drachma piece."

Herr Hall replied, "My stock is rather low; I have only twenty or thirty at the moment."

Then I remembered my first London days and meeting one of my brother's famous literary friends, Arthur Machen, whose book of stories, *The Three Impostors,* had been imported by Professor Copeland for his English 12 class at Harvard. The story I remembered was called "The Adventure of the Gold Tiberius"; it was tense, thrilling, even frightening in its history of the things that befell each owner in turn from the day the Emperor Tiberius made this one coin for himself. No other existed.

So I said to Herr Hall, "And so now may I have a look at *the* gold Tiberius?"

"I have only three at present," Herr Hall replied; "I once had seven or eight. They are rather scarce." He showed me the three.

Although I had long ago passed through my stamp collecting days, I could not resist buying many fine U.S. stamps as gifts to my friends: I remember once finding a U.S. ninety-cent stamp; it was black, and I think it showed Commander Perry. It was unused, and although the price in millions made the dealer happy, it also made me happy because it was just one-tenth face value for me that day, nine cents for a ninety-cent unused U.S. stamp of many years ago, already worth a lot of dollars.

Before I took over the CTFNS Berlin office the Kaiser's and later the Republic's mark was the usual 4.2 to the dollar. I was in and out of Germany many times during the inflation and did not record all the changes, but according to my records the inflation figures are as follows:

```
Early 1922, marks to dollar.....................................75
Mid-1922 .........................................................400
January 1923 .................................................7,000
August 1923...........................................1,000,000
October 1, 1923...................................200,000,000
```

November 4 (A.M.) ....4,200,000,000 to the dollar
Later
    the same day ....4.2 Rentenmark to the dollar

What we, the new millionaires of the Adlon, did not see and did not report, because we were in the midst of it, was that the majority of Germans, the working people, did not have enough to eat; that Ludendorff-Hitler Naziism had found a great appeal to the masses, almost equal to the *Dolchstosslegende,* an appeal to an empty stomach.

We did see clearly, however, that as money became worthless, morals became worthless. One had only to cross to the far corner of the Wilhelmstrasse from the Adlon to see a vast parade of not only whores but male prostitutes, transvestites, homosexuals, lesbians, almost shouting offers of what to the perhaps pure midwestern American mind seemed incredible experiences. For reasons known only to the Berlin police, immorality—conventional and perverted—had to stop at the corner, it could not turn into the Wilhelmstrasse nor could it cross to the Adlon.

In the hotel itself there was a daily sale of sex. Everyone knew the Adlon was an annex of Hollywood—and Hollywood was heaven to many European beauties. Somehow the word had spread throughout Europe that the way to fame and fortune was via the Adlon bedrooms; I do not remember ever hearing the term "casting couch" in the 1920s. Not uniquely but almost daily the American correspondents would be approached by Berlin, Vienna, Budapest, Scandinavian, and Balkan beauties with offers to spend the night if tomorrow introductions to Hollywood producers would follow.

One of the short-time residents of the Adlon was the famous—or notorious—dancer, Anita Berger. To see her walk down the main staircase of the Adlon from her suite on the second floor was a grand sight—almost worth applauding. She was always dressed, or partly dressed, unconventionally; she was the best-known naked dancer in Europe. Her face was chalk-white, and across it was a crimson line, her lips. We who had seen her and her six girls, most of them teenagers, all dancing stark naked, never suspected until a writer in Berlin later revealed it that Anita sniffed cocaine before every performance. This helped produce an almost incredible wildness rarely if ever before seen in a cabaret or theater.

The Anita Berger show was only one of a hundred or more pieces of evidence that Berlin during the inflation was the most sinful city in Europe, if not in the world. Sin was blamed on inflation, although by the end of 1924 solid money was restored. Hitler in 1925 added inflation to his *Kriegschuldüge*—"the lie that Germany alone was responsible for the First World War"—and the *Dolschstosslegende,* the "stab-in-back-legend" which blamed the Jews for losing the war. *"Die Juden haben schuld"* ("The Jews are to blame"), Hitler shouted at all his crowded meetings, and Germany, being historically anti-Semitic, never questioned him. The important fact, the one we did not even suspect then, was that after the Munich fiasco and the restoration of good money, the real owners of Germany, the great industrialists, the mine and coal operators, the steel kings, the merchants of death, the great bankers, met secretly and decided to subsidize Naziism and take over Germany in the way Mussolini had taken over Italy.

We at the Adlon did not suspect in those days that a fellow resident, Hugo Stinnes, known already as the richest man in Germany (in hard money), was then engaged in business operations that did more to ruin Germany than the actions of any other person, dead or alive. It was not until 1927, on my "re-Americanization" trip to Chicago, that I was able to say this in a series of articles I wrote on what newspapers call "the general situation."

How wrong our press, how wrong the world press can be, is evident from another fact: that Stinnes—the greatest looter, the chief destroyer of the German Republic, the man who must bear more guilt than Thyssen (who confessed his part, in the book *I Paid Hitler*), Alfred Hugenberg, the film tycoon and press lord, Kirdorff and Father Voegeler, and other secret backers of Hitler—was actually described as "a symbol of a resurrected Germany."

Stinnes was also known as the greatest man of mystery of

the time. He talked to no one but those who surrounded and shielded him. He rarely said *"Guten Tag"* to anyone at the Adlon, employee or prince. Sometimes I went up to the third floor in the same elevator with him. The operators had been ordered to close the doors the moment he entered, but there were accidental encounters. I would say "Herr Stinnes" and he would turn his face to the wall. The *Saturday Evening Post,* then the most popular weekly in America, sent its star, Isaac Marcosson, to interview the giant after all of us had failed. A few days later he announced at the Adlon Bar that he had been successful, and in proof of his claim showed us Hugo Stinnes's business card on which was plainly written: *"Der Herr Stinnes bedauert Er kann Sie nicht emphangen,"* which translates, "Mr. Stinnes regrets he cannot see you."

From the waiters we learned that Stinnes never dined with anyone, he merely ate peasant food in his rooms, ordering the Adlon French and German chefs to prepare simple sausages and at least twice a week his favorite dish, Kasseler Rippespear with sauerkraut. From the maids we learned that the bathtub was used rather infrequently.

Stinnes was the sole owner of a large part of the Ruhr industrial belt, coal and iron and steel. He employed 600,000 men. He also owned outright or had a controlling interest in sixty-three newspapers and one of the major political parties, which he financed. He and the lesser German tycoons borrowed millions of dollars' worth of marks from the Reichsbank, dug their coal, produced steel and machinery, sold everything abroad for pounds, dollars, pesos, any hard money, anywhere. All these hundreds of millions, eventually billions of dollars in foreign money were kept in banks abroad, while at home the mark dropped every day, sometimes to half its value in twenty-four hours. Stinnes would exchange enough pounds in London to meet his fortnightly payroll for the half million or more men he employed, giving them marks that cost him half, some weeks a tenth as much at the end of a fortnight as on the first day.

Stinnes may not have been the originator but he was the most successful practitioner in Europe of the vertical trust. The horizontal trust was an American idea—the best example being J. P. Morgan's steel trust. Stinnes's vertical trust was based on the idea that if you owned forests, you could make paper; if you had paper you could publish newspapers; if you owned mines you could make steel rails, you could build railroads, you could manufacture locomotives, you could ship your own products anywhere on your own lines.

With the dollars, pounds and other hard currency abroad, Stinnes used the favorable exchange to buy up more mines, build steel plants, buy ore deposits, also hotels, banks, steamship lines, real estate, anything at bargain prices in Germany, and when he had enough, he went abroad, to Austria, Russia, Poland, Switzerland and South America. The "German Colossus" also dominated the chancellors of various parties—Wirth, Cuno, Marx, Stresemann. He dominated the political as well as the economic life of the country.

The day inflation stopped in 1923 Stinnes was worth billions of dollars in coal mines, twenty-five or thirty in Germany, whole oil fields abroad, refineries, three telegraph companies in Central Europe, at least half a hundred gas and oil lighting and heating companies, threescore owned or controlled newspapers, and several large banks. All had been bought with depreciated paper marks—while he kept his hard money abroad.

For every cent Stinnes gained this way another German had to take a loss. The McKenna Report to the House of Commons in 1924 estimated that one million Germans, men of some wealth, not working men, had been ruined by the inflation.

The stabilization of the mark in 1923 saved Germany. It ruined Hugo Stinnes.

There were no more worlds to conquer.

The richest man in the world died April 10, 1924, at the age of fifty-four. One report said he died in a delirium, screaming about "reds" under his bed.

He had never taken another man into his confidence. His heirs knew little about his affairs and were not trained to run an empire. It went to pieces in 1925.

Part V

~~~~~~~~~~~~~~~~~~~~~~~~~~~~

Trotsky, Lenin,
Lenin's America

Chapter 20

How the United States Saved Russia

B y 1922 the Soviet Russians were no longer able to hide the fact that there was famine in the land and that thousands, perhaps hundreds of thousands, were dying. The most logical explanation for secrecy was this: the peasantry, which usually raised great crops that fed the cities, now refused to do so because they hated the Bolshevik regime and its new laws, so they raised enough for themselves only, and let the people in the cities die. The first appeals for help came from Maksim Gorky and the Norwegian explorer Nansen, who had reported conditions in Samara so unbelievably bad that instances of cannibalism had resulted.

When the Bolshevik regime could no longer conceal the famine—the rumors in Berlin said the dead now numbered in the millions—it appealed to Herbert Hoover to save the children of Russia as he had once saved the people of Belgium. Hoover immediately sent his first assistant, Walter Lyman Brown, to meet the Soviet diplomat Litvinov in the then neutral city of Riga, in Latvia.

Up to this time, late summer 1922, Soviet Russia had been sealed to all journalists except Communists and fellow travelers, but one of the conditions the American Relief Administration—shortly to be known in Russia as "the Arrah"—made before coming to Riga was that American correspondents, regardless of their politics or those of their newspapers, would be free to go to Moscow and to the famine zone to report on Arrah's activities.

It followed naturally that the majority of American press representatives at the Riga conference, and toward the end of August 1922 in Moscow and the famine zone, were the Berlin correspondents. Some newspapers sent their stars from the Paris office.

Hoover's man Brown insisted that the press be present at even the most important political meetings with Litvinov. Imagine our surprise, or shock perhaps, at listening to an almost angry confrontation in which Comrade Litvinov was trying to lay down rules under which Russia would accept the food to save its millions of children. Mr. Brown was pure American: frank, friendly, candid. "To save your children," I heard him say to Litvinov, "we will send you as fast as we can get transportation, millions of tons of food, wheat, powdered milk, cocoa, rice; we'll send you hospitals and ambulances if you need them, and we'll send along thousands of our fine young men, the former army officers trained to direct transportation and distribution. . . . "

As Brown uttered the last of the "We'll send yous," Litvinov interrupted with a shout: "No! No! No!"

Walter Lyman Brown appeared stunned. We of the press were not stunned but merely surprised. In Berlin we had been hearing what a large part of the world thought were incredible stories of how the Soviet system and Soviet officials worked, but none as surprising as this rejection of perhaps fifty million dollars' worth of aid.

While Mr. Brown was able only to utter a surprised "Why?" we of the press began shouting perhaps rude questions at Mr. Litvinov. He replied that he knew all about the American government's using food in Hungary to overthrow the Communist regime of Béla Kun. Moreover, he wanted no ex-army officers of any kind visiting Soviet Russia, even if they came as relief workers.

Relief was delayed. Children died. Brown cabled for instructions. The American press attacked Litvinov for biting the hand that was about to feed him. But eventually a compromise was made. Mr. Brown called us in and told us we could go to Russia without any special visa on our passports and that we would be free to travel anywhere and to report on the famine and the relief expedition.*

The first train from Riga to Moscow had on it the heads of the Berlin bureaus of many American papers and news services, notably Jim Howe of the AP, Graudenz of the UP, George Popoff of the INS, Sam Spewack of the New York *World*. The *New York Times* man was Walter Duranty of Paris. We had been instructed to proceed to the Hotel Savoy, a small hostelry near the Kremlin, and we were assigned rooms on the second or third floor. But Floyd Gibbons had beaten all of us to Moscow. We heard that he was now in Samara, the worst-hit city in the famine zone. Floyd had flown in from Paris and then Berlin on hired airplanes. He had given Litvinov an ultimatum: a visa to go immediately to Russia, or he would fly and land his plane in the middle of Red Square and cause a scandal. The ultimatum worked.

In Samara Floyd found three or four "journalists" who had preceded him—they were all persons of some note in the Communist Party of America, and they either did not want to send

---

* It is one of history's great ironies that many of the men ruling Soviet Russia in the past several years—Brezhnev, Kosygin, Podgorny, Suslov, Shelepin, Gorbachev, the heads of the Politburo, the heads of the KGB (newest successor to the old Chekah), all the leaders of the Communist party who are alive today, owe their lives to the sixty million dollars—real 1922 dollars—the United States spent for food. At first we fed young children from newborn babies to age five or six, then we extended the age into the teens. Generally it is estimated that the United States saved the lives of at least six million Russians during the years 1922 and 1923. And thanks to Stalin, there is not one word about American help in the *Great Encyclopedia* or any book or magazine published in Soviet Russia.

out details of the famine or thought that it was useless to try, owing to the fact that all the postal and telegraph office employees were thought to have died of starvation.

Floyd, in his usual brisk *Chicago Tribune* manner, proceeded to get the news and write it. Then, stepping over bodies of men, women and children lying dead in the streets, he walked to the Samara post office and found one man still there—alive but half-starved. Floyd immediately made a deal with him. He supplied food, and the telegraph operator that day and for several days afterward telegraphed all of Floyd's stories of the famine to me at the Hotel Savoy in Moscow. I immediately re-telegraphed them to London. Our London chief, Steele, cabled them to Chicago, and from Chicago, they were sent to every newspaper-reading nation in the world.

On the fifth day of Gibbons's Samara trip, I received a cable from Chicago congratulating him on "scooping everyone by four days on the biggest story of the year."

Floyd now returned to Moscow, made me officially his Russian correspondent, and sent me off to Samara, instructing me to evade the censorship by every trick known to the profession. By the time I was able to go to Samara—about a month later—there were no longer people lying dead on the streets, the Arrah was functioning marvelously, and every American was treated as a benefactor. (In Moscow officialdom tried its best to make believe there was no famine, no American aid saving millions of lives.)

The heads of the Bolshevik government, totally ignorant of the idea Edward Bernays popularized in the States and now known as "public relations," shunned rather than sought contact with "capitalist reporters." When I got a cable from Colonel McCormick saying INTERVIEW TROTSKY, I found he was the most difficult man in Russia to see. The best I could do was interview his chief of staff, General Danieloff. The subject is today of no importance whatever—some Balkan affair—but one thing did impress me. On leaving, I had said, "How can you, a Tsarist officer, support the Bolshevik regime?"

"Because I am a Russian," General Danieloff replied.

That was his only explanation.

In November 1922 the RSFSR celebrated the fifth anniversary of the Bolshevik Revolution and the armed forces paraded through Red Square, Trotsky taking the salute.

Inasmuch as the Russian censor had not forbidden photographs, I walked into the space between Trotsky and the marchers and aimed my Leica at him. I had bought that camera in Coblenz in December 1918. It used a filmpack with twelve exposures, and I hoped, always an amateur, to produce one good picture. I knew my first shot was spoiled. I had been given a great push, almost falling to the ground. My assailant also carried a camera. He spoke angrily to me in Russian, then German. I replied I was an American foreign correspondent and had the right to take pictures. The Russian photographer yelled at me that no one but he had that right, he had the monopoly. He started to shove me out of the Square.

Trotsky heard or saw the commotion. *"Was ist hier los?"* he said—literally, "What is going on here?"

"Herr Trotsky," I started, then switched to English, remembering the Red Army commander's New York Second Avenue café days, "I am an American journalist trying to photograph you, and this man says he has a monopoly. I thought that under the Communist system you had abolished capitalism and all monopolies . . . "

Trotsky smiled, laughed, then turned angrily on the Russian monopolist and shouted the equivalent of "Beat it." Then, smiling again, he turned to me and said, "What pictures do you want? How do you want me to stand?"

I told him to keep saluting and took eleven shots in a row, as army, navy, and a few insignificant cannon went by.

Next day the filmpack was on its way to our London office via the American Relief Administration diplomatic pouch. All eleven prints were perfect, and I had a five-day scoop. Steele, in London, sold one print to the *Times* of London for ten pounds, about fifty dollars then. Other prints, copyright by P & A Photographs, a *Chicago Tribune* subsidiary, were sold around the world. Somehow or other Chicago pretended it knew nothing about Floyd Gibbons's promise to his staff to reward them for photographs.

Many years later when I asked for a print of this Trotsky episode to illustrate a book, I got it—with a bill for five dollars.

Chapter 21

The Lenin Interview

For the great fifth anniversary of the Revolution the Soviet leaders did relax their disdain of the capitalist press enough to provide sleeping-car accommodations—for which we paid—to Petrograd, the former St. Petersburg and the present Leningrad, where the Kerensky and the Bolshevik revolutions had both started.

Nothing but oratory. Nothing to cable. But there was a sight the afternoon of November 7 that remains as vivid as only yesterday. The city had been decorated with millions of yards of red cloth, important buildings five stories high completely covered, and there were a million banners, all red of course, and all apparently dyed with the same cheap non-waterproof color.

There were two or three feet of snow in the streets, and it snowed early in the day, but sometime in the afternoon, during the oratory, the snow turned to rain, and the wind began to blow, whipping and tearing the red sheets and banners and flags, and all the ragged edges began to shed red drops like blood, and later there were showers of blood, and the snow began to melt and what looked like streams of blood ran in the streets of Petersburg.

Outside of this memory, the most notable was the discovery that an old tsarist custom of selling sleeping-car berths—four to a compartment—to men and women indiscriminately, still prevailed. We had all come to Petrograd on a special train, but we returned to Moscow individually.

I bought a sleeping car ticket. I went to the compartment, opened the door and found . . . a woman undressing.

I have a record of having spent 180 days and nights on the Orient Express, where of course nothing like this had ever happened to me. To my surprise must be added stupidity because, without thinking, I said, or rather shouted, something, I forget the exact words, but it amounted to "What the hell kind of management is this?" and the lady apparently understood the astonishment of an American, picked up her clothes, and immediately left the compartment.

It may have taken me a whole minute to recover. Nor did it make matters any better when I learned that the beauty I had driven out of my compartment was one of the leading actresses of the Moscow Art Theatre.

The celebration of the fifth anniversary of the Great Bolshevik Revolution that had begun on November 7 in Petrograd now moved to Moscow. I do not know the exact date, but it was still November, when we at the press tables in the Tsar's throne room of the Kremlin were trying to keep awake while all the heads of the Soviet government, one after another, were making one- or two-hour speeches of which we understood not one word.

Suddenly we who were near the first of the five doors of the huge hall noticed a little man arguing with the armed soldier standing there. Each of the five soldiers had been chosen because he was illiterate, each had been given a large piece of cardboard on which were pasted five or six cards, each a different color, one for delegates, one for journalists, one for Comintern members, and so on, and no person without a card matching one of the five could enter.

The little man—he was probably the classic Napoleonic five-foot-five—finally was permitted to enter. I was immediately impressed by his consideration for the speaker, because as he passed by our press table he walked on tiptoes so as not to make a noise. Suddenly he was recognized, and there was an uproar.

Lenin, however, insisted that Zinoviev conclude his high-pitched oration, and then he spoke. First in Russian, and then in German (which I understood), and perhaps again in French. But he spoke breifly in each language, with humor, and his eyes twinkled and he smiled, all of which was strange and unusual in Soviet Russia.

Fortunately for those at the American press table, we were closest to him when the session ended and the shoving began toward an adjoining room where historic photographs marking Lenin's first appearance after his stroke were to be taken. It was during this mob scene that we had what we later called our "one man—one minute—one question" interview—an almost childish affair, except for the mention of an American angle—which, however, I could not enlarge upon until my return home.

First, some bright boy asked, "Do you speak English?"

Lenin replied: "I speak she, ze English language, not-so-ver-goot."

We were jostled, shoved, pushed around by some of the most famous people in the world. But another question was managed, and Lenin replied:

"I occupy a good portion of my time with American affairs. I am reading Pettigrew's *Plutocratic Democracy.* I am interested in everything Senator Borah says or does. I watch all events regarding Japanese-American relations. I am interested in the American elections."

Then, laughingly, he concluded, "Your American newspapers frequently report me dead. Let them fool themselves. Don't take away the last hope of a dying bourgeoisie by saying you spoke to me."

We had to go where we were being shoved. Just as we got separated Lenin said, "How do you like Moscow? Not like New York." We were now in the small room where the photographers were taking group pictures. No one had asked a serious question. No one had asked about "selling revolution abroad," no one had mentioned the "red terror," no one had even gotten a word from Lenin about the American relief effort, which right at that moment was feeding more than six million babies, children and teenagers. The greatest living man in the world—and a lot of small talk.

For many weeks Oscar Cesare, the noted artist of *The New York Times,* was privileged to sit in Lenin's office daily and make sketches. Sometimes Lenin talked. When Spewack of the *World* and I heard of these conversations, we primed Cesare with questions—and thus we had a secondhand running interview.

To our questions, "Will you ever permit another political party to exist in Soviet Russia?" Lenin replied:

"The two-party system is a luxury which only long-established and secure nations can afford. However, eventually we will have a two-party system such as the British have—a left party and a right party—but two Bolshevik parties, of course." Cesare said that Lenin's eyes twinkled when he said "two-party system," and that he finished his talk with a knowing laugh.

Another story Lenin told—which again illustrates my belief that Lenin was the only dictator, past or present, who had a sense of humor—concerns the time he lived in exile in London. In Marxist circles, of course. Frequently working men's delegations who had chosen arbitration rather than going on strike would come to him asking that he represent them.

"On one occasion," said Lenin, "the delegates themselves could not agree on terms. They argued. Several of them shouted. They made a mess of things.

"I said, 'Go home, come to an agreement on terms, come here again tomorrow, and tell me in a few words.'

"The delegation returned the next day. The spokesman said: 'All we want is world revolution, and better toilets.' "

Chapter 22

~~~~~~~~~~~~~~

Lenin Speaks of
His American Mentors

Thanks to Lenin's chaotic press interview and to Oscar Cesare, I learned something of the origins of Bolshevism that to this day I have not seen or heard reported anywhere: the American inspiration for the Leninist interpretation of Marxism and the names of two of Lenin's American mentors.

I no longer remember the questions with which Spewack and I primed Cesare every day before he went to sketch Lenin, but I was so greatly impressed with one of Lenin's answers, as conveyed via Cesare, that I wrote it in my Russian daybook immediately. Lenin, chiding Cesare for the intense and violent American reaction against the Russian system of government, said:

> Bolshevism, our reading of Marxism, actually originated in America. Daniel De Leon left the Socialist Party, he resigned, he founded a more radical party, a more truly Marxist party, which he called the Socialist Workers Party of America. What we have done in Russia is accept the De

Leon interpretation of Marxism, that is what the Bolsheviki adopted in 1917.

Strange as it may seem, these words of Lenin (via Cesare) hit me with a certain shock—I cannot think of a stronger word—because in my childhood years I had heard the name of De Leon as a friend and a fellow worker with my father, not as a socialist, or as a Communist, but as a Single Taxer.

What Lenin did not say, and probably did not know, was that in origin De Leon was not an American—in the sense that he was not born in the United States but on the West Indian island of Curaçao, of Dutch parentage; and in 1886, when Henry George ran for mayor of New York City, he came as a volunteer worker to Single Tax headquarters.

Suddenly I had this strange feeling about the personal significance of this historical event, because my father, a bachelor of twenty-five or twenty-six in 1886, then employed as a librarian, was also a Single Taxer, and also a volunteer worker in the same campaign. I had heard him speak of that group of idealists and notably of De Leon, Louis F. Post, and Father Edward McGlynn (who was soon after excommunicated for his political views and activities). The Democratic Party candidate was Abram S. Hewitt, my father had told me, and the race was between Hewitt and George, with George picked to win. But the Republicans then nominated a demagogic upstart who ruined the election although he was roundly (or soundly) defeated: Theodore Roosevelt. Had it not been a three-way race, Henry George would have been mayor and Single Tax might have become a national political party. Moreover, it was later revealed that Tammany Hall not only stuffed the ballot boxes for Hewitt but threw many Henry George ballots and boxes into one of the rivers. Henry George was counted out. He died three or four years later.

Lenin revealed another American mentor in that famous running interview the first time the press saw him in 1922 when he casually remarked on his reading an American book that he called *Plutocratic Democracy*. As I later found, no such title exists in any language. Fortunately Lenin did name the author as Pettigrew, and that is all I had to work with when I went to the New York Public Library years later to do some research. The library believed that *Plutocratic Democracy* was a Russian mistranslation of the American title. It finally did find a listing of a book by Senator R. F. Pettigrew of South Dakota, which was undoubtedly the one Lenin was reading and which so greatly influenced him. It took me many years to get a copy from secondhand and antique book dealers. The American title is *The Course of Empire,* published by Boni & Liveright in 1920, introduction by Scott Nearing, as devastating a muckraking work as any Lincoln Steffens ever wrote about corruption in the cities, or Upton Sinclair about the press, or Chicago meatpacking.

Pettigrew's book is made up of his Senate speeches, which were generally suppressed in the press of his time, exposing what he called "American imperialist policies" in Cuba, the Philippines, Latin America—and the press itself. Pettigrew documents American army atrocities in the Philippines, he boldly mentions and attacks the House of Morgan in its international dealings, he accuses big business interests of controlling both the Republican and Democratic parties.

In the original edition, Lenin could read (page 688) Senator Pettigrew's letter to the American Red Cross saying,

> I believe the new century will open with many bloody revolutions as a result of the protest of the masses against the tyranny and oppression of the wealth of the world in the hands of a few, resulting in great progress towards Socialism and the more mutual distribution of the products of human toil and as a result the moral and spiritual uplifting of the races.

Or Lenin could find these views on the American press:

> The great corporate newspapers of this country are owned by special interests and run in these interests, or they sell their editorial columns for cash for any interest that may come along.
> They are anonymous; they have no character; no one is behind them. They hire men to write editorials who write

against their convictions, the same as a man hires a lawyer to try his case. They recall these falsehoods for the purpose of influencing the people of this country in behalf of the special interests which they always represent, sometimes because their stock is owned by men whose interests are promoted thereby; and their editorials are ordered from the business office, oftentimes by men who do not and cannot speak the English language; and again, the editorial columns are sold, purchased, for the purpose of promoting an interest for which they receive pay.

In his last chapter, "Summing It Up," Pettigrew says:

Daniel Webster lays down these principles. He says: "Liberty cannot long endure in a country where the tendency is to concentrate wealth into the hands of a few.' Such is the testimony of the wisest of mankind, almost from the creation down to the present time. . . .

Here are the millionaires. Four thousand, or three one-hundredths of the population. Average wealth, three millions apiece. Total wealth twelve billion, or 20 percent of the total wealth of the country. I say a country is not rich where such conditions are brought about or are shown by that table.

These are the conditions that we protest against.

And the last, the very last words of the book that Lenin read and approved were these: "We propose second: to enact those laws which will destroy the trusts and syndicates and control the corporations so that they will be our servants rather than our masters."

(Not exactly Bolshevism!)

Chapter 23

Inside the Dread Chekah

Next to interviewing Lenin, the great objective of all foreign correspondents in Moscow in the early 1920s was getting an "inside" story on the Chekah.

The Russians called it the Vai-Che-Kah, an acronym for Extraordinary Commission for Combating Counter-Revolution—we called it Chekah—and its first chief in 1917 was Feliks Dzerdzinsky.*

When Russia was forcibly opened to non-Communist journalists and we took the four-day Riga trip to Moscow and were told we must stay at the Savoy Hotel, we learned immediately that the real head of the police and terrorism department was a Lett named Peters—Yakov Khristoforovich Peters.*

Dzerdzinsky was visible only at public affairs. He was old and sick, a broken man; we were permitted to say only hello to him. By the end of 1922 the Chekah changed its name to

---

* The spellings are Solzhenitsyn's.

195

GPU—Gay-pay-oo, we called it—it was officially the State Political Administration, and Peters was its head.

This man, I learned, was actually the famous, or notorious, "Peters the Painter" who had written a page in Churchill's, if not Britain's, history. He had lived in Sidney Street. When London police came to arrest him as a dangerous revolutionist, he barricaded himself with his followers. A frightened Churchill, instead of sending a few more policemen, called out the regular army and fought—to the delight of the yellow press—"The Battle of Sidney Street," in which the "revolution" was put down, and its leader, the Lett, Peters, captured and imprisoned.

To see Peters in his office required a special pass for me and my interpreter. Chekah headquarters was in the largest building on Lyubianka Square, former offices of Rossiya Insurance Co. The Bolsheviks, after expropriating the company, did little to alter the building. (A picture in the Paris *Herald,* December 24, 1975, shows it exactly as I saw it in 1922.) However, in the basement was installed the most dreadful prison in all Russia, and in the courtyard, according to report, executions took place every night, the machine guns accompanied by the roaring of motor trucks from which the mufflers had been removed. In this building, devoted to terrorism and death, I found in 1922 all the old insurance company signs, "Insure your life *NOW*" and "Protect your wife and children when you are gone—insure *NOW.*" None of the Russians seemed to sense the tragic irony.

The majority of persons who entered Lyubianka never came out alive. You had to have a pass to enter, a pass to go to another floor, and most important of all, a pass to leave.

From the first words spoken I realized that Peters of the Chekah, whom I took to be Peters the Painter, knew English, although he pretended he did not. His eyes, his smile, betrayed him. The first thing he said was "There is no red terror."

When I suggested that both Lenin and Trotsky had said or written that terrorism is necessary in a revolutionary period, Peters countered with the White terror. "For every spy or traitor we have executed," he said, "the White generals, notably Mannerheim, the hero of Finland, has executed a score, a hundred." (I thought this was nonsense, but see the *Encyclopaedia Britannica:* the Mannerheim terror and bloodshed were appalling.)

"As for the 'red terror' which has so upset the bourgeois mind," continued Peters, "it was instituted in time of war. There was an enemy advancing against us and an enemy within preparing to join the foreign enemy. So we declared war on him. We openly called it 'The Terror.' In 1918 we executed only five hundred eighty persons."

In the following years when the Lenin-Trotsky regime was attacked by the White generals on all sides—the Ukraine, the Cossack country, the Crimea, Siberia, and by the Allies in Archangel—"we had to arrest and execute many thousands," continued Peters, "but not a million, several hundred thousand, as Northcliffe says."

To my surprise Peters actually found among the mass of papers on his desk the page of the *Daily Mail* of London listing 1.7 million Chekah terror executions.

"Look," said Peters, "at the groups of our victims by professions. For example, six thousand college professors. Six thousand! How could we execute six thousand professors of any kind when Russia never had near that number? So with the other professions. All these figures are falsifications."

There was nothing new in this denial. The Northcliffe hoax had been exposed for years.

"Mr. Peters," I asked, "why don't you tell me just how many persons have been executed?"

"I said," he replied, "a few thousand."

"Two thousand?"

"No. More than that."

"A hundred thousand?"

"Much less than that."

"Split the difference? Fifty thousand?"

"That's about right," said Peters. "A few thousand more or less. In wartime, mind you. Traitors, spies, enemies of the Revolution!"

He spoke with passion and anger.

If I had said in my cable that I knew many of the persons Peters called spies and traitors were revolutionaries—Mensheviks, anarchists, social revolutionaries and others who had helped overthrow the Tsar and then Kerensky—the censor would have killed the entire interview.

However, for my own information I did bring up the subject. "Mr. Peters," I said through my interpreter—his name was Heidkin and I had to fire him later when I found him spying on me for the Chekah—"isn't it true that among the fifty thousand traitors and spies you executed there were also revolutionaries of the March 1917 Revolution, and others who fought alongside the Bolsheviki in the November 1917 Revolution, and even later—not spies or traitors but revolutionaries whose interpretation of Marxism or Communism differed from that of the Bolsheviks?"

For the first time in the long, calm and friendly interview Peters was angry at me. He got up. He shouted at me, "Every one had a fair trial. Every one a traitor."

Simultaneously, without being called, a Red Army soldier appeared and handed us two red exit passes. He gestured to the door. He seemed to rush us. We barely got in a thank-you to Mr. Peters.

(Mr. Peters was "liquidated" by Stalin in 1942.)

It must also be said, perhaps emphasized, that in all those grim and tragic days of the 1920s in Moscow, when the nightly executions at the Lyubianka were being covered up by roaring motors, there was also laughter in the vaudeville houses and circuses, and there were great presentations in the theatre, and a cultural life still flourished freely, not underground as it does now.

In the days of Lenin and Trotsky clowns were so free they could even joke about Bolshevism—and the men who created the Revolution. My favorite—everybody's favorite—clown was Bim Bom. There may have been two clowns, Bim and Bom, in tsarist times, but in my time I am sure the one great clown was named Bim Bom. He was the only free Russian of the time.

Imagine this: the curtain goes up, this clown in conventional makeup, vertical lines through the middle of his eyes, bulbous nose, enormously painted mouth, pantaloons, comes on stage. The only difference is, he carries two posters, like the sandwich men who went about the streets a generation ago advertising something or other. Bim Bom comes rushing in all directions, perplexed. As he turns here and there everyone sees that the two placards he carries are pictures of Lenin and Trotsky.

Then someone—a straight man or a man in the audience—calls out: "What are you going to do with them?"

"Put one against the wall," replies Bim Bom, "and hang the other." The Russian clown is not silent. He talks.

In the uproar that follows there is more than laughter, there is political dissent expressed in laughter.

Then there is Bim Bom's story about Lenin. Lenin is in the country, talking to an old peasant:

"Well, *dedushka* [little father], you should be happy now, you have the land, the cow, the chickens, you have everything."

The peasant to Lenin: "Yes, God be praised, little father, the land is mine—but you have the bread; the cow is mine—but you get the milk; the chickens are mine—but yours the eggs. The Lord be praised, *dedushka*."

Everyone in Moscow knew a good Bim Bom story. The act changed every year and the stories were dated like good wine—from 1917 on. Every Muscovite who went to another citytold the current Bim Bom stories to many others, so that millions must have heard them.*

It seems as though somebody, it might have been Lenin (who did indeed have a sense of humor), or perhaps Trotsky the book-made Napoleon, may have gotten the suggestion that humor might be the safety valve of the Soviet steamroller. A dictator could arrest a hundred thousand men and send them to

---

* Rene Fülöp-Muller in his masterpiece, *The Mind and Face of Bolshevism,* recounts the successes of "Bim and Bom"—he says they were two clowns. I swear there was only one Bim Bom in 1922. He also reports many people so amazed by the liberties taken by the clowns that they spread the word, time and again, that the actors had been arrested, deported or shot.

die while building a canal in the Arctic Circle leading to the Volga, he could send men to be machine-gunned to death every night at Chekah headquarters, but he also needed Bim Bom to relieve the hearts and minds of millions who could not accept the new system of living.

(Whether humor was permitted under Stalin I do not know. The traveling Russian circuses I saw in Europe had only conventional silent clowns—and trained pigs that played football.)

One day toward the end of August 1923, Spewack of the *World,* Noel of the *Ledger,* McCullough of the *Herald,* and I received notice that Mr. Chicherin, who in Soviet Russia occupied a post equivalent to Vice President and Secretary of State in the United States—wanted to talk to us; please come to his office at two o'clock. A few minutes before 2:00 P.M. the four of us climbed the five flights of stairs to his office, and although we found it a very busy place, there was no Chicherin there, no appointment for us listed.

Someone then explained: Mr. Chicherin was an old revolutionary conspirator of the tsarist time; in every foreign country where he hid, he worked only at night: "Mr. Chicherin will receive you at two A.M." And so the four of us had to climb the five flights of stairs again.

Mr. Chicherin was friendly, even cordial. "Gentlemen," he said, "I suppose you have guessed the reason for the call. You have violated your pledge to send all your news via the censorship, and you know what the penalty is. But we are not a cruel people, as some journalists have so frequently reported. Should you miss Wednesday's train to Riga, you may take Saturday's."

This is what had happened: the four of us who were caught—and very likely our colleagues who were not Communists (Graudenz of the United Press was a Communist) or pro-Communists, of whom there were at least three, had found a way of defeating the censorship—were allowed to use the diplomatic pouch of Hoover's Relief Administration (the Arrah) for our personal mail, so each of us merely put a "Dear John" or "Dear Harry" at the heads of our big news stories, signed them under the words "Cordially yours" and mailed them to London. Within a day or two they were front-page news throughout the world.

The Soviets never caught on. Until one day the police had a rumor that some Arrah men were smuggling diamonds in the Arrah diplomatic pouch. At this time of famine and semi-starvation, anyone who had the right to buy at the American PX could have become a millionaire by collecting diamonds or paintings in exchange for flour. Although no correspondent to my knowledge engaged in this business, each of us did make at least one deal. Spewack got a sable coat for his wife and fellow journalist, Bella, and I exchanged ten boxes of Park & Tilford chocolates, priced one dollar each at the commissary, for a mink coat. (When my sister-in-law had it altered in Paris the furrier found each mink skin stamped with the tsarist coat of arms, and numbered. In other words, the man who traded it to me was telling the truth when he said his father was a grand duke, and had received the mink skins from the Tsar of Russia.)

Spewack, Noel, McCullough, and I took the Wednesday train to Riga, and proceeded to Berlin. Each of us wrote a series of articles at great length telling what we believed to be the whole truth about the Soviet system: the common people of Russia; everyone we knew; those who stopped us in the streets— recognizing us by our good clothes—begging us to save their lives by helping them get out of the country; the new Red Army we had seen parading and had secretly watched being indoctrinated with Bolshevist propaganda in special schools; in short, everything we could not get by the censor in the year or more we had been in Russia.

I had no sooner finished my Russian series when I got orders from Colonel McCormick to come to Chicago to be "re-Americanized." The *Chicago Tribune* half-owner—the other half belonged to Joe Patterson, the second heir to the great Joseph Medill's fortune, now estimated at $220 million—hated everything European and therefore planned a trip home for us every three years.

Before going to Chicago I went to Washington to meet

President Coolidge. I attended the regular press conference. Afterward Arthur Sears Henning introduced me to the President. Coolidge's questions surprised me. Although I had not believed in the myth of "Silent Cal" then almost universally accepted, I had not expected a long series of questions that in themselves betrayed the President to be as well aware of Soviet Russian affairs and politics as most European leaders.

Naturally, he asked first about the famine and the functioning of the American Relief Administration. He then switched to Bolshevik propaganda abroad, its success or failure, the morale of the common people in Russia, their attitude toward their leaders; he asked me if there was any opposition then existing, or the possibility of an opposition; he asked if there was consent or dissent, and he wanted to know how the Chekah functioned, and if there was terrorism in the country. Mr. Coolidge, I would say, was better informed about Soviet Russia than many of his own diplomatic representatives abroad.

After half an hour or more of questioning me, the President asked me to repeat all I had told him to Secretary of State Hughes. He phoned. Within a few minutes I was talking to Mr. Hughes.

Having been instructed not to put any questions to the President, I now proceeded to put them to the Secretary of State. "Is it true," I asked, "that American business is bringing pressure on Congress to recognize the Soviets?" Mr. Hughes said, yes, it was true. "Would the U.S. for reasons of expediency, for dollars, for *realpolitik,* recognize the Soviets?"

"No," replied Mr. Hughes, "there are still moral reasons in American politics."

At least I got something out of Mr. Hughes.

The Soviets were not recognized until a decade later, during the Great Depression, in 1933.

The Colonel's plan for re-Americanization, believe it or not, was to make each of his foreign correspondents, several of whom were already internationally noted, go back to the very beginning of reporter training—the central police station. The only difference I found between J. J. Kirby's Pittsburgh police court in 1909 and Chicago in the 1920s was that in Chicago I was under the instruction of the *Tribune*'s chief police reporter, a man named Alfred Lingle, better known as "Jake." Every day there was the same lineup in Chicago as there had been in Pittsburgh: prostitutes, streetwalkers rounded up by the police during the night to whom the magistrate said "ten or ten," and for repeaters, who got a little lecture, "thirty or thirty." Occasionally, as in Pittsburgh, there were muggers, pickpockets and criminals who were held for trials in the criminal courts. What all this had to do with "re-Americanization" I never found out, and of course no employee had the courage to ask Colonel McCormick to explain.

Some years later, one day in June 1930 when I no longer worked for the *Tribune,* the papers throughout the nation reported the revival of the great war between Chicago's rival gangs for the control of the city. Most papers reported that a newspaperman was caught in the crossfire and killed. *Editor and Publisher* (June 14) declared editorially that Jake Lingle "joined Don Mellett," late editor of the Canton *Daily News,* "among the martyrs of the Fourth Estate."

But next time I saw John Gunther, he showed me clippings from the *Tribune*'s rival papers in Chicago: all agreed that Jake Lingle was actually a member of the Al Capone gang and in fact the liaison officer of McCormick's *Tribune* and Capone. (This also accounted for the fact that a plain newspaper reporter could be wearing a belt into which no less than fifty thousand dollars' worth of diamonds had been set.)

Part VI

Rome, Mussolini, and Fascism

Chapter 24

Vincent Sheean in Trouble

Having reported to President Coolidge and having undergone the first of my two McCormick "re-Americanizations" in Chicago, I returned to my Berlin office but did not stay there long. It was probably in January 1924 that I received Gibbons's telegraphic order: PROCEED ROME. SHEEAN IN TROUBLE WITH VIRGIN MARY. GIBBONS.

(Now, if any devout person thinks the above telegram is vulgar or truly blasphemous, I must say this for my director: Floyd Gibbons and his entire family were members of the Roman Catholic Church, the majority mass and confession-going members, always in a state of grace. Floyd went to mass occasionally, he never mentioned going to confession, but he was certainly not anti-clerical. He had chosen James Sheean for Rome largely because of his name, but insisted "James" was too shanty-Irish, which Gibbons admitted he and his family were, and decided on Vincent as a fine lace-curtain Irish name.)

But what was Sheean's "trouble with the Virgin Mary"?

Readers who can remember back to 1950 or who have read of the Holy Year the Pope then proclaimed, will perhaps remember the Vatican announcement of a new dogma, the assumption of the Virgin. Newsmen will realize that Sheean, instead of being transferred from Rome, should have been congratulated for getting a great world scoop; he had cabled the news of the proposed new dogma at the time the Pope was discussing the matter *in camera* with only the bishops of the Church, years before it was to be announced officially. But in Chicago the *Tribune,* which had had an old, and deserved, reputation of favoring the Ku Klux Klan, was accused of dirty journalism when it published Sheean's report. It was attacked in many pulpits and denounced in *Our Sunday Visitor,* a national weekly with at least one million readers.

My first task in Rome, therefore, was to make peace with the Vatican. But how to go about it. I then did not speak a word of Italian, I had no sources of information, I had no friends. Fortunately for the *Tribune* our interpreter was a wise, or wily, man who was also quite a diplomat, and he said he would introduce me to the right person to plead the *Tribune* case, a certain Monsignor Pucci, the man who helped all foreign journalists—for a fee.

Pucci arranged an interview with a prominent Cardinal. He also translated the Sheean story, about three hundred words long. The Cardinal explained that it was not the matter of the assumption of the Virgin Mary that had offended the Church but a few lines about papal infallibility. Contrary to popular belief, he said, the dogma of papal infallibility and the dogma of the Immaculate Conception, papal actions which had helped divide rather than unite Christendom, were modern, the first dating from 1854, the second in the memory of then living men, in 1870. The assertion that a new dogma would soon be announced, the Cardinal believed, would raise the question of papal infallibility anew, and that was why the Vatican wanted nothing said about new dogmas.

What could the *Tribune* do about it? The Cardinal offered to write a statement, and he did. But in answer to Sheean's three hundred words he wrote six thousand, almost all theological. I condensed the answer to one thousand words at first, leaving out all qualifying phrases—all the buts and howevers and perhapses—but it was still too long. When I got it down to three hundred in cablese I found that what the Cardinal was saying was what Sheean had said: that a study was being made, the bishops of the Catholic world were being consulted, and that the common belief in the assumption of the Virgin Mary might result in a dogma sometime in the future. Inasmuch as the Cardinal had permitted me to use his name, I cabled his repeat of the Sheean story.

The Virgin Mary dogma was proclaimed decades later, on November 1, 1950. Newspapers then stated that this was the first time that the power of papal infallibility had been exercised since 1870.

One of my first assignments in Rome was to get for Colonel McCormick a stone each from two of the most famous buildings in the world, St. Peter's and the Colosseum. Fellow correspondents got orders for stones from the Taj Mahal, the Parthenon, the Louvre, St. Sofia, the Kremlin, and the Kaaba in Mecca if someone could be bribed to get one from the most sacred shrine of Mohammedanism; also the Alamo, Notre Dame Cathedral, Westminster Abbey, Independence Hall and from any and all the Seven Wonders of the World if they were still around. So far as I know, I was the only one ordered to get two. All the stones the Colonel collected were embedded in the entrance hall of Tribune Tower, which he had built in Chicago, and the names of the correspondents were cut into the plaster. As I mentioned earlier, the Colonel had my name chiseled out when I resigned.

The Colosseum was easy. Every tourist who cared to could pick up a stone from the rubbish heap in the middle court and put it in his pocket. But the Colonel demanded a certificate of authenticity with each one, and that made all the difference. However, as Fascism's other name was Corruption, I got the Colosseum stone and documentary proof for a price. St. Peter's was different. The great cathedral is always being improved and there is always a courtyard filled with debris. Again, I could have a stone for nothing, but the document was another matter.

As was usual with every foreign correspondent in Rome in those days, I had to see Monsignor Pucci at the Vatican. If I had called him the Pope's public relations man or press agent, it might have sounded unfair. Let us say he was the ombudsman for the Vatican and the press. Or maybe a paid fixer. Monsignor Pucci introduced me to the director of restoration at the Vatican, who graciously offered me not only a stone but a free authentication. But he also asked me to accompany him into the very heart of St. Peter's.

The great dome of Michaelangelo is supported by four enormous red pillars, obviously porphyry. The director rapped each of the four with his knuckles. "Two of them are real," he said, "two are plaster, painted imitations."

Then he made us this proposition: he would not only give the *Chicago Tribune* any stone it wanted, he would give us one of the imitation columns, provided we gave St. Peter's a genuine porphyry one in return.

"What would that cost?" I asked. The price was about $25,000.

Then the director went a step further. "If you give a gift to St. Peter's," he said, "you are entitled, as others have been, to have a bronze plate on it—it would hang right here, at eye level, right on the new column. Think of it, *signore,* a sign millions would see, saying, 'This column presented by the *Chicago Tribune,* the World's Greatest Newspaper'; you could say that, too, it is your slogan."

I cabled. Colonel McCormick accepted the same day, delighted. But next day, second thoughts: it might make a bad impression on the Protestants—wasn't there a Protestant Church in Rome that could use a similar donation of $25,000?

I found the Rome Methodists planning a church on Monte Mario and other American Protestant groups, but all refused the money because of the St. Peter's deal. Finally I paid Monsignor Pucci a considerable sum and he got me a stone from the debris of St. Peter's, with its pedigree and credentials.

(When Mussolini was shot and hanged on public view in a Milan filling station, all the Fascist records were made public. Monsignor Pucci was listed as a secret Fascist agent—all the time that he was also the Vatican public relations man.)

Chapter 25

Mussolini: "My Dear Colleague"

Every reporter, journalist, freelance, or editor who ever came to Rome in the Duce's early years asked for an interview, but it was no easy matter for the men. The visiting "lady journalists," as we then called them, found it less difficult, and those willing to make the front page via the bedroom found it almost too easy. Even in those prudish post-Victorian days "lady journalists" at gatherings of the profession were liberated enough to hint, even speak, of their experiences; several even boasted of the amorous prowess of that great man, the Duce. (I put "lady journalists" in quotations to distinguish them from women journalists, my colleagues, resident in Rome or elsewhere in Europe, who may or may not have had interviews, but who never strayed from the ethical and accepted ways of getting them. It was almost always the visitors, the strays, who came and saw and were conquered—and whom the regulars generally despised.)

For the foreign press corps in Rome the early Mussolini years were truly unique. Even those of us who had no liking for

Fascism and the armed Blackshirt terrorism and murder of unarmed men did like the fact that a regular "working journalist" had become the ruler of a country. Some of us had known him for several years, a fellow worker, a colleague; we had met at the same reporters' hangouts, had exchanged news and views. I had not only reported the miscalled "Red Revolution" of 1919 with him, I had seen him almost every day of the Genoa Conference of April 1922, and of course after I was assigned to Rome in 1924 and stayed for more than a year I saw him many times and interviewed him once, for several hours.

It was Eyre of the *World* who told me of his investigation of Mussolini's secret rise via the power of the press. He got his information from a friend in the Quai d'Orsay, but it was later confirmed when Mussolini was tried on a charge of corruption and expelled from the Lombardia Journalists' Association. The facts were these:

Although Italy was aligned with the Central Powers by treaty during World War I, it could not join the fighting alongside its old enemy the Austro-Hungarian monarchy, so it stayed neutral. Clever men in the French Foreign Office then sent a noted socialist leader, Jules Guesde, one-time co-worker with Karl Marx, to ask Mussolini, the editor of the Socialist Party daily, *Avanti,* if he would be willing to accept 200,000 francs ($40,000) to establish a newspaper favoring the Allied Cause and urging Italy into the war on our side. Mussolini would also receive a monthly sum of thousands of francs, enough to keep the daily going, until such time as it earned its own way.

Mussolini saw the dream of his life come true. Along with every man in journalism the world over, so it is reported, he hoped one day to publish a paper of his own, so he took the money and founded the Milan *Popolo d'Italia* and editorialized the news to fit the Allied cause. Eventually the day came when Italy declared war on Germany and Austro-Hungary.

When Eyre and I called on Mussolini in 1919, he was cordiality itself. The first thing he said when we told him we had been sent to Turin to cover the strike was that he had offered his Blackshirts to the labor unions because he considered this one "a creative strike." He then added, "My dear colleagues, I am still a socialist." He also proposed a union between labor and his new force, which he called Fascismo Italiani di Combattimento. Together, they could take over the government as well as the factories. "I spit upon the legal social democracy of the labor unions," he said, illustrating the verb.

Throughout history, he continued, "the armed forces have conquered and the unarmed have been destroyed," pausing to note whether his less intelligent colleagues knew he was quoting his favorite writer, Machiavelli. "That's Machiavelli," he added, and after another pause, "Machiavelli was the first Fascist."

What was the secret of this doubletalk: I am still a socialist, I am a Fascist? Late in 1922 in Paris the former Italian Premier Nitti introduced me to the exiled head of the Italian labor unions, Buozzi, who permitted me to copy an important document written at the time of the Turin "uprising." The Buozzi document concludes:

> This is the secret. Animated by an unhampered ambition, Mussolini sought to keep one door open be it the Right or the Left, so that no matter what would happen after the occupation of the factories, he would always be able to emerge, be it at the head of a revolutionary movement or a reactionary movement.

My next meeting with Mussolini was at the 1922 Genoa Conference, which attracted about four hundred foreign correspondents. Mussolini appeared as the reporter for the *Popolo.* The main source of news was David Lloyd George's daily press conference—for Britons only. We Americans begged to attend and were welcomed. Then all the continental Europeans were admitted. Immediately there was trouble. One journalist, instead of asking questions, began making speeches. He took issue with Mr. George on many subjects. He roared defiance.

"Who is this man making trouble?" Mr. Lloyd George asked.

Someone told him it was an Italian journalist from the *Popolo d'Italia* named Mussolini.

"Then throw him out," said Mr. Lloyd George, and two British guards did so. Many of us applauded.

The third time I saw him it was a new Mussolini—a sort of statesman in striped pants, sitting with a scowl behind his big desk in the map room of the Chigi Palace—it was the 29th of February, 1924. Having in fact forgotten it was leap year, he had made no appointments for the twenty-ninth and gave me a two-hour interview about everything in his life except politics. "There are books. Read the books," he said. What would he talk about? His pets. His lion cubs. His chief sport: driving dangerously. He was not a prohibitionist but "drinking is useless—alcohol bores me." His hobby was the violin. "It is my refuge." "Music sometimes brings tears to my eyes . . . I am not ashamed to admit it." The greatest composer of all time was Vivaldi.

Religion? (I did not ask, "Are you still an atheist?" but I had obtained a rare copy of his first writing, the pamphlet "Dieu n'existe pas" ["God Does Not Exist"], published in Switzerland.) "I am a fatalist," he replied, "I believe in the star of destiny. I am not afraid of anything in the world. I am not afraid of death."

His whole life had been shaped by books. Who was his favorite author? He replied, "Sorel, Machiavelli, Nietzsche. Nietzsche has influenced me more than any man, alive or dead." He used the titles of Nietzsche's books in conversation, watching to see if I knew them; he spoke of being *Human, All Too Human,* of *Beyond Good and Evil.* He went beyond Nietzsche's "Thou goest to woman, do not forget thy whip" by saying his own epigram was *La fortuna é donna—bisogne prenderla e batterla.* ("Fortune is a woman—you must beseige her and overpower her.") This was straight out of Machiavelli, but he passed it on as his own.

Probably the most interesting thing he said was that in his early youth, when he was in Switzerland on his first job, he had, along with millions of Italians, considered emigrating to America where the pay of a bricklayer or stonemason was very good.

What decided him?

"I was nineteen," he replied. "I thought of trying my fortune in America. I tossed a coin."

He was silent it seemed to me a long time.

"Youth! Youth!" he said and sighed. "A dream! A dream! I wonder what would have become of me had I gone to America?"

He might have become chief organizer or president of the stonemasons' union, AFL—or is it CIO?

When I rose to leave, Mussolini took a photograph of himself and his lion cub from the large stack that he kept handy on top of his desk and addressed it to his "Dear colleague, Giorgio Seldes," signed it and dated it.

When late in 1924 I was appointed to Rome permanently, I went from Berlin via Paris and the Café Select. At this cafe I met William Bolitho, with whom I had worked in Germany on several big news stories. He had then been known as William Ryall of the *Manchester Guardian*. He now preferred his middle name, his mother's name, Bolitho.

When he heard the word Rome he became intensely interested; he told me my first job was to collect the facts and early documents on Fascism that Mussolini was attempting to wipe out of history.

"In about five years," he said, "Mussolini will have destroyed past history and substituted forgeries. The truth is being suppressed every day. We will probably never get the facts about Mussolini being bribed by the French Foreign Office in 1914, but you can still pick up the Mussolini manifestos, statements, radical socialist speeches, and get reports from thousands of persons about the Blackshirt terrorism and bloodshed in many cities that began before 1920."

One of the best examples of suppression was the original Fascist program, which, Bolitho said, consisted of sixteen points, and included several of the ten points made by Marx and Engels in the Communist Manifesto: all land to be divided up, "partial expropriation of all riches," a "graduated income tax," the railroads to be given to the railroad workers, and other national undertakings to be handled in the same way.

Bolitho knew that Mussolini and his Blackshirts had been

bought and paid for ever since the general strike of 1919–1920 by the Confederazione Generale dell'Industria, the equivalent of the American National Association of Manufacturers or the Federation of British Industries.

The General Confederation of Industry, said Bolitho, had given Mussolini twenty million lire, then worth a million dollars, which provided barracks, guns, uniforms, clubs, and castor oil—Fascism's modern addition to the history of torture and slow, painful death. The other subsidizers of Fascism named by Bolitho were:

Lega Industriele (equivalent to the Associated Industries)

Associazone fra Industriali Metallurgica (equivalent to our Iron & Steel Institute)

Ente Nazionale per le Industria Turistici (a chamber of commerce of the tourist industry)

Associazone Grandi Alberghi (the big hotel owners)

Bolitho could name all those business interests who stood to make money from Mussolini's Fascismo. The *Manchester Guardian* has always been regarded as one of the greatest, if not the greatest newspaper, of the time. In the United States the New York *World* and its sister paper, the St. Louis *Post-Dispatch,* would reprint the *Guardian* stories, but the Associated Press and the International News Service (Hearst) and most newspapers were more likely to print tourists' reports of trains running on time than stories about corporate interests bribing Mussolini.

"But first of all," said Bolitho, "try to get the facts on the assassination of Matteotti—you know that he was killed just after he announced he would expose a deal between the Sinclair Oil Company and prominent Fascist leaders. Go after this story: it will rock the world."

Suppressed News: Matteotti Assassination

The first thing I did on taking over the *Tribune* office in the Hotel Excelsior in the Via Veneto was to clean out the desk of my predecessor. He was a man named De Santo, and it was immediately obvious from the letters I found that he had been a voluntary worker in the Mussolini camp. He also had been receiving, along with many other correspondents representing not only the American but the world press, a monthly bribe from Mussolini in the form of five thousand words free via telegraph or cable.

Then I found an assistant interpreter, Camillo Cianfarra, and the first thing I asked him was, is there anything to the rumors we heard in Paris that Mussolini was implicated in some way in the assassination of his rival, the Socialist Party head, Giacomo Matteotti?

"Rumor?" exclaimed Cianfarra. "The documents proving it, the confessions of Mussolini's men, can be had at almost any Rome newsstand."

But, I asked, why hasn't the story that would "rock the world" been sent out?

The answer in short: Salvatore Cortesi of the Associated Press, the greatest news service in the world, the U.S. self-styled cooperative that serviced almost every morning paper in the country, most of North, Central and South America, and exchanged news with Reuters, Havas, WolffBuro, Tass and other national services, was a noted Fascist—he did not carry a card or pay dues, but he was Mussolini's chief publicity man. Arnaldo Cortesi, his son, was the Rome correspondent of *The New York Times.* He also was a super-Fascist. De Santo was a Fascist, and that added the *Chicago Tribune* to the list of the biggest and most powerful dailies suppressing the news and thereby supporting Fascism. As for the several liberal journalists resident in Rome, each without exception warned me that if I sent out the true story of Mussolini's guilt, the Duce would not hesitate to have me killed. Each of my colleagues had photographic copies of the confessions made by Cesare Rossi, head of the Italian Press Bureau and Filippo Filippelli, director of the *Corriere Italiano.* My colleagues also told me that there were two front-page American angles to the news. The man who had done most of the stabbing was an American gangster. His name was Amerigo Dumini, he was born in St. Louis, and although his father had an Italian name, his mother was the American-born Jessie Williams. Dumini was not only a hired murderer, he was on friendly terms with Mussolini, visiting the Duce not only in his office, but in his home. The second angle was Matteotti's speech in the Chamber of Deputies scheduled for the day he was assassinated, in which he said the Sinclair Oil Company and its head, Harry F. Sinclair, had been intriguing—that is, bribing men close to Mussolini including cabinet members—in an effort to obtain an oil monopoly in Italy.

It was indeed a story to rock the world. I sent it by mail via the Paris office of the *Tribune* and warned them not to let the Paris edition print it because I might be killed if they did. The next morning the Paris edition was sold throughout Europe with the Matteotti assassination featured, my name signed to it.

When I was ordered to leave Italy immediately, the entire American press with the exception of the two Cortesis protested and were told by Dino Grandi, who was known as Mussolini's right-hand man, that he would rescind the order. I invited my colleagues to a celebration that night—I then had an apartment on the Via Lombardia. We ate and drank and sang the hours away. Then there was a knock on the door. Four men, two in police uniform, ordered me to pack my things; they would take me to the train for Paris. I packed.

For reasons I was never to know, the Orient Express stopped for an hour this side of the French border. The town was called Modena. After about a half-hour's wait I heard shouting, a commotion in the sleeping cars and eventually the words *"Dové Seldes?"* ("Where is Seldes?") Then I saw the Blackshirts with their clubs and realized that Mussolini had sent word to the Modena *squadristi* to beat me up, or perhaps pour a pint or quart of castor oil into me—either method would result in death, not immediate death which might be called Fascist murder, but slow lingering and painful death.

In the third compartment from mine I had seen four men, two obviously British naval officers. I hated to barge in on English strangers, but I did. "Pardon me," I said, "but I am about to be killed by the Fascisti—they are searching the sleeping cars for me and they'll be here in a minute. I'm the correspondent for the *Chicago Tribune* and I'm being deported by Mussolini . . . "

"Please sit down," said the senior officer; "we are four admirals from Malta, two in civvies . . . "

And at this moment the *squadristi* arrived, pulled open the door, looked at the three in civilian clothes, and shouted "Dové Seldes?"

The admiral in charge then rose and issued his command: "Out! Get out, you *porco fascisti.*" And the "pig Fascists" stopped shouting, they groveled before the admirals, whispering *Perdone, perdone, signori,* and fled.

Twenty minutes or so later we were at the French border for passport inspection. For a moment I felt like kissing the ground.*

---

* From the New York *Post,* Leonard Lyons's column, 1944:

"In George Seldes's book *Sawdust Caesar,* one of the earliest biographies of Mussolini, the author concludes with the statement that 'the day will surely come when in all the noble cities of Italy there will arise the statue of Giacomo Matteotti. A free people will then decide if there will be room also for those of our Sawdust Caesar.' Sergeant Martin Watkins now reports that in Rome the first statue of Matteotti has been set up on an old pedestal from which the bust of Il Duce was thrown."

From *Basic News,* U.S. Army newspaper in Italy, October 17, 1944:

"Rome, Oct. 16.—It was announced here today that the busts of Giacomo

Matteotti and Giovanni Amendola will be placed in the Chamber of Deputies....

"Matteotti, a Socialist deputy, was murdered on 10 June 1924 by thugs on direct orders from Mussolini."

From *The New York Times,* June 11, 1945:

"Rome, June 10.—Today was the twenty-first anniversary of the murder of Giacomo Matteotti and the fifth anniversary of Italy's declaration of war against France and Britain.

"Both acts are recalled today as among Benito Mussolini's greatest sins.... A bust of Matteotti was among three unveiled today at the Montecitorio Palace where the Chamber of Deputies used to meet. . . . "

From *The New York Times,* June 10, 1964 (Letter from Vanni Montana, editor of *Giustizi*):

"June 10 marks the 40th anniversary of the kidnapping and murder by a Fascist gang in Rome of Giacomo Matteotti. . . .

"Mussolini felt strong enough to declare in a speech to Parliament January 3, 1925, that he assumed the "historical responsibility" for the murder of Matteotti. . . . "

Footnotes to a footnote: Martin Watkins, sergeant in the U.S. Army which liberated Rome, is the man who climbed onto the famous balcony of the Chigi Palace, from which Mussolini harangued his followers, and, mimicking the Duce, drew the applause and laughter of all Rome. He is now an American college professor.

Chapter 26

Cianfarra, Sturzo, Pirandello

Shortly after I was thrown out of Italy and escaped being murdered on the Orient Express by Mussolini's *squadristi,* I received word from Rome that Cianfarra had been beaten up by the Fascists, and although castor oil was not forced down his throat, he could never recover with so many of his bones broken and splintered. I had foreseen such a tragedy and had cabled Colonel McCormick to ask the State Department to safeguard the life of my assistant. Colonel McCormick did this. Unfortunately the U.S. Embassy in Rome was at this time, as were the embassies in several other countries, in the hands of self-styled diplomats—men who contributed big money and got embassies in exchange from victorious Presidents—who were in reality an American brand of Fascisti. Ambassadors and ministers representing the United States were the worst offenders in labeling, branding, name-calling: liberals and especially Socialists were all called "Reds" and "Communists" and therefore everything done against them was justified. It was the same in Mexico, as I later found, as in Rome of my time. No one would listen to the view that the very best way to fight the Communist dictatorship movement in any country was to aid the liberal Socialist Party in winning the elections.

Cianfarra at one time had been in the Italian diplomatic service, a member of its embassy in Washington. One of his jobs, he told me, was to investigate Italian immigration into the United States. His most interesting finding concerned the Mafia and other criminal elements. Cianfarra told me:

Italian judges, notably Sicilians, when Mafia members, murderers, cutthroats and bandits came up for sentence, usually sent them to the nation's Siberia, the Liparian and other islands—later used by Mussolini for intellectuals and anti-Fascist socialists.

Since Italy had no death penalty, and the cost of keeping men imprisoned for life was incredibly high, the judges frequently suggested that Mafia members and other criminals emigrate to the United States. They frequently suggested the names of boats and named sailing dates and suggested where help could be had with passports and visas.

However, when Mussolini took over, he ended this practice. He had other uses for the Mafia: he incorporated it into his Blackshirts. You may remember the Mussolini proclamation that appeared in most of the newspapers throughout the world some years ago, headlined something like 'Mussolini Abolished Mafia.' Technically true. He abolished the Mafia by making it part of his armed forces."

It was sometime in 1924 that Cianfarra took me to the cathedral in Naples to be a witness to the regularly expected miracle—to see the blood of Saint Gennero liquefy and give Italy another good year. On the rare occasions it remained congealed there would be another great earthquake or similar disaster. Usually a miracle occurred.

How Cianfarra was able to get us standing room so we could see the altar was itself almost a miracle. Perhaps the word "press" still had power in those days.

"Note," said Cianfarra, "how the Cardinal displays the monstrance as he prays for the miracle to happen. Note the big candles with the big flaming wicks. Note that somehow he passes the monstrance through the flame of one or another of these big candles. In no time at all the metal monstrance and the glass vial within will be hot enough to melt the solidified matter—blood, or whatever it may be—inside."

In no time at all the Cardinal held up the monstrance and the crowd began to shout *"Miracolo! Miracolo!"*

Another good year for Italy.*

Don Luigi Sturzo

One of the greatest myths of modern history was originated by Mussolini and promoted by the great banking houses of America that financed Fascism: it was that the Fascisti were fighting the Communists, the "reds." This justified bloodshed and murder.

In fact and in truth the most powerful opposition to Mussolini in the 1920s was the Popular Party, headed by the priest Don Luigi Sturzo. Every foreign correspondent in Italy knew this.

The first time I interviewed Don Sturzo was two years before Mussolini abolished all opposition parties. Don Sturzo said:

> The King should have acted, he should have dismissed Mussolini and called out the army the day he learned that Mussolini was implicated in the assassination of his Socialist rival Matteotti.
>
> The King showed no courage whatever. Neither did the living ex-premiers, Salandra, Giolitti and Orlando. Maybe the King was afraid the Army would not be loyal, maybe he was afraid that the bankers and big industrialists who had subsidized Fascism would turn against him.
>
> We, the Popolari, did our best to combat the Fascists. But we had no capitalists, no generals, no prime ministers on our side—only a vast majority of the people.

* In the May 1976 Saint Gennero festival, however, as *Time* reported from Naples on the seventeenth, there was a failure, and a great disaster was expected. "But Naples' Cardinal Ursi," said *Time,* "calling for intensified prayer, identified the threat as neopaganism, which his flock interpreted as an oblique or unmistakable reference to the rise of Italian Communism."

• • •

When opposition parties were outlawed in 1926, Don Sturzo fled into exile in the then largest Catholic diocese in America, Brooklyn. He became guest professor in history in several universities.

In 1948 I found him again in Italy. When we talked of Fascism and the new Republic he said proudly: "The Partito Popolari which I founded to fight Fascism is now the Partito Democracia Christiana—the most powerful party in Italy."*

In Italy the two notable literary figures D'Annunzio and Pirandello were famous before Fascism arrived. D'Annunzio got a villa and the title of Prince Snowymountain from the Duce.

While in Rome I got to know Pirandello well enough to ask him if he was a Fascist. On the opening night of his *Sagra della Madonna de la Nava* I said to him, "You are the only writer who has joined the party; how do you account for it?"

Pirandello shrugged, shook his head and replied good-humoredly: "This is my theatre. It is subsidized by Mussolini. I can produce every play that I write here, I can produce any play that I like. I have no money problems. So long as this situation remains, I have no complaint."

There is perhaps more explanation in this little statement than in whole books written to solve the Pirandello "riddle."

---

* Italy's Fascist dictatorship, two decades long, produced nothing. The Spanish dictatorship, 1939–1975, produced nothing. In 1917 when the Bolsheviki overthrew the tsarist dictatorship, it released for a while the genius of the people. All the arts and sciences flourished. Today the only intellectual activity in this dictatorship is that of dissenters, opponents, enemies of the system, exiles and would-be exiles. The U.S.S.R. is the only great nation where intellectuals hope for exile.

Chapter 27

Dr. Alfred Adler on Mussolini

After my expulsion from Italy by Mussolini in 1925 I went immediately from Paris to Berlin, still in the belief I was technically at least head of that office and not a roving correspondent. One of the great advantages of being Berlin correspondent was always having Vienna included in the territory. Unfortunately there were few great or sensational events taking place in Austria and therefore few excuses for spending more than a few days on each visit.

Whenever I stayed in Vienna at least a week I never failed to attend the receptions that Dr. Alfred Adler—whom I have always considered one of the greatest human beings I have ever met—gave for doctors, foreign, or rather mostly American, medical students and interested laymen.

At my first visit, late in 1926, I was eager to ask the man commonly (but wrongly) called "the father of the inferiority complex" about Mussolini. (Dr. Adler hated the title because as he frequently said, a complex is a serious matter, a mental illness, and the man who suffers from it needs psychiatric help. Few suffer complexes. He, Dr. Adler, was willing to be called "the father of the school of individual psychology," and he differed from Freud in many essential ways. He did insist that his pupils and his weekly visitors study the *feeling* of inferiority, with which every human being is born, and the lifelong struggle for its opposite, the *feeling* of superiority.)

I told Dr. Adler of my expulsion. I also told him that in 1919 and 1920 Benito Mussolini, Lincoln Eyre and I had met as fellow journalists, good friends on an equal basis. Dr. Adler showed great interest. He questioned me about Mussolini as a common laborer in Switzerland, as a socialist, a labor leader; why Mussolini had sold out to the French Foreign Office; and his subsequent change into a man of violence and terrorism.

Although he made no attempt to analyze Mussolini at long distance, his views on inferiority and superiority, with the occasional references to Mussolini, made an exellent feature story, which I sold to the New York *World Sunday Magazine* (December 16, 1926) and, as Dr. Adler said on my return to Vienna in 1927, "You introduced me to America."

In his weekly talks Dr. Adler always emphasized the behavior pattern of all human beings set in the earliest years of their lives. Nevertheless I feel that his views shaped my pattern almost as much as those of my libertarian, nonconformist, freethinking father in my childhood. I did not become Dr. Adler's patient. But during the weeks and months I worked in Vienna I never missed the Adler afternoons—I think they were on Wednesdays—where quite a number of us not only sat at the feet of the master but also drank Mrs. Adler's tea or coffee and ate her cookies. (Later, when I wrote of these afternoons and said there was a silver dish in the Adler hallway on which Wednesday guests were supposed to leave three Austrian schillings—about fifty-one cents—this memory which I reported as a fact was denied by the family.)

When Dr. Adler first said that every man and woman had experienced the feeling of inferiority, and that from childhood on everyone struggles to overcome it, that all of us seek "the equation of one's individual inferiority, the tests of one's behavior pattern through relationship to society, to one's work, and to sex," speaking the common language at these Wednesday meetings, it came as a revelation to me and set me reconsidering my whole history so far as I could remember it, reconsidering, meditating, judging and deciding upon the future.

I was especially interested in the Adlerian view of compensating for the universal feeling of inferiority. I realized that my choice of a trade (or profession) had been explained by Dr. Adler. I had been a timid child, fearful of adventures. Adler told us that youth meets the feeling of inferiority in many ways—one person might become a bully, seeking compensation in fighting; and another would become a humanitarian. He himself, Dr. Adler told his groups, as a child was nearsighted and timid, was beaten up by older boys, and more often was just ignored by his peers. In his own childhood, when he felt inferior to many, he had determined that he would become a famous man, a doctor, a humanitarian; and this feeling drove him onward the rest of his life.

Those Wednesdays at the Adler apartment first made me want to quit newspaper work and attempt writing of more lasting value than headline news.

Part *VII*

~~~~~~~~~~~~~~~~~~~~~~~~~~~~~~

Damascus and Mexico via Chicago

Chapter 28

Sarrail: A Tragic General

Within a year after my expulsion from Rome I was made "roving" correspondent for Eastern Europe, Berlin to Baghdad, but I was not given the title because "roving" hitherto had meant a considerable increase in pay, and neither "Black Jack" Hummel in Paris nor the Colonel in Chicago liked to part with money. (I never got more than sixty dollars a week in my ten *ChiTrib* years.)

Twice a year, however, I was to visit every country on the route of the Orient Express, all expenses paid: Vienna, Budapest, Belgrade, Athens, Bucharest, Constantinople, with automobile sidetrips to Damascus and Baghdad. In 180 days and nights on the Orient Express I never saw a king or a crook, a millionaire or a refugee, a smuggler, a prima donna, a beautiful adventuress or a courtesan.

Six months on the Orient Express and the most interesting thing I can recall is one of the conductors warning passengers about those famous, but fictitious, slinky beautiful blondes with whom we might get in trouble. He said: "In your compartment it's rape. In theirs, it's commerce."

And once, somewhere between the Greek and Turkish frontiers, where the League of Nations had arranged an exchange of populations to prevent religious wars, Muslims vs. Christians, our train caught up with the League's and we had to wait for hours. I tried to photograph a field with hundreds of men, women and children, Mohammedans obviously, from their clothes. But Mohammed, apparently, had once abolished photography, and one of his followers, a long knife in his hand, rushed at me, and also tried to smash my camera. The conductor saved me.

Although Kaiser Wilhelm dreamed of a Berlin-to-Baghdad empire, it remained a dream. Beirut, Damascus and Baghdad were three of my stringer cities, and it was in Damascus in 1925 that I chanced upon one of the notable tragic figures of modern history—General Maurice Sarrail, who governed Syria for the French under the League mandate.

It was also the occasion of what I consider one of the greatest falsifications of history in our time—by the news service considered the best and most reliable, as well as the most powerful, in the world, our Associated Press. I am referring to its report of a massacre of 25,000 men, women and children by the French army in the bombardment of Damascus.

For more than half a century I have been trying to set this historic incident right. I was there. I was the only reporter there. I saw the last part of the three-day bombardment. I took photographs of the refugees streaming from the Muslim section to the foreigners' section. I went with an officer later and counted the dead. Although I saw only 308 bodies I reported there might be more dead in the rubble—and that a maximum might be one thousand. But MASSACRE OF 25,000 MEN, WOMEN AND CHILDREN IN DAMASCUS, a common headline, remains to this day, in less sensational wording, in responsible history books.

When the Muslims, who had rebelled, threatened to kill all the Christians, General Sarrail gave the civilian population time to evacuate, then ordered Fort Gouraud to fire some warning shots, then shell the rebel sector. Unfortunately for truth and history, the Associated Press representative, who had sailed from Marseilles with Henri de Jouvanal, the governor chosen to replace Sarrail, heard rumors from various Arab liberation groups and Arab nationalists about a massacre and cabled the "news" to America.*

The important and historic result of this perversion was the impetus it gave the Arab independence movement. Beirut, Jerusalem and Cairo joined in telling a shocked world of this terrible French atrocity. The Arabs were fundamentally right in demanding independence. France, Britain, the League of Nations, every occupying country was in the wrong. If the Arab propaganda groups did not know during the three-day bombardment that they were spreading a great falsehood, they knew it shortly afterward, but as the atrocity story had raised sympathy throughout the Christian world and made Arab nationalism known, the authors of the massacre myth continued to exploit it. The end justifying the means is probably not an original Arab nationalist idea, but it worked in the Near East with great success.

However, if you looked for facts, even facts *sub specie Chicago Tribune,* you found an instance of historic irony. The facts were that this man, this governor, this general who stood accused before the whole world as one reponsible for a great atrocity, was the one and only man, governor and general, among those ruling colonial empires, mandated territories, who was an idealist, a democrat in the Jeffersonian sense, a would-be liberator of the Arabs—and other suppressed people—in the Near East.

Of course I went to interview General Sarrail and later came to talk to him man-to-man several times. This is his report as I confirmed it with the few unprejudiced sources, Christian and Muslim, in Damascus:

On arriving at his new post, Sarrail said, he had found the religious and economic problems he had expected, but he was

---

* In my previous reports I was perhaps wrong in naming the AP correspondent as the falsifier; but the AP itself can never be excused for accepting a French politician's rumors as fact and Arab nationalist propaganda as truth.

immediately shocked to find twenty-nine varieties of organized religions, several of them fanatically willing to murder the communicants of rival sects. He had found, as expected, ignorance, poverty and misery among the vast majority of people, and a ruling class of Arab emirs, sheiks, pashas, most of them holding titles from the previous oppressive Turkish regime, all wealthy, all living on the blood and sweat and tears of their fellow Mohammedans.

He had found slavery. Not the conventional kind such as once existed in America, but the Arab kind—which incidentally existed until the League of Nations finally took up the matter and published a report on it in Geneva in the early 1930s. This is the slavery Sarrail told me he found: every wealthy emir, sheik, pasha, had not only the four wives in his harem that Mohammed in the Koran told him he could have but a larger number of concubines, and to serve the harem women and frequently the emir himself, black slave girls from Africa. These black slave girls were usually Sudanese, many of them were beautiful; their price was the equivalent of five hundred American dollars. The Muslim master used them until he tired of them, then sold them into houses of prostitution, preferably in Beirut, which had the largest red-light district outside of Port Said and Alexandria; the going price was generally also five hundred dollars. (In 1925–1926 and 1927 in visits to Beirut and Damascus I frequently saw processions of these pashas followed by their wives wearing yashmaks to cover their faces, several concubines all dressed in some sort of blue linen, almost a uniform, and two or three black girls. In Beirut foreign correspondents frequently went to bargain sales in the big department store—I think it was a branch of the Galéries Lafayette—where Arab girls and women in their eagerness for bargains forgot Mohammed and removed their veils; many were really beautiful.)

"But, worst of all," continued General Sarrail in our first interview, "I found serfdom, which was general, and almost as bad as slavery. These Arab rulers had vast land holdings, and the serfs went with them, they were bought and sold with the land just as they once had been in Russia.

21 Lady Astor on the campaign front—"Save your votes for me."

22 Isadora Duncan at the time of Seldes's 1924 interview.

23 *Right:* Gabriele D'Annunzio, Seldes's first SOB.

24 *Below:* "Otto" Hitler in the Beer Hall Putsch days — a man of "startling insignificance."

25   "Of all the grand hotels in the world the grandest was the Adlon in Berlin."

26   Seldes hard at work in the Adlon offices, 1923.
The celebrated 25¢ Van Gogh lithograph graces the wall
(far left).

27   Ernst Udet, dashing
German aviator and one
of many Adlon habitués —
photo taken by Seldes.

28 *Right:* Seldes (center) with correspondents covering the Fifth Anniversary of the Bolshevik Revolution, November 1922.

29 *Below:* The day the American press met Lenin — the Kremlin, November 1922. Circled from left Trotsky, Lenin, and Seldes.

30 *Above:* Leon Trotsky saluting his troops at the height of the anniversary festivities—photo taken by Seldes.

31 *Below:* A member takes the "Red Oath" in a forbidden photo of the "dread" Russian Vai-Che-Kah.

32 *Right: ChiTrib* boss Colonel Robert McCormick in 1929, shortly after Seldes's name disappeared from the roll of honor.

33 *Below:* Seldes photographing Syrians in 1925 at time of revolution. With this photo the U.S. press credited Seldes as an "instructor" of Syrian rebels.

34 Seldes's Vatican I.D.—a momento of the Monsignor Pucci days.

35 The Rome *ChiTrib* office Seldes established in 1924, across the street from Mussolini's favorite balcony.

36 *Above:* Il Duce, fellow journalist and former "dear colleague."

37 *Right:* American journalists
expelled from Italy by Mussolini in
1925 (Seldes bottom right).

"I determined first of all to free the serfs. I did not need new laws to do so. The laws were there. I merely ordered the enforcement of the laws already on the books. The law said that anyone who broke this law, sheik or peasant, would be tried and, if found guilty, would be sentenced to work out his duty to the state by breaking stones and building roads, usually near his own town or village. Of course in this matter all the lawbreakers without exception were the rich landowners, the Arab sheiks, emirs and pashas. I had them arrested, tried, and when they were found guilty, their own courts sentenced them to break stones and build roads, along with the other criminals, the common thieves and the rest of them."

What happened then?

"The serfs, the masses of common people I hoped to free, revolted in favor of their old masters," said the old socialist general, and there was a world of tragedy in his voice.

One of the great secrets of the Great War (now demoted to World War I) concerned the actions, against orders, by three generals, the men who saved France. The one I knew quite well, General Sarrail, one day showed me the published diary of his colleague, General Gallieni, commandant of Paris:

25 Sept, 1914. General Headquarters instruction, 2 Sept., orders the Armies to retire to the Seine and the withdrawal of two army corps from Nancy. Thus, evacuation of Nancy and Verdun.

General de Castlenau disobeys orders (from Marshal Joffre), resists on the Grande Couronne, saves Nancy. General Sarrail gives battle before Verdun despite orders to retreat. He saves Verdun. I take the offensive before Paris while G.H.Q. are moved far to the rear at Chatillon.

These were actions independent of the will of the Commander-in-Chief, carried out by commanders of army corps, but premeditated by G.H.Q.?—*jamais!*

Joffre was replaced by Foch. Pershing arrived and won the war for him. Castlenau fought and won great honors. Gallieni was the hero of a hundred cabaret songs despite the fact that about seventy-five percent of the story of "the taxicab army that saved Paris" is a myth. (Most of his army came in other vehicles, mostly trucks.) These three generals saved France by disobeying orders. Two of them received the highest honors. One was treated shabbily. Sarrail, who saved Verdun, and therefore could be called the greatest hero of World War I, was demoted. He was "exiled" to a command in Salonika, Greece.

Why was General Sarrail deprived of honors and justice? In 1925 when I talked to him in Damascus, it was not impudent to ask. He replied:

"I was always anti-clerical in a country where the clericals controlled the army at all times and the government a large part of the time. Moreover, I was a socialist—I do not mean a member of the Socialist Party of France, but my views were socialistic. This combination was fatal."

Nevertheless, here he was, governor of the mandated territory of Syria, and commander of the French Army in the Near East. How did that happen?

"In 1924 there was a political upset. The Radical Socialist Party—which, as you may know is neither radical nor socialist, but a truly liberal party, was elected to power. Edouard Herriot was premier. One of his first acts was to recall General Weygand and give me this post."

Chapter 29

~~~~~~~~~~

The Suppressed Mexico Series

From Damascus, at the end of 1926 or early in 1927, I went by auto caravan to Baghdad, knowing in advance that under the British mandate all would be peaceful—i.e., producing no news. Within an hour of my arrival a British officer invited me to his club and bought me a whiskey and soda. I had just one drink. The next thing I remember was opening my eyes in my hotel room bed two days later. I had probably set a record in getting malaria.

I could not do a day's work. When I got to Berlin I went immediately to see my doctor—he was now head of the medical school of Berlin University—and he told me that he was experimenting with a new drug which someone had invented for curing malaria: would I care to be one of the guinea pigs? I would.

Within a few days my fevers seemed to slacken. I cabled Colonel McCormick about taking sick leave but he refused it. I came back to the States on my own and stayed for several months. Then I got a telegram from the Colonel telling me to come to Chicago if my health permitted. The day I reported to him he said my being in America was a lucky coincidence. The United States was going to declare war on Mexico in a few days, and he needed a trained war correspondent. He ordered me to go to Fort Worth and tell the commanding general, whose name he gave me, that I was ready to report the war.

My old pal Ferdinand Reyher drove me to Fort Worth. When I brought the commanding general word from his old pal Colonel McCormick, the general said: "We always considered Bertie McCormick a ——— fool when we were all in the First Division. I see he still is. There won't be any war. Why don't you go to Mexico City and enjoy yourself?"

Instead of a war or even rumors of war, all Ferd and I found was a tremendous intrigue carried on by the American oil companies and various agents, spies, counterfeiters and irresponsible persons. The center of intrigue seemed to be the Hotel Regis, best in Mexico, where I was staying. Everyone seemed to be there: the press, the oil interests, the intriguers, the warmongers—it was the Hotel Adlon again, the epicenter of journalism in miniature. Among the little differences: at the Adlon the forged documents for sale by tsarist princes and others concerned the Soviets; here the forgeries were peddled by Mexicans and Mexican-Americans hostile to the government in power. Another difference was that the real center of anti-Mexican intrigue was the American Embassy.

For the first and only time, I heard the slogan: "The United States, from Alaska to the Isthmus of Panama!" I did not know then that it dates from the days of the Civil War and had now been revived by interventionists who wanted Mexico's oil and pretended it was "for Mexico's own good."

The embassy was in the charge of its first secretary, Mr. Arthur Bliss Lane. I went to see him on the advice of a man who asked $25,000 for several documents that named several American senators, the most outstanding liberals of both the Republican and Democratic parties, as receiving money secretly from Mexican sources—the document peddler called them "traitors."

The documents, he said, were in the embassy safe and the peddler's bona fides would be established by the U.S. chargé d'affaires.

And that is just as it happened. I saw the documents, the chargé vouched for the seller, who confided to me that he was really a secret agent of the U.S. government—this was in the days the initials FBI and CIA were unknown.

It was not until, somehow in conversation, I mentioned talking to a certain few Americans opposed to both war with Mexico and the exploitation of Mexicans by American oil and hacienda interests—notably the writer Ernest Gruening, who was later to be governor of Alaska and a U.S. senator—that Mr. Lane lost his diplomatic calm.

"Skunks—liars—traitors—all of them," he shouted at me; "they are all paid agents of the Mexican Bolshevik regime. . . . "

Mr. Lane was also of the opinion that Mr. Gruening, the two Americans who edited and published magazines in Mexico City, and Robert Hammond Murray, a noted foreign correspondent now in Mexico for the *New York World,* should all be hanged. He believed, on the other hand, that the Associated Press dispatch dated November 17, 1926, published November 18 (stating that "the spectre of a Mexican-fostered Bolshevist hegemony intervening between the U.S. and the Canal has thrust itself into American-Mexican relations"), was true, although it had already been proved in American liberal weeklies to be a falsification. There was no "spectre," there was no Bolshevism. If the AP had stated that the Bolshevik Russian Embassy, in charge of Madame Kollontai, and the Third International, were hoping and planning to win Mexico—as they were hoping and planning to win every country in the world including the United States—that would have been the truth. This was, is, and probably will be Soviet policy so long as the Soviets last.

The "secret agent" who had the documents for sale was named Miguel Avila. The documents, he said, and Lane confirmed him, were stolen from the offices of El Sol Petroleum Company, the only oil producer cooperating with the Mexican government. According to Avila he would supply me with documents naming not only senators but writers of books and newspaper correspondents, every man who had expressed sympathy for Mexico, as having been bribed by either El Sol or the Mexican government itself.

At that time I did not know a word of Spanish, but who would not be suspicious of "documents" on the letterheads of the Department of Education on which Education was crossed out and Treasury typed in. I therefore, even at the risk of sharing a scoop, consulted Mr. Murray. He no sooner read a line or two than he began laughing. What's the joke?

"This document," Murray said, "was written by an ignorant peasant, or a Mexican Texan or someone who never even had a high school education: every third word is misspelled and the grammar is unbelievable. They are either Avila's own faking—he is totally ignorant—or one of his pals'."

When I confronted Avila with my charge that these documents were forgeries, he made no denial. Instead, he offered to bring me another set of documents which he said would expose the real forgers.

I telegraphed Colonel McCormick immediately that I had had the documents which he had previously agreed to buy for $25,000 tested and found false. I said good-bye to Mr. Avila. However, he had no difficulty whatever in selling his works to the Hearst correspondent in Mexico City, and within a few days they were spread all over the front pages of the nineteen Hearst dailies and many other newspapers which bought press lord Hearst's services. (Later, a congressional committee investigated and declared the documents forgeries—but the denial did not get a tenth the front-page publicity the falsehoods did. I had saved Colonel McCormick what might be called a journalistic black eye, and $25,000, and got no thanks for it.)

On the other hand I did find several authentic documents that proved beyond doubt that the U.S. Embassy in Mexico City had been implicated in the assassination of a Mexican president in 1913. These documents were available, free, to every American correspondent in the capital—it was a parallel to the case of the confessions of the slayers of Mussolini's rival Matteotti in

Rome two years earlier. There was another coincidence: in Rome the suppressors of anti-Fascist news were chiefly the Cortesis, who represented the AP and *The New York Times,* while according to Murray, in Mexico City the chief suppressor was the *Times* correspondent, who, unknown to his employers, was trying to get an oil concession for himself and financial backers in the American oil industry.

I sent the most important authentic document to the *Tribune.* It was suppressed. It can be summed up as follows:

> The U.S. ambassador to Mexico, Henry Lane Wilson, had prior knowledge of a plot by a general named Huerta to overthrow the government and imprison its president, the liberal leader, Madero.
>
> The State Department, informed of the plot, did nothing—it did not suggest to Huerta to refrain from rebellion, it did not discourage treason, it did not warn the President.
>
> That by failure to act, although informed, both the embassy and the State Department were—at least in Mexican eyes—guilty of participation in the rebellion which followed and the assassination of both President Madero and Vice President Suarez.*

This document is signed by Sara Perez de Madero, widow of the murdered president. She further states under oath that the day after her husband was imprisoned she called on U.S. Ambassador Wilson and in reply to her request to "Use your influence to protect the life of my husband," Wilson replied, "That is a responsibility I do not care to undertake, either for myself or for my government." Moreover, an appeal that Madero's mother made to President Taft to save the Mexican president from assassination, which Wilson agreed to forward, did not reach Taft until a later time when he was no longer in office.

When I returned to Chicago I was introduced to E. M. Beck, the *Tribune*'s managing editor, with whom I discussed the series of reports I was planning. I had already prepared a list of several subjects, the most important of which was oil. Others

---

* The full text may be found in my first book, *You Can't Print That,* 1929.

were the hacienda interest, and the Mexican republic's attempt to follow the Jeffersonian principle of "a wall of separation between church and state." This plan to force the Roman Catholic Church out of its place as part of the government had already resulted in bloodshed in several Mexican states.

I proposed to take each subject and write two or perhaps four one-column articles on it, one or two giving the American oil, hacienda and embassy side of the question, the others giving the Mexican government side. I would write ten or twelve columns, which Mr. Beck could publish in any manner he thought best, either the two opposing views side by side, or five or six days giving the Mexican side, followed by an equal number of days giving the opposition side. Mr. Beck was delighted with the plan. I wrote twenty column stories.

When I returned to Europe I went again to Berlin. In those benighted days it was possible to get letters from America in less than a week, and also the office copy of the *Tribune,* which we displayed on our reading table and which was sent by letter-mail. Within a few days the paper arrived. Five days in succession I was on the front page with a story of how the American oil, hacienda and other interests had helped make Mexico a rich and successful country, and what hardships the Mexicans were now putting in the way of American business. Then days, weeks passed and there was no sign of my other five columns. I cabled Mr. Beck and was informed that it had been editorially decided not to use them because they were not of much interest.

This was total censorship and suppression. It had never happened to me in the more than eight *Tribune* years. The reason was obvious: the xenophobic Colonel hated Europe so much he did not care what our corps sent as news every day. With Mexico it was different. I then and there decided to quit the *Tribune* as soon as financially possible.

Chapter 30

Katherine Medill McCormick

When I had been Americanized, Chicago style, via the police courts and Jake Lingle, in 1927, Colonel McCormick sent me back to Europe after assuring me that I would have to be re-Americanized in about three years. As a personal favor he asked me to look after the welfare of his mother, Katherine Medill McCormick who, with her two nurses and her French maid, was going to Karlsbad for the cure.

Everyone on the *Tribune* knew that this newspaper and various other corporations including the Canadian paper and power companies (and in 1919 the New York *Daily News*) belonged not to the Colonel and Captain Joseph Medill Patterson but to the Medill Trust, which Abraham Lincoln's great friend Joseph Medill had established for his two daughters, and that the Colonel's mother was now the real owner and director of all these enterprises.

Is truth stranger than fiction? What follows is a truthful account of the few days I knew the old lady. I wrote it first, as now, in plain journalism, but it was so incredible a story that Edward Titus, the publisher of *This Quarter* in Paris, told me to change the names of all concerned and he would publish it as fiction. I did.*

The Colonel told me to hire a special train from Paris to Karlsbad, but the French authorities just laughed. We got one of those twenty- or thirty-berth wagons-lit for the five of us and were hitched on to the regular train.

The day before our journey I was taken to the Ritz in Paris and introduced. Mrs. McCormick did not catch my name, but heard me described as "our Berlin correspondent." She replied: "God damn the Germans."

Then she added: "God damn the French, too. I fell out of bed in this country."

She was silent, summoning her forces for her final attack.

"And God damn the Japanese, too. And God damn the Jews and God damn the Catholics—I hate them all."

Two days later, at the Hotel Pupp, Karlsbad, the nurses, the doctor and I were playing bridge in the reception parlor of her suite. We discussed the patient's universal hatreds.

"But you are Catholics," I said to one of the McCleary sisters. (I am changing the Irish name slightly because I do not know if they want it used.)

"And I am a Jew," Dr. Toepfer said. (I am using his real name.)

"Her former doctor was named Blumenthal. Now she has you. Can you explain?" I asked.

The elder Miss McCleary explained. It was simple. Mrs. McCormick had said time and again that she found the most conscientious nurses were Catholics, and Jewish doctors everywhere the best doctors. She would never have any other nurses

---

* I called the story "Someone to Hate" and if any reader cares about it he may turn to page 387 of *The Best Short Stories of 1931*, edited by Edward J. O'Brien, where he will find this listing: "Seldes, George. Someone to Hate. T.Q. . . . " The asterisk means it received one star; the ten greatest short stories, which received three stars, were by Faulkner, Fitzgerald and other such masters.

than Catholics, other doctors than Jews; she had always asked religious belief whenever she needed either.

One day reading the Paris edition of her paper, obituary page first, she expressed satisfaction with the demise of a person, no relative, also named McCormick—"the reaper McCormicks," she called them. "How I love the reaper McCormicks," she said to us, "how I love to go to their funerals."

Then, without stopping, apropos of nothing, she said: "I remember Abraham Lincoln. Nasty old man. Mother always said when we had to go to their house to play with the Lincoln children, Mother said, 'Kate and Elinor, be very careful—don't let that nasty old man kiss you. Don't let him play with you. He may be President of the United States, but he has dirty finger-nails.' "

(My first and only encounter with anyone who had really known Lincoln. When I reported G.A.R. reunions circa 1909 to 1912, every veteran, without exception, said he had spoken to or at least seen Lincoln, but no one ever believed veterans in those days.)

One afternoon, when we were as usual playing bridge, there was a great ringing of bells and a pounding of things in the next room, and then we heard Mrs. McCormick's slightly drunken voice saying: "Miss McCleary, Miss Agnes McCleary, come into my room this minute and tell me the name of that man from St. Louis whom I hate."

The man she hated was Charles A. Lindbergh, Jr.

The next day she asked, "What's in the papers?" and a Miss McCleary said, "Only Lindbergh."

"What's he ever done?" asked the patient. "Yes, I know. If I were a man I could have done that. My son Medill" (for some reason she pronounced the Senator's name Medal) "could have done that. Call them up at once and tell them I won't have any more Lindbergh in my newspapers. . . . No, wait a minute. Tell the paper to announce that the *Chicago Tribune* is awarding a prize to Lindbergh for flying the ocean. Tell it to announce I will award Lindbergh ten dollars."

The nurses, at Dr. Toepfer's suggestion, diluted the whiskey with something called condurango because Mrs. McCormick insisted on a full bottle every day. She frequently complained that whiskey was losing its taste; Scotch wasn't what it used to be in the old days.

Once, sober, she spoke confidentially to me: "You all think I won't get into heaven. I'll fool all of you. I'll go to heaven all right. I'll get in. I'll go right up to St. Peter, I'll—I won't even say 'Saint' to him. I'll say, 'Peter,' just 'Peter.' I'll say, 'Peter you, *you*. YOU denied the Lord three times. . . . You let *me* in."

She made a motion with her elbow as if she was actually shoving huge St. Peter aside, and stepping through the gates of heaven.

When I returned to Berlin I began preparations to resign from the *Tribune* foreign service. Fortunately, my brother's literary agent sent me an offer from a new publisher, Payson & Clarke, to write a book about foreign correspondents, and so I sent Colonel McCormick my resignation, dated either December 31, 1928, or January 1, 1929, and wrote my first book.

Part VIII

France: Artists
and Writers

Chapter 31

The One-Man Lost Generation

Freedom from the press came in 1929—twenty years from the time I got my first job on a newspaper—a year in which Paris was still attracting writers and artists from all the world.

Montparnasse was unquestionably still the intellectual center. Its cafés were meeting places of thousands who worked all day at their professional callings, as well as tens of thousands of frauds who were tolerated, and gaping tourists who were despised. The two rivals were Raspail-Montparnasse and the Saint-Germain-des-Prés corners. The Dôme, which had many German and Scandinavian customers as well as the most tourists, and the Rotonde, of whose many French artists several were said to sit nightly under their own canvases, were the best known on the Raspail-Montparnasse corner, but Americans preferred Le Select, a hundred feet or a hundred yards away; and the fourth noted place was the new Coupole, occupying a former lumberyard, a large terrace now and a restaurant with good food at a fair price.

The other center of culture and bohemianism was the Café

des Deux Magots facing the church of Saint-Germain-des-Prés, the Café Lipps opposite the Deux Magots, and the Café Flore a few hundred feet away on the Boulevard St. Germain. This section of Montparnasse was almost totally French except for the tourists of many lands who came at first in twos and threes and eventually by the thousands—and of course ruined everything. In my time, and for several years thereafter, we could catch a glimpse of Gide dining at Lipps or sitting on the Deux Magots terrace, and perhaps even Picasso walking by. But in later years when I passed the Deux Magots I found it filled almost completely with German tourists, and their buses, each marked with the name of a big German city, parked nearby. The commercialism and degeneration of this once great intellectual center can be illustrated by the words on the cash register slips of the Deux Magots: "*Rendez-vous des élites intellectuels.*"

But there was one phenomenon we never had in the years 1918 to 1933 when I visited or lived in France, and that was a lost generation. Hemingway was responsible for this myth. In *The Sun Also Rises* he uses this epigraph: " 'You are all a lost generation.'—Gertrude Stein in conversation" and it is now as impossible to rectify this fraud as it is to correct the false reports in history books of our time—the Damascus "massacre," for example.

The facts are simply:

1. Gertrude Stein was quoting someone.
2. The reference was to postwar workers, auto mechanics, and not to arts and letters.

As Miss Stein herself told it: when she complained to her garage owner about the bad job of repairing her auto, he replied that ever since the war he could no longer get skilled, responsible craftsmen of the good old days, and it was in this connection, and with no relation to the perhaps 100,000 artists, writers, expatriates crowding Paris, of which he probably knew nothing, that he remarked on a generation being lost.

Moreover, in all my years in Paris, I spotted only one "intellectual" who might be classified under the Hemingway misquotation. I wrote his story. I entitled it "The One-Man Lost Generation," and it was published in, of all places, the magazine edited by Professor Tom Wood of the University of Arkansas, and his wife, Delores, and called *The Lost Generation Journal.* This is the story:

Harold E(dmund) Stearns personified the suspicion of someone "lost." Here was a young man, brilliant in America, on the threshold if not within the portals of fame, editor of two books which entitled him to be a spokesman for his times. Stearns's *America and the Young Intellects* expressed the beliefs of the post-war generation; and his *Civilization in the United States,* the book he edited and to which he contributed, certainly placed him among the rising stars of American letters.

And then he went to Paris and took to drink.

And so he was "lost."

There were many drunkards and do-nothings in the foreign colonies of Paris and other European cities hospitable to American literati, newspapermen, artists, escapists. But if there is a second *notable* person who became as lost as Harold, I do not know his name. I never met him, saw him, in my seventeen European years, 1916–1933. Along with others I saw Scott Fitzgerald and Hemingway drunk on at least one occasion worth perhaps a chapter in a book. But I know of no one who began a brilliant career—as Harold Stearns did so obviously—and, shortly after uprooting himself and joining the American colony in Paris, became a nobody, as Harold did; therefore, in my article I made the point that the "lost generation" consisted entirely of one lost man, Harold E. Stearns.

When I first saw him on a stool at the bar of the Select—he never joined the terrace crowd—he was a fellow employee of the *Chicago Tribune.* The Paris edition hired him to do its horse racing column under the title "Peter Pickem." I do not know what the *Tribune* paid him, but it was probably the same half-price that either Colonel McCormick or his financial watchdog Hummel paid most of the Paris staff, i.e., twenty-five dollars a week. (All of us, foreign bureau heads, roving correspondents, were paid less than any other group employed by any other news service—we were all eager to be in Europe and willing to work for almost nothing.)

If Harold got the usual *Tribune* twenty-five a week, it was the equivalent of the wage of a French journalist, and therefore not quite enough to live on. Many French journalists supported themselves in those days by all sorts of journalistic dirty tricks, which produced many francs. Almost all the Paris newspaper owners, it was documentarily proved when the Bolsheviks released the Tsar's archives, were corrupted by Russian money, and this corruption continued into the 1920s. As for Harold, he needed at least twenty-five dollars a week for his Select bar bill, and he was clever enough to find a way of getting it.

Peter Pickem was known to most English-speaking people in Paris and to many tourists. Many asked him for tips on the races, and he always concluded his reply with the suggestion that if the questioner could not get to the track today—or tomorrow—he would place the bet. In this way he collected quite a number of fifty-franc notes (two dollars at the time) and could pay his bar bill, and did not go begging for loans as did the fraudulent Prince Romanoff.

Peter Pickem did not give his clients the name of the horse he himself picked—he gave the names of all the horses running in the race. But he was an honest man. The next day he returned the fifty francs to each man whose horse had won, saying, sorry, he had not been able to get there after all; and of course he kept the losers' money. The short-time visitors and tourists never found him out.

And then, toward the end of my stay in France, Harold had a new line. A French millionaire, a Rothschild, it was whispered, had given him a filly as a gift, and Harold needed money to board her and train her until she could enter the big race and make him a fortune. Everyone was sympathetic. Everyone contributed. But after a long time went by and people began to ask when the mare was going to run, Harold had to answer.

My finest memory of Harold Stearns is of that night at the Select when, surrounded by a group of his friends at the bar, he told a long story of the sudden tragic end of a great dream. He told it brilliantly, and I shall not attempt to repeat but one line of it—the last line. The Stearns mind was still unclouded by alcohol; it was a literary chronicle that should have been recorded. It was a little epic of effort and heroism and devotion, of sickness and mystery and the final fading away of the Rothschild filly:

"She died in my arms," Harold concluded.

Whatever became of Peter Pickem?

He returned to America.

He was completely rehabilitated. He wrote *The Street I Knew* in 1935 and *America: A Re-Appraisal* in 1937, a symposium and a companion volume to *Civilization in the United States,* which had once brought him fame.

He died in 1943.

And so even the one person who for more than a decade was pointed out to every visiting fireman at the Select as illustrating Gertrude Stein's garage owner's lost generation remark was not really lost after all.

Chapter 32

Adventures in the Latin Quarter

In contrast to the myth of one temporarily lost soul in one Montparnasse cafe constituting a whole lost generation, there was the daily life of the Latin Quarter in the fourteen years I visited or lived in Paris, each day a new adventure with people, each day worth recording.

A score of writers, painters, composers—and perhaps as many pseudos and pretenders—lived at the Hotel Liberia, just around the courner of the intersection of the boulevards Raspail and Montparnasse, for two dollars a day, running water but no bath. So did I. (When the *Chicago Tribune* paid I had always stopped at grand hotels—Imperials, Bristols and Excelsiors, even Ritzes; on my own it was the Liberia. The bathroom was at the end of the corridor.) From morning walks to evenings at the Dôme, Rotonde, Select and later the Coupole, it was impossible to avoid men and women who were already noted or who would become world famous. Neither Hemingway nor Sinclair Lewis—respectively the fifth and first American Nobel Prize laureates in literature—underestimated himself in his Café Select days.

One noonday walk it might be two hungry young American artists suggesting I take them to lunch—on my *Tribune* salary I was considered one of the well-off dwellers in bohemia of that time. And so, on my farmhouse wall at Hartland-4-Corners in Vermont today there is this drawing made by a grateful artist, exaggerating my hat and the turn of my raincoat somewhat to represent the generally accepted picture of a "dashing" foreign correspondent; and on the page is written:

> Sold to George Seldes for 10 francs
> Au Rendezvous des Chauffeurs
> pres de la rue de la Gde.
> Chaumiere
> at, or about Oct. 19, 1926
> Sandy Calder

The other hungry artist was Adolf Dehn, who became one of America's leading lithographers. He made no new drawing, but tore a page from his sketchbook that showed two chauffeurs, and wrote it was not a sale but a loan of ten francs—the equivalent then of fifty cents.

Another day it could be Colonel Charles Sweeney, known to all as "Sweeney of the Legion," with the reputation of a romantic and dramatic career in the French Foreign Legion, sometimes called "the greatest soldier of fortune of the century." He always carried an armful of books, and everyone suspected he was writing his history. Once I asked him. He replied, "Hell, no, I'm writing a life of Jesus."

It was Colonel Sweeney who organized the Kosciusko Squadron when war began in 1920 between Soviet Russia and Poland. Of his hundred volunteers, Captain Marion Cooper became the best known. One night at the Select, Cooper told me this terrible story:

He had been shot down. He was lying wounded beside his wrecked plane when a squad or company or horde of Russian

Cossacks came thundering toward him. But they did not kill him. They did not take him prisoner. They just played a game with him—as some of their fellows did in circuses. As each Cossack galloped up to Captain Cooper he whirled his horse around with his left hand and with his right drew his sword and swished it over Cooper's face, each Cossack in turn, each laughing, each apparently seeing how close he could get with his sword without cutting through Cooper's nose or his eyes or his throat. Cooper said he was scared—almost scared to death, which he thought inevitable. But the Cossacks rode away, and he could hear their laughter mingled with the sounds of hoofbeats.

One evening Jonathan Cape might be sitting at a Select table with a cluster of writers. Or the Paris publisher Edward Titus, whose home and office were just around a corner. Titus was known as a book collector; as the husband of Helena Rubinstein, whose cosmetics he had made internationally famous when he was in New York advertising; and as the publisher of *This Quarter* beginning with Volume 2. Once when I mentioned meeting Arnold Bennett, Titus invited me to see his two manuscripts. Whether they were short stories or books I do not remember, but they were surprising. One was written in tiny letters, the other was bold and defiant. The little handwriting, Titus explained, was the young, uncertain Bennett, the large letters a product of recent success and fame.

One night there was more excitement at the Select than was ever made by any supposedly "intellectual" prince—the arrival of the unmistakable and still beautiful Aimee Semple McPherson. She may have been slumming, but she drank her beer with the others, her saucers piled up as high. And then she said she would also like to see what the Right Bank was like, and would we take her to Place Pigalle, Montmartre. We did— and she drank the obligatory drinks at all the joints we had to visit. (What year that was I have forgotten—it was certainly after 1926, the year she disappeared on a beach near Los Angeles and sent five thousand searching for her body—in vain. Then she came starved and staggering out of the nearby Mexican desert saying, as she dropped to the ground, that she had been kidnapped.)

There was the night I met Oskar Kokoschka—a painter I thought in the same great class with Picasso, Braque, Juan Gris.

During the long evening I happened to mention the amusement Americans expressed about Kokoschka's signature. The artist was not amused. He was surprised. He had signed every canvas, year after year, with only his initials—in a corner, rather large: "O. K."

"Has no one ever told you what O.K. means to an American?" I asked.

No one ever had.

I told him.

He smiled. But he continued to sign his pictures "O. K."

One day I met the painter Jerome Blum on the boulevard. He was calling on James Stephens and invited me to go along. No one had ever mentioned the author of *The Crock of Gold* living in Paris, no one except Blum ever mentioned him. (I recalled AE [George Russell] speaking of him as one of the Irish writers he had urged to visit the Aran Islands.)

On our way we came upon Leo Stein, who may have been known in America as "Gertrude's brother" but in Montparnasse was respected as a great art critic and the real discoverer of the new artists, Picasso included, for whom Gertrude got the credit. Blum told Leo to come along.

Stephens himself opened the door. He was surprisingly a little man, not much over five feet; he seemed to be fifty, and his Irish brogue seemed acted. Blum introduced me first, then Leo Stein, saying "Mr. Stein is the author of *The A B C of Esthetics*."

Stephens put on a grave look and said: "Esthetics, eh? *The A B C of Esthetics*." He paused. "You sholl go to Heaven for thot."

Although Gertrude Stein's literary salon has been immortalized, there were other such Wednesday evenings or Sunday afternoons in Paris, usually in the apartments of noted writers, or a literary agent, and in one instance of a couple from Philadelphia who, during the Depression, had their usual income from mortgages and could afford the drinks. Their salon was crowded with the hungry and thirsty, but no one had anything to say to the host and hostess and they had nothing to say to their guests, and a good time was had by all.

Next in fame to Gertrude's salon was Ford Madox Ford's in the Rue Vaugirard—it was a long walk upstairs and for guiding signs the famous author had clipped the word FORD from auto advertisements, pasted them on each floor, and drawn arrows through the name.

He regaled his guests with stories of the great days of English literature, and although his tales about Henry James were later called fictionalized, he could not exaggerate his relationship with Conrad. He had met the unknown Polish-born British sea captain who had great tales to tell and little experience in writing, and made him famous. When I told Ford that in the early 1900s Professor Copeland at Harvard introduced Conrad to America and that some twenty classes in twenty years were "indoctrinated" by "Copey," Ford was delighted and somehow I felt that we became closer friends.

I asked him the technique of their collaboration. Ford replied:

"When it was possible, when there were two characters talking, Conrad would be one and I the other; Conrad would write one line or one paragraph and I would write the reply, or the next paragraph."

Ford said that one day they decided to write a romantic novel. They would outromanticize the romantic writers. "We will call the novel just that," Ford said, and so they wrote *Romance.*

In it there is a scene dealing with a trial for treason against an important person, and a peasant, a shepherd, is also involved. The judge thunders questions. "What were you doing on such and such a day and in such a such a place?" Conrad did the thundering.

"A few goats, exellency," replied the shepherd (Ford).

Then Ford said to me: "At this reply Conrad jumped from his chair and said, 'A stroke of genius, Ford. "A few goats, exellency." A stroke of genius.' "

One night—it was probably in 1932—when guests were leaving, Ford said: "Seldes, will you stay?" and of course I stayed.

Ford found a small bottle of real Napoleon brandy—say an 1880 or 1890 vintage, nevertheless a prize. When we had consumed most of it Ford said:

"Seldes, I'm getting to be an old man—I spent years helping Joseph Conrad, and at first the publishers put both our names on the books we wrote together, but do you know they are now issuing a definitive edition of Conrad and my name does not appear on the dust cover or even on the back of any book?

"I made Hemingway. I published his first work and later I let him edit my *Transatlantic Review,* and he disowns me now that he has become better known than I am."

Tears now came to Ford's eyes.

"I helped Joseph Conrad. I helped Hemingway. I helped a dozen, a score of writers, and many of them have beaten me. I'm now an old man and I'll die without making a name like Hemingway."

At this climax Ford began to sob. Then he began to cry.

We were never good friends again. He had confided too much.

(Moral: If you value a friendship, never let the friend confess to you.)

When Harper's published Claude McKay's *Banjo* in New York, his Paris literary agent, William Aspinwall Bradley, gave him a party at Stella Bowen's studio, to which the entire cast of *Blackbirds* was invited. Bradley asked me to come early—midnight—to be the bartender.

When I arrived, I found twenty guests grouped about a

large low table, the French (white) literati—M. X de l'Académie Française, Mme. Y, the noted novelist, one or two publishers and their women in evening clothes, all surrounding Mme. Bradley—while sitting uneasily on a trunk or standing uneasily near the entrance were several American Negroes (that term, rather than Blacks, was considered correct in the late 1920s and the 1930s.) Between the two groups there was a long refectory table splendid with glassware, eighteen quarts of champagne, ten quarts of gin, and ten quarts of vermouth—Mr. Bradley thought a martini was a fifty-fifty affair—several quarts of cognac, bowls of lemons, heaps of ice. But the ice between the Blacks and whites was more apparent.

Mrs. Sylvia Lewis, a fellow journalist, came with me. Countee Cullen recognized her and immediately there was a white woman in conversation with a black man, and the atmosphere warmed. Lee and Virginia Hersh—he a painter, she a novelist—arrived, were introduced in the impersonal French way, were taken over by Mrs. Lewis and joined the Negro faction. Thus the melting began.

No one had served a drink before I came. I said, "Hit them in the ribs with a cocktail," but Bradley said, no, give them champagne, and I did, and this is probably why nothing happened for a long time.

Just before 2:00 A.M. the chorus of *Blackbirds* arrived. The social line between principals and chorus of *Blackbirds* and the Blacks and whites already present remained distinct. All the Negroes had been told they must always remember they were in France and among white French.

Finally I began shaking martinis. Several hundred glasses of champagne had had no effect. Nothing had happened but a violent thunderstorm, which crashed over the studio and imprisoned us for hours with chains of rain.

Principals and chorus of *Blackbirds,* without requiring the insistent pleading and flattery that seem so necessary to white artists, now gave their numbers—but in a more refined way than on the stage. Mrs. Lewis danced with "Snaky Hips" and other

Negro men and the women of the chorus danced with white partners, but in a very dignified manner. "He hardly touched me. He kept at a distance," Mrs. Hersh (née Virginia Davis of New Orleans), observed.

I put cognac into the champagne and reduced the vermouth in the martinis from one in three to one in five, and at about 3:30 A.M. one of the Negro musicians began a low *tom-tom, tom-tom-tom* rhythm on the piano. A beautiful girl, one of the chorus, her body golden as the marble of the Parthenon vibrant with the sun of twenty-four centuries, lifted her blue dress and shook her silken limbs. Several began to beat time with their hands. There was a frightening flash, an almost simultaneous crack of thunder, and in one moment nature and alcohol had stripped the veneer of white civilization. In one moment it became madness.

All the Blacks and many of the whites joined. Some clutched each other, body to body, legs to legs, cheeks to cheeks. Some stood apart and swayed and shouted. Thunderclap after thunderclap rolled over the house, scarcely heard because of the rhythmic roar of voices, the pounding of feet in unison, the frenzied *tom-tom, tom-tom-tom, tom-tom, tom-tom-tom* of the desperate piano player. The walls shook, the floor sank and rose, threatening to carry us all down in one wild mass of wood, broken bottles, and wet bodies.

They lifted their skirts. They embraced with hands and thighs and lips, clutching each other, swaying, drunk with alcohol and passion and the frenzy of music. It was savage and delirious and even frightening. *"Je me sauve! Je me sauve!"* cried Mme. Bradley as she fled the studio, into thunder and lightning and rain.

Ecstasy, black and white, remained with us in the studio the rest of the night. A night to remember.

Poet and Traitor: Ezra Pound

If American traitors, rather than expatriate drunks, tramps, do-nothings in sufficient numbers, constitute a lost generation, this denigrating title might fit a little better. There were quite a number of journalists and literary lights of the "long armistice" between the two great wars and during the Second World War who betrayed their country to Hitler and Mussolini. Several had been my onetime friends and colleagues, I knew them well, but the most notable, the one I knew least, apparently hated me (and my brother) most: Ezra Pound.

The reason for this hatred, I learned later, was a misunderstanding, not with me but with my brother, Gilbert, who in 1920 as editor of *The Dial*—once considered the leading literary magazine in America—had published T. S. Eliot's masterpiece, "The Waste Land," for whose greatness Pound was partly responsible. On a report that Pound was moving to Italy, the owner of *The Dial,* Scofield Thayer, sent its editor, my brother, Gilbert, to find a replacement for Pound as Paris contributor or editor. Pound spread the word that he had been fired by Gilbert, and ever afterward defamed not only my brother, but me.

When Pound became a Fascist—on his way to becoming a Nazi and eventually a traitor to the United States—he wrote in a book entitled *Jefferson and/or Mussolini:* "I see a member of the Seldes family giving half an underdone damn whether their yawps do harm or have any other effect save of getting themselves advertised." I cannot understand the meaning of this sentence or the malice behind it. I never met the man except at a few parties or on a café terrace. Nor can I understand the concern the American "intellectual class" had for Pound when in 1942 he went over entirely to Hitler and between Pearl Harbor and 1942 made three hundred broadcasts attacking the United States and praising the Nazi and Italian fascist systems. When finally the Allies won the war and the traitors either died in the ruins of enemy cities or were brought back to America, Pound was sent to an insane asylum instead of the gallows— thanks to the powerful influence of fellow American writers.

To conclude the story of a man I hardly knew who hated me as if we had once been friends, I must relate the findings of the German writer Eva Hesse of Munich who, in doing research for her next book, wrote me recently that she had found among Pound's books a copy of the British edition of my 1929 *You Can't Print That.* In that book I mentioned that Mussolini, in my 1924 interview, declared Vivaldi the greatest composer of all time. Miss Hesse wrote me that Pound, who met Mussolini in January 1933, suddenly, in 1936, developed a vigorous interest in Vivaldi scores and concerts.

Chapter 33

The French Riviera

The chief difference between the literary-artistic colonies of Montparnasse and the Riviera in the 1920s and 1930s was this: the Paris Latin Quarter was filled with tens of thousands of hopeful men and women, quite a number of writers and painters and poets, and thousands of fakers, whereas on the Riviera everyone worked.

There were no clutters of cafés, there was not even one (fake) story about a lost generation. Two of the Riviera's centers were Bandol, where for some reason most of the Guggenheim fellowship winners gathered at the same hotel, and Saint-Paul-de-Vence, where a little hotel, the Colombe d'Or, owned by a modern Maecenas, known simply as Monsieur Roux or Roy, housed and fed writers for two or three dollars a day and took paintings from unknowns for payment. The outstanding Riviera personages in my time, 1929 to 1932, were D. H. Lawrence, Frank Harris, William Seabrook, H. G. Wells—whom I was to meet again in Vermont—and Dr. Angelica Balabanoff.

At the Colombe d'Or all the summer of 1930 we debated calling on the most celebrated of the Riviera colony, D. H. Lawrence, who lived in the nearby town of Vence. Always the question of intrusion came up, and the non-intruders won. But the day came when we were defeated, and so four or five writers and painters walked to Vence and inquired of strangers where the Lawrences lived. The fact is, no one seemed to know, and we got lost. So much time passed that the non-intruders again raised the question. So we went to a florist shop, bought a huge bundle of roses, wrote out our names and the name of the Colombe d'Or on a sheet of paper, and had the flowers delivered to Lawrence before walking home.

Early the next morning I was called to the telephone by M. Roy. It was Frieda Lawrence. She had mistaken me for my brother, Gilbert, who had first published her husband in *The Dial* in 1920 and is credited with introducing him to America.

"Your flowers," said Mrs. Lawrence, "were the very first to arrive after Lawrence's death yesterday."

She described the great writer's last hours.

"The doctor had told me recently he had only a little time left. I did not tell Lawrence. The day before yesterday he said, 'Read to me, read some Persian philosophy.' I read to him: 'When man is in the best of health and has no fear of death, he should make his testament.' Lawrence stopped me. 'Perhaps,' he said, 'I should make mine now,' and he laughed.

"I replied, 'No. You've got years to live.'

"That was the day before he died."

All of us came to the dismal funeral. Aldous Huxley was there.

One day in 1931 a one-horse shay drove through the gates of this ancient Crusaders' walled town and into the courtyard of the Colombe d'Or, and out stepped both a beautiful lady I had known in Paris and the famous Frank Harris, the author of many books, including *My Life and Loves,* a *succès de scandale,* which he was living up to.

For several days Frank Harris entertained the English-speaking guests of the inn with the most outrageous stories of late Victorian literati. This I thought was his best:

> We all happened to be in Paris at the time. We saw each other every day—Oscar Wilde, Ernest Dowson, Aubrey Beardsley, and I. We were people who could talk to each other. I do not think anyone in our circle, either in Paris or London, thought homosexuality a great crime. It was of course the great secret. But with Oscar you could talk; you could argue. And I did. I nagged him. I said, "Oscar, why don't you give heterosexuality a chance—just once?"
>
> Eventually he agreed. We found him an excellent bordello. All of us accompanied Oscar. He entered, we remained outside. We serenaded him. Beardsley played the guitar. We were all very merry.
>
> Shortly after he entered, Oscar reappeared.
>
> "Cold mutton, gentlemen; cold mutton," was all he said.*

All my previous visits to the Riviera dated from my *Tribune* decade, when my summer vacations coincided with my brother's visits to France. I remember Cap d'Antibes and Juan-les-Pins when they were "discovered" by Gilbert's friends, Gerald and Sara Murphy, and Cole and Linda Porter. These couples had homes nearby and on my first visit I went through the ritual of swearing a solemn oath never to betray this last paradise on earth.

One of my most notable days in almost half a long lifetime spent in Europe was the one when the Murphys had as their guests Rebecca West, Max Eastman, Crystal Eastman, my brother and his wife, Amanda, and Picasso without any wife or mistress.

Picasso never forgot that it was *The Dial* that introduced him to America. That very year, when Gilbert and Amanda were married in Paris, he had brought along to the wedding breakfast in Armenonville one of his drawings of the Minotaur series,

---

* This is the way Frank Harris told the story at the Colombe d'Or circa 1930. But I found it also in Hesketh Pearson's biography of Wilde, the scene set in Dieppe, and no Frank Harris present. There are other versions and there are rumors that Mr. Harris was lying and that he stole not only this but many another good story, and that *My Life and Loves* is, putting it nicely, nothing but fiction.

which he inscribed *"Pour le ménage Seldes."* With Picasso on the beach at Juan-les-Pins all the talk was about painting, not books, not "literature." I cannot remember who asked the question—I think it was my brother—but I do remember that only I, the "hardened" and "blasé" and "tough" newspaper reporter, was shocked when Picasso replied, "You know, *I* paint with my penis." (He had said it before, and he was to say it again, as numerous books and articles testify.)

The Cole Porters later moved on to the Palazzo Rezzonico on the Grand Canal of Venice—then known as the Palazzo Curtis, after an American family from whom the Porters rented. The only work of art there I can remember was a glass-covered watercolor of a gondolier by Sargent. It interested me because it seemed to me that Sargent, on a later visit, dissatisfied with his original work, had repainted the gondolier, giving him more movement and color—but on the glass rather than on the original paper.

I was invited to a formal luncheon there, apparently for the purpose of provoking an argument with several Fascist politicos and one or two members of Italian royalty—the year must have been after my expulsion from Rome by the Duce, which had been widely reported in the European press.

I never saw Mrs. Porter smile, heard her laugh, or saw her betray an emotion. According to my brother, who knew the Porters well, she was the famous beauty Linda Lee of Louisville, and she had been married before, for money, to a man named Thomas; she had refused to share his bed and had driven him to drink. Then, for one million dollars, she had let him get a divorce.

Linda was at least seven years older than Cole when she married him—her enemies said nine—and she was terribly afraid of losing him. Her entire life was devoted to beautifying herself, trying to make herself look younger than her age, and that is why she never laughed or smiled and suppressed all her emotions. Zelda Fitzgerald, another of my brother's friends, had told me at one of the Antibes parties that "Linda considers every woman younger than herself her enemy." Zelda felt she was never wanted at the Cole Porter parties; my sister-in-law, Gilbert's wife, Amanda, said almost the same thing—adding, "Linda has an obsession against youth."

At the Juan-les-Pins gathering—I think it was in 1924— Cole Porter was probably in the middle of writing one of his famous songs, "You're the Top" because almost every time we met on the beach he would try out some new lines. "You're the top, you're the Queen of Sheba" is one I remember, but there was another tryout that showed how naïve a person Cole Porter was when it came to practical politics. If all of us, with one voice, had not protested, that famous song would have included a verse that began with the words, "You're the top, you're Mussolini."

Of course, being only a fortnight-a-year visitor to the Riviera, I cannot say I really got to know its famous American residents, but I could not help hearing the gossip: everyone said that Linda never permitted Cole to come to bed with her, and that Cole probably had other erotic interests. Rumors, but persistent.

William E. Seabrook

Of all the writers I have known, the greatest certainly was not Willie Seabrook, but he was certainly the most interesting. He was the only sadist—self-confessed or rumored—I have ever met. (If Willie had not later publicly so declared himself I would not during his lifetime or even now have said anything about it. But Willie, so he said, had been advised by his psychoanalyst— at times he said it was a friendly priest to whom he had confessed although he was not a Catholic—who advised him to stop keeping his sadism a secret, to treat it as if it were normal behavior—and he had done so.)

Everything Seabrook wrote was fictionalized. All his books claiming to be truthful accounts of great experiences, notably voodoo in Haiti, magic in Africa, cannibalism, were wholly or partly fiction. One day when we went to a shop in Paris dealing in African art—we were looking for gorilla masks—and I mentioned cannibalism. Willie said it was a technical question: it was true that the story of eating part of a warrior freshly killed by an African tribe with which he was living was untrue—but he had in fact eaten human flesh on another occasion, so there was no fakery.

I asked where and when.

"Right here, in Paris," Willie replied.

Then he told me this story, which is stranger—and probably a greater falsehood—than his African writing:

He had joined a group of devil worshippers in Paris, white, brown, and black. They performed the "black mass" over the body of a naked woman (white) on an altar in their "church" in a cellar. (But I cannot repeat the details.)

As for cannibalism: Willie boasted that a group of these devil worshippers engaged in that only once—and just as with African tribes who ate one of the enemy it killed, so his group ate just token pieces of the man who had betrayed them, and whom they had killed. What did human flesh taste like? Willie used the same terms heard in Africa and found in older books, "coarse veal" or "long pork," all probably false.

But his sadism was real. Willie practiced sadism à la the Marquis de Sade, whom he had obviously studied. In the early 1930s in Toulon it was no longer a secret. In fact Willie himself told us why he had moved from a loft in New York City to a loft in Toulon: sadism is too noisy an event for an apartment house, anywhere, and when it proved too noisy in a New York loft, Willie packed his long black gloves and considerable equipment and sailed away.

"When we were going through French customs," Willie told me, "the guard insisted I open all my baggage—others opened only one piece. He looked at my handcuffs, chains, whips and other paraphernalia.

" '*Voilà*,' one inspector shouted to the others, '*un gangster Américain.*'

" '*Monsieur*,' I protested, '*je ne suis pas gangster Américain, je suis sadist.*' I explained the ways of the Marquis de Sade.

" '*Comprends, comprends*,' said the chief inspector, who had now taken over. '*Entrez, monsieur, entrez. Bienvenue en France.*' "

In the Toulon loft overlooking the Mediterranean, Willie showed us what he called his lion's cage—and all sorts of riggings from the wooden ceiling, chains and pulleys. He said he preferred to hang his women by their feet while he whipped them. (He had actually placed an advertisement in the personals column of an American literary weekly saying: "Wanted: Beautiful girls for scientific experimentation.") He now asked the beautiful blonde from Moody, Texas, whom I had brought along, if she would be willing to spend some time in the lion's cage and be treated like a wild animal—and to my amazement Miss Texas agreed.

When I saw her the next day, she was very angry at Willie. "Seabrook is a faker," she said, "that is not a lion's cage, that is a monkey's cage!"

Willie himself had sometime earlier spent five days in it. He insisted on being chained inside, being whipped, having his food thrown at him and on being spoken to as if he were a wild animal. He wore a black mask over his eyes.

Describing those five days, Willie said:

"I wanted darkness, blindness and physical pressures. I wanted a great spiritual experience. I wanted to cast out the devil within me. I wanted to see the face of God!"

Another time he said of the same episode:

"I wanted to walk along the borderland of genius and insanity, the dividing line, the crest, I wanted to look at the other side, I wanted to see the face of God, and yet return."

But instead of seeing "the face of God," Willie took to alcohol.

His first wife, who could have been typecast for the role of "beautiful Southern aristocrat," which she was, divorced him. She grew tired of being whipped. His second wife, who years later wrote a biography in which she called Willie "a fine, intelligent and lovable man with a touch of genius as well as madness," ran away from the loft several times and stayed at the apartment of my friends nearby. Once she showed us the welts made on her back by Willie's whips. But she always went back.

Willie's first best-seller, *Asylum*, purported to tell the inside story of an alcoholic being cured. *Jungle Ways* has cannibalism as its climax. His books on magic, witchcraft, Haiti and voodooism, his adventures among the Bedouins and the whirling dervishes were probably partly or totally faked. But, as Julius Caesar* and others, have said, "Men want to be deceived." Willie was never without a book contract. Publishers kept offering him ideas. In the early thirties in Toulon he was planning to do a book on all the miracles that had occurred at Lourdes. There were many afternoons and evenings in the Seabrook loft spent in arguments: Do miracles occur today? Are the cures—even a small percentage of the many claimed—real? Someone had actually seen a man, a man he knew well, a cripple, throw away his crutches and walk. Someone suggested it was hysteria, someone said it was ecstasy, which caused a temporary "cure" or "miracle."

Weeks and weeks of discussion. Willie was wise. He realized that no matter what he wrote in a book about Lourdes, that book, even if a truthful account, would get him into trouble at once, with either the true believers or the true doubters. This was a place too close to civilization. Willie went searching for miracles in faraway places.

---

* Fere libenter homines id quod volunt credent.—*Comentarii de bello Gallico.*

Chapter 34

Angelica Balabanoff

The Duce frequently said that, along with Lincoln, all he was he owed to his mother. But there was a long period in his life, from the days he fled to Switzerland in the early 1900s to escape military duty to the time he was chief editor of the Socialist Party official newspaper, *Avanti!*, when he told everyone he owed everything to his comrade, Angelica Balabanoff.

Almost unknown now, forgotten except for a few chapters in books on Fascism and Mussolini, Dr. Angelica Balabanoff was one of the great radical leaders of the early decades of the twentieth century. Long before the ten days that shook the world also split the Marxist movement in two, she had been the friend and had worked with Liebknecht and Rosa Luxembourg in Germany as well as Jean Juarès in France, and in Swiss exile she was the co-worker of both Lenin and Trotsky. So important a leader was she that when the Cominform was established she was chosen to preside at its first congress.

In July 1902, when an Italian émigré worker arrested for

vagabondage in Lausanne was let out of jail, Dr. Balabanoff spotted him at one of her meetings. He was such a forlorn tramp that her heart was moved. She spoke to him and began to help him at once. She translated the ten points of the Communist Manifesto of 1848 for him. (He repaid her in a curious way: he incorporated seven of them in his fourteen-point Fascist program of 1919. In 1923, when the Duce threw me out of Italy, it was five years in exile on the Liparian Islands for any Italian who reprinted the two sets of points side by side, as I had.)

When I was in Bandol, in southern France, writing a book on Mussolini in 1931, I was told that Dr. Balabanoff, who had split with Lenin and Trotsky and returned to her first interpretation of Marxian socialism, was now living nearby. I wrote her about my book and she came to Bandol. She not only corrected my manuscript, but talked to me a full day and later contributed several pages of Mussolini's early history, for which I credited her in the text.

Although in 1902 he was unwashed, his clothes showing grains of the sand under the bridge where he had been sleeping, although he seemed to cringe, although his dark protruding eyes seemed stricken with fright, Dr. Balabanoff told me, there was something in his bulging jaw and bellicose manner that seemed paradoxical, and she could not resist taking an interest in him.

"Nobody can help me," Mussolini told her. "I am condemned to remain a wretched vagabond all my life." When she insisted, he said: "My father was a drunkard, and besides, I have a congenital disease for which I have to thank him. I can't work. I can't be militant. I will have to live as miserably as I am living."

"No, no," Dr. Balabanoff replied. "I'll see that something is done for you."

Mussolini never did name his disease, and Dr. Balabanoff in 1931 was conventional enough not to name it to me—the word "syphilis" for centuries was the most tabu word in all languages, and even advanced thinkers who sometimes used the forbidden four-letter words refrained from naming the disease.

The first thing she did, Dr. Balabanoff told me, was to translate Kautsky's pamphlet, "The Coming Revolution," for which Mussolini got the editor's price, fifty Swiss francs, good money in those days. It was the turning point in his life. About ten years later Mussolini, now a bellicose street orator, was so well known a journalist, thanks to this woman's help, that he was offered the chief editorship of the Italian Socialist Party's daily newspaper, *Avanti!* He agreed on one condition: "that Comrade Angelica work with me as assistant editor."

In the two years they had desks side by side as editors of the official organ of the Socialist Party, Mussolini frequently had fits of incredible physical fear. He was afraid of the dark, and the job took them through at least half the night. The future Duce begged Dr. Balabanoff to see him safely home, as they lived in the same street, and she took him to his door. "What am I afraid of?" he said to her repeating her question. "Myself. A dog. My own shadow."

He would not of course confide to other comrades what his disease was, but frequently he would burst into tears, complaining of the treatment he was undergoing because it meant a visit to a clinic every day of the year. Dr. Balabanoff then took Mussolini to a comrade doctor. The Wasserman test was positive.

From December 1912 to November 1914 they wrote editorials denouncing war preparations and then the war. Italy had been pledged to defend Austria but had remained neutral. Mussolini, Comrade Angelica said, frequently ridiculed the French and favored the Germans. But almost overnight his tone changed, he resigned from *Avanti!* and in Milan started his own newspaper, *Popolo d'Italia.* He was totally committed to the Franco-British side. "We could only suspect that some sort of an offer had been made him by the French," said Dr. Balabanoff.

In 1931 in Bandol she said: "I did not want to suspect that the man whom I taught socialism from his youth to this rise to power would or could betray our ideals. I never in all the years of our collaboration was blind to some of his inherent traits, his fundamental weaknesses, to his physical cowardice in personal encounters contrasted with his heroic gestures when surrounded by numbers; to his inability to resist temptation for personal power, to his unbridled egotism."

One subject remained: Mussolini's women. Many, perhaps most of the laudatory biographies of Il Duce, and almost all the long interviews written by young and passably beautiful lady journalists of the 1930s, and perhaps later, were written just this side of idolatry and after at least one wonderful amorous experience.

It is true, Dr. Balabanoff told me, that in addition to all these adventures Mussolini also had two women with whom he lived for years and with whom he fathered children. They came to the *Avanti!* office in 1915, when Italy entered the war and Mussolini was called to serve. One was Rachele Guidi, daughter of Papa Mussolini's mistress, and the family servant (whom he finally married after signing the Concordat with the Pope in 1929), and the other, Irene Desler, who came with her son and a birth certificate from Trento, which named him Benito Mussolini, Jr. Each castoff mistress, mother of one or more children, asked help in getting Mussolini's army pay.*

---

* The tragic story of Irene Desler, her internment as an enemy [Austrian] and Mussolini's final disposal of her by sending her to an insane asylum, a method antedating Stalin's disposal of intellectuals by more than a generation, is told briefly in *Sawdust Caesar*, pp. 60–64. When later I wrote to Dr. Balabanoff, mentioning the subject, she replied:

"I have seen Irene Desler and read her letters and documents, but neither Serrati (Mussolini's boyhood friend, now a Socialist Party leader) nor I thought it fair at that time (1915), despite Mussolini's betrayal of our paper and our cause, to take up her case. Mussolini was still claiming to be a Socialist and Fascism still did not exist."

Part IX

Return to the
U.S.A.

Chapter 35

∼∼∼∼∼∼∼∼

Paris: Marriage;
Honeymoon in Spain

I
t was the accepted custom in Montparnasse, rather than a
breach of social behavior in the Latin Quarter, for anyone having
an invitation to a party of any sort to drag along another person,
and so one day in 1929 I found myself at the apartment of a lady
journalist to whom the newspaper crowd was giving a farewell
(she had been recalled by the New York *World,* which was
replacing her with a man). There I met another non-invitee and
non-journalist in whom I immediately became interested.

Her name was Helen Larkin, and at the age of twenty-four,
she was in her third year at the Sorbonne, having graduated from
Washington University, in her home town, St. Louis, at the age
of sixteen. What was she studying at the Sorbonne? She said she
was taking biochemical physics, and next year, when she could
call herself a physicist, she intended to go to Moscow and offer
her services to the great Pavlov.

When I heard mention of Russia I became even more
interested, and of course took the opportunity to tell a stranger

of all the difficulties and terrors of life in Moscow, which I presumed had not changed since my expulsion six years earlier: the bad food, the rat- and bug-infested Savoy Hotel, where she would probably be quartered, and the many difficulties of ordinary daily life. I went on to attack the Soviet Communist dictators and the regime's denial of civil liberties to the masses, and Miss Larkin, who obviously was getting angrier and angrier, cut me short with the remark, "I don't think I ever want to see you again, Mr. Seldes."

Whether or not my 1929 encounter with Helen was a true case of "love at first sight" I cannot say, but our next meeting in 1932 was without a question "love at second sight."

The occasion was again a cocktail party. But this one was given by a Frenchman, and like most Europeans he was under the impression that every American could make cocktails. He was inviting a group of Americans, and would I please come and shake martinis. I would. But I did consult with the Select bartenders on the all-important matter of how much vermouth to add to how much gin, and how much ice to put in the shaker. I came early and was introduced to the Frenchman's lovely wife, who immediately told me she hailed from Salt Lake City and her maiden name was Young.

"Young? Salt Lake City?" I said.

"Yes," she replied, "I am one of Brigham Young's two hundred and twenty grandchildren."

Among the first guests to arrive was a writer I knew slightly, Dorothy Dudley, whose *Forgotten Frontier—Dreiser and the Land of the Free* is a great biography of a great writer. Miss Dudley had brought along the usual non-invitee, whom I remembered immediately as the Miss Larkin who never wanted to see me again in her lifetime. She actually seemed pleased when we shook hands, and did not get angry when I asked her what had become of her proposed Russian adventure. She told me she had, for reasons she did not explain, given up that idea and planned instead to stay on in Paris on the small allowance she got from her widowed mother. (Her father, she told me, had been one of the salaried chemists working for Procter & Gamble, in Cincinnati, Ohio, who had invented floating soap but had to spend years in changing the formula so they could package it. All he got when Ivory Soap came on the market and made billions of dollars was his weekly pay, but when he died, the company paid his widow his pension.)

I do not remember if I asked Helen to dinner the night of the party or for the next night, but when we met again and talked, we found that we really cared for each other. I told her I wanted to see her the next day also, and the next and the next.

And so, for three weeks or more, we were together every day. But unlike so many lovely American girls who came to Paris to have their fling, Helen never did invite me up to her apartment on the Rue de Froideveau, and, respecting her, I never suggested that she come up to my room at the Hotel Liberia.

Then one night, when she told me she had spent a summer or two on the Isle of Mallorca, had a sailboat there, and spoke passable Spanish, I said, "Let's get married and go to Spain on our honeymoon." We were married next day by the mayor of one of the Montparnasse arrondissements.

Spain was one of the only two countries which I had not visited for my newspaper. Switzerland, which is generally acknowledged as the most beautiful place in Europe, never had wars and uprisings, revolutionary strikes and other forms of violence and bloodshed which make up so much of the news, so no one was ever stationed there. I found Mallorca living up to all the advertising Helen gave it—we went back to it many times until the tourists overran it, bringing with them pickpockets and muggers. After a month's honeymoon, we went to the Peninsula, as the Mallorcans would say, and settled down for me to write my next book.

We chose Granada for the winter, staying first for a week or so at the parador San Francisco, which I believe is built right into the wall of the Alhambra, then moved to the Hotel Washington Irving, where I finally went to work. But one day a week for practically the entire five months we visited the Alhambra and found new wonders each time, or old wonders in which we saw new beauties. When I sent my brother, Gilbert, the book,

World Panorama, he wrote me a letter saying, "This is the only decent writing you've ever done—all the others are just journalism." But, of course, Gilbert was a highbrow. . . .

Shortly after taking office in 1933, President Roosevelt declared a "bank holiday," which stranded every American abroad. Our money, not only cash, but traveler's checks, letters of credit, even solid silver dollars were not accepted, and every shop and every restaurant was closed to us. The situation seemed desperate.

And then, for the first time, Helen and I learned that the Spaniards differed from other Europeans—and for that matter, Americans and all the people of all the countries in which we had lived. It so happened that on the morning of the "holiday" I went to Ramirez, the best tailor in Granada, to get two suits, one grey, and one brown flannel, for which I was paying thousands of pesetas—in American money. (It was great, being on the other side of inflation, as I was several times during my seventeen years in Europe. For quite a number of years I was quite a rich man. I could have, had I cared to exploit my host country, made a real dollar fortune buying almost anything. I could have bought a castle with land and a lake for $10,000, as the Hearst man, Karl von Wiegand did, pay quintillions of marks and sell it back in "hard" money a year or two later for a mere 440,000 Rentenmarks, pocketing exactly $100,000 in American dollars' profit on the $10,000 investment, but all I did was live well.)

Said Mr. Ramirez: "I'm sorry, I can't accept your American money, but here are the two suits. Take them home and wear them in good health. America is a great country and soon enough its money will be good again, and then you can send me a check or a money order."

That same day the manager of the Washington Irving called us to his office. Helen and I thought we were going to be put out on the street, but what he said was, "I know that you have been living here about five months and I know you have planned to stay on one month more. Feel free to do so. But you will have to have all your meals here and all your drinks in our bar because no other place will accept your dollars. And then, in a few months or a year, America will recover, its money will be good again, and you can send me a check. Meanwhile don't worry about living here."

I cannot imagine a tailor or a hotelkeeper in the United States or any European country doing what the Spaniards did, and these are but two illustrations of the kindnesses we received in our last month of our Spanish visit in 1933, and also in twelve or thirteen winters when we owned a summer house in Vermont and wintered in Spain.

I do wonder, however, whether the manager of the Spanish steamship line would have given Helen and me two tickets back to America on the chance we were honest and would some day remit several hundred dollars. Fortunately, I had paid for them in advance, and we sailed on the *Marquis de Camillas* for New York in early spring, 1933.

We were home again! Our money was good, and we could pay for a hotel room, go to a restaurant—even buy a newspaper. But this great feeling of relief did not last long. When all the banks of the United States of America were reopened for business, there was one exception, and that was the Harriman National of New York, in which I not only had every cent I owned but also a share of stock which Mr. Harriman had persuaded me to buy many years earlier at a price of $1,800 or so.

Moreover, Little, Brown & Company of Boston now informed me that the salesmen who had taken the six leading books on their list from city to city had not been able to sell one copy during the bank holiday, and so there was not one cent in royalties due me. We were indeed desperate. But thanks to help from my brother and my cousin, Bill Randorf, we managed to survive.

Translation from the cultural—or pseudocultural—centers of Europe to an America in which I had not lived for seventeen years, and had visited only for my "re-Americanization" by Colonel McCormick in Chicago, also frightened me at first, but here again I was in luck.

Chapter 36

*Encounters With
Theodore Dreiser*

That chance meeting with Dorothy Dudley in Paris had brought me Helen and a quarrel-free marriage (which lasted for forty-seven years); and here in New York Miss Dudley invited us to her dinners and parties at which she introduced us to the literary world of the metropolis, and at which Dreiser was always the main attraction.

There was one evening, more than forty years ago, which I cannot forget: it was the dinner at which Dorothy's chief guest was the leader of the Russian Mensheviks, the man who led the March 1917 uprising which drove the Tsar and his family into exile and tried to establish a liberal, socialist republic in Russia, Alexander Kerensky. He had been overthrown by the Bolsheviks under Trotsky, forced to flee his beloved country, and was so bitter about Bolshevism that he refused to spend so much as a minute in the company of a Russian Communist. (It was for this reason that Miss Dudley was obliged to ask each of her guests, before she allowed him or her to enter her apartment, whether or not he or she had any sympathy for the regime now in power in Russia. All of us who said "No" were welcome.)

Dinner over, the guests clustered around the two notables, eager for the great confrontation. The topic of the times was: what is going to happen next in Soviet Russia? Kerensky would predict. Dreiser would predict the opposite. Dreiser would make a flat statement. Kerensky would deny it.

"Because," Kerensky would say, "ze Roshin peepel eez deefrent."

"Nonsense," Dreiser would reply, "there are no differences between people. All people are fundamentally the same."

Kerensky: "But you do not understand ze Roshin soul . . . "

Dreiser: "There is no such thing as soul. There are no Russian souls, there are no American souls. We all, Russians, Americans, all people, are compounded of certain chemicals and made by physical processes . . . "

Kerensky: "Ze Roshin soul eez meestical . . . "

"Souls!" shouted Dreiser, "Theological myths! The genes and the chromosomes influence intelligence, aggression, all human sensibilities. Biologically we are not different."

It was obvious to us neutrals that Kerensky did not understand a word of Dreiser's statement.

Kerensky: "Ze Roshin peepel . . . "

Dreiser: "The Russians, like all human beings, are governed by the same elements. We have the same genes, the same number of chromosomes, molecules, atoms, electrons, protons. The Russian people will be ruled by those who know and understand this, and they will do just what other people will do. The same genes and chromosomes make Russian intelligence, Russian aggression, all Russian actions, just as they make American—or any other people."

"No, no, no," cried the exasperated Kerensky. "We Roshins are not like other peepel. We are deefrent . . . "

"Nonsense," said Theodore Dreiser in conclusion.

Kerensky did not hear Dreiser. Dreiser did not hear Kerensky. Each had his one fixed idea, each repeated it, sometimes varying the words, the manner, the tone, but never the one and only idea—the different Russian soul, the same genes and chromosomes making all peoples, races, ethnic groups, the same, now and forever. . . .

When my wife and I returned from reporting the war in Spain, late in 1937, it seemed as if the whole American literary world wanted to hear about the conflict between the Republic and the Fascist Internationale. Dreiser was interested in only one subject; he insisted on asking us about the destruction of churches, if the Church itself in Spain would be destroyed.

The press of the whole world had been overflowing with sensational news: in Barcelona every church had been set on fire, in the countryside peasants had killed priests; and atrocities were blamed on the Republicans, who were called "reds." I told Dreiser the facts: in the first week of the war, when the fascist generals had committed treason and attacked their own government, anarchists, of whom there were about a million in Catalonia, ran wild in the cities, attacking churches, as had been done in 1931, when the monarchy was overthrown, and a century before. "Moreover," I insisted, "all this destruction, all violence, committed by mobs, led by anarchists, was under control within a week—the Republic never burned a church, or shot a priest."

To my surprise Dreiser was displeased. He was disappointed.

"I would have given half my life to have been there then," he said and his eyes glowed. "I would have been one of the mob. I would have set fire to every church. I would have danced in the streets while the churches burned."

Anyone who had read a Dreiser biography or talked to him knew he was born and brought up in a strict religious household, his father was a bigot, and Theodore had publicly declared he hated his father, and that his whole career had been a rebellion against his parochial childhood. But what Dreiser said next shocked all who heard him.

"All my life," he said, "I have always wanted to get a Cardinal. Of course this was an idle thought in America. But last year in Spain I might have got one—I could at least have got a monsignor."

Of the occasional meetings with Dreiser from 1933 on, the foregoing are the only ones of any significance I remember. However, from November 1940, about six months after I began publishing *In fact,* he became an enthusiastic contributor, a supporter and an adviser.

His first contribution was an original item he had written for the American Newspaper Publishers Association (ANPA), which had asked hundreds of leading citizens, noteworthy persons, to help celebrate Newspaper Week—in a somewhat more civilized manner than Cheese Week and Apple Week and other great national achievements. The laudatory statements, the ANPA announced, would be printed in *Editor & Publisher.*

Dreiser wrote four paragraphs. Either the ANPA or *Editor & Publisher,* or both, suppressed Dreiser.

He told me he was stunned by the "unmitigated gall" of the owners of the American newspaper press who had written him boasting that the U.S. was one of the few countries in the world with an uncensored press. And now he was censored again. He told me to emphasize this fact when I printed his rejected (free) contribution. Dreiser told me that the American press had either lied about him or resorted to silence—which to a writer of books means total censorship. His masterpiece, *Sister Carrie,* even today considered one of the greatest works of fiction ever written by an American, was met with silence by the literary elite—probably at the order of the owners or their publishers.

When I opened the columns of my newsweekly to him, Dreiser wrote some very radical views. For example, the item the ANPA and *Editor & Publisher* suppressed, and I published, declared that in all labor troubles, "the press invariably sprang into action in behalf of capital, and violently against labor." He accused the big corporations, the main advertisers, of controlling the newspapers of our country—as well as, incidentally, the radio, the politicians, the majority of judges, the state legislatures, both houses of Congress, the mayors, police, chambers of commerce, banks, clergy of all denominations—practically every person and every group in power.

Two years later Dreiser suggested that coincident with Free Press Week I help him organize "Kept Press Week," with the support of several liberal weeklies, the labor press, a few honest journalists and a few honest newspapers. I agreed. We wrote and talked to writers, editors and publishers, but unfortunately neither Dreiser nor I got enough favorable responses to engage in this venture.

Dreiser was without doubt the most noted literary man to contribute to *In fact.* Although he never received the Nobel Prize, he was in the opinion of many writers in all parts of the world the most worthy of it of all Americans. Among those who thought so was Sinclair Lewis, and this was not just a gracious pose, as several New York columnists hinted; when I got to know Lewis better, he showed me that every year from 1931 on when the committee awarding the prize asked holders of it to send in suggestions, he nominated Dreiser. Lewis said frequently that Dreiser was America's greatest writer; he had done more than any other to liberate American writing from reaction, insincerity and trashiness. The fact that he was not a stylist—he was, as many critics did not hesitate to say, "a very sloppy writer"—should not have mattered, Mr. Lewis thought; Dreiser was a great writer despite every drawback. (In 1933 there was no award for literature. That was the year Lewis was angriest with the judges. There was no award in 1943, but by then Lewis and I no longer saw each other. When Dreiser died the critics generally agreed that it was he, not Lewis, who had dominated the twentieth century in American letters.)

It has always seemed significant to me that three of the writers generally accepted as giants of the age—Dreiser, Lewis and Hemingway—were all professional newspaper men. I do not mean by this term young men who went into newspaper work to use it as a steppingstone toward other work, such as novel writing. Each had gotten jobs as reporters with the intention of making journalism his profession—and each fortunately quit before printer's ink corroded his blood.

Chapter 37

Sinclair Lewis in Vermont

In 1933 my wife and I, who had been guests of the Paul Osborns in Brattleboro, Vermont, decided to stay on that summer at a nearby boardinghouse. One day Lewis and his wife, Dorothy Thompson, driving home to Barnard, Vermont, from New York City, stopped by and urged Helen and me to buy a house in their neighborhood. Lewis said, "You'll be near the best college library [Baker, at Dartmouth] and the best hospital in New England [Mary Hitchcock Memorial Hospital and Hitchcock Clinic, Hanover, New Hampshire]."

I replied, "That's great, except for the fact Helen and I haven't got any money."

"But I have too much," Red replied, and persuaded us to come with him to Woodstock.

We liked the first little house the real estate agent showed us: it was built in 1783, the last year of the Revolutionary War, and had wooden pins, not nails, holding it together. It had a gravity water supply. It had no heating except fireplaces, no electric light, no telephone within miles. It did have 125 beautiful acres, and a view of the entire Green Mountain range. The price was $4,500.

Mr. Lewis took out a checkbook and made out a check to me for two thousand dollars. He then told the agent he would guarantee the mortgage—which was also two thousand dollars. Helen and I, with help from Gilbert, raised five hundred dollars, and later that summer we moved in, bought an automobile, which Helen knew how to drive, and registered as voters.

Of all the great writers I have known in my seven European and American working decades, only one became a real friend. Hemingway chose to exhibit his dislike of my brother by attacking me; Theodore Dreiser was too difficult a person for anyone but adoring women to call more than an acquaintance; but of the great men of the literature of our time Sinclair Lewis was the one easy to become friendly with; and when my wife and I were his neighbors in Vermont we became good friends even before we had the chance, not once but several times, to save him from delirium tremens, perhaps even to save his life. He became so good a friend he could in sober as well as alcoholic moments confess the most intimate details of his life and still remain a friend.

I met him first in Paris in the 1920s with his friend and guide, Ramon Guthrie, when they returned from a walking trip in the Dordogne, the most beautiful part of France, totally unknown to tourists; and again in 1927, when Dorothy Thompson persuaded him to go with her in her hired airplane to Vienna— where I had had a world scoop on a revolutionary uprising.

While Dorothy was still winding up the affairs of the Ledger Syndicate in Berlin and Vienna, Red and I met frequently in Paris at the Select. One night Red wrote five words on the back of an envelope and told me to read them, letter by letter:

FUNEX
SVFX
FUNEM
SVFM
MNX

• • •

When I said I could not understand it, Red said, "This is a slightly anti-Semitic joke. You have to read it aloud with a ghetto Jewish accent. This man is saying to the waitress, 'Eff you any eggx?' and she replies 'Ess, ve eff eggx' and he asks, 'Eff you any 'am?' and when she says, 'Ess ve eff 'am,' he orders, 'Am and eggx.' "

Lewis, all the years I knew him, loved to act out his stories, testing some for future publication, such as Lowell Schmaltz's monologue for "The Man Who Knew Coolidge," or the following for purely entertainment.

It concerns a newly rich, very Babbitt-type American who had laid in a great, expensive, wine cellar, and his best friend who drank and also criticized every bottle. One day the newly rich American says, I hear the Monsieur DuBois is in town, he is a great connoisseur, so let's invite him to try some of my best vintages.

At some length, for Lewis had a great imagination and could make repetition interesting, the story goes through a dozen famous châteaux and a dozen famous years. Eventually the American opens a bottle of his prize Château Lafite, 1922. A good year, says M. DuBois, but 1921 would have cost you even less, and is a more noble wine. Montrachet 1924. You cannot go wrong on Montrachet of any year. But if I had my choice, said Mr. DuBois, I would have bought 1925. It is a wine of great authority. And so it went for a long time.

Eventually the rich American got very angry. So he went into another part of his cellar, found an old bottle which had contained Château d'Yquem, a famous white wine, and urinated in it. He then came back, pretended to pull the cork, found a new glass for the Frenchman.

Now Lewis acted Mr. DuBois. He held the glass under his nose, swirled it slightly, and took a little sip.

Then, Red's eyes lighting up and raising a glass that stood before him on the café table, he quoted the Frenchman ecstatically saying, "*Mon Dieu*, this isn't wine. This is piss!"—and drinking it all down to the last drop.

• • •

One day Red took me to a Right Bank restaurant. At a table nearby were two American women, obvious tourists and female Babbitts. Their talk was so banal that I said to Lewis, you couldn't do better. I began writing down the dialogue on the large menu card. Red said, "Don't waste your time. I'll do it word for word for you when we get back to the Select." And he did.

It was at this lunch that he also said:

"Mencken and I are two of the best one-hundred-percent Americans alive. We are accused of running down America, writing about nothing but her faults. We both criticize America, true, but it is because we want perfection. Others who boast they are one-hundred-percent American close their eyes and walk in dirt. We go with open eyes, and we clean out the dirt. If Mencken and I didn't love America so much, we would not criticize what is wrong with her."

There was never any small talk at the Lewis table in Vermont. Sometimes there was an obvious subject—doctors for *Arrowsmith,* preachers for *Elmer Gantry,* Naziism and Fascism for *It Can't Happen Here.* But a recurring topic over many years was the great American labor novel that was to be the Lewis masterpiece. It haunted him, it was discussed between each successful book, and labor writers were at Lewis's table year after year. He probably accumulated filing cases of notes, but he never wrote the book. Perhaps it was because he had not come from a working-class family.

Sometimes, when not trying out parts of his work in progress, Lewis would talk about anything at all—from religion to his relations with his first wife. He once said, "God is *lachryma Christi*"—or Christ's tears of doubt—and once he said something that so impressed me I wrote it down immediately: "The Christian Church today is either an apology for no God at all or for God's mistakes."

Of his first wife he made a sort of fiction character; he may have been trying out the stories for a future novel about her. I always had a feeling Lewis never wasted words. He said Gracie came from a simple background, and later when he began making money and they were getting ahead, she had delusions of grandeur. He illustrated his point with this story: One of her high school classmates was in the hospital for an appendectomy. "Gracie called on her and asked the usual question. 'It was nothing,' the classmate replied, 'I'll be out in no time.' Gracie then said, 'I know. It's your healthy American peasant blood.' "

On another occasion Gracie was very critical of everything American. One of her listeners asked, "But you were born in America, weren't you?" "Oh, yes," Gracie replied, "but I was *conceived* in Vienna."

Much talk about fellow writers. And experiences in the hinterland as a lecturer. One story ends: "And then the chairman introduced me as Upton Sinclair."

"I love Upton," said Lewis once, "but look what he says about me in *Money Writes.* He says I am one of those writers spoiled by success, by big money. He says, 'Sinclair Lewis has a million dollars.' I give you my word, George, I haven't more than $600,000 and he calls me a millionaire." The usual Lewisian sense of humor was not present.

When Red's marriage to Dorothy began to go bad, Red took the conventional road to alcohol. In his half-drunken times he would say cruel things about Dorothy, such as, "Tell me, George, why did I have to marry a *senator?*" And on one of our trips to Barnard in reply to frantic telephone calls from the Viennese couple who kept house for the Lewises—it was mid-April 1936—Red said, after my wife had fed him black coffee and partly sobered him, "George, you don't know anyone around here who is looking for a job as a mistress—at least a part-time mistress—do you?"

Strangely enough neither Sinclair Lewis nor Dorothy's first husband, whom I also knew—he was a Viennese poet whom my brother had published in America—ever suspected that the failure of their marriages was due to Dorothy's being bisexual, and at times, lasting years, wholly lesbian, as her recent biographer has disclosed. Red thought she was a senator; her first husband told me one day that Dorothy had made his life unbearable by "dominating me—as a man would his employees."

Nevertheless, Sinclair Lewis owes several books to Dorothy, most notably *It Can't Happen Here,* written in 1934 and published the next year. She inspired the book, gave him the story of Nazi-Fascist dictatorships in Europe as she had experienced them, and invited her colleagues to Barnard to help Lewis.

As was his habit of pumping everyone for information, he especially pumped me on this subject. I had to relate every meeting with Mussolini, every glimpse of him, every day I could remember of the year and more in Rome under Fascism. He pumped day and night, lunch and dinner, cocktail hour and auto trips. In payment to several who helped him on this book he lists us on page 264 as journalists imprisoned by the American fascist dictator, "Buzz" Windrip.

It was a brave thing for Lewis to take on Fascism at that time. The Un-American Activities Committee witch-hunts were directed always against the left, General Butler had testified to a fascist plot to seize Washington and the news had been suppressed. Lewis has someone say to his crusading Vermont editor: "Why are you afraid of the word Fascism, Doremus? Just a word—just a word! And it might not be so bad . . . not so worse to have a real Strongman, like Hitler or Mussolini—Napoleon or Bismarck in the good old days—and have 'em really *run* the country and make it efficient and prosperous again." No one in the 1930s dared attack American fascism. (And few dare, even now.)

There was a time when the two most influential women in America were Eleanor Roosevelt and Dorothy Thompson; there was a time when Dorothy Thompson was being talked about as the right person to make the first woman's bid for the Presidency of the United States.

All the years we had been colleagues and rivals in Europe we had not become friends. We almost became friends in Vermont. But it did not last long that way because I published a story she had told not only me but everyone, every group of dinner guests every week for perhaps years, so that it was known not only in Vermont but in New York and throughout the journalistic world. Dorothy told this story to illustrate corruption in American politics, and I printed it in *In fact*.

In the early 1930s, but after Roosevelt was already implementing the New Deal and making millions of friends among people and thousands of enemies among the powerful and special interests, Dorothy happened to be crossing the Atlantic, Le Havre to New York, and happened to meet Harry F. Sinclair of Teapot Dome fame and infamy, on the boat. He invited her to sit at his table and meet his friends, the most notable of whom was Elisha Walker, a Giannini banker; the others were industrialists or corporation heads. Continued Dorothy:

"One day at lunch Sinclair remarked that the big business interests bought the Presidency and controlled American politics no matter which party, Republican or Democratic, won.

"'What about FDR?' I asked.

"'A slight error there,' replied Sinclair. 'Of course we had our money up on him as well as the opposition, and we expected him to make those talks about economic royalists, money changers, and all that bunk, but we did not expect him to take action.'

"I asked Sinclair what his group was planning to do next.

"'I do not think we can defeat him [i.e., FDR in 1936],' he replied, 'but my friends do. It will take more than five million dollars but they say they will raise it easily. Even if it takes twenty million dollars. Make no mistake about it, we buy and control our Presidents. And by we I mean the five men seated here, right here at this table, and our friends back home. We make mistakes sometimes, but usually we win no matter which party wins.'"

Having heard Dorothy tell this story to hundreds and over the years, I thought it a public statement and so published it. There were many other stories I did not publish. We were always talking politics at the Lewis home. In the year when the main subject was Fascism, Dorothy would say, "If I had to choose between Communism and Fascism, if there were no democratic choice, I would *prefer* the lesser evil, Communism, but I would *choose* Fascism." (She pronounced the word "facism.") "I hate it but I would have to choose it, because I have a son, I have a family, I have a home, and I am afraid everything would be lost under Communism. I would want Fascism only as long as I lived and brought up my son."

As Dorothy became more and more famous and Red became more and more unhappy in his marriage and took to drinking more and more, our friendship with Red increased. I had never been friendly with Dorothy—not even in the journalistic colleague sense. Although Helen and I did return to Vermont after our coverage of the Spanish War (1936–1939), I never saw Dorothy again.

Chapter 38

Woodward, Boyd, H. G. Wells Again

By the time Sinclair Lewis was awarded the Nobel Prize in 1930, he had already made the words "Babbitt" and "Babbittry" part of the English language. To save time and explanation many people now refer to a certain type of hypocrite-preacher as an Elmer Gantry. The phrase "it can't happen here" is also current after fifty years.

And yet, today, when Laurance Rockefeller in his Woodstock Inn advertising lists the historic events of our Vermont neighborhood, he mentions Woodstock as the birthplace of the Morgan horse and forgets the years Sinclair Lewis made this part of New England one of the cultural and literary centers of America.

Among those who came as guests and then rented homes for the summers in the Lewis neighborhood were William E. Woodward and his wife, Helen Woodward, who wrote *It's an Art,* a debunking of the advertising profession. William was the one and only begetter of the word "debunking," a variation of "bunk," which was the title of a Woodward novel. Both words derived from Buncombe County. Woodward's debunking historical works were *George Washington: Image and Man, Meet General Grant,* and *A New American History.* Woodward may also be called one of the founding fathers of revisionist history, preceding and perhaps inspiring his friends Charles and Mary Beard's *The Rise of American Civilization* (1937) and *Basic History of the United States* (1944). In these six books many great truths of American history replace the myths, bunk and falsehoods which, unfortunately are still being taught in many public schools and some colleges.

A great event of one of the summers in which Vermont was a cultural center was the cocktail party and dinner given by the Woodwards to celebrate Bill's being commissioned by the Rosenwald family of Chicago, and paid an advance royalty of $25,000 (no mean sum in the 1930s), to write a history of the great mail order house, Sears, Roebuck and Company, which the Rosenwalds had owned for decades.

Woodward went to Chicago and came back with a fascinating story on which he worked all one summer in Vermont and probably many seasons in New York. Among the amusing or amazing stories Bill told us were the following:

Mr. Richard Warren Sears and Mr. Alvah Curtis Roebuck had operated one of the greatest swindles in the world when they started their company. For example: they had advertised "An engraving of the first President, George Washington, made by the U.S. government, and only $1." This was a genuine government-made engraving of Washington—the two-cent postage stamp. The advertisement had not been false; the persons who threatened to sue had no case.

"A houseful of bijou furniture: living room, kitchen, three bedrooms, bathroom, lamps, pictures, all for $25." Unbelievable. But thousands of persons answered the ad and each of these thousands got a houseful of miniatures—"bijou" furniture: look the word up in the dictionary.

And so it went.

Then came the experience that brought Mr. Rosenwald into the company and finally made him its owner. Mr. Sears and

Mr. Roebuck had advertised a "high-grade all-wool three-piece gent's suit—coat, vest and pants—only $3."

They had at the time about a thousand miscellaneous suits in their warehouse, some twenty years old, all misfits, torn, stained, almost worthless, and this was one way to get rid of them.

But the response overwhelmed them: ten thousand persons each sent in three dollars for a suit.

Mr. Sears and Mr. Roebuck were desperate: they went to every manufacturer in Chicago and bought up all the junk they found, useless jackets, leftover vests, all sorts of sizes and colors of pants including overalls; and one of the manufacturers they dealt with was Julius Rosenwald. The price was low, but he got rid of years' worth of junk. He was intrigued by the deal. Mr. Sears and Mr. Roebuck later assured Mr. Rosenwald that they had filled every order: they did not send matching clothes, they had the clerks put one jacket, one vest, one pair of pants, no matter what size or color, no matter what was ordered, into a package, and ten thousand were sent out.

Surely, Mr. Rosenwald suggested, the majority sent the stuff back, protested, demanded their money. Not at all, replied the two enterprising merchants, "Ninety percent of the people kept their three-dollar suits."

Mr. Rosenwald, according to Woodward's account, then said to himself, if a couple of crooks can make a lot of money in a crooked way, what could an honest man do in this newfangled mail order merchandising?

He made them a proposition: he would take over the coat and suit business, send out good wares at a fair price and split the profits. Sears and Roebuck paid Mr. Rosenwald in stock.

Eventually he bought out Sears and Roebuck.

Why was Woodward's manuscript suppressed? Sears and Roebuck were dead long ago, but the present owners didn't think this sort of history would do them any good.

Thomas Boyd, sergeant, 6th Marines, fought at Belleau Wood and at Château-Thierry, and in 1923 wrote a novel,

Through the Wheat, which several critics said was one of the three great war books, the equal of *Three Soldiers* by John Dos Passos and *The Enormous Room* by e. e. cummings.

When Tom came to join the summer colony of writers that Sinclair Lewis had attracted, he devoted all his time to researching the career of John Fitch, the ancestor of his wife, Ruth Fitch. The statement that Robert Fulton invented the steamboat, although it also appears in the *Britannica* (11th edition) is not true. John Fitch did. Tom wrote *Poor John Fitch,* and although it got excellent reviews, history was not changed—and probably cannot ever be changed.

The Boyds apparently stayed in the Woodstock neighborhood long enough to become Vermont voters. I do not remember whether or not U.S. Marine Sergeant Boyd registered as a Communist or independent, but I do remember that U.S. Marine Sergeant Boyd filed for the office of governor of Vermont in the 1934 election on the Communist Party ticket.

When the votes in the Woodstock district were counted that November, Tom Boyd had a total of four. Everyone suspected that he had voted for himself and had his wife, the descendant of John Fitch, vote for him also. But to this very day the town and county still ask, who were the other two persons in this town, among the richest and most aristocratic in America, who could have cast a Communist ballot? We never did find out.

H. G. Wells Again

Another notable person I also encountered in the mid-1930s at the Lewises' house or as a dinner guest was H. G. Wells, whom I had visited once in Grasse, in southern France, when I was living at the Colombe d'Or. In 1931 I was writing an exposé of the international armaments makers, which I proposed to call *Merchants of Death*—this title was vetoed by Harpers—and needed permission to quote Mr. Wells. I wrote him. He invited me to visit him. Friends, an artist and his novelist wife, drove me over.

We were introduced to the beautiful Levantine, Odette Keun, with whom Wells was then living. We thought it conventional un-Wellsian sentimentality when we read, cut into the stone mantel of his fireplace, the words "TWO LOVERS BUILT THIS HOUSE." Then, later in the day, Odette took my friend, the novelist Virginia Davis, to see the upstairs rooms, and there was another fireplace, and again in the stone there were the words "TWO LOVERS BUILT THIS HOUSE." Virginia did not get to see the third-floor guest rooms, but we suspected a third fireplace.

What surprised me most, the moment I came to the Lewises' several years later, was Mr. H. G. Wells's remembering not only me but also my name. As we shook hands he pulled me aside and whispered:

"Not a word about Odette, Seldes. You understand."

I did not utter a word. Obviously Mr. Wells had changed mistresses.

After a grand lunch we surrounded Wells, listening to every word he had to say on history, politics, world affairs. Kyle Crichton, an editor of *Collier's*, who moonlighted as Robert Forsythe of the *New Masses*, asked the sharpest questions. This annoyed Mr. Wells.

"The trouble with you Americans," he said, pausing, "is that you are still too much under the influence of that second-rate—shall I say third-rate—mind, Karl Marx."

This declaration from on high blew up a storm. Although Kyle Crichton was the only true Marxist in the group of ten or twelve, almost everyone present had taken some interest in some form of Marxism, even to being Marxist anti-Communists, and most were sympathetic to some form of socialism. Everyone seemed to shout a question at Wells at the same time.

He then expounded his world philosophy for an hour or so—he had already written books on the subject and would write more. His great idea was to replace capitalism, Communism, and socialism with his own ideology, which he called Cosmopolitanism. He gave us a long detailed outline of Cosmopolitanism. It included cooperatives, a great Cooperative Commonwealth, and a score of well-known Marxist socialistic ideas. But it had a new name; Mr. Wells's.

Part X

~~~~~~~~~~~~~~~~

The Spanish War–and After

We can at least refuse to join in the plan to suppress, distort and mutilate the history of those days. . . . History is the torch that is meant to illuminate the past, to guard us against repetition of our mistakes in those days. We cannot join in the rewriting of history to make it conform to our comfort and our convenience. . . .

Claude Bowers, *My Mission to Madrid*

Chapter 39

"Spain Broke the Heart of the World"

Every civilized democratic nation in the world except one—Mexico—either turned against a fellow democracy, the Republic of Spain, or did nothing. Every intelligent person in the world who knew what was happening—with the exception of a few individual pro-Nazis or pro-Fascists in the United States, Britain, France and other countries—favored the Spanish Republic.

Nevertheless the British Foreign Office proposal of "neutrality" was accepted almost universally. It permitted no food or medicine or armies, navies, tank corps or aviation squadrons to be sent to Spain to aid the Republic, while Hitler and Mussolini shipped in armies and tank corps and air squadrons, and Portugal crossed the frontier with another army in support of Franco. (This also was news suppressed throughout the world—I learned about it years later at a solemn requiem mass in Lisbon for nine thousand Portuguese soldiers killed aiding the fascists.) The Russians flew in a few aviators, sent a few officers, and even a few doctors, a total of perhaps five hundred to seven hundred men—and later Stalin betrayed the Republic, and this news again was either suppressed or falsified.

Today historians speculate on what would have happened if the neutrality pact had been honestly enforced, Hitler and Mussolini had kept out of Spain, or the democracies had supported the Spanish democracy. Everyone agrees World War II would have been postponed, most likely prevented. Without one exception every correspondent in Madrid informed the world that Hitler and Mussolini were trying out infantry, tanks, airplanes and other weapons for an imminent world war, but no one listened. In 1939 Hitler was able to review Goering's Condor Legion of fifty thousand men, all of whom had had combat experience in Spain and were ready to fly against Czechoslovakia, France and England.

"Spain broke the heart of the world," wrote Ruth McKenney from the left, and old rightist curmudgeon Malcolm Muggeridge admitted that the younger generation saw the Spanish War as "the last occasion on which people were confronted with a clear choice between good and evil." Camus wrote, "The tragedy of Spain remains to haunt the conscience of mankind," and again, "It was in Spain that man learned that one can be right and yet be beaten, that force can vanquish spirit, that there are times when courage is not its own recompense." Hemingway predicted in 1939, the year the Fascist International triumphed, that "Spain will rise again as they have always risen before tyranny." (After thirty-nine years of fascism and stagnation Franco died in November 1975 and was totally forgotten almost that very day. In the election that followed more than seventy-two percent of the people—despite fascist indoctrination the execution by Franco of at least ten thousand Republicans each year of his first ten years of rule, and eight new death penalty laws, one for the execution of every union labor organizer or leader of a strike—voted for democracy.)

How was it possible, given a free press in the free nations such as the United States, Britain and France, and a pro-democratic people in at least half the world, that one small free and democratic country, the Spanish Republic, could be abandoned by its alleged friends and destroyed by its fascist enemies? One answer, the one that interests me especially, is that the free press of the world was free to publish the greatest series of falsehoods in modern history—or to remain silent when it feared the truth might offend a great Church or lose it a lot of department store advertising.

The press lords of this era still dominated the United States. Public opinion was still being made by them. Hearst Sr., who once had made his $400,000-a-year deal with Hitler, now gave orders that the Spanish Republic was to be denounced editorially and always referred to as "reds" whereas the traitor generals and their forces, supplied by Mussolini and Hitler, were to be called "Nationalists." When I challenged Kent Cooper on a violation of Associated Press regulations by Hearst, he told this press lord to stop altering AP news. But when Webb Miller got an interview with Franco in which Franco said he would establish a corporate state on the German and Italian plan, press lord Roy Howard of the United Press altered the Caudillo's words. Press lords McCormick of the *Chicago Tribune* and Patterson of the New York *Daily News* decided it would not do to save Spain from Fascism because the result would be another "red," or Communist, victory, which was worse. No press lord in America would believe the war correspondents who were in Madrid and who reported there was not one red or Russian soldier there—only a few hundred men, aviators, tank crews and doctors, but not one infantry soldier.

There was only one publisher in America who had a "chain" of papers and who was a liberal: J. David Stern of the New York *Post,* Philadelphia *Record,* Camden *Courier* and Camden *Post.* He fought Nazi fascism and therefore supported the Spanish Republic in July 1936. I had talked to him several times in previous years, and once, when O. K. Bovard, editor of the nation's best and most powerful liberal daily, the St. Louis *Post-Dispatch,* was visiting me in New York, I telephoned Stern. He came to my apartment, and we spent the whole night in an angry dispute over freedom of the press. As in all my previous battles with Stern over the silent and atrophied code of ethics of the profession, and the hope of a free press in the United States, Stern won this battle with Bovard and me as he won all others, with just this simple statement: "What do you want me to do, take a quixotic stand, print the truth about everything including bad medicine, impure food and crooked stock market offerings, and lose all my advertising contracts and go out of business—or make compromises with all the evil elements and continue to publish the best liberal newspaper possible under these compromising circumstances?"

Mr. Stern compromised. He had to. He remained in business, and his newspapers were among the best published in the East.

Despite perversion and falsehood of the news in most of the daily papers in America about the Spanish War, hundreds of persons, scores of journalists, scores of writers came to Barcelona, Valencia and Madrid, eager to help the Republic. From the beginning of the war it had the support of only the few liberal (honest) weeklies which, unfortunately, had small circulations and therefore no mass impact. Near the end of 1936 I asked Mr. Stern to send me to Madrid. He agreed to publish the reports my wife and I would send, but he offered no money to pay our way over. Nevertheless, one of the bravest episodes in American journalism of that decade was the publication by J. David Stern in his four daily newspapers of our twenty-four reports from Loyalist Spain, at a time other press lords were falsifying the news, publishing horrible stories of atrocities on the Loyalist side, suppressing the eyewitness accounts of officially ordered atrocities by the German Nazis, the Moors, Franco's Foreign Legion—everyone on Franco's side except his Italian troops.

My wife, Helen, and I interviewed captured Italian infantrymen and reported whole divisions present sent by Mussolini—

an obvious fact the Fascists denied; we described the anarchist excesses of July 1936 but stated none was ever committed by the Republic, whereas the Nazi German air services had destroyed Guernica and killed two thousand in one square block in Barcelona, a Goering experiment for the next war; we also named priests on the Loyalist side whom we had interviewed and gave the name of the Cardinal (Vidal y Barraquer) who supported the Republic.

Our series ran for months in Stern's four papers in three cities. During that time Cardinal Daugherty in Philadelphia demanded of Stern that he stop it, but he refused. The Cardinal then issued a pastoral letter, which was read at mass in every church in Philadelphia and Camden, calling for a boycott of the Stern papers; it was also published in the official diocesan organ, *Catholic Standard and Times.*

Stern took a poll of Catholic readers and found that the majority supported the Spanish Loyalists and refused to obey the Cardinal's boycott order. The Gallup Poll at this time showed only thirty-eight percent of America's twenty-two million Catholics favoring the Franco fascist side.

Having failed with his pastoral letter, the Philadelphia Cardinal went to work on the big advertisers, department store owners, Protestant, Catholic and Jewish, all of whom were immediately intimidated by the word "boycott"; they in turn frightened and intimidated Mr. Stern.

Mr. Stern came to Canossa. On August 20, 1937 (when, incidentally, our most important reports had already been published), he sent a letter of humble apology to Cardinal Daugherty and enclosed an editorial he was publishing "denouncing the Spanish government's action against the Catholic Church," adding he hoped "it would offset any unfriendly impression created by a previous editorial." In conclusion, figuratively down on his knees as Henry IV before Pope Gregory VII, the owner of the only liberal newspaper chain in America said to the Cardinal: "I would very much appreciate your advice as to what I should or should not do in the matter."

The Cardinal accepted, graciously.

I never spoke to J. David Stern again.

The Spanish government was red-baited to death.*

---

* On June 28, 1939, James Benet and Bruce Bliven, Jr., published their report, "Who Lied About Spain?" in *The New Republic,* naming seven persons and three publications in the following order:
1. William Carney of *The New York Times.*
2. *The Brooklyn Tablet,* diocesan weekly.
3. Robert Davis, professor of history, Middlebury.
4. Sir Henry Lunn and Arnold Lunn of London.
5. Ellery Sedgwick, editor, *The Atlantic.*
6. Dr. Joseph B. Code, Catholic University, Washington.
7. Cardinal Hayes, who announced publicly he prayed for a Franco victory.

Chapter 40

Hemingway: Man and Myth

There were two episodes in Hemingway's life that I shared and that I consider of importance, perhaps turning points on his road from the Select to the Nobel Prize for literature: first, his discovery of "cablese," or a new way of writing, as he called it, during the Genoa Conference of 1922, and second, his part in the war in Spain, which may not have broken his heart but which did present him with a situation. It was because of Spain that Hemingway became, as his friend the French poet Robert Desnos called him, *un homme engagé,* a committed man.

Before sharing more than a year with Hemingway in the Hotel Florida, Madrid, during the Spanish War, I had met him only occasionally in Paris, two or three times at the Select, once or twice at Gertrude Stein's, where he was a weekly guest and I an outsider fortunately dragged there by a regular; and again during the great conference in Genoa, Italy, in the spring of 1922 on which the hopes of all the world were centered. The Italians heralded it as *"il piu grande conferencia dell'historia del mondo"* (the greatest conference in the history of the world), and that was actually its purpose: to right all the evils in the world caused by the Versailles Treaty, and thus produce an age of peace and prosperity—all that Woodrow Wilson had hoped for when in 1918 he called the conflict "the war to end all wars."

The largest number of correspondents ever gathered, about double the number who were in Paris for the peace treaty, came to Genoa. When I spotted Lincoln Steffens and recalled meeting him in Paris in 1919, when he was returning from a mission to Russia, Steffens asked me to round up a few foreign correspondents with friendly views and meet him at a trattoria he had found in the working-class section of Genoa. On one of its walls appeared the graffito, *"Viva Lenin."*

We met almost every night. I brought along Spewack of the New York *World* and Hemingway of the Toronto *Star.* Steffens's other occasional guests were Jo Davidson, the sculptor; William Bird, who published unknowns in Paris; and George Slocombe of the *Daily Herald* of London. Hemingway taught us how to hold our glasses with the thumb and last three fingers while pulling forward the neck of the two-gallon bottle, which was on a swivel, with the index finger, filling the glass by using only one hand. We usually drank up a gallon or all of the large container.

Hemingway also taught us to sing his translation of the once treasonable song he had learned at the time of the Italian defeat at Caporetto:

> *The General Cadorna*
> *Wrote a letter to the Queen:*
> *If you ever want to see Trieste,*
> *Buy yourself a picture postcard.*
>
> *Boom, boom, boom, boom,*
> *Viva la Cannonado!*

But mostly we listened to Steffens. He was one of the great journalists of all time, undoubtedly the greatest of our time—an "investigative" reporter, until Theodore Roosevelt labeled him and his fellows—at a time when he, T.R., not they, had changed political colors and made peace with the ruling powers—"Muck-rakers."

I think I am right in saying that the Genoa Conference was Hemingway's first experience with filing cable news, with writing "cablese," and that this encounter affected the famous Hemingway style and made him a world-known writer. I do remember Hemingway asking questions about "cablese" of those who used it daily, and the suggestions the cable correspondents made to him. "Cablese" was more than cutting down on words, or skeletonizing—business firms throughout the world practice it to some extent. It meant not only removing all the surplus fat, yet including all the facts, using simple and direct words, new word combinations, word inventions, condensations—everything to save words and therefore money for the paper—but also it meant employing the language to give the recipient abroad, the man who had to make an excellent column story of a thousand words out of the two hundred he received, hints and suggestions to stir his memory. Something like impressionism in painting.

Hemingway was so pleased with cablese that one night he brought to the trattoria samples of his latest messages to Toronto to show Steffens. He said that cablese was not only "a great language"; he said to all of us, "This is a *new* language." He spoke with great seriousness, as if he had discovered—or invented—it himself.*

My next encounter with Hemingway was years later, when by coincidence he had left starving Madrid to get something to eat, at the same time as my wife and I. We met in Paris, at the Select naturally. This was the night Hemingway expressed his

---

* In the past twenty years perhaps twenty biographers have asked me what I remember about as many men and women, each worthy of at least one book. On May 26, 1979, for example, I was corresponding with writers interested in Ezra Pound, Josephine Herbst and Jack Reed. When Carlos Baker, Woodrow Wilson Professor of Literature at Princeton, wrote his life of Hemingway, I sent him the Genoa Conference episode, and to this day I insist the trattoria meetings with Steffens were in that city in 1922 and not in Lausanne (which I have never visited) and not a year later (when I was reporting Soviet Russia).

commitment, not only to Loyalist Spain—everyone had done so except a Nazi or two or a fascist in each civilized country—but also to the great cause that this conflict represented and that Camus wrote would "haunt the conscience of mankind."

On this occasion Hemingway was not only friendly, he invited Helen and me to his table and introduced us to Robert Desnos. We talked Spain until midnight. Then Desnos invited us to his apartment on the Rue de Seine nearby. We were joined by several others, Americans and French. The night passed. The subject was always Spain—the threat that Hitler and Mussolini would overrun the Republic and then start a European, perhaps a world war; the failure of the democracies to take any action; the failure of the world press to tell the truth about the obvious Nazi-Fascist conspiracy. Webb Miller of the London United Press Office not only agreed to everything we said but also gave us details of almost incredible perversion of the news. It was now morning.

As we stumbled (more from lack of sleep than alcohol) down the staircase from the Desnos apartment to the street, Hemingway turned to us and said:

"And I had to go to Spain before you liberal bastards would believe that I was on your side."*

Hemingway created myths and legends about himself and so was forced to live up to them. His hairy-chested masculinity and his victories as a boxer, his feats as a hunter, and his literary wars with Stendhal or Tolstoy or Dostoevsky, with the intention

---

* At the second Writers Congress in New York a year later Hemingway said, "There is only one form of government which cannot produce good writers, and that system is fascism. For fascism is a lie told by bullies. A writer who will not lie cannot live and work under fascism." For the *New Masses,* a Communist weekly, he wrote an article—actually a poem—"On the American Dead in Spain," in which he said, " . . . our dead are a part of the earth of Spain now and the earth of Spain can never die." (A score of novelists and journalists also contributed, including Sinclair Lewis and the present writer, and all of us were attacked and red-baited by the Dies Committee, and later the McCarthyites, but not one of us was a Communist. Nor was the Spanish Republic Communist.)

Desnos was killed by the Nazis in a concentration camp in France in 1941.

of defeating them all, make fascinating chapters in many writers' books. As I remember it, the first myth Hemingway originated dates from 1923 when his first work, a little pamphlet he called "three stories and ten poems," was published. His first bound book was *In Our Time* (Liveright, 1925), which credits the short stories to *Transatlantic, The Little Review* and *This Quarter.*

The myth began with the commonplace among writers: "I was rejected when I began. I am now a success." However, Hemingway, to make himself more interesting, chose to be rejected by what was unquestionably the leading literary publication in the United States, *The Dial,* and to make the myth more believable invented a letter from *The Dial*'s editor that— Hemingway told all Paris—said he would never become a writer, so better stick to newspaper journalism, or (in a later version) get an honest job as a truck driver.

The Dial had been bought by two of Gilbert Seldes's rich friends, J. S. Watson and Scofield Thayer, all formerly associated on the *Harvard Monthly,* and although Thayer was listed as editor-in-chief, Gilbert was editor in fact, and it was he who first published T. S. Eliot ("The Waste Land") in America, D. H. Lawrence, James Joyce and an appreciation of the unknown Pablo Picasso. Gilbert Seldes made it the outstanding literary magazine in America. In 1925 he resigned and Marianne Moore became editor, and the publication gradually began to fade away. It was Marianne Moore who returned Hemingway's story "The Undefeated" to him in 1925 with a covering letter saying it was too strong for American readers. But 1925 was too late for the Hemingway myth.*

---

* In 1924, editing *Transatlantic* during Ford Madox Ford's trip abroad, Hemingway had already "impugned the talents of Tristan Tzara, Cocteau and Gilbert Seldes, whose book on *The Seven Lively Arts* was more or less favorably reviewed in the same issue" (Carlos Baker, *Hemingway,* page 128). In the autumn of 1934 Hemingway sent Arnold Gingrich, editor of *Esquire,* his regular contribution, this one attacking Gilbert Seldes more cruelly than before. Asked by Gingrich to send some proof of his statements, Ernest replied that the Seldes letter "was locked up with his papers in Paris . . . he could finish off Seldes whenever he wished. . . . He had no quarrel with people unless they lied about questions of fact or repeated old lies." But, said Ernest, "when I lie myself

Hemingway's Lady Brett

*T*he fictional Lady Brett is quoted by Hemingway as saying on one occasion, "I won't be one of those bitches," and on another, a little while later, "You know it makes one feel rather good deciding not to be a bitch"; and so for the benefit of novel readers who know Lady Brett and might want to know what Lady Duff really was like, here is a personal encounter.

It was in Paris in the early thirties, after I had quit the newspapers. One night I had a phone call from an old friend, the Countess Monici, whom I had first met in 1924 when she was helping Sheean pack up at the Hotel Excelsior, in Rome, so that I could replace him there as correspondent.

A year later, when I was expelled from Rome by Mussolini, I went to Paris and again met the Countess Monici. She introduced me to her Captain Patterson. They were both heroes of a great romantic adventure. Having been refused visas for England many times, they had bought a rowboat and attempted to cross the Channel. They were overturned, saved by a passing ship, taken to England, and immediately deported to France. They lived on a small allowance the captain received from home.

The evening of the phone call I found the Countess, Patterson and their guest, Lady Duff, at the Montmartre club. They were apparently finishing their second bottle of champagne—champagne was obligatory and the price was triple or more the market value. In my honor, Lady Duff said she was ordering a third bottle.

We had a happy hour. Then Duff had to visit the ladies' room and the Countess said she would join her, and away they went. Captain Patterson and I talked about the war. And then he too had a call and went away and I sat alone drinking my second glass. And so a quarter of an hour passed. Then the waiter came

---

its Hokay" (Baker, page 613). This letter is dated October 24.

Watson and Thayer had donated the literary remains of *The Dial* to Yale, and a search was made of the files. The magazine had kept a careful account of every manuscript received and its disposition. No Hemingway until 1925, eliminating false and libelous matter. Hemingway never produced the alleged Seldes letter on which the entire legend rested.

by and presented me with the bill for three bottles and various sundries, such as cigarets at one dollar a pack, and sandwiches. I said I was a guest, I had ordered nothing. The waiter mentioned the police. I gave him all the money I had.

It was not I who spread the story at the Dingo and the Select. It could only have been the gold-diggers themselves. Everyone laughed at the poor sucker from the provinces who had fallen into the trap. Didn't I know that Lady Brett Ashley (Lady Duff Twysden, née Mary Byron) was capitalizing on her Hemingway fame for lunches and dinners and night clubs and drinks every night of the year; and that the suckers usually paid gladly for the honor of meeting the real Hemingway character? Hadn't we heard in Berlin or Rome?

Thomas Wolfe

Dreiser, Hemingway, Lewis—the giants of American literature—had declared for Spain publicly. The four undecided or neutral writers included only one notable: e. e. cummings. But where did Thomas Wolfe stand? Was he apolitical, uncommitted, above the conflict?

I did not know Thomas Wolfe until sometime in 1938 when, on our return from Spain, our temporary apartment in New York City became a meeting place for friends and strangers, writers and poets, everyone interested in the Spanish War, everyone asking how he or she could help the Republic.

The most interesting night I remember was when a dozen or more persons, including Josephine Herbst and Thomas Wolfe, were present. Miss Herbst was one of the best writers of our time, for some reason almost completely overlooked by the critical profession.

She skillfully brought out the best in Wolfe. A tape recording of that evening's conversation between the two would be one of the literary gems of the century. I think Wolfe spoke for almost a full hour about his nights among the castoffs of society who found shelter under the New York terminus of the Brooklyn Bridge. His talking did not seem to require the editing and cutting that Max Perkins found necessary for his over-written manuscripts. Every word Wolfe spoke was interesting and seemed necessary. The rest of the evening was spent on talk about Spain. Josephine had been there, too. Before the night was over Wolfe declared himself for the Spanish Republic and offered to do what he could.

We discussed a plan for a group of friends of Loyalist Spain to go to Washington and picket the White House. Our placards would demand that Roosevelt lift the embargo on the Republic. No date for our trip to Washington was set. A few days later I heard from Wolfe:

Hotel Chelsea

April 25, 1938.

Dear Seldes:

I would like to know when the committee is going to Washington. . . . I am going to Purdue University May 19, and want to accomplish all I can before I go. I had not thought of making any more trips at the present time. But let me know about it, and I will see what I can do.

Tom Wolfe

The trip was never made. That very year Wolfe was dead of a brain tumor and Mike Gold in the *Daily Worker* said he was "definitely a fellow-traveler of Communism and was wrestling in his mind as to going the whole way . . . a muddled introspective. . . . But he found his way out of the bourgeois swamp, onto the high road of Communism."

This is nonsense. At no time in the last year of his life did Tom Wolfe show any signs of fellow-traveling, nor was he on any high or low road to Communism. That he had ceased being neutral or apolitical was the important thing of the last year of his life; he was anti-totalitarian, he was more anti-fascist than anything else, and the cause of the Spanish Republic was the deciding factor.

Chapter 41

A Hero, a Villain, and an SOB

As in all wars, there were heroes and villains, traitors and SOBs in the Spanish War, as well as the vast majority— not Thoreau's masses who lived lives of quiet desperation but Garrison's millions whose apathy "is enough to make every statue leap from its pedestal and to hasten the resurrection of the dead."

The overwhelming majority of the writers, poets, artists, civilized people of the world were committed to the Spanish cause, and not only did many vote for it, speak for it and raise money for it, but also thousands in a score of countries enlisted and fought for it. The man considered the greatest living author in France, André Malraux, now known as Colonel Malraux, commanded the Espagne Squadron, which is about all the aviation the Republic had outside a few Russian pilots and their planes who, despite the French and British and American blockade, somehow managed to reach Spain.

When my wife and I recognized Malraux one day in the

Hotel Victoria in Valencia, we could not resist speaking to him. To our surprise he spoke to us like an old friend.

"Our group," he told us, "consists of antiquated French planes, Potezes, and a few Douglas passenger planes. We do not have war planes. We go on bombing missions—but we have no means of sighting our targets. We have to fly almost directly over them. I am at the controls—Lieutenant Pons here"—he introduced us—"is in the passenger section. When we see that we are over our target by looking through the window, I begin circling, Pons takes up a bomb, sights with his eyes, and throws the bomb out the window."

Lieutenant Pons appeared to me the best-fed man I ever saw in Loyalist Spain during the war—except for the occasional visitors. He looked as if he weighed considerably more than two hundred pounds. Said Malraux:

"When they assigned Pons to this antiquated plane I fly we had to test it on the ground: would Pons break through the old wooden floor? Pons was not allowed to set foot in several of the old crates in our squadron."

Among the influential advisers who succeeded in getting President Roosevelt to accept the British Foreign Office's plan for "neutrality" in the Spanish War were Joseph P. Kennedy, Ambassador to London; Congressman John McCormack, the Democratic Party leader James A. Farley; and the Ambassador to France, William C. Bullitt.

I had met William Bullitt with Steffens in Paris in 1919 when they returned to report to Wilson on Lenin's views on world peace—would Bolshevik Russia come to the conference, would Lenin cooperate, what were his views, what were Lenin's terms?

Steffens and Bullitt achieved the supposedly impossible. Lenin had accepted Wilson's terms, which he had previously declared he would never accept. All he asked in return was one act of friendship: the withdrawal of British, French and American troops from Archangel, Siberia, and other parts of Russia; the lifting of the blockade; and some agricultural machines with which to produce food and end the already visible famine.

When Lloyd George not only refused to agree but also repudiated the Steffens-Bullitt mission, the U.S. State Department joined him and double-crossed Wilson, denying even the fact that the mission had been authorized by the President himself.

Steffens, an old-time newspaperman, merely shrugged. But the idealist aristocrat from Rittenhouse Square, Philadelphia, Mr. Bullitt, was disillusioned, depressed, almost shattered; in reaction he joined the opposition. He became an enthusiastic follower of Lenin and the chief advocate in America of the recognition of the Bolshevik regime. When Roosevelt finally did so in 1933 he made Bullitt the first U.S. ambassador to the Soviets.

Steffens had introduced me to Bullitt in Paris. I met him only two or three times. However, on my return from the Spanish War in 1938, when I was stopping at the obscure Hotel Liberia, I was told there was a telephone call for me downstairs. I went down. "That you, George," said an unfamiliar voice; "this is Bill—Bill Bullitt." He had never before called me George and certainly never before referred to his aristocratic self as Bill. He invited me to visit him at the embassy on the Place de la Concorde.

He cross-examined me on the Spanish War and I repeated the facts of the twenty-four articles my wife, Helen, and I had sent the New York *Post*—nothing more. I have never in my lifetime given ambassadors, diplomatic personnel, generals or anyone information I had not published or would not publish. I did not, for example, tell Bullitt that the Republic had almost no machine guns, rifles or cannon behind the trenches, little ammunition, almost no medicine, almost no food. I did mention the foreigners, the whole Italian armies in Spain, and Hitler's tanks and his Condor Legion of thousands of aviators, and I added that despite what the papers in foreign countries said, there were no Russian *troops* in Spain.

"But there are Russians in Spain," Bullitt insisted.

"If you mean some officers and technicians, yes," I replied;

"there is a general named Gal or Gall or Hal—I talked to him; he claims he is a Hungarian but he is Russian; there are some three hundred or four hundred Russians altogether." (Later, historians were to place the number of Russians at five hundred to seven hundred.) "A few aviators, I've seen three mechanics; tankmen, specialists, generals and doctors. No troops. No infantry."

"I know differently," said the ambassador; "we have reliable information."

"Then you are misinformed," I replied. "The American military attaché General Fuqua, and Captain [Townsend] Griffis, your own air attaché, they told me there is not one Russian soldier—infantryman—in Spain. They could not possibly have told you otherwise."

"I have other sources," the ambassador replied angrily.

We began to argue, our voices rose, he certainly lost his diplomatic coolness, and I suppose I lost my temper. Then Mr. Bullitt apparently pushed a button, a clerk appeared, and I was practically bounced from the embassy. We did not shake hands.

Bullitt continued to misinform the State Department and FDR. He also intrigued with the ambassador to London, Joseph P. Kennedy, and Lord Lothian, who headed the Cliveden Set, with friends of Nazi Germany; when the Spanish War was over, he insisted on immediate recognition of fascist leader Franco.

What had happened to the man? He had risked his career at a time when to say a kind word for Lenin or the Soviet system meant ruin, and for fourteen years he had fought for Russian recognition. Now, four years later, an ambassador, he had become the chief intriguer for the overthrow of the government he had defended.

The explanation of this strange behavior—if it is an explanation—may possibly be found in the famous French cliché, *cherchez la femme*. I cannot of course reveal the name of the minor American diplomat who served under Bullitt in the Moscow embassy, but I believe he told me the truth. Mr. Bullitt fell in love with one of the ballerinas—I will not of course disclose her name—of the great Bolshoi Ballet, and this somehow coincided with the greatest period of his pro-Soviet activities. When the lady informed him she might consider his affections if they were directed toward a marriage, but would under no circumstance become his mistress, the American ambassador to Soviet Russia coincidentally had a change of mind regarding his attitude toward that new system of government.

Whatever the cause of this man's 180-degree turn in politics, in my opinion Bullitt was and remains one of the great villains in American diplomacy, one of the many pro-fascists in British, French and American diplomatic posts who are all partly responsible for the destruction of the Spanish democratic Republic. In a historic sense Bullitt was a greater force for evil than Errol Flynn, to whom I have given second place in my proposed Hall of Infamy—for which only SOBs are eligible.

My Second SOB

*M*y hesitation to use the term SOB, properly restricted in my youthful journalistic years almost exclusively to liberated newspaper people and other such ruffians, ended the day Mr. Studs Terkel came to Hartland-4-Corners to talk to me. He insisted it was now one of the milder of the many words once banned by public opinion from newspapers and books, and later on radio and television. All four-letter words may now be found in most publications, including the women's magazines.

Mr. Terkel's first question was: who are your three favorite SOBs? I have already named one, Gabriele D'Annunzio, a great poet and novelist—but whether he is to be ranked first or second to Errol Flynn I must leave to my readers. In a concluding chapter I will nominate three noted newspaper columnists for a choice of third place in my proposed SOB Hall of Infamy.

My wife, Helen, and I first met the noted Hollywood star and his beautiful wife of the moment, Lili Damita, at the main Paris police station on the Île-de-la-Cité where the French, probably illegally, decided on who was to get a permit to travel to Spain and who was to be refused. We sat on the same bench and talked. We were curious about this Hollywood type wanting to go to Spain: almost all the writers and poets and artists in the world were siding with the Republic, but who could imagine Errol Flynn favoring the Loyalist cause—or any cause?

He told us he was going to Madrid as representative of scores of Hollywood people, he was bringing a million dollars, he and his friends would supply a hospital for the Republican soldiers and for the International Brigade, medicines, and food.

In Valencia while we waited for transportation to the front, Flynn was given a banquet by government officials at a time when most of the country was starving. He asked for a car and chauffeur—which he got at a time when human lives could be counted in gasoline, "a pint of blood, a pint of gasoline."

All of us lived in the Hotel Florida in Madrid, press head-quarters, a penny subway ride from the front-line trenches, and the cars were running in the subway. Hemingway and Matthews of the *Times* had a special place, a half-ruined house in University City, then in no-man's-land, from which the trenches of both sides could be seen. Flynn asked if he could go along with them.

When the shooting began and the building was hit and hit again, Errol Flynn, the hero of a hundred fighting films, decided to go back—but not to the Florida directly. "Do any of you know of a good, clean whorehouse?" he asked—and was told the direction of the old red-light district.

The next day Flynn went the short distance to the Telefonica—the ITT building—which housed the censorship. He had the censors pass an apparently harmless personal telegram to Paris. But it was a pre-arranged code—and it released a hoax planned in Hollywood.

The next day the New York *Daily News* published the headline: ERROL FLYNN KILLED ON SPANISH FRONT, on the entire front page. This was followed by a statement from Warner Brothers, Paris, which was headlined ERROL FLYNN WOUNDED ON SPANISH FRONT. (The *Daily News* had Flynn "killed by machine gun bullets on the Guadalajara front," and the next day, "wounded on the head.")

Meanwhile Flynn, still having the use of a car and priceless gasoline, drove to Barcelona where, questioned by correspondents, he rolled up his left sleeve and showed a bandage over what might have been a self-inflicted scratch. The next day he left Spain.

There were no ambulances, no hospital, no medical supplies, no food for the Spanish Republic, and not one cent of money. The war correspondents said bitterly it was the cruelest hoax of the time. Flynn was one of the most despicable human beings that ever lived, and had used a terrible war just to advertise one of his cheap movies.

Flynn remained a hero in the American press. Not one newspaper, so far as I was able to learn, published the story of Flynn's night in a whorehouse, and when it did appear in a book Flynn instituted a suit for two million dollars in damages. All of us who had been at the Hotel Florida offered to testify against Flynn, and when both Hemingway and Matthews of *The New York Times* informed attorney Melville Cane they would come to Hollywood, or go anywhere to testify about the whorehouse incident, Flynn realized that he might not be able to get the entire press to suppress this news, so he withdrew his suit.*

---

* If any reader wants more information on this despicable human being Errol Flynn, he can get some two hundred documents from the U.S. government under the Freedom of Information Act, which show that Errol Flynn was also a Nazi spy not only before Pearl Harbor, but also throughout World War II, and that both the FBI and Naval Intelligence kept watch on him and tried to stop him from making a movie at the San Diego naval base. They were overruled. Flynn took photographs of U.S. naval installations and sent them to Japan. All of these facts are included in Charles Higham's biography, *Errol Flynn: the Untold Story.*

Chapter 42

Esquire's *Mr. Smart—*
Wasn't

Everyone who came to Spain from 1936 to 1939 knew the war was not just a small fascist adventure but the prologue of a world war in which the Nazi-Fascist International (Germany, Italy and Japan) planned to take all of Europe and Asia, and then turn on Russia, and eventually face the United States.

Almost everyone, but notably writers and newspapermen returning to America, searched for a means of mass communication for these obvious but alarming views they considered facts. But the British Foreign Office, the French Quai d'Orsay and the U.S. State Department, as well as the British, French and American press (with rare exceptions—the newspapers honest enough to report the Loyalist side as Republican and not Communist) destroyed Spanish civilization—at least temporarily. Not only visitors but also diplomatic and military observers in Madrid and Barcelona, notably Ambassador Bowers, the military attaché General Fuqua and air attaché Captain Griffis, warned their government that the day Spain was occupied by Hitler's and

Mussolini's forces the next world war would begin. In Britain the Hitler appeasers, the Cliveden Set, were in control. In France the premier, Léon Blum, was either frightened by Naziism or such a weakling that the reactionaries began writing on the walls of Paris the slogan *"Mieux Hitler que Blum"*—"Better Hitler than Blum"—and in the United States President Roosevelt—afterward the only leader in the world ever to confess his error—failed to act in time.

In America, more than anywhere else, the press made public opinion, and public opinion from the earliest days of the Republic still was either powerful or was everything.*

Returning from Spain we found the conventional lineup: committed to the Spanish Republic without exception, one entire medium consisting of nine or ten liberal weeklies, with a total circulation of perhaps one-tenth of any one of the Hearst magazines or one-hundredth the circulation of the Hearst newspaper chain and the papers served by Hearst's International News; or the pro-Mussolini New York *Daily News* or the pro-Mussolini *Chicago Tribune* under the Patterson-McCormick editorship of the time; or a hundredth the circulation of press lord Henry Luce's magazines—in 1934 he devoted an entire issue of *Fortune* to glorifying Mussolini and Fascism, and in *Time* he permitted an outright pro-fascist, Laird Goldsborough, to slant and pervert the news every week.

As always, there were a few roll-of-honor newspapers, outstanding honest dailies, notably the *Christian Science Monitor* and the St. Louis *Post-Dispatch,* and of course a larger number of small-town papers such as Gitt's *Gazette & Daily* of York, Pennsylvania, which published the facts fairly and honestly. (It must also be noted that whereas the reactionary or pro-fascist newspapers and magazines slanted and perverted the news, the honest

---

* " . . . it is essential that public opinion be enlightened."—George Washington.

"The only security of all is in a free press. The force of public opinion cannot be resisted, when permitted freely to be expressed."—Jefferson.

"With public opinion nothing can fail; without it nothing can succeed."—Lincoln.

media always remained ethical; they confined their views or emotions to the editorial page.)

In this tragic era of the 1930s the reader must imagine the international rejoicing that followed the "epoch-making" announcement in 1937 by *Esquire*'s owner, David Smart, that he was about to issue a big, popular, illustrated magazine, *Ken*. It would be a rival to *Look* or *Life,* a rival also to *Collier's* and the *Saturday Evening Post; Ken* was to be the first mass-circulation, public-opinion-forming magazine in history on the liberal side— "one step left of center," as Smart described it. The editors were to be Ernest Hemingway, Paul DeKruif, Raymond Gram Swing and George Seldes.

It was Arnold Gingrich, editor of *Esquire,* who paid my way to Chicago to explain my proposed press column to Smart. I had already contributed to such a department in *The Guild Reporter.* One after another, as Smart nodded approval, I suggested:

> "Nail That Lie" column, reprinting newspaper items contrasted to reports a day or year later.
>
> A column of parallel quotations and photographs of "notable" citizens, showing up their endorsements of Mussolini or Hitler—it would include Martin Dies, Father Coughlin.
>
> A series of in-depth exposés, based on investigations, similar to the New York *World*'s Ku Klux Klan stories of the 1920s.
>
> Series of articles: "The Inside Story of the American Legion," founded in Paris by insurance corporation heads and bankers for the purpose of stopping "radicalism" from spreading in America when "the boys" came home.
>
> Series of big articles: "The Private Lives of the Dictators."
>
> Spain: including "The International Brigade, the greatest shock troops in modern history." Hemingway to do a weekly or monthly Spanish story.

Before I had finished my suggestions, owner Smart turned to editor Gingrich and said I was to be a regular editor, not merely a contributor of one press column. Then, in great surprise, he asked me what I meant by Legion "exposés"—he could

not imagine there was anything to expose. Obviously he had
never seen *The Guild Reporter,* the organ of the American Newspaper Guild, or read the annual reports of the American Civil
Liberties Union, so I began by quoting Guild President Heywood
Broun ("The Legion breaks more strikes than the National
Guard and the police") and the commandant of the U.S. Marines,
General Smedley Butler ("I have never known one commander
of the American Legion who has not sold them out") and the
headlines I remembered:

GUILD PAPER ASSAILS
LEGION AS NO. 1 ENEMY

LIBERTIES UNION
CALLS LEGION FIRST
IN REPRESSION

"Great!" said Smart. "We'll run a Legion story in the first
issue: it'll make America sit up; we'll sell a million copies."

Both Smart and Gingrich seemed unaware that the big-
business interests, which originally subsidized the Legion, and to
some extent still do so today in presenting posts with club houses,
could destroy *Ken* through an advertising boycott; they could
even destroy *Esquire,* I said.

"Couldn't touch us," replied Smart; "we're mostly men's
clothes and liquor. These people need us as much as we need
them. Some ask to advertise . . . "

And so a new world under a bright journalistic heaven was
born and I wrote eighty-three items for *Ken* about evenly divided
between one-column press criticism and "Nail That Lie" columns, and three-thousand- to five-thousand-word investigative
exposés. I sat alone in an office, one of many on an entire floor of
the Esquire Building on Madison Avenue, in New York. Soon
enough I learned that Hemingway, De Kruif, and Swing were
not editors but contributors; a clever artist named Sharp drew our
four pictures and *Ken* issued a prospectus boasting our four
names, but this was a Smart hoax and falsehood. No "editor"
ever showed up. Gingrich in Chicago was the real editor.

Although sitting in New York I was occupied every day in editorial work: authors came and went, scores of manuscripts arrived and had to be forwarded to Chicago, every day men and women applied for jobs—but I was never allowed to make a final decision.

I documented every chapter about the Legion. Broun's charge of strikebreaking was officially confirmed when Commander Colmery issued his order that "in the future" all strikebreaking by Legion posts would be done by Legionnaires in civilian clothes—no longer would Legion uniforms be worn. In addition to official quotations of Legion invitations and honors for Mussolini, I confirmed the statement of one of its commanders that he was ready "if ever needed" to take over the government in Washington.

(Incidentally, Smart paid me $150 a week—a fortune; I had never made more than sixty dollars a week in my life.)

One day the advertising offices of *Ken* filled up. A score of solicitors with the editorial prospectus and the usual displays called not only on clothing, liquor and cigaret advertising companies, but also on drug and auto manufacturers, and makers of everything sold to the general public. Every afternoon the solicitors came back and told the boss, a Mr. Weintraub, they had not sold a page, not even for the first issue.

When, in the middle of this boycott, a telephone rang and someone contracted for a page every month, the advertising men thought the boycott was broken. But Mr. Weintraub looked at the order. "Hell, no!" he shouted, "This is from Consumers Union, it tests goods and rates them, the greatest menace to the advertising industry in the country. Tell them 'over my dead body.' " Consumers Union in 1937 was about one year old at the time and I was one of its original sponsors.

One day there was a meeting in the board room of *Esquire* at which all Madison Avenue was present. One of the new advertising men, whose name I have never disclosed until now, Mr. Perley O'Gorman, told me later that Young & Rubicam, J. Walter Thompson, N. W. Ayer, and Batten, Barton, Durstine & Osborn were there, along with a dozen lesser powers, and their

38 *Above:* In Montparnasse cafés like Le Dôme it was virtually impossible to avoid those already, or soon to be, famous.

39 *Left:* Seldes's profile as captured by a professional artist at the Café Select, 1929.

40 James Joyce, Ezra Pound, and Ford Madox Ford — the last two figured prominently in Seldes's Latin Quarter adventures.

41 Lazy days in the south of France—Gilbert Seldes center,
Pablo Picasso in hat.

42 Gilbert Seldes and his wife, Amanda.

43 Theodore Dreiser, the main attraction of Dorothy Dudley's dinner parties.

44 H.G. Wells in 1931, the year Seldes visited the house "two lovers built."

45 *Above:* Brook Hollow Farm, Woodstock, Vermont—the house bought at "Red" Lewis's suggestion.

46 *Left:* George and Helen in the early Vermont days.

47 and 48 The Seldes's Vermont neighbors Sinclair Lewis, *left,* and Dorothy Thompson, *below.*

51 The metal fragment Seldes holds at left — a grim, ironic message.

49 and 50 *Above and right:* The Seldes surveying the ruins in Brihuega after the Battle of Guadalajara, March 1937.

52 *Above:* Spanish refugees en route from Barcelona to the French border.

53 *Left:* A message from the Republic: "The antifascist militia needs you."

54 *Right:* "The Spanish Civil War" on the American homefront.

55 Ernest Hemingway covering the war in Madrid.

56 Errol Flynn — Seldes's slippery second SOB.

decision was "Publish one item 'one step left of center' and you'll never see one dollar in advertising money." Moreover, one of the Big Four—my friend would not confirm it was J. Walter Thompson—added that he would withdraw eight color pages, costing $64,000 an issue, from *Esquire* if *Ken* was in any way a "leftist" magazine. (To these people "one step left of center" meant "leftist," and leftist meant "red," and "red" of course meant "Communist.")

Mr. David Smart not only surrendered to the advertising agencies, he instructed me to cease and desist on the Legion series and the press columns. I heard from Gingrich that Smart was looking around for some articles and pictures of a red-baiting nature. He had employed the one journalist in the country who fully answered to the now disused term "press prostitute," George Sokolsky, and some Hearst men and some popular ex-Communists turned red-baiters.

I telegraphed Hemingway in Key West where he was temporarily between his trips to Spain:

TYPEWRITTEN PROSPECTUS KEN DEFINITELY
LEFTWING ANTIFASCIST[.] ADVERTISERS DEMAND
REACTIONARY ANTILABOR POLICY SUBTHREAT BOYCOTT[.]
SMART COLDFOOTEDLY SURRENDERED[.]
KEN ENTIRELY PHONY[.] CONFIDENTIAL

Hemingway replied:

RUSH AIRMAIL PROSPECTUS ALL MATERIAL ASK
DEKRUIF WRITE ME IMMEDIATELY ERNEST

I sent the documentation to him as well as copies to DeKruif and Swing. DeKruif wrote me: "Gingrich got me into this thing on the idea that it was going to be more than liberal, really progressive." DeKruif resigned. Swing resigned. I resigned. Hemingway protested to Smart, demanding a disclaimer in the first issue of *Ken* that he was ever an editor, as advertised. He told everyone he would continue contributing articles representing the Spanish Republican side, and did so. One gossip columnist reported him saying he would be "boring from within" the now reactionary *Ken*.

Smart's first issue had on its cover a Moor in typical head-dress in full color. Instead of "the big story that would make America sit up and take notice," the story of the American Legion, there was "The Coming Revolt in Morocco." Nobody bought issue No. 1. It also contained some quickly bought red-baiting cartoons—and very little advertising despite the last-minute switch. Poor Gingrich did his best to save the stillborn "liberal" slick and popular weekly. It struggled for a while on *Esquire* money. Shortly afterward Mr. David Smart was sentenced to two years in prison and fined $10,000 for manipulating the stock of his own company, rigging, and profiting by $1,075,000 of stockholders' money. *Ken* died and no one missed it.

Chapter 43

~~~~~~~~~~~~~~~~~~~~~~

Ken's Engraved
Letterheads

With my $150 a week and a magnificent office in the Esquire Building there was another valuable asset: engraved stationary. I could now write to notable people at home and abroad and, to my surprise, receive answers. Bernard M. Baruch agreed to an interview, the great Bernard Shaw sent a personal card, an ambassador who had once been the commander of the American Legion frankly answered what was meant to be an embarrassing question.

In doing research for my proposed *Ken* series on the American Legion I learned that a half dozen commanders in as many years had endorsed Mussolini, invited him to a convention, even tried to make him an honorary member (which would have been a violation of the Legion constitution). I wrote all of them. I asked Commander Alvin Owsley if this press report was correct:

> "If ever needed, the American Legion stands ready to protect our country's institutions and ideals as the Fascisti

dealt with the destructionists who menaced Italy."
(Owsley)

By taking over the government? he was asked.

"Exactly that," declared Owsley.

"Do not forget," he added, "that the Fascisti are to Italy what the American Legion is to the United States, and that Mussolini, the new premier, was the commander of the Legion, the ex-servicemen of Italy."

Legion Commander Owsley was now U.S. ambassador to Denmark. He replied from Copenhagen, January 6, 1938: "No doubt I at the time reflected the real sentiment of the hopeful and confident Legionnaire in the light of history."

The rest of the letter explained that as a member of the diplomatic service he was not allowed to express his opinions. He did not deny that six Legion commanders had endorsed Mussolini and Fascism.

(And at no time after his retirement from the diplomatic service, when he was again free to express his opinions, did he deny the above statements he had made to the NEA, which were syndicated throughout the world by the Scripps-Howard press service.)

When I wrote to Mr. Baruch, "the friend and adviser of many Presidents," I mentioned meeting him in Paris at the time the Versailles Treaty was being made—and being introduced by Lincoln Steffens. Mr. Baruch had said to meet him at Jensen's next day at eleven.

A little early for lunch? But I went to the restaurant and waited. No Mr. Baruch. No reservation. Then a wise waiter who knew the statesman, said, "Maybe Jensen the shoemaker—Mr. Baruch has his shoes made to order."

I found Mr. Baruch at Jensen's, barefooted.

He was very angry at writers he termed muckrakers who had estimated his fortune at a certain figure—say $100 million.

"This is outrageous," said Mr. Baruch. "I haven't a

cent over eighty-nine million." He was as sincere as he was indignant.

When, in one question, I used the word "speculating," he became even angrier.

"I'll have you know, Mr. Seldes, that I never made a cent in my whole life *speculating.*"

He then told me the secret of his success:

"When I was a young man and had a few thousand dollars to invest, I decided to do my own investigation first. I would get a job, any job, with a corporation; I was on the loading platform hauling the product if no other job was open. I waited. I would get a job as a clerk—shipping clerk. I knew exactly what the business was doing. I would get a job as a bookkeeper. I assure you that in three or four months I knew more about this company than the chairman of the board or the president or any member of the board of directors, or anyone.

"I then weighed the facts: this company would soon have a boom, it would split its stock many times, raise dividends, make records. So I put my money in it. And went and got a job, any job, at another likely company. After a month or two as book-keeper I would quit, and do the same thing elsewhere. This is true investigation, this is true investment—I never speculated a cent."

And then as an afterthought Mr. Baruch said:

"I have made millions but I never made a cent out of the sweat and blood of any other man."

The third and last time I saw Mr. Baruch was in Paris, in 1938 or 1939. The Spanish Republic had just disbanded the International Brigade, and one of its components, the Abraham Lincoln Battalion, or what was left of it, was in Paris, stranded. Mr. Baruch paid the passage to America of several hundred men. Secretly.

All in all, a remarkable man. A multimillionaire with a social conscience? A man of rare courage, brave enough to withstand the waves of red-baiting which he knew would follow his aid to the Lincoln Battalion. (This American contribution to the tens of thousands who came from thirty or forty countries to fight fascism in Spain, lost a large percentage of its men in great battles. It was heroic. And, because the American Communist Party had organized the transportation of the volunteers to France, it was attacked almost universally as "red" although the majority of the battalion were neither party members nor fellow travelers.)

When I was writing a series of articles on the American Legion and reread the Legion's constitution, which states as its aim: "To perpetuate one-hundred-percent Americanism," I remembered that at the time Shaw made his famous lecture trip to America he had said in his first interview that "anyone who is one-hundred-percent anything is generally ninety-percent a fool," so I looked up his London address in *Who's Who* and asked him to confirm or deny the statement and also whether he was referring to the Legion constitution or certain types of patriots in general.

Shaw's reply was handwritten on one of his famous blue cards, which gives his address and also his cable address as "Socialist-London." He wrote:

> Dear Mr. Seldes:
> I cannot remember the exact wording of the statement to which you allude; but what I meant was that in my experience a man who calls himself 100% American and is proud of it is generally 150% an idiot politically. But the designation may be good business for war veterans. Having bled for their country in 1861 and 1918, they have bled it all they could subsequently. And why not?
> G. Bernard Shaw.

When Mussolini ran over a child and said to his companion, Cornelius Vanderbilt, the young multimillionaire temporarily playing journalist, "Never look backward, Vanderbilt. What is one life in the affairs of a nation?" the commandant of the U.S. Marines in a public lecture denounced the Duce as a "mad dog let loose in Europe." At the time, unable to get a hearing in the

American newspapers, General Smedley D. Butler went on a lecture tour telling the American people that Grayson M. P. Murphy of Wall Street and two Legion Post commanders had asked him to lead a march of Legionnaires and throw FDR out of office. The McCormack-Dickstein Committee—actually the first Un-American Activities Committee—published the documentary evidence, but the press suppressed the news, as was usual in those dark and primitive days.

It was because of the Mussolini episode that I got to know General Butler. The (Fascist) Italian government and the Duce were outraged and insisted that President Hoover punish General Butler and force him to apologize publicly. Butler refused. Instead, aided by Paul Comley French of the Philadelphia *Record* (and later head of CARE), he began collecting documentation on Mussolini. They asked me for the facts on Mussolini's criminal participation in the assassination of the socialist leader Matteotti in 1924—news that, although published in a few newspapers and weekly magazines, was still not generally known throughout the world. I was able to send General Butler my photostats of the Filippelli confession, which the A.P. had suppressed.

When Mr. French published an article listing the documentation General Butler was preparing to make public, notably the items I sent him, President Hoover dropped pressure for an apology. Nor did he demote General Butler. Why? The general wrote me this was the reason:

"Hoover sent his aide to see me. I said, 'Put me on the stand and you'll hear the story of the Boxer Rebellion.' That was all."

During the 1928 election campaign Hoover, "the great engineer," had also been touted as a hero of the siege of Tientsin during the Chinese uprising there. Two thousand foreigners were besieged by some thirty thousand fanatics. Every able-bodied man was called to defend the women and children.

"When we got to Tientsin," General Butler continued,

"we found all the able-bodied men on the wall with guns protecting the foreign section. Where were the women and children? We were told they were hiding in a cellar.*

"When I arrived I found one man cowering among the frightened women and children. I kicked his ass and him into the street. I did not ask his name, nor did I care to know who that coward was. Someone said later it was an engineer named Hoover."**

---

* John Hamill, in *The Strange Career of Mr. Hoover,* locates the cellar in the house of a Mrs. E. M. Drew.

** This is General Smedley Butler's statement, uncensored, unedited. As Hoover and Butler were both members of the Society of Friends (Quakers) it is obvious that the latter did not practice the religious precepts of his childhood when he became a soldier. If Hoover did, it might explain his refuge in the cellar, and the words "cowering" and "coward" might become irrelevant.

Chapter 44

~~~~~~~~

You May Owe Your Life to Mr. Ickes

I f readers of this book—I am sure of at least two—stopped
smoking or never began because they heard or read of the
relationship of tobacco, especially cigarets, to lung cancer, emphysema, heart disease and the general shortening of smokers' lives
by at least five years, they may be among the hundreds of
thousands of Americans whose lives were saved in the past forty
years by Secretary of the Interior Harold L. Ickes. It was he who
broke the "non-conspiracy" of the nation's newspapers to suppress the news. (In this instance the "non-conspiracy" paid them
about $50 million a year in cigaret advertising; today tobacco
advertising amounts to about $1.5 billion a year.)

I first met FDR's Secretary of the Interior in December
1937, at a birthday celebration of the founding of the American
Civil Liberties Union. He spoke on "Nations in Nightshirts,"
assailing two sacred idols of his first profession—he had been a
newspaperman himself, a *Chicago Tribune* reporter. He used the
word "fascists" for the conservative, reactionary, rightists and

their organizations (just as Mussolini did), and he said they controlled most of the wealth and power of the country, including the press, which was the chief maker of public opinion and therefore made this possible. He continued:

> As a matter of fact, it is the fascist-minded men of America who are the real enemies of our institutions. They have solidarity, a common interest in seizing more power and greater riches for themselves and ability and willingness to turn the concentrated wealth of America against the welfare of America. It is these men who, pretending that they would save us from dreadful Communism, would superimpose upon America an equally dreadful Fascism. . . .
>
> Our ancestors fought to prevent a state censorship of news and ideas. Our ancestors did not fight for the right of a few lords of the press to have almost exclusive control of and censorship over the dissemination of news and ideas. Yet, under the stress of economic forces, our press and news agencies are coming more and more under the domination of a handful of corporate publishers who may print such news as they wish to print and omit such news as they do not wish to print. They may even color the news. [This paragraph was totally suppressed in *The New York Times,* partly in the *Sun.*]

One day in 1939 I received a letter from Mr. Ickes saying he had been invited by "Town Meeting of the Air," the great radio program that probably did reach its claimed ten million listeners, to debate the question, "Do We Have a Free Press?" with press lord Frank E. Gannett. Mr. Ickes naturally took the negative. He asked me to send him facts, illustrations, documented proof, and I was happy to send a few items from the mountains of materials that I had collected for years. Even laymen knew that a report of an elevator crash in a city department store that killed two or seven persons would (1) be entirely suppressed, or (2) have the name of the store omitted. I told Mr. Ickes about the Pittsburgh department store owner's son who raped the prettiest salesgirls regularly—a sort of modernized, and therefore vulgarized, *jus primae noctis* or *droit du seigneur.* I sent him not only department store episodes that newspapers generally suppressed, but also the really big news of the connection between tobacco and cancer, emphysema, the shortening of life, and tens of thousands of deaths.

The Johns Hopkins Medical School and Dr. Raymond Pearl, chief biologist, were not the first to attack tobacco. As early as 1604 no less a person than King James I of England wrote "A Counterblast to Tobacco," saying smoking was "a custom loathesome to the eye, hateful to the nose, harmful to the brain, dangerous to the lungs, and in the black stinking fume thereof, nearest to the horrible Stygian smoke of the pit that is bottomless."

Although King James had no scientific knowledge whatever and wrote out of emotional hatred, he somehow in one of his several unproved but regal allegations hit the vital and deadly fact that Johns Hopkins documented just 334 years later: smoking is dangerous to the lungs because it is one of the main causes of lung cancer and emphysema.

Between 1604 and 1938 no one knows how many attacks were made on smoking mostly for fanatical moral-religious reasons, none based on research, none supported by facts. But when Dr. Pearl and Johns Hopkins produced their charts and their studies, the press, which lived well on such things as patent medicines and cigaret advertising, made no attempt to start or keep the world informed: the media raised curtains of silence a hundred times more powerful than any iron curtains of modern politics.

What Mr. Ickes did in 1939 for the first time since 1604 was reach a mass audience—ten million Americans to begin with—about one-fourth of our country's newspaper readers. (To the credit of the three great news services—AP, UP and INS— research shows that they did send the news to every one of the 1,750 or more daily newspapers of the United States, and this makes the crime of suppression by the press only the greater.)

Mr. Ickes broke the three-hundred-year-old barrier; it was due to his radio statement that the movement began—depite the

tobacco lobby in Washington, and the newspapers—to place
warnings on every package of cigarets, to list tar and nicotine,
perhaps ban smoking in all public places—and in some more
civilized countries, or perhaps countries with less corruption than
that present in the American House of Representatives and
Senate, Iceland for example—to ban cigaret advertising altogether.

Part XI
~~~~~~~~~~~~~~~~~~~~~~~~~~~~~

The *In fact* Decade

Chapter 45

~~~~~~~~~~~~~~~~

Now It Can Be Told

During all the years Mussolini was sending his armies to fight in Spain for Franco fascism, some historians estimate the Italian army at 100,000, others estimate it to have been 200,000, but in either case it was the main land force on the fascist side. The entire German air force saw service in Spain. Goering's plan was to have each and every squadron get actual war experience in preparation for the world war Hitler was planning the year the Spanish conflict was ended.

When *Ken* failed us as a weekly journal "one step left of center" and not one newspaper or magazine with a million circulation or more did an honest job of reporting the Fascist International's plan to take over all of Europe and the rest of the world, all of us who were friends of the Spanish Republic were desperate. There was a meeting in Carnegie Hall in New York at which notable persons spoke. There were plans for a protest march on Washington to picket the White House—we accused FDR of overlooking the facts that Germany and Italy had violated the neutrality pact by sending fighters and military supplies to Franco. And so while the Fascist armies and navies were fighting a war, the American friends of the Republic were making speeches and taking a poll of all the writers of the country.*

One year after the *Ken* disaster a stranger called on me and proposed starting a new popular illustrated weekly that would support the Loyalist cause. I applauded his plan and his idea, but I said that it would take about one million dollars just to get out the first issue.

"Well," replied the stranger, "I've got a million dollars."

He put his hand in his jacket pocket and took out a bulging leather thing. He opened it. There were bonds, certificates of deposit, bank statements, and the like, all for large sums of money.

When the stranger was leaving I asked him to repeat his name because I did not get it when he phoned me. It was Gilmor—without an e; his father was or had been a noted admiral in the U.S. Navy. I never saw Mr. Gilmor again. I had been certain the reason for the meeting was to offer me an editorial job, but that never eventuated. What did eventuate was a weekly called *Friday,* an amateurish sort of thing that lasted a little while, made no impact, and disappeared.

In 1939 the Italian infantry and German aviation, aided by a very few Spaniards, finally captured Madrid and established a fascist dictatorship. The Republic had held out for three years with no military aid, no armaments from abroad and no food.**

*Of five hundred replies those who favored the Republic numbered 495, neutrals numbered four, and there was one pro-Franco vote, a woman named Atherton who wrote a novel entitled *Black Oxen.* Among the neutrals there was one noted name: e. e. cummings. The anti-Franco 495 were headed by Dreiser, Lewis and Hemingway.

**In the eighteen months, 1936–1937, when Helen and I were in Madrid for the New York *Post,* one of the less than one percent of the entire American press favoring the Republic, we lived on four starches: bread, potatoes, rice and churos—something that looked like doughnuts but was extruded from a machine and sold by the meter; it was made of dough. We journalists, however, were the fortunate ones, for every four months or so we could take the train, cross the border into France and eat. The Spanish Republicans had no guns,

After the failure of *Friday*, several friends meeting at my rented house near Wilton, Connecticut, talked about starting a modest four-page weekly newsletter, printed on cheap newsprint, selling for fifty cents or one dollar a year. We figured we could get a start with, say, five thousand dollars. Inasmuch as the commercial press was, as usual, about ninety percent anti-labor, we decided to appeal to the new union labor movement known as the CIO for subscriptions at the beginning. Bruce Minton, who would edit the weekly newsletter with me, had a friend who would sound out the CIO immediately. We discussed a name. I spoke up for making the weekly absolutely fair and factual, printing straight news, no slanted pro-labor news, just the facts. I proposed several names that included the word fact or facts. Helen said, "Why not just call it *In fact?*" By May 1940 our CIO subscription solicitor presented us with a subscription-in-advance list of six thousand names and three thousand dollars in the bank. From the first issue on we were successful. Our subscription list approached 200,000—which we figured would be about one million readers; and we would have gone far beyond that had not almost every newspaper in the country and every crooked and prostituted journalist in the country united in red-baiting us—and finally destroying *In fact*.

Although the majority of friends of my newsletter did not ask that their names remain secret, the situation that Representative Martin Dies and Senator Joseph McCarthy created, the atmosphere of fear that prevailed for years, the complete irresponsibility of these two men, made it almost certain that every friend, no matter how firm and powerful he was, would be harmed and perhaps destroyed. Here are the names of the most notable individuals and groups that contributed news items or encouragement to my publication:

— A senator who became President of the United States: Harry S Truman, whom I had known as Captain Harry in the Rainbow Division, and who in exposing the Nazi

---

food or medicines and the world press published falsehoods about them, called them "reds" and let them die.

I. G. Farben deal with American oil companies accused them of treason.

— A senator who became a Justice of the Supreme Court: Sherman Minton. Shortly after I began publication in 1940, he not only subscribed but sent me money and names of a score of liberal senators to enter as subscribers.

— The wife of the President of the United States: Eleanor Roosevelt.

— George Polk, the CBS Radio correspondent in Greece, later murdered by the rightists—although the press blamed the left; now a journalism martyr.

— Drew Pearson, who contributed several items he feared to syndicate.

— Charles Malcolmson, press attaché, Department of Justice.

— Henry A. Wallace, Vice President of the United States, whose great "Century of the Common Man" speech was suppressed.

— Harold L. Ickes, Secretary of the Interior.

— Editors of the chief labor weeklies, notably Len De Caux of the *CIO News* and Edward Keating of the Railroad Brotherhoods' *Labor*.. Also Claud Cockburn of *The Week*, London, and the editors of the London *Tribune*.

— Members of the American Newspaper Guild: in ten years some two hundred of them contributed one or more items, usually news their papers suppressed or distorted.

— More than a score of leading senators and representatives.

— And, perhaps most important of all, the CIO unions, notably the autoworkers, oil workers and rubber workers. My first six thousand subscribers were CIO men and women; at all times at least one third of my subscription list was from the CIO.

• • •

Among the enemies of my newsletter, naturally enough, almost all were the large-circulation and powerful newspapers of the country, notably the press chains, Scripps-Howard, Hearst and Gannett, which either permitted or encouraged their syndicated columnists to attack *In fact* and libel its publisher. Equally disastrous for us was the silence of the great "respectable" press, notably *The New York Times,* whose managing editor, Edwin L. James, had given orders to his staff never to mention my newsletter or my books or my name. (I had testified for the Newspaper Guild in its NLRB suit against *The Times* in 1934 and James frankly told me on leaving the hearing that he would revenge himself in this way.) Other enemies included:

— Almost all of the six hundred stations of Mutual Radio network, whose chief oracle, Fulton Lewis, Jr., I had exposed.

— At least a score of members of the House and Senate whose pro-Mussolini and pro-Franco speeches and votes, and anti-Semitic remarks (frequently censored out of the *Congressional Record*), were known but never reported in the press. Our list included J. Parnell Thomas, who later went to jail as a common crook.

— Secret agencies, such as the FBI, and probably the U.S. Post office, which frightened not a few but eventually the majority of our subscribers enough to cancel or refrain from renewing.

— All the most powerful business organizations in the United States, notably the National Association of Manufacturers, all exposed by numerous Congressional Committees, but never in the press.

— Hundreds of leading reactionaries and pro-fascists, many named by Senator Black's lobbying investigation but never exposed by the press. (Note: everything called "left" was attacked by the press in those dark days, but "rightist" was sacred.)

• • •

Here are some facts about two sample enemies of my newsletter, the journalist Randolph Churchill and Congressman Karl Mundt:

When Roy Howard's United Features Syndicate employed Sir Winston Churchill's son, Randolph, as a columnist I pointed out in *In fact* that this man had favored both Hitler and Mussolini and helped to overthrow the Spanish Republic by writing a series of falsehoods favoring the traitor Franco. The article concluded with the statement that Randolph Churchill was more pro-fascist than any journalist in America.

A few weeks before Randolph Churchill's last visit to Franco Spain, *Reynolds News,* a great liberal London newspaper, said, "The Spanish embassy here is on the lookout for an English journalist who will visit Spain to write up the Franco scene. This report will be submitted to newspapers as an 'objective' account. Franco is offering a fat salary for this 'independent' review."

Churchill returned. He wrote a series in praise of Franco. The articles were distributed in Europe and America.

Imagine my surprise when I was notified that I would be sued by Churchill for libel if I did not retract the item I had reprinted from *Reynolds News.*

It had been my policy to correct every error of fact whether a correction was asked for or not. I insisted not only on truthfulness but also fairness. On receiving the request I wrote a simple statement, saying the item had appeared in *Reynolds News* and that Churchill objected. Meanwhile *Reynolds News* wrote me it was not being sued for libel or threatened; it stood by its story that Churchill was being paid by Fascist Spain. I so notified Churchill's lawyer. He again threatened to sue me despite the fact that the item was not challenged in England where the libel laws are a hundred times as severe as in America.

My lawyer told me it would cost $25,000 to defend a libel suit. I had no money. I had to apologize in print to Randolph Churchill for facts he could not deny in his native land.

One of the best illustrations of the difficulties of printing facts in the dark Dies-McCarthy era is the case of Karl Mundt and three others who constituted the South Dakota delegation in Congress.

The chairman of the Democratic Party organization in South Dakota, Walter H. Burke, wrote me, asking if I could identify a dozen easterners who had raised a slush fund and bought four Republicans: Mundt, Bushfield, Case and Gurney.

I easily identified Iréneé Du Pont, Lammot Du Pont, Alfred E. Sloan of General Motors, Joseph Pew of Sunoco and Sun Shipbuilding, members of the Mellon family and others who incidentally were the controlling interests of the National Association of Manufacturers (N.A.M.), and whose names were also listed in one of the La Follette Committee reports and the Temporary National Economic Committee reports as among the 207 who controlled American industry and business.

The Democratic Party issued a sensational statement denouncing these eastern interests for buying the South Dakota election, but with the exception of the little Mollala, S.D., *Pioneer,* not one newspaper reported this news. I sent the story to a friend, Senator Joseph Guffey of Pennsylvania, who inserted it in the *Congressional Record* after denouncing the Mundt slush fund in a speech on the floor. But this news was again suppressed with the following exceptions: columnist Drew Pearson and the St. Louis *Post-Dispatch*—which said editorially that the Pews, Du Ponts and other corporate heads "got away with murder in South Dakota."

Not one commercial newspaper or magazine investigated this scandal.

For years *In fact* noted the votes of Messrs. Mundt, Bushfield, Case and Gurney on measures favored by the great lobbies in Washington, notably that of the N.A.M., and in every instance every bill big business wanted and the labor unions opposed was supported by the South Dakota quartet.

Mr. Mundt replied to *In fact*'s exposure of the slush fund by making slanderous statements in the House and inserting libelous statements in the *Record,* secure in the knowledge that the only place in America where slander and libel are privileged are the houses of Congress and their daily publication. Mr. Mundt, by this outrageous although legal action, thus armed all the obviously dishonest columnists, notably Lewis and Sokolsky, who were beneficiaries of the same N.A.M. money that had helped him to repeat the falsehoods that eventually destroyed my newsletter.

Chapter 46

How We Defeated Martin Dies

A far greater enemy than Karl Mundt or the several members of Congress who, taking advantage of their immunity, committed criminal actions was Martin Dies, House Un-American Activities Committee chairman, and in my opinion the most un-American of them all—if by Americanism we mean American democratic principles. McCarthy, who gave the era its bad name, was at least American enough to permit the men he planned to pillory to defend themselves; Dies did not. Still more important, the atmosphere of the decades had changed, so that when the Wisconsin senator made speeches saying he held in his hand the list of names of 207 or 87 or whatever number of employees of the State Department "who are members of the Communist Party," enough good newspapers and commentators called public attention to the absurdities and contradictions, causing laughter and ridicule and a growing conviction that McCarthy was either lying or drunk, or both—and eventually helping his downfall.

But no one outside the small liberal weeklies, certainly not the free press, made any attempt to look for facts when Dies in the 1940s told the reporters there were exactly 1,121 federal employees who were subversives, and that altogether there were seven million dangerous "reds" in the United States. Attorney General Biddle and his staff devoted a long time to the list of 1,121 and found exactly three persons of "doubtful status" and fired them. News columnists, cartoonists and editorial writers overlooked this Dies fiasco. They also overlooked the fate of the 1,118 persons who had been cleared but whose careers might have been ruined. Mr. Dies made another public speech naming thirty government officials as subversives. Every one of them lost his job, although only two or three were of any doubtful standing and not one of them was found subversive.

President Roosevelt told his press conference—for quotation: "Martin Dies is a liar." Wendell Willkie told his press conference: "The Dies Un-American Committee is undermining the democratic process." The Hitler radio service endorsed Martin Dies and in the first years of World War II quoted him favorably in broadcasts aimed at the American forces in Europe. But the great American press either suppressed these news stories or buried them, so that no public opinion was created unfavorable to the representative—and he flourished.

And then, to the great surprise of the uninformed public, an election was held in Texas, and Martin Dies was defeated— by 34,916 to 5 votes (to be exact). But even this newsworthy political Waterloo was not commented upon by the press.

This, then, is "the rest of the story." From the day the Texas oil workers' union decided to throw Dies out of Congress, *In fact* cooperated with its leaders, supplying documentary evidence that was used to defeat him. If the Colt was the gun that won the West, *In fact* was the gun that blew Martin Dies into oblivion—although naturally, no one outside the unions ever gave it any credit.

All the newspapers in this Texas district, notably those in Port Arthur, were anti-labor. They fought the CIO with the foulest falsehoods, repeating Martin Dies's charge that the entire CIO, now almost half the organized labor strength of the nation, millions of Americans, was a Communist Party affiliate, or "Communist-dominated," or "Moscow-directed."

Along with many others who found they could never get an honest deal in the press of that era—labor unions, the chairmen of two state Democratic Party committees, Mr. Ickes, a score of senators—the Texas CIO oil workers turned to *In fact* for documentation with which to fight the Texas press. I sent President C. A. Knight of the Oil Workers International considerable evidence I had collected on the activities of Tidewater, Gulf and other companies, their records from government reports on labor spying, use of machine guns, strikebreaking, which should have been front-page news when issued by senate investigating committees, notably those of several La Follette committees and Senator O'Mahoney's Temporary National Economic Committee reports, No. 6 and No. 26.

Not one word of Knight's charges was published in Texas, but when Martin Dies, unable to answer documented facts, replied by again calling the CIO a "Communist outfit," he was headlined in the Port Arthur newspapers. Violence and bloodshed followed. An oil worker was killed in the town's streets, and the CIO demanded intervention by the Department of Justice. When the National Maritime Union announced it was unionizing one thousand black workers of Gulf Oil, Texas newspapers were outraged.

The Ku Klux Klan and the Nazi Bund joined the Texas press in supporting Dies. In *The Fiery Cross*, Imperial Wizard J. A. Colescott expressed the Klan view under this headline:

KLAN URGES THAT WORK OF
DIES COMMITTEE BE CONTINUED
Calls on Congress to Provide Ample Funds for
Further Investigation of Un-American Activities

and when the Bund in New York gave a reception for Dies, the newspaper headline read:

KUHN AT LUNCHEON HONORING DIES DECLARES
FOR CONTINUANCE OF QUIZ OF UN-AMERICANS

When Dies announced he would run again for the House of Representatives, the CIO oil union in Texas announced it had six thousand members who with their wives and friends would cast at least ten thousand votes for any man brave enough to run against him. (The oil union locals in Texas at that time subscribed en bloc to *In fact.*) Judge Combs agreed to run.

When the polls, one after another, showed that Dies would be defeated, he withdrew his candidacy suddenly, saying he was in ill health; then he told the Associated Press, which sent the statement to every morning newspaper in the country, that "It will become obvious to the people that the CIO will become the Communist Party of America."

This was the parting shot. The Houston *Post,* one of the few Texas newspapers that reported the situation fairly, later announced that Martin Dies, in retirement, was working on "a documented denunciation of the New Deal."

And that was the end of the most un-American of Americans.

Chapter 47

~~~~~~

Face to Face With Joe McCarthy

Unlike the war with Martin Dies in which my newsletter supplied part of the best munitions for the oil workers' union's heaviest artillery but nevertheless remained behind the scenes, my war with Joe McCarthy, carried on for years by *In fact,* ended in a face-to-face confrontation in Washington.

And, to this very day, every friend I have questions my opinion that of the two most notorious members of Congress of their times Dies was a more truly evil and despicable human being than was Joe McCarthy. (I am tempted to put an exclamation point at the end of that sentence. It surprises me, too; it is hard to believe, nevertheless true.)

When the FBI agent came to my house with a subpoena—mid-June 1953, it was almost three years after the demise of *In fact,* which, next to the Madison, Wisconsin, *Capital-Times* (William Evjue, editor), had been most active throughout McCarthy's public life in exposing his falsifications of his own record, his policy of character assassination, and the crookedness

357

of his income-tax returns and other financial matters for which a plain American citizen would have been arrested and sent to the penitentiary. Here are two sample *In fact* headlines:

U.S. SENATOR "NEGLECTS" TO REPORT
$43,000 PROFIT IN STOCK DEALS,
NEWS SERVICES KILL TAX SCANDAL
—February 14, 1948

McCARTHY DATA ON STATE DEPT.
"REDS" LIFTED
VERBATIM FROM ANTI-SEMITE'S SMEAR PAMPHLET
—April 17, 1950

The senator's income-tax falsification story was credited to the *Capital-Times* and the Milwaukee *Journal.* The news story naming the source of the most important (and sensational) of all the McCarthy charges—that the State Department was riddled with red termites—was sent me by Dr. Leon Birkhead of Friends of Democracy, who, comparing the listings in the pamphlet "America Betrayed" and the McCarthy speeches, found that the senator was repeating, frequently verbatim, the words of one Joe Kamp, co-publisher with Lawrence Dennis of *The Awakener,* the first openly fascist magazine in America, a man whose writings met with Hitler's enthusiastic approval, and who in 1948 was convicted of contempt of Congress and sentenced to four months in prison. Dr. Birkhead first sent his documentation to Senator McCarthy, asking for an explanation, and, receiving no reply, sent it to the press. But the newspapers of the nation in those days were not owned or directed by the type of men and women who twenty years later exposed Nixon, and so *In fact* devoted an entire issue, five thousand words, to news that should have made the front page of every conventional newspaper.

McCarthy himself probably never heard of *In fact,* but there can be no doubt that his attorney, Roy Cohn, and his chief investigator, J. B. Matthews, knew my newsletter and me very well. Although the senator gave me a square deal, as I have said, every question asked by Cohn and Matthews was loaded, slanted, a piece of entrapment. Throughout the hearing McCarthy, although sober that day, showed little interest in what I said, once I had taken the oath that "I am not now and never have been a member of the Communist Party." At least twice, perhaps three times, that great lawyer Cohn got in questions such as this: "What was the number of the Communist Party cell you belonged to in Connecticut?" and Matthews, an ex-liberal, who on turning sour became a red-baiter, and whose name had formerly appeared on the letterheads of twenty-three liberal, anti-fascist, or pro-Republican Spain organizations, kept nagging me about my name appearing on the letterheads of some fifty groups.

When I replied that I knew nothing of certain letterheads but was proud to appear on those of every group favoring Spain against the Fascist International of Franco, Hitler and Mussolini, the line changed and Matthews accused me of writing "anti-Catholic books."

"If you are referring to *The Vatican—Yesterday, Today and Tomorrow*," I replied, "it was made the choice of the Catholic Book Club—the Catholic book-of-the-month club." This shut Matthews up and brought a friendly smile from McCarthy.

Cohn then read extracts of my previous writings on the American Legion, the American Civil Liberties Union, my defense of Tito (who had defied Stalin, although Cohn chose to omit this fact), the "merchants of death" making money out of the war. In reply I mentioned "my friend General Smedley Butler" and the ACLU reports on the Legion plot to march on Washington and take over the government; also Legion strike-breaking activities, my reports on Spain and the little aid the Soviets had sent, and finally my *In fact* Tito interview and the disclosure that Stalin had tried to use Yugoslavia as a colony, to exploit and rob it.

McCarthy seemed bored. He brushed Cohn aside and asked me, "When did you stop publishing *In fact*?"

When I gave the date, 1950, McCarthy questioned me about my stand on the Korean War. Apparently this was a most important matter. I had in that year published a statement based on facts received from a former colleague, William Powell, Far

East correspondent of the *Tribune,* and I now repeated it: "I published facts, I did not take an editorial stand. The facts were that obviously the North Koreans, or Communists, were the aggressors militarily. It was proved by logistics. They could not have marched all the way from Pusan, defeated the South Koreans, conquering almost the entire nation, if they had not *planned* the entire military campaign. There had been a hundred border clashes before this. This was a planned war—I accused the North of aggression and said so in *In fact.*"

McCarthy suddenly broke off the questioning. "How many witnesses have we?" he asked. Cohn said, "One." McCarthy then said to me, "Wait outside, I'll call you back," and I went outside and immediately wrote out my experiences and talked with the AP, UP and other correspondents also waiting.

Wilkerson was the last of the four called that day. Suddenly, the hearing room doors opened and McCarthy, Senator Symington, Cohn, Matthews, and others came out, McCarthy stopping for a moment to speak to the newspapermen: "Seldes and Freeman," said the senator, "are cleared. I am holding Kent and Wilkerson over for tomorrow," meaning for the almost daily Hollywood-production-style public hearing.

I do not know what I was "cleared" of, but I do remember that that word was used, and that Freeman and I were among the few of the hundreds of persons called before this senator who could ever afterward say we were "cleared by Joe McCarthy." I am also sure that my colleagues with whom I had had a friendly conversation sent out the news and did not censor or change that word. Nevertheless there was almost no mention of this fact anywhere. *The New York Times* was one of the few newspapers which, reporting on page one that Kent was held over, said in its last paragraph on page fourteen that Freeman and I were "not held over." No one ever told the public, which for years had been reading libelous attacks on us, that we had been "cleared."

As I walked alongside the famous (or notorious) McCarthy I could not help saying to him: "Senator, do you know that I came to this hearing *voluntarily*?"

"Hell you did," he replied. "I subpoenaed you. I sent an FBI agent to Connecticut after you."

I then showed him the supposed subpoena. It was not the original, but a carbon copy, unsigned, useless. A secretary probably had filed the original in the senator's office.

McCarthy looked at the worthless paper, laughed and said, "Well, I'll fix that up for you," and signed the duplicate "Joe McCarthy." Then he added, "Just for that, I'll let you ride in the senators' elevator with me," and we rode, shook hands cordially and went our ways.

To this day I cannot understand this man who had given this era a bad name (as Nixon did to another, about two decades later), and whom I had exposed as a crook and a liar and a repeater of fascist and anti-Semitic propoganda: why did he give me a square deal?

The answer might very well be that McCarthy was a nobody, a puppet with ambition, manipulated by others, and most notably by his three foremost newspaper friends, Fulton Lewis, Jr., Westbrook Pegler and George E. Sokolsky.

Chapter 48

〰〰〰

The Third SOB:
Reader's Choice

It may be a mere coincidence or it may be an illustration of the low state of the media of the time, but it is a fact frequently published and frequently approved that McCarthy had voluntarily helping him three of America's most powerful columnists and radio commentators; the very three (in my opinion) who are the likeliest candidates for a place in my proposed Hall of Infamy. I would leave it to readers to choose the one to occupy a niche alongside Gabriele D'Annunzio and Errol Flynn.

All my five, elected and candidates, fit well with Dr. Johnson's view: he once wrote that he knew of no crime a man could commit greater than "poisoning the sources of eternal truth." Two of the three did it for money—for big money; one honestly admitted he was a crook; the other hid his connections. The third candidate named here developed a warped mind, as his advocacy of lynching clearly showed, which may, to a psychiatrist perhaps, excuse him from inclusion in modern journalism's most disgraceful trinity.

An attorney for all three, perhaps a devil's advocate, could argue that not one of the three is as guilty as his employer who agreed with him, aired or published him, encouraged him and possibly directed and plotted his activities. Although this view has merit, my relations with all three convince me each was quite satisfied with himself and enjoyed his work of character assassination.

The four radio oracles earning the most money and influencing the largest audience at that time, according to statistics published in September 1950, were:

Commentator	Estimated Audience	Income
Walter Winchell	25,000,000	$650,000
Drew Pearson	15,000,000	$400,000
Fulton Lewis, Jr.	10,000,000	$350,000
Westbrook Pegler	45,000,000	$ 90,000

This table is not complete because in two cases, Pearson and Pegler, their newspaper readers added tens of millions each, and radio was confined to Sunday night broadcasts. Of the four men read and listened to by the majority of the people of the United States one, Winchell, was fairly neutral in politics, and one, Pearson, courageously published exposés of McCarthy's illegal activities as well as his unethical and immoral actions. Two, Pegler and Lewis, were the main members of the journalistic trio who not only favored McCarthy, slanted the news for him or omitted unfavorable news, but voluntarily worked for him.

Although not listed among the radio giants with tens of millions of readers, Don Hollenbeck must be named as one of the two men with a large following—the other of course being Pearson—who during the months and years of McCarthy's growing power spoke out against him. But most of the press lords, notably Howard, Hearst and Gannett, and the group that then owned the Mutual Network, share responsibility for what is now known as the shameful McCarthy Era.

Before considering the candidates for my third SOB, I would like to repeat and emphasize this important fact: every word that follows appeared in print during the lifetimes of these three men, and although all three engaged almost daily in libels and slanders and were frequently sued for libel, and lost, and paid out money, none of the three was ever able to sue *In fact* because everything it published—for example, a Nazi document seized by the U.S. Army proving Fulton Lewis, Jr., a voluntary helper of Hitler—was not only true but also libel-proof.

Lewis in McCarthy's time had the largest radio hookup of all, 406 of Mutual's six hundred or more stations, each one paying him money for his secretly subsidized National Association of Manufacturers' propaganda and anti-labor views, and an additional 225 stations, which could find no sponsors for Lewis but approved of his character assassinations and libels and reactionary slant of the news so much that they paid him out of their own pockets. (The New York *Post* called Lewis "the golden voice of reaction," adding another proof to the declaration of the noted educator, John Dewey, that reactionaries controlled not only the army and police, but also the schools—and the press.)

The entire issue of *In fact* for August 7, 1950, was devoted to a single news item, headlined:

OFFICIAL STATE DEPARTMENT DOCUMENTS
SHOWING FULTON LEWIS, JR., AS A
HITLER ADVISER ARE SUPPRESSED

The reader can find the entire documentation in the *Congressional Record* of July 14, 1950, pages 10295–8. It was Senator Hubert H. Humphrey who exposed Lewis and, after obtaining a certificate of authenticity from the Department of State—its Secretary, Dean Acheson, was accused of suppressing them—placed translations in the daily journal of Congress. Here is Number one, the most important:

> Habana: July 26, 1940, 00.45 o'clock. . . .
> Arrival: July 26, 1940, 15.05 o'clock
> No. 140 of July 25
> Press adviser Washington Embassy (Kurt) Sell transmits following memorandum. . . .
> One Washington journalist . . . told me quite positively Roosevelt will declare war on Germany in October. . . .

Fulton Lewis approached me yesterday. [Lewis] . . . has been friendly with me for twelve years. . . . He requests therefore he be allowed to expound the following idea . . . have the Führer send a telegram to Roosevelt of not more than two hundred words . . . of approximately the following content: "You, Mr. Roosevelt, have many times turned to me with appeals and have constantly expressed the wish to see a bloody war avoided. I have not declared war on England. . . . I request of you, for your part, to approach Churchill and to talk him out of his senseless pigheadedness." Lewis added, Roosevelt would naturally answer with incivility and animosity; that didn't matter. But upon the North American people, and above all, South Americans, the appeal will make a deep impression. . . . Tauchnitz.

Sell refers to Lewis as "an American journalist admiring Germany and the Führer." In another letter he warns Lewis that Drew Pearson "has got hold of a telegram from Habana. . . . I have done my best to kill the thing so far as you are concerned."

"With these letters and these documents, the facts are now public, and available for judgment by the American people," concluded Senator Humphrey. He was wrong. The documents and facts were suppressed in the big press, never mentioned on any one of the radio networks. Only one New York newspaper, the *Post,* published them, whereupon Lewis attacked this daily.

On the other hand, when Lewis made one of his outrageous false charges, the press generally repeated it without investigating the matter. Illustration: Mr. Lewis's December 5, 1949, broadcast, which Mutual advertised in a press release headed: REDS GOT ATOM ORE IN '43. The newspapers gladly picked it up, many headlines reading

SALE OF A-BOMB ORE TO REDS
NEW DEAL RELEASED URANIUM IN 1943

Hopkins was named as the villain. He was no longer alive and could not defend himself. But ex–Vice President Wallace was also libeled, and he telegraphed the Un-American Activities Committee to investigate "the continuous character assassination over the Mutual Broadcasting network, and through the press by the *World-Telegram* [Lewis's New York outlet for his United Press articles]." The Atomic Energy Commission, the U.S. Army and the U.S. Air Force intelligence service all gave the lie to Lewis. But no correction was ever made. (In this instance when I refer to "the press" I mean the Republican Party–supporting press.)

Public Opinion Quarterly named Lewis as the prime example of "irresponsibility on the air." In a detailed study it found that the statements made by Lewis were "wrong" at least seventy percent of the time—among the "wrong" items were outright falsifications and libels, as for example a red-baiting attack on an educator named Pearl Wanamaker, who sued Lewis for libel and got $55,000 from him, and another $100,000 from his Mutual Network.

My first contact with Lewis was a note from him, evidently a subscriber, when *In fact* published a suppressed news item: Senator Harry Truman had just declared, "It is treason," when his committee, investigating the practices of great corporations during the war, found the trade agreement between Standard Oil and I. G. Farben that gave the Nazis synthetic rubber. Mr. Lewis kindly wrote: "Your little publication has tremendous influence and a tremendous and loyal following. You have built up what I have tried to build up over the air—a feeling among your readers that you are telling them the truth, and the whole truth, and nothing but the truth—and I think that you do that within the usual human qualifications of all of us." (Could this man, who was seventy percent wrong always, and who engaged in red-baiting, slander and character assassination, be capable of totally deceiving himself also? A subject for Dr. Freud.)

When, later, *In fact* mentioned Lewis's failure to report certain news items he wrote me he had never heard of the La Follette Investigations or other Senate reports on the great corporations, or of "Thirteen Ruling Families of America," or Senator Black's Lobbying Committee investigation, which named pro-fascist organizations and their financial supporters, or any of these numerous significant events in Washington during the many years in which he had been broadcasting. "I heartily disapprove of anti-labor propaganda," he wrote in conclusion.

But most amazing of all was Lewis's letter indignantly denying he was broadcasting the propaganda of the National Industrial Information Committee, the propaganda branch of the N.A.M.—he was merely in the pay of the National Association of Manufacturers, he said, and had never heard of its press and publicity department, the N.I.I.C. I sent him the complete documentation.*

When these reports gave them documented evidence, the United Auto Workers protested Lewis's biased and false reporting against labor, asking the Federal Communications Commission to cancel the licenses of certain Mutual stations. The National Maritime Union protested Lewis's "malicious lies," also asking station cancellations. The FCC acted, and Mutual forced Lewis to apologize to both unions, to say he had been one hundred percent wrong. This somewhat tarnished the golden voice of reaction for a while but never stopped it from slandering liberal and New Deal organizations and leaders, and scores of individuals who did not have the large sums necessary to start libel suits and see them through.

The concluding word on this character assassin could well be the report in *Time*, November 24, 1961, which quotes Mr. Lewis criticizing the moderation of the John Birch Society in merely asking for the impeachment of the Chief Justice. "I would lynch Earl Warren," *Time* quotes Lewis as saying.

As for advocacy of lynching, it is a fact that the very first item Westbrook Pegler wrote when he was elevated to the position of columnist by Roy Howard of the Scripps-Howard press was in favor of lynching. Mr. Howard thought it a bit too strong, so he held it over from Monday to Wednesday!

---

*Readers will find it, with photostats, on pages 184–199 of *Facts and Fascism*, which I published in 1943; and they can look up the La Follette Committee on Education and Labor, 76th Congress, 1st session, Report 6, part 6: the N.A.M.; also TNEC Monograph 26.

Pegler and I once worked in the London offices of the United Press, and by coincidence each of us got an appointment in 1918 to the press section, G-2D, of the U.S. Army in France. Pegler was the youngest member, an individualist, a brilliant writer, a dissenter, an iconoclast; he believed in no rules and thought laws were meant to be broken, and so I admired him greatly.

However, even before the American divisions were in the field, and long before the A.E.F. took part in any important action, General Pershing requested the United Press to replace Pegler because of "undisciplined" and "irresponsible" behavior, and this was done, and at twenty-seven and a half years of age I became the youngest member. We heard later that Pegler had enlisted in the navy.

Although Helen and I had our home in Vermont, we spent winters in the late 1930s in houses in Connecticut and there renewed friendship with the Peglers. In 1937 when he wrote in one of his columns, "As for General Franco, I'd rather see him in hell than in church," I told Peg he was the only person read by millions of Americans who was on the Spanish Republican side. The year before, he had been sent to Berlin to report the Olympics and had denounced Hitler, and Naziism, and for a while the liberal-democratic movement in America thought that at last it had a champion in the press, more powerful than its one friend on the radio, Don Hollenbeck of CBS.

We corresponded. He signed his letters "Love, Peg." But I never saw him again after the Spanish War, and no one has ever explained what happened that turned him into one of the meanest, cruelest, most slanderous reactionaries in the country. A mutual friend and fellow member of G-2D, Heywood Broun, said "Pegler was bitten by an income-tax return," but I cannot believe it was money. Perhaps it was the tragic loss of his wife. Whatever the cause, he began to use his columns not only to slander but to lie about FDR and the New Deal and eventually make outrageous personal attacks on Eleanor Roosevelt.

When Pegler's falsehoods, libels and irrational attacks on people made it impossible for Roy Howard to continue publishing him, Pegler naturally moved to a more hospitable place; he became a Hearst columnist. Among the persons he libeled was Quentin Reynolds, who sued him, employed the noted attorney Louis Nizer, and won an award of one million dollars, the biggest libel award in history to that date. Hearst had to pay part of it. By 1962 even Hearst found it impossible to put up with Pegler, so the columnist found his haven at last with the John Birch Society; he became a contributor to their *American Opinion.*

When Eleanor Roosevelt died, Pegler published an article comparing her to Polly Adler, who had been the madame of the most notorious bordello in New York City. In another contribution to the Birch magazine Pegler, recalling the attempted assassination of President Roosevelt, said that if Zangara had been a better marksman "he would have been a great benefactor to mankind."

Along with the rest of the political and journalistic exponents of all forms of Fascism (and more recently Russian Communism), Pegler became more and more an anti-Semite in his Birch Society writings. He made anti-Semitic speeches and eventually became a barroom brawler, shouting anti-Semitic obscenities. Addressing a Hollywood women's club called "Friends of Westbrook Pegler," he said of Hitler's murder of six million Jews that "the victims were of course Communists," and so it didn't matter at all. At the famous Stork Club in New York City he created a scene shouting "Jew-Communist" at several other guests and challenging them to a fistfight. He was thrown out by Sherman Billingsley. A passer-by tried to lift him from the gutter but Pegler began screaming "Nigger-bastard" at the good Samaritan, a black chauffeur. The Anti-Defamation League protested to *American Opinion* about not only Pegler's writings but also its distribution of anti-Semitic pamphlets, and eight months later received a letter from Robert Welch saying he was "quite unhappy" with certain of Pegler's writings. By May 1964 even the Birch Society could no longer keep Pegler.

The third of the McCarthy masterminds—persons with millions of followers who not only approved of the senator but were his friends and advisers on relations with the press and other members of the media—was George E. Sokolsky, or "Sok," as he was pleased to have himself called by his friends. My second or third encounter with him is perhaps worth reporting. It was at the apartment of a very successful lawyer, on either upper Fifth Avenue or Central Park West, circa 1938, and the conversation, as I now recall it, went something like this:

"What are you doing now, Seldes?"

"Freelancing. Writing another book."

"Making a lot of money?"

"Just getting by." (I had not had a best-seller for years, or ever since the newspapers or their book reviewers or both, in revenge for criticism of the press, decided that boycott was better than personal attacks.)

"You'll never make a good living that way. The only way for a newspaperman to make a good living nowadays is to be a crook!"

(He stopped at his own exclamation point, and everyone at the dinner table heard him and became interested.)

"Be a crook, Seldes; but don't be a little crook. Be a big crook. I'm a big crook. I've made a lot of money. Be a big crook, Seldes."

The fact that Sokolsky was a crook was not news, but his confession was interesting to all present. He had been exposed by at least three Senate investigating committees and by the liberal weeklies. The time I first came on his name was in 1933 when, returning from Europe, I offered Harpers a book I proposed to call *Merchants of Death*. (Editor Eugene Saxton changed the title to *Iron, Blood and Profits* because the British League for Industrial Democracy had once published a little pamphlet with my proposed title and Saxton respected it.) Searching for material for my American chapters, I found that at the time Sokolsky was correspondent for *The New York Times* in the Far East he was also double-dealing by selling 7.9 cartridges to T. V. Soong, Chinese finance minister.

But Sok was even more than that: he was a triple-dealer. Because at the time he was selling munitions he was also in the pay, secretly, of the Chinese government and edited a propaganda weekly for it. However, being in the pay of China did not stop Sok from, again secretly, working for the potential enemy, Japan. (On December 2, 1941, five days before Pearl Harbor, this man, who had already been exposed—not by the press, but by the liberal weekly, *The Nation*, as a Japanese paid agent—wrote in his syndicated column: "In spite of bellicose talk, the Japanese want no war with us." Sok certainly earned his Japanese money.)

To the credit of the *Times* it must be emphasized that it had no knowledge either of the merchant-of-death episode or the China and Japan employment. When *The Nation* published the facts, the *Times* let Sokolsky go, but the *Herald-Tribune* took him on when he returned to America.

One of the foulest episodes in modern newspaper history is contained in the report of the Committee on Education and Labor.*

The La Follette Committee states that the National Association of Manufacturers, once investigated by Congress and exposed for bribing members of the House and the Senate to pass anti-labor and anti-union legislation, had changed its tactics and now sought to corrupt public opinion in the United States via the press: everything from comic strips to editorials was supplied free to newspapers, daily and weekly, and a majority of the smaller publications—some five thousand of them—accepted and published this propaganda.

Concerning the self-confessed "big crook" Sokolsky, the La Follette Committee made disclosures that were known to *In fact* readers but previously suppressed and now again suppressed in the majority commercial press: that he had been put on the monthly payroll for one thousand dollars by the American Iron and Steel Institute (for making speeches attacking unionization) while still in the employ of the *Herald Tribune*; and been paid $7,133.32 by Hills & Knowlton, now one of the most successful public relations agencies and the agency employed at the time

---

*The La Follette Committee, No. 6, Part 6. See especially pages 159, 162 and 163.

by almost all corporations which tried to destroy the unions and which were, generally speaking, supporting the big interests and against the general welfare.

It is one of the nice ironies of the McCarthy case that, although he was the darling of the press and largely the successful creation of Lewis, Pegler and Sokolsky, it was a journalist—but not a newspaper writer—who at the moment of truth delivered the deathblow to McCarthyism.

McCarthy had never lost a battle until, without or against the advice of his three mentors—or it may have been because he was drunk at the time—he attacked the U.S. Army and met his Waterloo. The courageous journalist, Edward R. Murrow of CBS, prepared a documentary that is now of historical value. But all Morrow did was give the facts; he presented McCarthy himself, year after year, contradictory statement after contradictory statement, until viewers with any intelligence whatever could see the crookedness and the falsehoods—shall we say "obvious lies"—of the great press hero. The facts, fairly and honestly presented, convinced the American public.

Only one powerful man remained faithful to the crooked idol he had helped create: Fulton Lewis, Jr., gave over his entire Mutual Radio Network program one day to permit McCarthy to attack Murrow and "segments of the press" with the usual but now dead and stinking charge of "association with reds."

Chapter 49

Friend or Enemy? J. Edgar Hoover

For many years I thought J. Edgar Hoover was a friend. Our correspondence began shortly after *In fact* was started and continued for five years. It began the day after I received a death threat—it was not my first and did not worry me. At the time Mussolini threw me out of Italy there were quite a number of them, all from Chicagoans who loved the fascist dictator and approved of his assassination of the socialist leader Matteotti. Most of these letters had no signature; one was signed "The Black Hand."

An American fascist outfit calling itself the White Shirts and commanded by George W. Christians had been exposed by my newsletter. Mr. Christians replied by threatening to kill me. This meant nothing. But there was a postscript that was a death threat against the President of the United States, and I knew from newspaper experiences with public safety agencies, local and national, that assassinations throughout centuries of history had followed threats spoken or written generally by crackpots or "patriots," all egotists, and frequently ignored by authorities. I mailed Mr. Christian's letter to Mr. Hoover thinking the FBI was the agency that protected President Roosevelt. Mr. Hoover replied:

> This is an acknowledgment of your letter . . . enclosing a letter addressed to you by George W. Christians of Chattanooga, Tenn.
>
> Please be advised that a copy of your letter and the original enclosure which accompanied same have been furnished Mr. Frank J. Wilson, chief, Secret Service Division . . . who is charged with the duty of protecting the life of the President.
>
> Your courtesy in communicating with this Bureau is appreciated.

Three or four days later two members of the Secret Service came to see me. They not only confirmed what I had previously heard about assassins betraying themselves, but also informed me that the U.S. Secret Service had compiled a thirty-volume history of assassinations, probably unique in the world, beginning with Egypt and the Bible, Julius Caesar, and the several Presidents of the United States. They also told me the Secret Service had a list of tens of thousands of names, "every radical, every crackpot" in every village, town and city in the country, each one to be watched or arrested whenever the President passed through or visited his vicinity.

When I suggested that such arrests could not be made legally, the Secret Service said there were many ways of dealing with "suspicious" characters. "If the suspect, of whom we have a complete record, frequents saloons," said one agent, "we follow him, get to talking with him, and start a fight with him. We have already arranged with the local police. And so the saloonkeeper calls the police and both of us are arrested for disorderly conduct and the suspect never realizes that the half-drunken guy who hit him is really a Secret Service agent. Both of us are locked up as 'drunk and disorderly,' and both of us are taken before a magistrate the next morning and fined or freed with a warning. Meanwhile the President has come and gone, and the suspect never knows anything."

(I forgot these friendly disclosures until the day the newspapers published the fact that the Secret Service had had Oswald on its list of suspicious persons who had bragged about "getting the President." Oswald should have been watched, followed, gotten out of the way that fatal day in Dallas.)

Christians continued to send me letters with death threats. In one of his footnotes he wrote of FDR: "What a neck for a noose." I continued to mail the letters to the Secret Service.

As for Mr. Hoover's letters,* nine of them in all, the majority of them are denials that the FBI engaged in such illegal and unholy activities as taking the names of persons receiving my newsletter or watching the mail my wife and I received. For example: a soldier at the training base in Marfa, Texas, wrote me saying the FBI had a man in the post office whose only duty was watching certain publications, mine included. Mr. Hoover denied it.

One year there was a flood of letters from subscribers saying letter carriers were taking names or warning their friends that the FBI agent in the local post office, or the city branch post office, compiled names not only of *In fact* subscribers, but also of all who read the four or five liberal weeklies then as now trying to reach a few more than the saturation point of twenty-five or thirty thousand. Mr. Hoover denied it. A score of my readers offered to send in enough money to have their weekly sent first-class in a sealed envelope with no evidence of its source.

And then, one day in January 1945, a strange thing happened. I received a communication in a "penalty envelope." It was from the Post Office, Norwalk, Connecticut—where I had moved in 1940 to be near the printers of *In fact*, in New York City—postmarked January 10, and although addressed to "Mrs. George Seldes," it was not intended for her. Here is the text in full:

---

* They may be read under certain conditions, since they repose with my "literary remains" in the library of the University of Pennsylvania.

UNITED STATES POST OFFICE   First Class
Norwalk, Connecticut
January 10, 1945.

Special Agent in Charge, F.B.I.
510 Trust Company Building
New Haven 10, Connecticut

My dear Sir:

The following pieces of mail have been received at this post office addressed to Mrs. Helen Seldes, Grist Mill Road, Norwalk, Connecticut, your file No. 100-6956.

Sender—(Card) League of Women Shoppers, Inc., 1133 Broadway, New York, N.Y.
    "   (Circular) Same as above.

Respectfully yours,
James H. Slattery,
Postmaster
Stephen R. Bray. [signature]
Assistant Postmaster

Here was documentary proof that the assistant postmaster of the town in which we lived was reporting every piece of mail, circulars as well as letters, my wife Helen (who was managing editor of *In fact*) and I (who sat at home and wrote all or most of it) were receiving daily. This was absolute proof of one of two things:

(1) J. Edgar Hoover was lying to me when he wrote me there was no FBI watch on our mail, or

(2) J. Edgar Hoover was ignorant of what was going on in the post office and the FBI.

It also raised a question: was the mailing of the FBI report to us an accident, or did we have a friend in the Norwalk post office who was more loyal to my newsletter than he (or she) was to the FBI?

I immediately made a photographic copy of envelope and letter and sent them to my friend J. Edgar Hoover. Mr. Hoover did not answer. Mr. Hoover never wrote me again.

Chapter 50

~~~~~~~~~~

Secret Friends:
Hollenbeck, Polk, Others

To this very day I have never disclosed the names of living friends and strangers who more or less secretly contributed to my weekly: all are younger than I and I hope they are still alive. In the 1940-to-1950 decade they would have lost their jobs; their careers might have been ruined if it were known that they helped a publication that the Dies Committee had denounced (and whose "clearance" by the McCarthy Committee had not been reported). Among my friends were:

Mr. X of the Hearst White House staff.

Miss X of the secretarial pool of the National Association of Manufacturers, who sent me the documentation of a score of N.A.M. campaigns.

Editors of two Scripps-Howard newspapers, who worked for Roy Howard but did not approve of many of his dirty journalistic tricks.

Editors of Hearst newspapers, who sent me seven originals

of Mr. Hearst's "Chief Says . . . " orders, each aimed at manipulating the news and the minds of Americans.

Both in number and importance my chief helpers were fellow newspapermen (notably Polk, Pearson, Hollenbeck and Malcolmson), and when you add the occasional contributions by the two hundred members of the Newspaper Guild, the fact becomes obvious that the employees of the press lords in those corrupt days were the true knights of the First Amendment. One of them today is known as a martyr in the cause of freedom of the press.

The Truth About George Polk

While the Truman-Marshall Plan was being ballyhooed as aiding nations endangered by the Russian advance in Europe, notably Greece and Turkey, objective American journalists outside the country were attempting to warn the American government that only too frequently it was helping elements totally opposed to the American ideal of democracy—in plain words, parties and governments ranging from reactionary to fascist.

In Greece there was a political struggle raging, which included everything from guerrilla attacks to civil war. On one side were the monarchists, rightists, reactionaries and fascists; on the other the republicans, democrats, leftists, socialists and communists. Whatever their own views, the majority of foreign correspondents were attempting to report objectively; the most notable were Homer Bigart of the New York *Herald-Tribune,* Ray Daniell of *The New York Times* and George Polk of CBS.

Polk had known of my newsletter *In fact* before going to Greece. The issue of March 22, 1948, mentioned Bigart's cable to the *Herald-Tribune* saying the Greek government had begun the execution of "leftists" as "the result of the Greek government's interpretation of the Truman Doctrine." But the big story of the week, three of the four pages, was headlined:

UNCENSORED: THE TRUTH ABOUT GREECE

• • •

and carried an editorial note intended to shield the secret contributor, George Polk. We had never written him, never asked for help—it was just one of the contributions of the two hundred newspapermen who, angry at the suppression of news, frustrated by their inability to get the facts published, found an outlet in *In fact*.

A large part of the Polk contribution is the story of the Greek rightists—who had U.S. government and U.S. press support—attacking U.S. journalists trying to do an honest job in Greece. Although he did not mention himself, we inserted a paragraph about Polk further to throw the pro-rightists off the trail. Polk's last paragraph, in light of the murder of this noted correspondent by the rightists, is significant. He wrote: "In addition, now that many correspondents are writing such critical stories on the dominant right faction of the government, there are any number of vague hints that "somebody is likely to get hurt."

Did Polk foresee his own death at the hands of the rightists?

If the American press instead of engaging in its "non-conspiracy of silence" about *In fact* from 1940 on, had read our May 31, 1948, issue it would have known most of the truth about George Polk—which it did not publish until about thirty years later. Here is our story in full:

WHO MURDERED POLK?

The murder of George Polk, correspondent in Greece of the Columbia Broadcasting System, has been a great shock to the world of journalism, and is especially shocking to the editors of *In fact*—and will be to its readers when they learn that the tremendously important exclusive and uncensored news item we printed in our issue of March 22 was by this writer.

As a rule *In fact* does not print items anonymously, but to protect our source and especially to protect Polk we not only did not indicate the source, but actually inserted a paragraph about Polk himself which would throw the Greek fascist dictatorship off the scent.

When Polk was murdered in Salonika the Greek government immediately blamed it on the "bandits and guerrillas," as the five anti-fascist groups fighting it are called by them. (Only one of the EAM-ELAS groups is communist.)

In the item which *In fact* published it is clearly shown that Polk was no friend of Greek monarchism, fascism, and reaction. He was not pro-EAM [which was Communist], but he was one of the fair and honest men who was willing to report both sides. He named *New York Times* correspondent A. C. Sedgwick and others as sending out pro-fascist Greek news.

"Somebody is likely to get hurt," Polk stated in the report to CBS which *In fact* published [and CBS did not broadcast]. He believed that if reporters told the truth—as he did—the Greek monarcho-fascist government would not hesitate to use physical violence.

The ancient Greeks believed that Truth would arrive eventually "limping on the arm of Time." The modern Greeks, the ruling monarchist-reactionary-fascist government of Polk's time, blamed the "reds." Neither CBS nor the U.S. press, which called Polk a martyr, made an effort then to find the assassins. *In fact* had neither the money nor the means of investigating. And so Greek truth limped along for some thirty years. On May 1, 1977, *The New York Times* published a full column under the heading

COVER-UP CHARGED IN REPORTER'S KILLING
U.S. Inquiries into 1948 Murder
in Greece Said to Have Left
Many Questions Unsolved

Again the statement is made that in the Greek civil war "Communist guerrillas were fighting royalist troops in northern Greece," whereas the truth is that one-fifth of the anti-government forces were Communists—just as in Spain in 1936, where the "red" percentage and power were even less. But three decades later the *Times* did report that Polk "had been making increasingly critical reports about the right-wing Greek government and was in Salonika on his way to interview General Vafaiades, leader of the left-wing guerrillas." If the press and

CBS had published these facts—which *In fact* did—in 1948, they might have stopped the Greek rightists from murdering Polk.

Don Hollenbeck of CBS

*A*lthough Don Hollenbeck was not murdered by rightists, he, like Polk, may be considered a martyr—along with Zenger and Lovejoy and Don Mellett—in the unending war for freedom of the press in America.

He was not a muckraker, or an investigative reporter or a crusader, but he was always a non-conformist, a dissenter, an individualist, a free and independent man who in the Shakespearean sense spoke truth and shamed the devil. He was the first, and so far as I know, the only liberal anti-reactionary journalist who in all history ever was heard or read by the millions.

My first communication with Hollenbeck was a request for permission to reprint a part of one of his "CBS Views the Press" broadcasts. Almost immediately afterwards he began contributing items, never asking that I keep the source secret—which I did—and eventually risking criticism and censure by sending me a signed story. He was also the one and only colleague, reporter or editor, in all the ten years *In fact* was red-baited, libeled, branded "red" and generally ostracized, who mentioned my weekly by name from coast to coast, complimented it on important exclusives, and in short, obeyed the unwritten and unused law that "news is news" no matter what its source, and must be reported.

For example, in May 1949 I published one of many general exposés of groups of newspapers, statewide and nationwide, this one originated by the Chicago *Daily News* and St. Louis *Post-Dispatch,* to which I added a similar exposé of New York city and state papers. My headline was:

ILLINOIS PUBLISHERS, EDITORS, PAID $305,000
FROM STATE SLUSH FUND
TO PRINT GOP PROPAGANDA.

Hollenbeck credited *In fact* for its share in the exposé but corrected it for saying the Associated Press had suppressed the news. My error was not quite an error. The AP held up the news fourteen days. And when it did send it out, not one newspaper of the circa 1,750 published daily in the country, with the two exceptions, the originators, printed it.

Mr. Hollenbeck obviously made few friends in the media. We shared many of the same enemies. Few who heard him realized the great courage this journalist had exposing not only the McCarthyites but also the newspapers and columnists who were much more responsible than the senator himself for blackening a decade. No one but his wife knew of the intimidations and pressures and threats Don Hollenbeck suffered.

Years later mutual friends told me he was "painfully depressed" in his last days. He spoke of "the Hearstlings" who were using not only the most powerful newspaper chain but also the hundreds of other newspapers that, despite Mr. Hearst's participation in the assassination of President McKinley and despite Mr. Hearst's $400,000-a-year deal with Hitler, voluntarily subscribed to his services—news, columnists, features as well as the necessary comic strips.

In the 1970s the Irving Caesar Foundation originated the Hollenbeck Award, donating a modest sum in the hope that greater and richer foundations would endow the award permanently.*

The Hollenbeck Award was administered by the New York University School of Journalism for several years, until the money gave out. Unfortunately it did not receive a large endowment, as have other journalism funds.

Charles T. Malcolmson

*E*very government official who contributed to *In fact* did so openly, with one exception. Although he did not request it, we

---

* Mr. Caesar, of course, is the man who would rather write the nation's songs than be its President. Incidentally, in every one of the thirty-seven countries in Europe, North Africa and the Near East in which I have worked I have heard "Tea for Two" sung, have seen freshly printed copies of the sheet music, and am convinced that this song is the best known and most popular in the world.

kept secret the name of Charles T. Malcolmson, who from 1940 to 1945 was director of public relations for the Department of Justice, and after that director of public relations for the U.S. War Crimes Commission. He died of a heart attack in Nuremberg on May 30, 1946, and this is the first time I have disclosed his name.

Malcolmson contributed many of the most important news items during the first years of *In fact*. He sent me the materials for the entire fifth issue, dated July 15, 1940, which was headlined "The Truth About Wendell Willkie" and it was the truth, it was news, and it was suppressed news about a man running for President with a likely chance of being elected. Here are the main points of the Malcolmson report:

1. In an address to the National Press Club in Washington Willkie spoke openly for industrial dictatorship in the United States. [I explained to readers that this approximated Mussolini's corporate totalitarian state.]
2. Willkie called for a let-down of New Deal social and economic welfare reforms.
3. End of all government interference with business.
4. All aid to the Allies short of war.
5. Willkie made no attempt to pose as a "liberal." The Malcolmson report states that this label was put on Willkie by Russell Davenport, former editor of *Fortune*, "who knew that the American people (scared stiff of the taint of Wall Street, public utilities and Big Business) want a 'liberal.'"

The fact that in the course of his campaign the Republican candidate for President actually changed his views in no way diminishes the great importance of the above declaration of a political philosophy as headline news. Nor is the usual "off-the-record" condition of National Press Club declarations an excuse for failure to publish, provided the rule of "no direct quotation" is respected.

In a letter to me Malcolmson notes that although Willkie for this declaration must not be called a "native American fascist," he showed himself "the 'closest thing' to one yet to receive serious consideration." "Willkie," continued Malcolmson, "appears to be more fascist-minded, American style, than any of the other candidates. . . . "

"As for the demagoguery, Willkie ran through the same old crap of how the New Deal had failed to build up national defense. . . . " The writer then confirms my important item of the Willkie meeting in New York with what he called "a flock of Lamont partners," meaning of course "Morgan partners," where he "advocated all aid to the Allies *including* another American Expeditionary Force. I got this straight from a member of the Senate who happened to be present. . . . "

(The Malcolmson reference is to the meeting in the home of Thomas W. Lamont, the most politically intelligent of all the Morgan partners, and generally known as the Secretary of State of the Morgan Empire. This was the meeting at which the Wall Street giants decided on Willkie as our next President; it was the first item published in the first issue of my newsletter *In fact.*)

Chapter 51

Public Friends:
Truman, Eleanor Roosevelt

Although my friends included noted people in high office, men and women of reputation and power, their support of my newsletter and their many efforts to alert the nation on subjects ranging from false news to treason in wartime had little effect. Public opinion is largely created and maintained by the press in a democracy; minds of human beings by the millions cannot be manipulated and directed in a free country as they could in Hitler's Germany and Mussolini's Italy, and as they still are in Soviet Russia. But the lords of the press and their hired writers and the big business sponsors of radio oracles for many years, notably the Dies-McCarthy era, did a comparatively successful job.

When a courageous congressman named two of the country's most widely heard and read commentators as the most dishonest, he was suppressed. When the head of the Senate committee investigating war profiteering stumbled upon the evidence of treason by a multi-billion-dollar corporation that aided the Nazis, he too was suppressed. The Vice President of the United States delivered a most important policy speech, but because he spoke in favor of "the common man," he was suppressed.

The best known of my newsletter's friends in public life were Senators Truman, Minton, O'Mahoney and Murray, Representatives Savage, Sabath and Celler; and in the White House Vice President Wallace and Eleanor Roosevelt. Without exception every friend here mentioned was a victim of a press that then called itself fair and honest and free.

Charles Savage of Washington is the congressman who took on two of the three candidates for the SOB list. In a speech on the floor of the House and in the *Congressional Record*, both libel-proof, he told his colleagues of the dirty journalism of Fulton Lewis, Jr., and Westbrook Pegler (whose chief victim was Eleanor Roosevelt). He called the two the most dishonest newspaper men of our time and concluded by proposing "The Westbrook Pegler Annual Award for Journalistic Infamy," with the first award to Pegler himself. This news was suppressed.

Senator Sherman Minton of Indiana, later a Supreme Court justice, was one of my first supporters. He sent me one day a copy of a bill dealing with the press that he had introduced, and also a statement he had made over the radio, suppressed in the newspapers. Minton suggested an investigation because "ninety-eight per cent of the metropolitan press are opposed to the Administration [of FDR] and do not hesitate to misrepresent it. . . . if you want to know the truth you won't find it in the metropolitan press."

In his letter enclosing the radio text Senator Minton wrote me, "You will find I am not attacking the free press. . . . you will also discover that this speech was misrepresented in the press, as everything else is that they don't like." Minton suggested that when editors and publishers are found guilty of publishing falsehoods deliberately they should be punished with imprisonment. At a press conference a few days later President Roosevelt said laughingly that if this were done the federal penitentiaries would not be able to house all the prisoners.

Senator Truman was one of my first subscribers. I do not

remember now whether he was on the list of twenty Senate colleagues for whom Senator Minton subscribed, or wrote me directly. Our correspondence began when an organization calling itself Moral Re-armament (MRA) but better known as Buchmanism after its founder, Frank N. D. Buchman, boasted that Truman was addressing its gatherings. I wrote the Senator, mentioning a fact I was sure he did not remember: my meeting him during the war when I was attached to the Rainbow Division and he commanded an artillery battery. The documentation on Buchmanism I sent him included:

—Buchman saying "I thank God for Adolf Hitler," in his United Press interview.

—endorsing fascist dictator Franco, saying "Spain has taught us what godless Communism can bring." (There were no godless Spaniards ever, and the Republic of 25 million people had less than 25,000 Communists, none in power.)

—Buchman exposed in the House of Commons as a "canting cheat," pro-Nazi, anti-labor and in the pay of the largest union-busting corporations in England, the United States, Germany and Japan—by A. P. Herbert and Tom Driberg (who sent me *Hansard,* giving the speeches).

—Buchmanism endorsed in the United States by Henry Ford; Harvey Firestone; David Lawrence, editor of *United States News*; and Howard Conley, president, National Association of Manufacturers, all anti-union; in Japan by Takasumi Mitsui, of one of the four corporations owning most of Japan; in Germany by leading Nazis, notably Himmler and Hess.

Senator Truman replied:

Dear Mr. Seldes:

I read your letter of the 8th with some interest. I am not personally acquainted with Dr. Buchman and I don't think I ever met him in my life.

However, Moral Re-armament on the West Coast and also in Detroit and Philadelphia did some excellent work in creating a friendly feeling between employers and employees. . . .

387

I don't know anything about the controversy and care less.

Sincerely yours,
[signed] Harry S. Truman

In reply I sent the Senator statements from the leading CIO and AFL unions in the United States unanimously denouncing Buchmanism as a hidden fascist outfit; the pastoral letter warning of excommunication of any Catholic joining MRA, issued by the primate of Great Britain, Cardinal Hinsley; the resolution passed at their national encampment by the Jewish War Veterans denouncing Buchman as a Nazi. I suggested to Truman that "sometime during this campaign this matter of your endorsing Buchmanism or MRA will probably come up," and shortly afterward the news weekly *Time* carried this paragraph:

> The Trumans. A member of the Grandview (Mo.) Baptist Church since his youth, Candidate Truman . . . once interested in Buchmanism . . . now disclaims any interest in the Oxford Group, has never met Founder Frank Buchman.

In March 1942, Thurman Arnold, the assistant attorney general, appearing before a Senate committee investigating war profiteering, testified that Ethyl Gasoline Corporation, General Motors, Standard Oil and I. G. Farben of Germany had an agreement by which the American corporations supplied Hitler with the secret of making tetra-ethyl lead for gasoline, without which Hitler could not have operated his air force or gone to war, and also supplied him with the secrets of making synthetic rubber. Truman, heading the committee, declared, "This is treason." *In fact* and other liberal small-circulation weeklies published the news; the big press did not. Henry Luce's *Time*, for example, ridiculed Truman on page sixteen one week and published a five-thousand-dollar Standard Oil advertisement on page eighty-nine.

When Henry A(gar) Wallace was Vice President of the United States he delivered (May 22, 1942) one of the most important addresses on the American policy of the New Deal administration.

The press ignored or suppressed the speech because it was called "The Century of the Common Man," and began with the declaration, "This is a fight between the slave world and a free world." It stated that "everywhere the common people are on the march" and proceeded to attack reaction—fascism and Nazism in other forms—the most forthright attack ever made by so high an official; it advocated the continuation of the American revolution for democracy everywhere. (Mr. Spanel, of the Latex Corp., later paid a number of big newspapers to print the speech. It was also inserted in the *Congressional Record* because it had been suppressed in Washington.) The few papers that used a paragraph or two headlined it WALLACE SEES ALASKA AS TARGET OF JAP ATTACK.

The speech was so totally suppressed that when my newsletter published it, 200,000 extra copies were called for. Mr. Wallace wrote me, pleased with the response the published speech had received.

When Mr. Wallace later moved to Salem, New York, which is close to where I lived temporarily in Connecticut, he frequently invited me to his farm. He was then hybridizing chickens and gladioli. I asked about the flowers: why bother when every garden book told how easy it was for anyone to cross two varieties. Wallace replied:

"My father, with the help of his sons, produced the first good hybrid corn—used everywhere in the world today. Of course anyone can cross two strains and produce hybrid corn—year after year—and for ages this was done and corn was a failure. Father's idea was to recross one strain with each of the parents. He called the result Hy-bred corn. This is the marvelous corn we now have.

"I am trying the same idea with chickens. I hope to produce chickens with a pound or two more white meat than any now existing. For some incredible reason people prefer white meat. I am crossing, then recrossing, Rhode Island Reds and Leghorns. This should also produce more eggs per chicken per annum.

"All this crossing and recrossing will take years and years. I will have to live a hundred years to see the results. I do believe that if a man has a goal like this he will live longer than a man who has nothing to look forward to."

His hobby kept him alive and healthy a long time, but unfortunately he didn't make the hundred mark.

Eleanor Roosevelt

*W*ith Eleanor Roosevelt as with Henry Wallace there was a personal as well as journalistic relationship: my wife and I had met her twice, and each time we talked freedom of the press and the unfair and dishonest reporting in the majority of newspapers concerning FDR and herself. It was therefore no surprise when as publisher of *In fact* I received a letter from the wife of the President asking me to contribute to her monthly department in the *Ladies' Home Journal* entitled "If You Ask Me . . . " in which she not only answered questions but gave her own opinions.

Moreover, as she planned to make my question and her answer cover the freedom of the press problem of the time, Mrs. Roosevelt encouraged me to write quite a lengthy letter, and it follows:

> Dear Mrs. Roosevelt:
>
> You are no doubt aware that many of our greatest Presidents while proclaiming the press a bulwark if not the cornerstone of our democratic liberties, also complained of the unfairness or the utter corruption of the newspapers of their times. President Jefferson at one time declared that if it were a choice, he would prefer government by the press to any other form, but during his two administrations he grew more and more bitter, until finally his denunciations of the American press equaled his former praise.
>
> President Lincoln actually suppressed newspapers (in wartime). As you know better than I do, in our own time the alignment of the press, its bias, its one-sidedness, and its fakery of the news has reached a historic low. I am of course referring to the press campaigns against President Franklin Delano Roosevelt.
>
> Before asking you a question I would like to make a statement as editor of the only publication in America which has in every issue for five years criticized and exposed

the American press. I have received thousands of letters, and actually hundreds of suggestions and plans for a free press. Some have been tried, many have been discussed. Only one has been found worthy of real consideration: a chain of standard newspapers to be started by the labor unions, or by one of their organizations such as the National Citizens Political Action Committee. The papers are to be standard papers, but honest papers, in competition with the dishonest self-styled free press.

What are your ideas on the plans for a free, fair, and honest press for the United States?

Cordially yours,
George Seldes

Mrs. Roosevelt's reply to the question she had suggested that I ask her was:

It is very difficult to have a free, fair and honest press anywhere in the world. In the first place, as a rule, papers are largely supported by advertising, and that immediately gives the advertiser a certain hold over the medium. . . .

I think the only hope for a really free press is for the public to recognize that the press *should not* express the point of view of the owners and their writers but be factual, whereas editorials *must* express the opinion of owners and writers. The news columns should be uncolored. The public can get to know the type of people whose publications they are reading and if they really want to get at the truth, they can read a variety of publications whose owners and writers have different points of view and in so doing they will be able to decide where they themselves stand.

If owners and writers express what they honestly believe and are not influenced by the advertisers or investors, we will have as nearly an honest press as it is possible to obtain.

(Not a very satisfactory solution to the free press problem).

In a small book she wrote in 1946 my letter and her answer appeared again, along with those of others including Einstein and Mme. Chiang Kai-shek. *In fact* was mentioned at a time when the red-baiting campaign against it was reaching its climax. It would be variously attacked by the Dies-Rankin-Nixon-McCarthy committees and all the professional red-baiters. The FBI had agents in post offices reporting on my mail, letter-carriers were warning subscribers their names were being reported to the FBI, and, for all I know, my temporary residence in Connecticut was wire-tapped. It took a brave person to mention *In fact* and its editor; and at this time when even the entire "liberal" medium, the magazines, were silent, Mrs. Roosevelt showed her truly remarkable courage.

Sometime later, when I returned from a six-month tour of several European countries and had written a series emphasizing news coverage behind the so-called Iron Curtain, I received a note from Mrs. Roosevelt asking about the Cardinal Mindszenty trial in Budapest. I sent her a short summary mentioning the outrageous falsehoods that were being published in the United States and Mrs. Roosevelt forthrightly mentioned it in her syndicated column. As a result Mrs. Roosevelt was viciously attacked by such fellow columnists as Westbrook Pegler—which did her no harm—and by Cardinal Spellman of New York. I then sent her all the documentation I had obtained and all the statements from most of the members of the British, Swiss and American press corps in Budapest refuting the New York Cardinal—but Mrs. Roosevelt was unable to get the facts published in the American press—no more able to do so than I.

Part XII

Through the
Iron Curtain

Chapter 52

Guglielmo Emmanuel vs. Mussolini

The more powerful *In fact* became—due largely to the support of labor, the AFL as well as the CIO and independent unions, and their national publications, and to liberal members of both houses of Congress making speeches or inserting items from my weekly in the *Congressional Record,* a number of them exposing the standard commercial big-city press—the more virulent became the campaign of libel, falsehood and slander against both me and my weekly.

It is true that the Commission on Freedom of the Press was brave enough when it issued its final report to accuse the press of "deliberate falsifications and reckless misstatements of fact," irresponsibility, ignoring "the errors and misrepresentations, the lies and scandals of which its members are guilty." But unless instances were given, newspapers named, even if they included those of the "great" newspapers which had created the commission, this report had little if any value. In editorial offices everyone knew that the Hearst chain, the Scripps-Howard chain and the *Chicago Tribune* of that time were regarded as the worst in the country. Hearst had boosted Hitler and Naziism for cash money, Roy Howard and Colonel McCormick had played the native fascist game, the chief move of which is to fight the labor unions.

As the 1947 report of the commission had no effect whatever, the attack on *In fact* grew more vicious. Libel is actionable, and libel was evident. The noted lawyer O. John Rogge, who as assistant attorney general of the United States had once prosecuted the alleged seditionist-traitors, and also represented this country at the Nuremberg trials of the Nazi war criminals, then stepped forward and offered to file a libel suit against the worst dishonest journalists who had attacked me and *In fact*. He said he would not charge me a cent for his services, but he said that if I did not have enough money to pay for filing briefs and other legal matters I had no chance at all in courts. When I replied that I did not have several thousand dollars for legal expenses, Attorney Rogge made the following offer: he himself would write me a letter denouncing the libelers and falsifiers, he would name them even if the biggest papers were behind them, and hundreds of millions of dollars. Rogge told me that he would welcome being sued by the crooked journalists so that he could go into court and expose them.

In his letter dated April 2, 1947, which I published, Mr. Rogge first named Eugene Lyons, whom I had known as a super-duper Communist in Moscow in 1922 and who had turned coat when caught cabling a false report, and gone so far right as to become a contributor to *Reader's Digest*, where his field was red-baiting liberals; Frederick Woltman, a columnist of the Scripps-Howard chain who wrote a half-page attack on *In fact* repeating such falsifications as the charge that it was subsidized with Russian money; and Fulton Lewis, Jr., one of whose broadcasts on the Mutual network repeated verbatim the Eugene Lyons libels. Wrote Mr. Rogge:

> While I am writing to you only as your attorney, I would advise you immediately to institute libel actions by filing

complaints against Lyons, Woltman, Lewis and others. . . . However, I must look at this case not only as your attorney, but also as an American citizen who has viewed with admiration your courageous fight for a free and untrammeled press and your sincere efforts through *In fact* to reveal to the American people the facts behind the news which appears in the daily press.

Mr. Rogge then mentioned the almost prohibitive costs for anyone except a wealthy person engaging in a libel suit—a poor man has no chance before the law. He also mentioned Eugene Lyons's writings after he became a red-baiter being used by the Nazi radio, which of course credited *Reader's Digest*. Mr. Rogge concluded: "I recommend that you continue to devote your main energies, time and resources to building *In fact* and getting a greater audience for it."

Neither Lyons, Woltman nor Lewis and their employers, *Reader's Digest*, the Scripps-Howard chain, and Mutual Broadcasting ever sued Mr. Rogge for exposing them. Rogge did silence them for a while, but did not prevent other, more careful press prostitutes, from continuing the effort to put me out of business. *In fact* was favorably mentioned in the *CIO News*; in *Labor*, the organ of the railroad brotherhoods; in J. W. Gitt's *Gazette & Daily* of York, Pennsylvania—which, incidentally would publish items I sent at times dealing with the suppression of news in the big press; and in Lyle Stuart's monthly, *The Independent*, which also opened its columns to me. I had perhaps fifty thousand press readers on my side compared to the millions who read nothing but red-baiting defamatory items. Our circulation crest of 176,000 was never surpassed. We kept losing subscribers every week because of the letter-carriers' warnings and the red-baiting campaign. We never again got three thousand subs a week, never again had a renewal rate of sixty three percent, never again hoped for a million circulation and a liberal national daily.

We held editorial conferences to which we invited knowledgeable persons, and one thing we thought might ease our dilemma was for me to make a trip back to the European countries I knew well, in which I had worked for at least seventeen years, and notably for me to penetrate the Iron Curtain. We were convinced that the news from certain lands was not being given to the American public fairly and honestly, that the red-baiting that marked the McCarthy era would include foreign parts, and that a six-month series of reports would attract a new field of readers.

In 1948 I went first to Rome and Milan to report on Italy without Mussolini, then to Yugoslavia to interview Tito, to Hungary for Rakosi, and to Budapest where I investigated the case of Cardinal Mindszenty, who was charged with treason.

Emmanuel Explains Mussolini

On the day following the night Mussolini's secret police knocked on my door and told me to pack for deportation, it also ordered the Rome editor of the *Corriere della Sera* of Milan, not only Italy's best newspaper but one of the great newspapers of the world, to leave the capital. Just two months after he was sent back to Milan the *Corriere* was suppressed by Mussolini. *The Times* of London then said editorially that it was "a serious loss to civilization." Of what other newspaper anywhere in the world could this be said?

In 1927 Mussolini ordered the total suppression of all non-Fascist publications—newspapers, magazines, periodicals of all sorts, all books, pamphlets, anything.

And so, at the very time Mussolini hung disgracefully upside down in the Milan filling station, the Milan *Corriere Della Sera* was revived and its former Rome correspondent, my colleague Emmanuel, named editor.

Now, Guglielmo Emmanuel was the *Corriere*'s editor-in-chief, known as the First Journalist of Italy, an Italian who had dared oppose Fascism when it was armed with guns—and castor oil. Mussolini was dead, and Fascismo was not only dead but intentionally forgotten. It was exactly twenty-five years since I had last talked to Emmanuel.

The first thing Emmanuel said, after agreeing with my

guess that Fascism had disappeared as completely as if it had never existed, was, "Moreover, Collego Seldes, I want to point out that no foreign army or military or social organization had to come here to purge our people of Fascism. We are self-purged."

But how is it possible that a system of government, an ideology if not a philosophy, that had lasted two decades, brought up a new generation, engaged in a great propaganda effort and seemed to have won the support of cheering millions could disappear so completely?

"One answer," said Emmanuel, "is this: Fascism was always contrary to the spirit and character of the Italian people—just as you might say, it was the right system or idea to appeal to the German mind and spirit.

"Where did Mussolini get his Fascism? Mussolini got Fascism out of books, and they were mostly German books.

"Moreover, Mussolini never ruled Italy as a statesman. Have you ever realized, Collego Seldes, that he was before seizing office, and after seizing office, always a journalist?

"Mussolini tried to rule Italy with words, not deeds. With newspaper headlines, not with public achievements."

Emmanuel illustrated his main thesis with many examples—from the days when Mussolini was an honest man, a socialist, editor of the party organ, *Avanti!* He then wrote that journalism was not a profession but a mission. It could lead to any goal—to victory. The First World War began in August, and within three months Mussolini was publishing his own daily, preaching against all the policies his father had taught him and that he had expressed in most of his thirty-one years. He had sold himself to the French for money because that was the only way he would ever have his own newspaper, his own means to power.

When the Allies won, continued Emmanuel, Mussolini could claim some credit. He also took the money sent to keep D'Annunzio in Fiume. "Did you know that almost all this money came from Italian Americans," Emmanuel said, "and that in using it to create the Fascist movement out of the one little

Milanese group—you do know that Mussolini was not the founder?—Mussolini made Italian-American money the basis of his movement?"

After that it was oratory—from the balcony, from his newspaper; oratory, promises, headlines. And, of course, censorship, suppression, deportation of all who stood in his way.

"I believe you were the only American journalist," continued the editor of the *Corriere*, "who noted the main fact about Fascism," that it was merely a new method by which a few enriched themselves at the expense of the many.

"While Mussolini was making the headlines, his industrial and financial backers were making money. And not by honest means. The heads of the Fascist Party became the heads of the Italian government and proceeded to sell their country for money. Fascism was corruption. Under Fascism the entire governing class became corrupt."

Chapter 53

A Man Named Sermonetti? Carlos? Vidali?

On my way from Milan to the Iron Curtain, which then encircled Tito's Yugoslavia, I had to stop at Trieste, a disputed city, from which D'Annunzio once had marched on Fiume and which was now occupied by the U.S. Army. The American officer in charge told me Trieste was the southern anchor of the Lübeck-Trieste line, which the Allied forces would hold against the Russians in the Third World War.

Although the U.S. Army ruled the city, the real "boss" everyone acknowledged was a man I had known fairly well when I had reported the war in Spain during 1936–1937. I had in fact witnessed one of the most dramatic episodes in modern military history. But to the American commander in Trieste and to newspaper reporters, even the name of the Trieste "boss" was in dispute. He was the international arch-villain of the time, if one believed U.S. press reports. His name was Sermonetti. He was "the number-one Russian agent in Europe and America." He was also Commandante Carlos of the Spanish War, the major who later became General Carlos Contreras. Now, in Trieste, he was plain Vittorio Vidali.

When I first met him outside Madrid his *nom de guerre* was Carlos. It was as Commandante Carlos that I saw him in action in Madrid the week the traitor generals and colonels began the Spanish Rebellion—falsely known as the Spanish Civil War. The officers deserted. The soldiers in Madrid remained faithful to the Republic, but Franco, Sanjurjo, Mola and other generals with their German aviation and Italian infantry were taking over the southern and western parts of the country. Rebellion? Foreign invasion? Yes. Civil war? No. The Republic armed every working man—and many women also who had volunteered—and tens of thousands came from abroad later on. But in mid-July 1936 Carlos called every Italian workman then in Madrid to join him. He formed the Fifth Brigade, known as "the Garibaldi Brigade," and it was he who saved Madrid.

In 1937, when Franco's forces, deploying four of Mussolini's "Arrow" divisions, were marching on the capital announcing as their first objective the city of Guadalajara, Carlos, now General Carlos Contreras, appeared at Briheuga, north of Guadalajara, with his Garibaldi Brigade. Almost singlehandedly, he defeated the entire Mussolini Blackshirt Army—without firing a shot. (I was there.)

Armed only with a loudspeaker, General Contreras advanced against the marching Italian divisions. He shouted:

> Fellow Italians! We are your brothers! We are Italians living in Spain!
> We are defending the Spanish Republic!
> You are in Spain, not in Ethiopia or Libya. What are you doing in Spain?
> Brother Italians, you have been betrayed. Mussolini has betrayed you!
> Go home. Go back to Italy. Throw down your arms. Fellow Italians, go back to Italy, to your wives and children. Throw down your arms. Go home!

The four Mussolini divisions dropped their rifles and ran as fast as they could. General Contreras's words had moved them figuratively and literally. Every Blackshirt soldier realized, slowly or suddenly, that he had been betrayed by Mussolini—for forty lire a day; he had been told he would be paid extra and sent to do police duty only, in Ethiopia or Libya, landing in northwestern ports. Every one of them was shocked by the unmistakable brotherly Italian voice over the loud speaker. Four divisions ran from the battlefield.

But it must be noted that the victors of the Battle of Briheuga, as well as the defeated, were also Italians. There was no brigade in Spain with a better record of bravery than the Garibaldis, and no greater a hero than the Italian Vittorio Vidali.*

In modern history few human beings of note have had so dirty a deal as Vidali-Contreras-Sermonetti. Under the third name, as a refugee from the defeated Spanish Republic now in fascist hands, he was denounced in the United States and deported to Mexico. When I saw him in Trieste, circa 1950, I had with me clippings and tearsheets that I showed him. For example:

> New York *Herald-Tribune:* For some time also he [Vidali or Carlos or Sermonetti] was one of the Communist agents in Spain . . . who damaged the Loyalist cause from within while the Fascists attacked it from without.
>
> *Saturday Evening Post:* After he went to Mexico he was named in connection with the Moscow-directed murder of Leon Trotsky. [The *SEP,* which had a reputation of checking and double-checking every item submitted, here presents an ugly rumor and does not say who "named" Vidali.]
>
> Hearst's INS, Madrid dateline: [For half a column the Hearst man in Franco-Spain boasts that he had obtained

---

* The term "Battle of Guadalajara" remains in history books although it is one of the thousands of historic falsifications, ancient and modern. We war correspondents went all over the ground of an almost totally destroyed Briheuga and an almost totally intact Guadalajara. We picked up the thousands of things a fleeing or evacuated military outfit leaves on the ground: letters, many from home, many unsent; photographs of wives and children; clothing; guns; blood-stained bandages; and even Fascist insignia. We interviewed many of the twelve hundred Italians who preferred to come over to Vidali's side rather than run. Imagine our surprise on returning to Madrid one day to find that Matthews of *The New York Times* had received a cable from his managing editor, E. L. James, saying that Carney, the *Times* man with Franco, had reported, "There are no Italians in Spain.")

authoritative information that Carlos was once arrested and sent to the Liparian Island prison as a "subversive." This is a press crime of omission. Vidali in fact had been arrested years ago, by Mussolini, and sent to the island for opposing Fascism.]

Joseph Alsop, syndicated columnist: Signor Vidali's major mission [in Trieste], however, is to bring Trieste under the eager heel of Marshal Tito.

This last clipping gave Vidali cause for an explosion of bitter laughter. "They lied about Spain," he said when he recovered, "now they lie about Trieste, and they always lie about me."

He suddenly became angry. "Tito!" he said. "I would like to get my hands on Tito. I'd strangle him to death. If I was sure I had a chance I would go to Belgrade today and shoot him. Tito has betrayed us." It was useless trying to explain how right Tito was and how evil Stalin had been.

When we finished our talk, Vidali took me in his car to see the Adriatic. I was more interested in the extraordinarily beautiful lilies growing wild along the hilly roads. I said as much. Vidali got out, rattled around in a toolbox, found something to dig with and got me several bulbs. But the U.S. consul would not allow me to take them home, so I took only the seeds. The Adriatic red Martagon Lily (*Lilium dalmaticum rubrum*) blooms in my border at Hartland-4-Corners, Vermont, today in memory of this archvillain Vidali.

Chapter 54

~~~~~~~~

My Last Hero:
Marshal Tito

T he summer of 1948 the headlines throughout the world read TITO DEFIES STALIN and TITO EXCOMMUNI-CATED, so I gave up my search for the house where James Joyce lived in Trieste and the school where he taught English, and rushed, along with a hundred or more foreign correspondents from Europe and America, to join the hundred already in Belgrade reporting the unsensational Danube Conference.

Two hundred men and women, many famous editors, powerful news magazine correspondents, clamored, begged, intrigued, maneuvered, pleaded for an interview with Tito, and a few angry men even insinuated reprisals. It was the first great postwar break in the monolithic Russian Communist ideological dictatorial system, which the "free world" had hoped for but never really believed would happen in Stalin's lifetime.

But Tito, unversed in modern or Madison Avenue–type public relations, failed to take advantage of his position. No ghostwriters issued statements, no "reliable sources" were available to anyone. Tito refused to talk. And so two hundred journalists went home via the Orient Express. I went to Paris.

Within a few weeks, however, thanks to the intervention of my old Yugoslav friend Vladimir Dedijer, now editor of *Borba,* the leading daily newspaper of the country, who was also Tito's closest friend, I was invited to Belgrade to interview Marshal Tito—if I cared to make the trip again. I did. I began our meeting with several questions. The world, or at least that part of it capable of reading, and rich enough to buy a newspaper, wanted to know if the Tito break with Stalin was genuine. And was it permanent? And if so, was it also a break with Communist ideology? And, again, expelled from the Comintern, where would Tito stand if the Third World War—then threatening the world—began with a Russian attack on the non-Communist European nations? (The fear of another war, the tension throughout the world, was greater then than it has been ever since, and this is the reason the Tito break with Stalin was for the time "the greatest story in the world.")

Inasmuch as I had said *Es freut mich sehr,* the equivalent of a conventional "Pleased to meet you," on shaking hands with Marshal Tito—I knew he had been a workingman in Wiener-Neustadt, Austria, and at a German General Electric plant in Zagreb, and spoke German—Tito replied in that language. "I will be very glad to talk about the economic and cultural program of my country, the five-year plan, about our progress in————"

"But doesn't everything," I interrupted, "economics, culture, progress, everything today depend on one thing: are we going to have war—or is it peace?"

Weighing each word, Tito replied: "In my opinion it is not war." There was a pause.

"To make war you have to have men who want war. Men, not people. People never want war. They are frequently led into war. The people of America do not want war. . . . Nor do the *people* of the Soviet Union want war. Nor do we want war. But there must be some Americans who do want war because America is talking about war and America is making preparations for the greatest war in history.

"The danger of war exists. The greatest danger is a provocation.

"We know the reasons wars are made. We know the causes of aggression, the causes for expansion, for expanding markets, for domination. But for Yugoslavia, now, there can be no reason for a new war." Then, with emphasis on each word, he continued: *"We have no cause for war. We have got what we want. We have freedom."* It could be translated "freedom" or "liberty." At times in the interview the Marshal would pause for a word in German and more often I would stumble, but our interpreter, Serge Prié (pronounced Pritzsa) would rescue us in English, German and Serbo-Croatian.

The large part of more than an hour was devoted to the war that then seemed possible—it was the time of great war scares, and it was also the height of the red-baiting era.

"Why are there so many war scares in America and Europe?" asked the Marshal.

"Why is there war hysteria in America?"

Tito fired these questions at me, stopping long enough after each to make its weight felt but not giving me a chance for a reply; I am sure he did not expect any.

"I ask these questions of every foreigner—I do not get an answer," he continued.

My next question was about fascism around the world, and the Marshal disposed of it immediately with the emphatic words, "In Europe fascism is dead, I can assure you."

Of course what the world most wanted to know at that time was the cause and sincerity of the break with Stalin, the "excommunication," and whether Tito would disavow not only Russian Communism but Communism in general, perhaps even Marxist socialism. If I had still been working for the *Chicago Tribune* or the conventional newspapers or a news service I would have had to ask that question quite bluntly. Luckily Tito saved me futile diplomatic maneuvers. He spoke of the economic plight of

Yugoslavia. He accused the United States of refusing to sell machinery that would have made Yugoslavia independent of other nations and described the Yugoslavs' own success in overcoming technical difficulties. He continued: "But the rumors in the foreign press that Yugoslavia will be on one side or the other side—the Russian Communist bloc or the anti-Communist bloc— as a result of this situation are real nonsense.

"Let there be no misunderstanding about these words 'one camp or the other, one side or the other.' We are staying in this camp. We are in the socialist camp, we are part of the people's democracies. No matter what happens in the whole world, we remain in this camp."

The Marshal may have caught my puzzled look. He continued: "We are going to establish democratic socialism. Democratic socialism, not social democracy, as it was in Germany under Ebert. True socialism has never been tried anywhere in the modern world. It may have existed for a little while when Lenin first came into power in Russia. But it soon disappeared. There is neither socialism nor Communism in Russia under Stalin."

He outlined in brief his plan for agriculture and industry.

"Our road is toward socialism, and we shall build a socialist state here. . . . The methods are not fixed but the goal is. . . . It is true democracy; it can be achieved only through socialism."

It was long past the hour promised me. One more question. "Did the Marshal say 'We shall change the face of the nation'?" This quotation was inscribed in many places, and Stalin had denounced Tito for "nationalism," too much nationalism. Tito, in replying, used the word "*zemlya*" which I remembered meant "country" rather than "nation." He insisted on the word "country."

As we shook hands Tito said: "We are on the road of human progress. We are on the road to democratic socialism, and we shall stay on that road no matter what happens."

This was the interview two hundred foreign correspondents had tried to get a few weeks earlier. It was still front-page news on October 12, 1948, when I offered it to *The New York Times* in Paris. The *Times* chief was delighted. But when I said I wanted no money, not even my expenses on the Orient Express, which were considerable, but I did expect that my newsletter *In fact* would get a credit line, New York had to be consulted. Managing Editor James refused to publish this exclusive story rather than mention my weekly.

About a year later *The New York Times* (September 1, 1949) published an interview with Tito on many of the subjects discussed above. The *Times* said in an editorial note: "The Marshal . . . received this correspondent in the first press interview he had granted since the dispute with the Cominform and the Belgrade government flared up."

This statement is not, shall we say, accurate. No one should know this better than this same Paris *Times* correspondent who first accepted and then on orders from New York returned my interview.

Helen and I returned to Yugoslavia in other years.

On one of the three occasions I talked to Tito, the first thing he said to me was, "You know of course, that Yugoslavia is the first country in history governed by a working man."

Having spent about ten years in Berlin and hearing a hundred times the story of Ebert "the saddlemaker" as the successor of the Hohenzollern Caesars, I ventured to mention his name. (Lenin had been a schoolteacher, Trotsky and Mussolini had been workingmen in their teens, but were journalists and politicians. Stalin was once a second-rate train robber.)

Tito replied:

"Ebert certainly began as a working man—a saddlemaker— true. But for how long? Almost all his adult life he was in politics, eventually an office holder. He went from being head of a political party, not a union, into the presidency.

"I was a worker in an electrical plant—Siemens-Schukert, the German General Electric. I worked in Wiener-Neustadt and in Zagreb. I never quit working—until the war. In Zagreb I had the idea of forming an electrical workers' union, and did so, and the men urged me to go to other cities and organize other plants, and that was my job, too, but all this time I still worked in the plant in Zagreb. When the Germans invaded Yugoslavia, I ran for the mountains—and then I began organizing the Partisans, and throughout the war we fought fifteen German divisions and kept them from the Western Front. And when the war was over the people elected me president of Yugoslavia."

My wife and I spent a large part of the year 1950 in that country, and one of the best illustrations of how impoverished it had become because of the war, and the Russian exploitation of its mineral wealth that followed, is our experience as guests of several of the leaders of this country.

Once, Helen and I were invited to a sort of state dinner given by the former ambassador to the United States, Dr. Bebler. We were eight or ten guests altogether, the food was excellent, the silver and the china sparkled, the service was extraordinary. We were impressed.

Sometime later another of our friends, the Vilfans—I believe he was an ambassador to the United Nations—invited us to their house, and again it was a banquet. My wife noticed the same silver and china, the same maid and waiters, and she told me later that the menu was the same, magnificent but *déja vu*.

Finally, when we were about to leave Yugoslavia, we received invitations from Tito's vice president and most likely successor, Kardelj, and it was again the same *haute cuisine*, the same silver and china, the same menu and apparently the same chef. Then both of us realized that Yugoslavia in the 1950s was still so poor, or had under Tito so honest a group of rulers, that there was not, as there was in Soviet Russia, a "ruling elite," an upper class in a supposedly classless society, living well and spending well; that all Yugoslav high officials up to and including the vice president, had their state dinners prepared and sent over from a sort of central office in the government. This was Tito's Yugoslavia, revealed at banquets.

Chapter 55

Rakosi, Dictator(?) of Hungary

From Belgrade, which in 1948 had just freed itself from Stalinist imperialism and colonialism (to use Moscow's most pejorative words to damn the West), my next Iron Curtain capital naturally was Budapest. Hungary, the world press said, was faithful to Stalin, and Matyas Rakosi was always labeled the "red dictator." It was quite a surprise, about one hour after I had arrived at my hotel, to learn from my former interpreter and for many years my (that is to say, the *Chicago Tribune*'s) "stringer," Eugen Szatmari, that Rakosi was vice premier, not premier, and that although the Communist Party was the strongest, the nation was governed by a coalition of four parties, the three others ranging from anti-Communist to Marxist-reformist.

The Hungarian electorate consisted of 5,761,000 persons and the 4,998,336 who went to the polls without fear or coercion (as they usually have when the regime proudly announces it got ninety-seven or ninety-nine percent of the vote), created a 284-member Parliament divided as follows:

Communist Party	100 seats
Social Democrats	67
Small Holders Party	61
National Peasants	56

These parties won on a program of separation of Church and State "as in America," the end of the feudal system, and the seizure of the vast landed estates, which was to be followed by a division making it possible for every peasant family to have enough land on which to make a living. The Social Democrats here as in other countries claimed they were the true interpreters of the gospel according to Saint Karl Marx; they actually were more anti-Communist than several other parties. However, the three non-Communist parties agreed that socialistic reforms were the goal of government, not Communist seizure; they had 164 votes among them, and although Rakosi, the vice premier, was a Communist, they could have ended his tenure at any session.

There was no doubt in Budapest at this time that Rakosi ran the country. Most of the program on which every party agreed was being fulfilled. After centuries of joint rule and at times Church rule, there was total separation from the State, and millions of acres that had belonged to the Church and the landlord nobility had been divided. The press was free, the churches were open, non-Communists approved of Rakosi.

I was early for my appointment. A quite short, stocky man wearing blue—a blue suit, blue shirt, blue necktie, three different shades of blue (I didn't see his socks) emerged from Mr. Rakosi's office, glanced at me, went out, came back. A moment later a little light flickered on the reception room secretary's desk. She beckoned me to the door. The man behind the desk was the man in blue. But before there could be any of the conventional small talk preceding the serious questions, Rakosi exploded in a torrent of words.

"You have just come from Belgrade," he shouted at me; "you have seen for yourself. You can be a witness of the truth— the Cominform is right and Tito is wrong." (He did not give me a chance to reply.)

"The shops are empty in Belgrade," he continued; "there is a serious lack of consumer goods. . . . The peasants have plenty of money but there is nothing for them to buy. . . . The agrarian reform was a fraud. The Cominform's strictures are correct."

He went on: Tito had betrayed the Cominform instead of expropriating the landlords; the rich peasants, the kulaks, still were in control; they refused to bring food to the cities. The industrial workers were starving. The people were unhappy. . . .

And so ten minutes, eighteen minutes passed and as we neared half an hour of my promised hour I still had not been able to say a word, but kept looking at my wristwatch.

Mr. Rakosi may have noticed this. He stopped as suddenly as he had started his tirade. He may also have noticed that I took no notes—I almost never did. He now asked in a changed, friendly, unimpassioned, calm voice what my questions were. I did have them written out:

— The danger of the Third World War (in 1948 the most frightening question of the year)?
— Reconstruction of your country without Marshall Plan aid; your next five-year-plan?
— Can the East outdo the West; will Europe swing Left or Right?
— Your chief enemy, Cardinal Mindszenty?

From similar interviews I could guess that the Communist leader would reply that the East would surpass the West, that all Europe, with the possible exception of England, would soon be in the Communist bloc—it would be treason not to believe it. Yet in the course of his reply, when he turned to the United States, Mr. Rakosi, brilliantly, I thought, stated a subject no one I had ever heard or read had mentioned before.

"Do you know what throughout history has been your greatest asset, the greatest source of your success, the real reason for the greatness of America?" he asked, and then answered:

"In the last century you imported forty million persons from Europe. This has been the most precious import you ever made. Even if you figure the material wealth, the worth to the nation, of these immigrants at the minimum figure of two thousand dollars each, then you have imported a value of eighty billion dollars—and it has not cost you a cent." He paused:

"Eighty billion dollars!

"And it has brought you interest at a terrific rate of increase."

Now there was a long pause. Did Mr. Rakosi realize he had perhaps hit upon a brilliant interpretation of the greatness of my country? I certainly felt so at that moment; I had to remember what he had said, and I quickly wrote "eighty billions" and "forty million immigrants in one hundred years" on the page with the questions.

On the subject of the threatening war, East vs. West, Rakosi also concluded with a brilliant remark—I am sure it was first made by a great historic figure. Assuring me that eventually the East would prevail over the West, he concluded:

"I say this because I know that ideas cannot be conquered by bayonets."

Finally he began to talk about Cardinal Mindszenty, a subject called "controversial" in the American press and tabu because it concerned one of the great religious bodies, the ruling party in many European countries but a minority sect in the United States—and probably the most sensitive to press reports.

"The Church," said Rakosi, "was not only a reactionary force in our country, supporting the monarchy and later the fascist dictatorship of Admiral Horthy, but it was the owner of more than a million acres of land." (He said half a million hectares.) "It was the largest landowner in Hungary. We took the land away."

At this point he gave me a short dissertation on feudalism. Did I know that Hungary was the last feudal state in Europe? Did I know that feudalism meant rule by Church and State united and serfdom—virtual slavery—for the majority, the peasantry? That had been the condition in Hungary throughout the ages; and Horthy's fascism had strengthened it.

"And this explains why Cardinal Mindszenty is putting up so hard a fight against land reform, nationalization of the land, and social justice, which the present regime has instituted," said

Rakosi—referring always to the "regime" or the coalition, not the Communist Party, as the foreign press invariably alleged. Rakosi continued:

"We gave this million acres of land to tens of thousands of poor, landless peasants.

"Thus, by one stroke, the Church lost its political and economic domination of the country. . . .

"The Church had one hundred thousand serfs. These hundred thousand miserable beings, hardly better off than slaves, worked for the bishops on the Church lands. . . .

"The Church remains the only reactionary force in this country. The Church everywhere has been and is on the side of reaction. . . . However, it is also true that many countries—France, Poland, Hungary—have stopped sending money to the Vatican. The power of the Vatican rests largely on one solvent nation: the United States. It is your Cardinal Spellman who is the man with the money. And money talks, even in Rome. . . .

"I say that Spellman dictates the reactionary policy of Rome, and Rome dictates the reactionary policy of the Church in Hungary, so that in an indirect way the Americans are paying for Hungarian reaction right now."

This was the only reference to Cardinal Mindszenty—except a remark about the government knowing all about the secret missions of Cardinal Spellman's agents bringing money to him.

At this moment the telephone rang—not for the first time—and Rakosi spoke yet another language into it. I had been told he spoke twenty. I mentioned this. He did not deny it. He had been in prison fifteen fascist years. "I had nothing else to do but learn languages," he said.

Somehow, as I was about to leave, we got back to the left-vs.-right movement in Europe. "Of course the left will triumph," said Rakosi.

"The left is the best organized, the most efficient, it has the most intelligent leaders in every country, especially in France and Italy. It knows what it wants. It knows where it is going.

"All that the right has got is the army, the Church, the

money, the political apparatus by which it rules. When a people becomes enlightened it goes left. In every nation in the world where there was a resistance movement against the Nazis in the war it was led by the left. We Communists claim a large part of the credit. There were others—but all of the left.

"After the war the Left gave the people of Europe leadership. You can check this move to the left with your money and your Marshall Plan, but not forever, not for long. . . . Your Marshall Plan helps Europe as the rope helps the man condemned to be hanged."

And then, as a parting shot, when I was already at the exit door, the dictator of Hungary called out:

"I am afraid we shall see all of Asia, and probably a large part of Africa, going left—before we shall see even a radical labor party in America." However, this last remark was said with laughter and with good humor.

Eight years later, when Hungarians overwhelmingly demanded the dismissal of Communist Erno Gero as premier, he called for Russian military aid. The Soviets sent 200,000 infantry and 2,500 tanks and armored cars. They killed many thousands of civilians in the streets of Budapest, and they ended coalition democracy.

Chapter 56

~~~~~~~~~~

Journalists and Cardinal Mindszenty

I t is perhaps necessary for me at this moment to state that although I have proposed a Hall of Infamy for certain journalists and named three candidates, leaving it to readers to choose which one deserves the title "SOB," I must emphasize the fact that in my decades in Europe, and notably in the press corps G-2D, U.S. Army, the 1922 Moscow group, and the staffs in most capitals of Europe, the corrupt journalist was the exception. The newspapers, not the newspapermen, were the guilty ones.

One of the best illustrations of this fact can be found in the actions of the Budapest press corps during the turbulent times following the Second World War, and the conflict between the head of the nation, Rakosi, and his chief opponent, Cardinal Mindszenty. (This is one of the main events I came to Europe to investigate in 1948.)

In more recent times, when I have been accused of growing mellow toward the American press, my reply has been that there is no comparison possible with the general situation at the turn of the century, when the Muckraking Era began and when Pittsburgh newspapers could be bribed with a two dollar-a-day advertisement—incidentally the same price streetwalkers and inmates of houses of prostitution charged—and the situation now. But, I have always noted, there are still several powerful sacred cows, and the two most important are the advertising of cigarets—a matter of about two billion dollars a year, one of the greatest causes of death from cancer, emphysema, heart failure and other diseases, which could be ended by state laws or an act of Congress—and the Church, any church, all churches, all religious sects, all preachers of any denomination. In one instance it is billions of dollars, in the other it is fear of offending millions of people of any faith or cult.

In 1948 the entire American section of the resident foreign press corps in Hungary implored me to report the facts about Cardinal Minszenty's collaboration with the Nazis during the war, his part in the deportation of the Jewish population to Hitler's death camps, and other criminal actions; and also to expose the scores of fraudulent news items coming from outside Hungary, from Vienna, London, Prague, and Rome especially, alleging drugging and torturing of the Cardinal.

There were in fact three notable churchmen who had been charged—in the European but never in the American press—with working for Hitler: Mindszenty, Monsignor Tiso, and Cardinal Stepinac of Yugoslavia—and I investigated all three, with little hope that any publication in America outside the liberal weeklies with their usual twenty-five or thirty-thousand circulation, would publish a single paragraph of facts.

Monsignor Tiso was actually set up as ruler, i.e., Nazi dictator, of Slovakia when Hitler's armies conquered that part of Czechoslovakia. I could have wagered a hundred dollars against a counterfeit dime that if a poll were taken in the U.S. Congress, or the entire membership of the American journalistic profession, there would not be ten men or women who could honestly say they had known during the war that Monsignor Tiso and the state of Slovakia had declared war on the United States. But it is a fact. When the war ended and before the war criminals' trials were held in Nuremberg, Tiso was captured by the anti-Nazi Slovaks, given a fair trial, found guilty of treason and shot. The world accepted this fact. But in the Mindszenty and Stepinac cases, thanks to almost total falsification of the news in the world press, Hungary and Yugoslavia were accused of great crimes against the Church.

On arriving in Budapest the first thing I did, after looking up my former colleague and employee Eugen Szatmari, was to request interviews with Rakosi and Mindszenty; and the first thing I learned was that Mindszenty, who previously had been only too happy to talk to the foreign press, now made it an absolute rule never to grant another interview. This is how my colleagues explained it:

Mindszenty had graciously received Miss Bertha Gaster, the Budapest representative of a great London newspaper, at a time a hundred foreign correspondents were clamoring for an interview. He answered all her questions very satisfactorily. And then, in conclusion, the Cardinal suddenly launched into his old enraged attack on "the Jews, the Jews"—the Jews were to blame for all the ills in the world, the Jews had stabbed Germany in the back, the Jews were trying to run the world their way.

Miss Gaster was more than interested. She made immediate notes, and when the Cardinal became calm she thanked him for what was now a really important news story—how important it was, only her London readers know; but Under-Secretary of State Ivor Boldizsar, on whom foreign journalists relied, told me that Miss Gaster on taking her leave, and somewhat emotionally upset, could not resist repeating her name to the Cardinal, and adding, "My father, Rabbi Gaster, is the chief rabbi of London."

Under-Secretary Boldizsar also told me something I had not known before, something which sets me thinking to this very day, that the main problems of many European countries—and I now think it is the main problem in Nicaragua, El Salvador and other Central and South American countries—is the land problem. Said Boldiszar:

"Land for the landless: this is the greatest problem facing our country. We have confiscated the land of the land barons and the Church, which owned more land than any man or institution, and given enough land for a living to 600,000 landless peasants. Will you believe it, the Church in Hungary did not protest this confiscation—but Cardinal Mindszenty did. His predecessor, Cardinal Szeredi, issued about two pastoral letters a year; Mindszenty issued one every week, each attacking the government. He cannot forgive the land distribution to the penniless peasants. He also makes treasonable statements—if he were not a Cardinal we would arrest him, try him, and let a jury decide whether he should be shot or not."

While I was still collecting material for the European series for *In fact,* the pro-Mindszenty campaign in the United States flourished. Here are a few samples:

— In the *Congressional Record,* which never in history has been known to correct any one of the falsehoods that representatives and senators place in it, which are officially immune from libel suits, Thomas Gordon of Illinois stated that the Hungarian people had been denied the right of worship. (Total falsehood.)
— John E. Fogarty of Rhode Island asked Congress to make an official protest to Hungary against persecution of the Church. (A total falsehood.)
— Kenneth Keating of New York likened the "torture" of Mindszenty to that of Stepinac in Yugoslavia. (A double falsehood.)
— Lowell Thomas, America's number-one radio oracle, detailed the "drugging" and "torture" of the Cardinal, inventing "beatings" and the Cardinal's "bloody face." (Total falsehood.) Thomas repeated the fake about the Cardinal being drugged with acetdron, despite the fact that throughout Europe and in the few liberal weeklies in America this European "drug" was identified as benzedrine. The New York *Post* was the only major paper in America to give the lie to this Lowell Thomas broadcast.

Eleanor Roosevelt, who was then writing a column for the Scripps-Howard chain, and whose attention had been called to her misuse of the drugging and torture stories, wrote a second column setting the record straight, whereupon she was attacked by Cardinal Spellman; he accused the President's widow of casting "yet another stone [upon] heroic, helpless men like Cardinal Martyr Mindszenty."

Before leaving Budapest I was given a copy of the following protest, which the Anglo-American press corps there had sent to all their newspapers, and which, they assured me, not one newspaper they represented had published:

> In view of the untrue reports written and broadcast abroad about the journalists' coverage of the Mindszenty trial the undersigned foreign correspondents wish to state that we regard these charges as unfounded . . . and we categorically wish to deny:
> 1. That censorship of any kind is being exercised. . . .
> 2. That the translation . . . is inaccurate. . . .
> 3. That the only correspondents granted visas or admitted to the courtroom are Communists or Communist sympathizers.
>
> Eugen (Jeno) Szatmari, *Basler Nachrichten*
> and Hearst newspapers and news service
> Dr. Endro Marton, the Associated Press
> Michael Burn, *The Times* of London
> Peter Furst, Reuters
> Rev. Stanley Evans, *Daily Worker*, London.
> [Although the *Worker* is the Communist organ, Dr. Evans was not a Communist, according to all his colleagues.]

At the 1949 convention of the American Newspaper Publishers Association, when its head, Allan Gould, praised its Budapest representative, Dr. Marton, who "was in a position to do a first-class reporting job and did it without censorship or physical interruption," the American publishers cheered or applauded. Whether or not one of the many who for two years had printed mostly falsehoods about the Mindszenty case ever corrected those reports or apologized for them is a subject for a long master's thesis.

Editor & Publisher, known as a sort of bible of the medium, held a panel discussion on the reporting of the Mindszenty case. The principal speaker was Gideon Seymour, executive editor of the Minneapolis *Star Tribune*, who said: " . . . the newspapers went overboard on this Mindszenty case, and there was great fault in their not properly developing the Hungarian background, the long-standing struggle between the Church and State for supremacy there, in the effort to break up the large landholdings. . . . " Mr. Seymour said that many newspapers "went back after that Mindszenty coverage and tried to redress the balance somewhat." The present writer could not find one item of "redress" in scores of newspapers he examined; no corrections, no apology for publishing falsehoods, not even one newspaper saying that the problems of Church and State, church land holdings, and church serfdom were the real issues in Hungary.

Don Hollenbeck was the only journalist in America with millions of followers who did an honest job, so far as I know. On "CBS Views the Press" he reported his investigation, which traced the origin of all the falsifications, and found that the worst of them came from an obscure London weekly called *The Tablet.* These false reports were picked up in Prague, Vienna and other cities by big newspapers and news agencies. Then, when the official organ of the Vatican, *L'Osservatore Romano*, without any investigation whatever, without any credit to any credible source, repeated this Hitlerian "big lie of which something always remains," the world press no longer could be restrained. It could now quote one of the truly "great" newspapers of the world, the official paper of the Vatican, as its source. And so Hollenbeck concluded his "CBS Views the Press" broadcast of the many Mindszenty falsifications by calling them "one of the biggest fakes in U.S. press history."

On February 5, 1974, Pope Paul VI removed Mindszenty from his post as Cardinal-Primate of Hungary. But the Cardinal still refused to return to Rome. Reuters quoted him defying the Pope, saying he "did not retire."

On May 7, 1974, Mindszenty came to New York to hold a press conference to advertise, as many authors do, his book, which he called *Memoirs*, in which he repeated every falsehood exposed by the *Basler Nachrichten*, *The Times* of London, the

Associated Press and Reuters, as well as the *Editor & Publisher* panel and the head of the AP, a quarter of a century earlier.

Newsweek now repeated the drugging story. Letters to the editor asking for a correction were ignored.

The John Birch Society magazine headlined its review, "Mindszenty: The True Story of His Courage."

The New York Times went along the same road, selecting William F. Buckley, Jr., to review the book. His first paragraph spoke of "phony defense lawyers, paid and intimidated witnesses."

When the Cardinal died *Newsweek* said he had been "tortured, tried on trumped-up treason charges," and *Time* added that he had been "stripped naked, drugged and thrashed repeatedly."

Part XIII

In Our Time

Chapter 57

Tito Interviews Us

A year or two after I had quit publishing *In fact* and was back in the precarious profession of making a living writing books, I was informed that there was a considerable sum of money due me in Yugoslavia from the sale of many thousands of copies of my little volume called *1000 Americans*. That is in dollars, sent to America, there would be very few, but in Yugoslav money a small fortune. Enough to live on for a year or so.

On previous trips to Yugoslavia and in talks to Americans who had visited the Adriatic, I had heard that an ancient town, with medieval walls, and houses and public buildings right on the sea front—Dubrovnik—was one of the most beautiful spots in Europe, and moreover, totally free of the plague of tourists. Helen and I flew to Paris, took the Orient Express to Belgrade, and called on our friends, the Dedijer family. A week later we were living at the Hotel Argentina, Dubrovnik, swimming in the Adriatic, and exploring the beauties of the town. To our surprise, a local official called on us and told us that Marshal Tito had heard—from Dedijer I have no doubt—that we were intending to spend the summer in his country, and so he was offering us the official guesthouse in Dubrovnik to which he usually sent his noted visitors from abroad. We could have it all summer, but not after a certain date, which was told us, when he had promised it to Anthony Eden.

This million-dollar building was named Villa Shahrazade—their spelling, not mine. It had been built by a mad Russian who had escaped from Moscow with his money; his name was Dimdin, and for some reason not disclosed to us, he had deserted the villa (or castle, or palace) and fled to Hollywood, where he spent the rest of his life.

Everyone, of course, knew the Villa Shahrazade: it was, for one thing, bigger than any other, except for the big hotels, anywhere within the country, and when not occupied had for a while been a tourist attraction. Our guide unlocked the door and ushered us into the place. The room was, as I later found out, exactly 60 by 120 feet, the entire downstairs, and known as the ballroom. We went upstairs. Here we found two rooms, each sixty by sixty feet, a bedroom and a bathroom. The ballroom was elegantly and richly furnished with "art," fairly bad paintings and sculpture and a style of furniture I had never heard of before which they called Chinese Chippendale. The bedroom had one large bed in it and a few other pieces of furniture. The bathroom was probably unique in this world: eleven baths in all, two rows of five, and in the center a tub large enough for six or eight persons to splash around in. No one could explain the ten baths, but eventually we identified a *sitzbad,* a special footbath, a showerbath, a sparkling water bath, and a perfumed water bath.

We were told that somewhere, perhaps downstairs adjoining the ballroom, was a Russian Orthodox chapel Dimdin had built for his one-man worship, and there was probably a tiny room for servants, and perhaps a kitchen; although Helen and I went exploring occasionally, we never found them. (One thing we did find out, and that was the origin of the fifteen or eighteen-foot tub: someone was able to crawl under it, and there he found the words "Kohler of Wisconsin.")

We continued to go to the Argentina for our meals and to fight off the tourists who tried to break in by day, and the thousands of mosquitoes that plagued us by night. The millionaire's villa had no window screens. If we needed air from the Adriatic, we got it with clouds of mosquitoes. I actually counted three hundred dead bodies the morning after our first night in residence. The next day I was able to round up men to tack cloth screening over several windows, and eventually we got rid of several hundred more mosquitoes that had entered the first night.

A few weeks later Dedijer's newspaper, *Borba*, published a long article about the book I had written with my Catholic wife Helen's aid, *The Vatican Yesterday, Today, and Tomorrow*. Almost immediately Tito's emissary came to see us again and said Tito wanted us to do him a favor and come for a day or two to Zagreb; "the Marshal would like to consult you on a very confidential and urgent matter." We suspected it had something to do with *The Vatican*.

We accompanied the emissary by train to Zagreb and were installed in the leading hotel. The next morning we were taken to see Marshal Tito. He immediately recalled the two previous visits, thanked us for making the long trip, and with no other small talk began a long history of the various traitors in World War II, the high churchmen who had helped Hitler and Mussolini, interrupting himself only to ask an occasional question: Were we aware of these facts? Did the American newspapers report these facts to the public? If so, why was there such a national uproar against Yugoslavia in America, because it had found the traitor Cardinal Stepinac guilty, and instead of executing him had politely asked him to leave the country?

I told him that I knew of the Tiso case and the execution of the traitor, and likewise of the two Cardinals, Stepinac and Mindszenty, of Yugoslavia and Hungary respectively, and the reaction to their arrests for treason in the United States. The Marshal then continued to fire questions:

— How powerful is the Roman Catholic Church in the United States?

— How powerful is it in the Congress; does it dominate the House and Senate, as it does in some European countries?

— Why does the United States, a Protestant country, favor Cardinal Stepinac, who is as guilty as Tiso? "You know he is a traitor; it was the Nazi newsreels we received from the American army that helped convict him."

— Why is the whole American press against Yugoslavia, while in the Catholic countries, such as France and Italy, it's not?

— Do the American people know that Stepinac is just as guilty as Hitler of genocide? Do the American people know that Stepinac was the chief chaplain of the Nazi forces that Hitler raised here? Do the American people know that Stepinac blessed the Nazi-Ustachi troops? Do the American people know that it was Stepinac who sent all the Jews and 60,000 Croatian Orthodox Christians to Hitler's death camps?

I tried to answer all of Marshal Tito's questions but realized it would take more than a day and more than a book to explain the sensitivity of the American press to any and all religious matters—from colonial times to the present. I mentioned the anti-Irish riots as late as my own time, 1906, in Pittsburgh; and the resurgence of the Ku Klux Klan, which was both anti-Catholic and anti-Jewish. I told him the people of these two faiths, these two minorities, were very sensitive to press reports about their religions. I illustrated the situation by telling the Marshal what had happened during the Spanish War—the very time he was in Paris organizing the Yugoslav Battalion to fight for the Loyalists. I told him that all the American Cardinals except Mundelein of Chicago were for Franco, and perhaps ninety-eight percent of the clergy, whereas the Gallup and other polls showed that the Catholic majority, along with the majority of Protestants and Jews, were for the Republic. Nevertheless, the American press, with such honorable exceptions as the New York *Post,* was either intimidated into silence editorially or blackmailed by threat of boycott, into favoring the Fascists. Moreover, the powers in the Democratic Party, notably Jim Farley, Father Walsh and Cardinal Spellman, had warned President Roosevelt—as he later confessed to Upton Sinclair—that he would lose the entire Catholic vote, which they controlled, if he did not adhere to the neutrality pact (which eventually killed the Republic).

"Spellman!" exclaimed Marshal Tito suddenly; "is it true he is raising a fund to build a Cardinal Stepinac High School in honor of this Nazi collaborator, this murderer, this traitor?" I did not know the answer to this one, and do not know if such a high school exists, but I have seen the Cardinal Mindszenty High School, and know from the evidence I myself have seen and almost all the journalists in Budapest have seen, and so reported, that Mindszenty was also guilty of both treason and mass murder of Jews in Hungary.

As for the State Department, I told him the facts as I had first heard them in 1937 in Madrid from Charles Duff, a member of the British Foreign Office for many years: Duff repeated what many already knew, that British foreign policy was largely made by the permanent staff of the F.O., but he said something I did not know and it even startled Tito: that by actual count, the permanent staff of the British Foreign Office was forty-one percent Roman Catholic. Moreover, Duff contended, this group collaborated with a similar group, not a majority but a cohesive minority and just as powerful, in the U.S. State Department.

As for the press, I told Tito my own experience with Mr. David Stern, owner of the New York *Post*.

I also told Tito about "the fascist phalanx in the bull pen"— the phrase is not mine but that of members of the *New York Times* staff who were powerless against Managing Editor James who perverted the news from Spain throughout the war. I told Tito that I had talked to the owner of the most important newspaper in America, Arthur Hays Sulzberger, on my return from the war in Spain, but unfortunately he was not a newspaperman himself, and he had the idea that total honesty and fairness meant giving equal headlines or equal space to both sides: to the proved Hitlerian "Big Lies" from his correspondents on the Franco side and to the eyewitness truthful accounts from Herbert Matthews on the Republican side.

Tito shook his head sadly. But he still could not quite understand how public opinion could be manipulated in one direction when the evidence was all in the opposite. Cardinal Stepinac himself, said Tito, never tried to deny the public speeches, his newsreel appearances with the traitors and their army, his Nazi affiliations, his own handwriting on the documents he had signed. "All he would say," said Tito, "was that what he had done was done for the best interest of his Church and for Croatia, and everything in collaboration with the Ustashi was done to save the country from the 'dangers of Communism.' "

Tito concluded by saying he had tried to avoid a public trial. He knew that world public opinion would be against him if the Cardinal was found guilty of treason no matter how conclusive the evidence—and the mandatory sentence for treason was death.

I asked Tito what his proposed solution had been.

"I asked Archbishop Stepinac to leave the country—go anywhere, go to Rome," replied Tito. "But he refused. I appealed to the Pope [Pius XII] to intervene but did not get a reply from the Vatican. There was at that time a papal nuncio in Belgrade, Bishop [Joseph Patrick] Hurley [of St. Augustine, Florida], so I asked him to intervene with the Vatican and get Stepinac out of the country. Bishop Hurley was sympathetic. He took the documentation of treason and sent it to Rome. But he also got no reply. It was only then that the authorities arrested Stepinac."

On hearing that the archbishop had been arrested, Pope Pius XII elevated him to Cardinal.

Although the mandatory sentence for treason is death—I was present once at a mass trial of a dozen men charged with treason and all were found guilty and executed and two or three of them were priests—the Yugoslav court decreed that as Stepinac had not fought with guns and grenades as had the other priests on the Nazi side, he would not be sentenced to death, but to five years' imprisonment.

"I would free him today if the Pope would recall him to Rome and send a new Cardinal in his place," Tito concluded.

The talk had now lasted two hours.

Several weeks afterward the Marshal announced that instead of keeping Stepinac in prison he was sending him home to his native village. He would be a prisoner, but he could say mass, he could engage in any political activity. At the end of one year, Tito freed Stepinac.

Postscript One: On the Orient Express leaving for Paris, I spotted an old acquaintance, a member of the European corps of correspondents with whom I had worked in several countries, now the Belgrade representative of the Associated Press.

In all his journalistic life, my colleague told me, he had not experienced such a reaction as that to the Stepinac story. His editors in New York cabled him almost every day that newspapers throughout the country were complaining that their readers were actually threatening violence as well as boycotts. The papers were also threatened with the loss of advertising, and eventual bankruptcy. Not one newspaper, my colleague told me, challenged the fairness or the truth of the AP reporting—scores of editors and owners, however, demanded that the AP "go easy" on Stepinac. According to my colleague they did not want published the fact that Stepinac had been the chief chaplain of Hitler's Nazi army, had become a traitor and had been rightly found guilty and had his life spared just because he was a high churchman and not a civilian or a soldier. The AP in New York cabled to "wrap it up."

"What did *you* do?" I asked my colleague.

"I wrapped it up," he replied.

"Meaning?" I asked.

"I wrote it the way they wanted it and kept my job," he replied.

Postscript Two: Of all the world political leaders, noted and notorious, or all the prominent men I ever met, good or evil, dictators and presidents, newsmakers all of whom I had the good or bad fortune to interview and in whose countries I sometimes lived for years, the one I knew longest was Benito Mussolini, 1919 to 1925. In 1919 and 1920 we worked together on an equal basis, I thought we were friends—did he not address me as *caro collego,* "dear colleague," and sometimes call me "caro Giorgio"?

In 1924 when I finally got an official interview with him, he pretended we had never met.

Tito talked to me as a friend.

Chapter 58

~~~~~~~~

Comrade Pavlov Owes Me $5,000

O nce or twice in each decade from the 1920s to the 1960s I would send my check to the Soviet consul in New York City with a request for a visa, and once or twice each decade the consul kept my two dollars and refused even an answer. I knew I was on Stalin's blacklist. But when the Committee for a Sane Nuclear Policy (SANE) sent eighty-four of its members on a trip to Moscow I was one of them, and no one ever looked at my passport. I was free to find out what had happened in the more than forty years since I had been deported from Soviet Russia (along with the New York *World,* New York *Herald* and Philadelphia *Ledger* correspondents). I used a trick for getting into a dictatorial country now so well known to so many thousands of people that I might as well tell it in print.

Every government, not only dictatorships but democracies, keeps a blacklist of "undesirables"—although none will admit it is a blacklist and each would define the word "undesirable" differently.

Here is how anyone, desirable or not, can get into any country at all—provided it is a country which in addition to blacklisting tens of thousands still wants millions to come as tourists, spend money, help its economy. (Fascist Franco Spain one year had 34 million tourists—its population then was about 32 million—and Palma de Mallorca was said to have one hundred visitors for each man, woman and child in the island capital city.)

All you do is join a group tour, twenty to a hundred persons. Go to your tourist agency, join up, hand in your passport. The host country's consul processes them without looking at the names. Then, just before flying date, go back and tell the clerk your grandmother has just died and you have to stay over for the funeral. Your passport is given back, correctly visaed, no questions asked.

A secondary reason for going to Moscow was to collect five thousand dollars I had been informed was due me, royalties on my book *1000 Americans*. Russia respects no copyright laws, steals whatever it wants, sometimes offers to pay, sometimes not. (In the case of Theodore Dreiser, at the time he became friendly to that country its consul brought him a check for $25,000 in royalties—at least so Dreiser told me.)

My first free day in Moscow, August 1964, I got in line near the Intourist hotel for a taxi. The Russian system is to load each auto with four persons going in the same direction—and incidentally charge each not one-fourth but the full price. The moment I told the driver I wanted the office of the director of the Publishing House of Foreign Literature he cocked his head, beckoning a man on the sidewalk, who jumped into the front seat. He was so obviously a KGB agent; he got out with me and was there, waiting to jump into any auto I might find to take me back to my hotel, half an hour later.

The director, one might say the dictator of foreign literature, Vladimir Pavlov, to whom I had previously telephoned, was very friendly. I mentioned the title of the book. He replied in the best British English—he spoke many languages:

"We have looked up the record. As you know we usually

436

publish 100,000 copies of each book from a foreign country we consider worth publishing, and the royalty depends on the sales price. In your case you will receive five thousand rubles." (In Germany I could have bought rubles eight to the dollar, but the Russians, suffering from a national superiority—or perhaps inferiority—complex, have to be better in everything in the world, from Olympic Games to rate of exchange, and therefore discount the dollar to about ninety cents.)

"Of course," Director Pavlov continued, "you will have to spend the money in the U.S.S.R."

I had known that.

"I have decided to donate the money to Harpur College," I said. "On the plane here I met a fellow member of the Committee for a Sane Nuclear Policy, Professor Pitcher, who told me his school was planning a large extension of its modern foreign literature, scientific and art books."

Mr. Pavlov was delighted. He said he would be happy to meet Dr. Pitcher and would advise him whom to consult in Moscow for the best and most representative books.

"One word more, Mr. Pavlov," I said. "A friend of mine, a publisher"—it was Lyle Stuart, who had made a small fortune in sex books but wanted to branch out into general books and had begun with Upton Sinclair, Ferdinand Lundberg and one of mine—"asked me to get in touch with Aleksei Adzhubei [editor of *Izvestia*], and I hope you will help me in this matter. This publisher will pay half a million dollars in advance for the autobiography of Khrushchev. . . . "*

At the mention of the name Khrushchev something strange happened to Mr. Pavlov. He jerked in his chair as if he had been electrocuted. (I had once seen a murderer go to the electric chair in a prison.) Then he waved both hands as if repelling a swarm of hornets. He shouted something, either "No" or "Go," but he was surely pushing me out of his office—I had a sudden memory of William Jennings Bryan in 1909—and I backed out.

---

*Every foreign newspaper on sale in Moscow and every Russian book spells the name as it is pronounced—Khrushchov—with an "o." However, standard western transliteration has it Khruschev.

This was the fatal August 1964 for Khrushchev. The SANE group, which had arranged the tour months earlier, had not been promised anything, but all of us somehow understood that we would not only be welcomed because of our opposition to nuclear power, but would be granted a meeting, most likely a conference, with the dictator. How were we to know the great secret of the time, that the vast intrigue to throw Khrushchev out would reach its climax during the very days of our visit to his country?

From that time to this I have never heard a word from Mr. Pavlov, and Harpur College has never received a book.

Immediately after my misadventure I put the matter in the hands of our Intourist guide and mentor, Katrina Demyanovakaya. On September 30 I returned signed papers she had sent me and incidentally offered her the usual literary agent's ten percent. On December 9, 1964, she wrote me of her visit to Mr. Pavlov and his assistant, Mr. Kuzolev, "who now deals with your matter. . . . They promise to do everything possible. . . . Merry Christmas." On January 14, 1965, I replied from Madrid. On March 4, Katrina wrote me of new difficulties: the book was not a recently published one; therefore I would have to make out new applications. I did so. More letters were exchanged. On November 10 I wrote Katrina again asking her to tell Comrade Pavlov and his associates at the Publishing House of Foreign Literature what a shame it was that Harpur College, which already had an excellent Russian literature department, should be deprived of this gift.

No reply, from anyone, ever.

Chapter 59

〜〜〜〜〜

Spain: Perico Chicote and Ernesto Emenwhey

In 1932 Helen and I had spent our honeymoon in Spain and fell in love with the country and its people; in 1936 and 1937 we witnessed the most noble expression of heroism, human suffering and human dignity of modern times, when we came back to report the war from the Republican side.

Between 1950, when I ceased publishing my newsletter and was free to live anywhere provided I had the price, and 1979, the last year I was able to make overseas journeys, Helen and I spent at least thirteen winters in Spain. We owe thanks to President Eisenhower's insistence in 1953 that Americans had the right to travel freely in this fascist dictatorship.

In the thirty-nine years of Franco fascism about ninety-nine percent of its intelligent, cultured, creative inhabitants either fled the country, remained abroad, were exiled, or were executed by the dictator. Picasso and Casals vowed they would never return to their beloved land until fascism ended, and both died in France. Unamuno was driven out of his university and died a week later. Spain's greatest poet, Lorca, was murdered along with scores of others and thrown into a common pit outside the cemetery of Granada. Miró alone remained in Spain, but in seclusion, working secretly against the dictator. La Pasionaria and many Communist leaders were helped to Moscow, and only one of the truly important men of the four decades remained in Madrid, the apolitical Perico Chicote.

It would be safe to say that for every thousand, perhaps ten thousand book readers or bullfight aficionados who know Hemingway and Harry's Bar, and the Floridita and various American bars, and everything about Pamplona, only one may be able to identify Chicote. But it is a fact that Chicote's café is mentioned five times in the Hemingway works—in three short stories, the one play, and *For Whom the Bell Tolls;* that one famous story, "The Butterfly and the Tank," appears just as it was told by the barman, my friend Turegano y Elvira; that Chicote was known throughout Europe and South America as the most famous barman of the century; and, most important of all, that it was Perico Chicote who did more to liberate the women of Spain than any man or woman or organization in that country's history.

How notable a man was Señor Chicote in European eyes? You did not have to be a newspaperman to realize his importance if you saw the front pages of Spanish papers the day after Christmas 1977. The entire center of the paper featured drawings or photographs of two men, and the headlines read EACH THE GREATEST OF HIS CALLING, CHARLES CHAPLIN AND PERICO CHICOTE, who had both passed away the night before.

Perico Chicote had won every honor and every known prize at every meeting or international convention anywhere in the world of café owners and barmen; he had a whole room filled with silver and gold, cups, statuettes, medals and ribbons and illuminated scrolls and other objects on which could be printed or engraved or written words calling him *numero uno.* He had been elected Madrid's favorite son one year, and he was the author of five books on drinks and drinking, read throughout the Spanish-speaking world.

There was another strange fact about Chicote: although his was the most named of Hemingway's places outside Pamplona, he was the only one so honored who refused to become part of what is now known as the Hemingway industry. In Pamplona they put up a bust on a pedestal to Hemingway—he has made the town rich; the population, thanks to *The Sun Also Rises,* has grown from 40,000 to 150,000, a vast number of people living on the million-a-year tourist trade; two noted Madrid restaurants have "Hemingway corners," and one hotel mentions Number 211 as "the Hemingway suite" to obvious Americanos; the Ministry of Information and Tourism has put Hemingway's picture on folders and in booklets; and as fame there is not barometric, as it is in America, Hemingway has given writers and critics in the publishing centers, Barcelona and Madrid, steady work for years.

In one of our winters in Madrid I asked one of the Chicote nephews, who now took care of the famous café while the owner busied himself in his office adjoining the famous museum in the basement, and he took me immediately to his bachelor uncle.

"I did not know Emenwhey in the first three years he was here and wrote about my café," said the owner in reply to my first natural question. "I was away. In 1936 on my return from London with a year's supply of whiskey the war broke out in mid-July and I stopped at the border. At Santander. I stayed until 1939. My employees, God will reward them, took care of the place." In the 1940s, when he was again able to visit Spain, "Eminwhey" was already famous. "I made him my guest. He would always say with pride to the score of friends, matadors, and hangers-on who came with him almost every night, 'I do not have to pay here. But *you* must pay.' When, later, I met him at a bar in Havana, he said, 'Sr. Chicote, I've had hundreds of drinks in your place and I never paid a cent for them. I'll buy you all the drinks here for as long as you stay.' I let him buy me one drink. I am a very small drinker."

"You don't make much of Hemingway's visits to your bar?"

"No."

"This clipping says you have been host to twenty-one winners of the Nobel Prize here—is that true?"

"I now count twenty-four."

"You don't consider Hemingway *numero uno*?"

"No."

"Who is your *numero uno*?"

"Dr. Fleming."

In Spain everyone knows, everyone reveres Dr. Fleming. Sir Dr. Alexander Fleming's penicillin may have saved lives by the millions elsewhere, but to Spaniards that is not as important as the lives of the bullfighters he has saved in Spain. Those who were gored frequently died of gangrene which, the Spaniards say, is caused by the filth or manure on the horn tips. The bullfighters have put up a statue of Dr. Fleming, and the nation's capital has named a street for him. Sr. Chicote had an additional personal reason for naming Dr. Fleming the most famous man who ever took a drink at his bar.

"My father, my beloved father," he told me, "died at the age of forty-two. After two days of a bronchial infection. I said to Dr. Fleming, 'If you had discovered penicillin earlier, you would have saved my father's life.'

"He was fascinated by my museum. He spent an hour or more asking questions. Then he returned to the English section and pointed to a bottle of Scotch with a label you no longer see.

" 'That is what I drank when I was a student at Oxford,' he said.

"It was terrible stuff. Worse than your American bootleg ever was. I told him it was probably the worst alcohol ever made, and he replied, 'But I drank it at Oxford; I have a nostalgia for it.'

"I gave him the bottle. It was the first and last time a bottle once in my museum has ever been lost, or stolen or given away. Dr. Fleming was very happy. He was a child—in a way."

In addition to twenty-four Nobel laureates, Sr. Chicote was

In fact

An Antidote for Falsehood In the Daily Press

GEORGE SELDES, Editor
Victor Weingarten, Associate

57   George and Helen, at the helm of *In fact*.

59 Westbrook Pegler—Second candidate.

58 Fulton Lewis, Jr.—First candidate.

60 George Sokolsky (center)—Third candidate, with Roy Cohn (left)
and Joseph McCarthy.

61 *Above:* Public reaction to Pegler's falsehoods, libels and anti-Semitism.

62 *Left:* Martin Dies, "the most un-American of Americans" before his *In fact* induced Waterloo.

63   Secretary of the Interior Harold Ickes, the anti-cigaret, "non-conspiracy" crusader.

64   J. Edgar Hoover — Seldes's friend or enemy?

65   Don Hollenbeck of CBS,
a courageous journalist and secret
friend of *In fact.*

66   Eleanor Roosevelt, a
staunch public friend of
In fact.

67 George and Helen with Marshal Tito in Belgrade—a gracious host of the Seldes.

68 *Above:* Matyas Rakosi, the garrulous vice-premier of Hungary.

69 *Right:* The Seldes in Dubrovnik, Yugoslavia, at the time of their visit to Villa Shahrazade.

70 The café of Spain's beloved Perico Chicote, the early "liberator" of
Spanish women.

71 Dolores Ibarruri, la Pasionaria, the fiery
orator of the New Spain.

72 William Allen White, a man not afraid
of the word "truth."

73 George Seldes today in Hartland-4-Corners, Vermont.

also the host to all the notables who had visited Spain since the days of Alfonso XIII in 1931: all the artists, film stars, scientists, nobility, politicos, bullfighters. "Between this café, this museum, and my small bar in the Cortes I have had all the kings, princes, presidents, prime ministers and generals of the past thirty years," he said. "I have served both Franco and La Pasionaria."

"And of them all, the most notable . . . ?"

" . . . is Dr. Fleming."

He then took me on a tour of his Museo Universal de Bebidas (or "Drinkables"). There were 28,000 full bottles—making it the largest museum of its kind in the world. The bottles came from more countries than are now members in the United Nations, 170 by recent count. For Americans Chicote had two showpieces: a bottle of champagne autographed by President Eisenhower in 1953, the time he came to sign the treaty for American bases—and incidentally embrace Franco and thereby fasten Fascism more heavily on the Spanish people; and a small sampling of the worst alcoholic and chemical concoctions ever made by civilized man, the whiskey, gin, applejack and other frauds of the dark ages of American prohibition.

He showed me genuine bottles from the Tsar's cellars in St. Petersburg that had somehow escaped the Bolsheviks, and vodka from the present Soviet factory in Leningrad, bottles from Spanish Cuba, Republican Cuba and Castro Cuba (a brand labeled Vodka Troika, made in Havana). When President Quirino of the Philippines was there, Chicote said, he wanted to buy his section, calling it "a history of my country," and when Aristotle Onassis was making the grand tour, he said to Sr. Chicote quite seriously that he would pay any price asked—he wanted every bottle packed, and the museum reopened in Athens so it looked exactly like it had in Madrid, and millions of dollars were no object.

Among the rare items, said Sr. Chicote, was a bottle of Napoleon brandy which, unlike the millions of bottles in France bearing that label and made from 1900 "up to yesterday," was actually distilled circa 1800; and one of the original little casks carried by the first of the St. Bernard dogs in Switzerland—their training began in 1839. The oldest full containers were amphoras

with wine found in sunken Greek and Roman ships. The smallest
exhibit was a vial containing, Sr. Chicote said, "one drop of
atomic energy"—it was probably radioactive because it glowed
in the dark. The largest bottle held thirty quarts of French
cognac. Many of these prizes were exhibited in the Spanish
Pavilion at the World's Fair in New York City and added
another gold medal to Perico's vast collection.

The Museo was insured for ten million pesetas—this may
not sound impressive to Americans who then got fifty-five to the
dollar, but for Spaniards in Perico's time it was equal roughly to
233 years' pay.

Chicote's branch café in the Cortes—the Congress of House
and Senate that now actually rules Spain—is open only to members and their guests. (Unfortunately, since Sr. Chicote's death it
has deteriorated greatly. When in 1977 Spain's vice president,
my friend Sra. Victoria Armesto, took my wife and me there for
a cocktail, the new barman put sweet vermouth into a martini.)

"All important men drink," said Sr. Chicote.

"Who are the biggest drinkers in Spain?"

"In Spain? Isn't it the same everywhere? Cinema actors,
artists in general, poets—and newspapermen."

"What do you drink?"

"An old-fashioned Spaniard, I drink sherry. With my meals
red wine with soda water, *tinto con sifon.*"

"What drinks do you recommend?"

"Straight drinks. Cognac, whiskey, gin, vodka."

"Why are there no drunks in your bar—or elsewhere in
Spain?"

"Because almost all my clientele is Spanish, middle or upper
class—but no class of Spaniards gets drunk. Not even today when
it is a sign of money and power to drink Scotch instead of sherry.
But have you ever seen a Spaniard order four or five drinks in an
evening—any drinks, even sherry?"

I have never seen a Spaniard order four or five drinks, one
after another. Of the three men I have seen cleverly and quietly
escorted through the revolving door, I was told later one was an
American, one was an inmate or a should-be inmate of an insane

asylum, and the third might or might not have been a Spaniard. Sometimes five winters have passed there without my seeing one man drunk.

However, a crime perhaps worse than drunkenness was being committed at Chicote's almost every night. A great urge to mention it to the owner came to me but I resisted it.

Almost every night for several years I had seen at least one Spaniard, a *nouveau riche*, obviously not a caballero, order a large Chivas Regal or a Ballantine, the price about four dollars, and one bottle of his favorite cola, Coca or Pepsi, which he himself poured into the Scotch whiskey!!!

Chapter 60

~~~~~~~~~~~

Women's Lib:
Chicote Style

Although he had never thought about it, never realized what he had done, this is how Perico Chicote liberated the women of Spain. He did it with a simple edict: everyone, he told his staff, man and woman, will be treated equally in my café.

The time was before the Republic—in the reign of Alfonso XIII (whom Americans, incidentally, called "Tracy" because thirteen sounds just that way in Spanish). It was a time when women were still in about as total a subjugation as they had been under the eight centuries of the Moors and five centuries of kings and queens. They were household workers and the means of producing male heirs to perpetuate the name, little more. Divorce was unknown, and one might almost say love was unknown. The Islamic ruler with four wives, concubines and even black slave girls was replaced by a ruling class with only one wife to do the work and produce the heir—and a mistress, who although a female and therefore an inferior, was worthy of some affection, if not true love.

446

The harem mentality, if not the buildings, persisted in Spain until just the other day. The 1931 republic was destroyed by the Nazi-Fascist International in 1936 and in 1939 Franco ended the emancipation women had enjoyed for only a short time. Thirty-nine years of stagnation and retrogression followed. On our first meeting I asked Don Perico how he came to be the first advocate of what is now regarded as the beginning of the Spanish women's liberation movement.

"Before we had the Republic," he replied, "even the bravest women in Spain, many with titles beyond reproach, did not dare enter a café or smoke a cigaret in public, or wear a skirt that proved they had ankles—we had a saying then, 'the Queen of Spain has no legs,' because even her slippers dared not be shown. But before the overthrow of King Alfonso, when many changes began, I had already told my men there were to be no distinctions in my place between men and women—nor between white and black and brown and yellow. No one was to be barred because of color or sex; no question of profession either. Absolute equality. Absolute freedom. If anyone wanted to come to my place, buy a drink, meet his friends, he or she was welcome. Provided all obeyed one rule. . . . "

"And that was . . . ?"

"Everyone here must behave like a lady or a gentleman. (*Señora o caballero.*) This needs no explanation."

He understood my unasked question.

"Common decency. Conventional decency. You must dress, you must comport yourself correctly. Have you ever seen in the many years you have visited my café any man make overtures to a woman or any woman making overtures to a man—what you call 'pickup'?"

No, but every night I had seen women, who usually sat at the small tables or at the bar, join a man in one of the loges.

"True. A man wants the company of a woman. He may invite her but only by asking a waiter to take her a message. She may accept, she may refuse. However, my idea of equality does not include women wanting the company of a man sending him

447

an invitation. And the man must act diplomatically. It must be done with propriety."

Besides the promulgated "one general rule of decency" there is also the inwritten Chicote law that no girl at the bar may ever have any but a business relationship with anyone employed there, from the proprietor to the shoeshine man. I know almost nothing about the mores of American cafés, but in the thirty-seven countries of Europe, the Near East, and North Africa in which I worked from 1916 to 1933 I found relationships, mostly illicit, between bar owners, bartenders, waiters, porters and the women who come to the cafés regularly. But not at Chicote's.

Moreover, every barman was instructed to give every woman who ordered a drink just what she ordered. Sitting alone or in couples they usually asked for a cola or an orangeade, sometimes a sherry, and when invited, they usually asked for Scotch. And they got it. The standard amount. Not so in the cafés I have visited from Berlin to Baghdad. If all the tepid tea in various shades of brown and yellow pretending to be Scotch or rye or bourbon served to women from Paris to Cairo to Damascus could be poured into the Hollywood tank where they make sea pictures, it would probably float the Spanish Armada.

There is also a door censorship on the Gran Via. No girl from the streets ever gets by the uniformed doorman, and he is immune to bribes.

No Chicote girl ever shows up during the day.

If the Greeks had a word for it, the Chicote girls have a whole lexicon. Their version is, never on my saint's day, never on any one of the holy days, never on Christmas, never on the day of the Three Kings, never during *Semana Santa* which is Holy Week—and of course, never on Sunday. There is no hypocrisy about the gold crosses many Chicote women wear; they go to church, to confession, to mass. "They reconstitute their faith," my friend and mentor Don Vicente used to say in his bookish English, quite seriously.

In the European press millions of words have been written about the Chicote women, all of them favorable: they have been likened to geisha, to Greek hetaerae, to India's devadases, by newspaper men and poets and novelists, all of whom warn their readers that Chicote girls must never be mistaken for their conventional half-sisters of conventional continental bars. Don Perico did not foresee them as the major female element at the late cocktail hour, nor did he realize that he was the instrument of a revolutionary idea whose time had come.

During the Franco stagnation, Chicote never wavered. Generals and their wives and children, señoras and caballeros and the ladies of the newly rich came weekdays before nightfall and all Sundays and holidays; the bar girls came only at late evenings. The café lived a double life.

Nevertheless, what Chicote had done was about as revolutionary as tearing the veils from the faces of Arab women—which is far from completed—or knocking fezzes off Mohammedan heads. (In Ankara once I watched soldiers with long sticks do that to newly arrived peasants trying to enter the gates. Kemal Pasha had ordered it. Peasants who persisted went to jail—there was a rumor that Kemal actually hanged chronic offenders.) The unveiled faces, the cap instead of the fez, and a woman, countess or bar girl, smoking a cigaret at Chicote's bar, were symbols of liberation. We live by symbols.

Our last winter in Madrid my wife and I passed a public school just at morning recess. A girl of eleven or twelve was handing out cigarets to a group of friends, one each, from an American pack of twenty. All lit up. My wife tried to say something in Spanish about cigaret smoking and cancer, but they all laughed at us. This too is part of the women's liberation in Spain, which one barman started.

Chapter 61

~~~~~~~~~~~~

La Pasionaria— the New Spain

In a newspaper poll for "greatest living women" reported in the European press in 1975 there was a tie for first place between Golda Meir and Dolores Ibarruri. By the time Helen and I had returned to Spain after the disappearance of Dictator Franco and his pseudo-fascism, and the restoration of liberal democracy only technically a monarchy, death had taken La Pasionaria's rival.

Dolores Ibarruri was born in the Basque country, sent to church but given no education whatever. She somehow managed to learn to read and write and made her living as a young woman selling fish out of a basket. She became a rebel at about the age of forty when the Asturian miner she had married and his fellow miners were shot down by government troops for going on strike. Those troops, mostly bloodthirsty Moors who killed not only men, but women—for a pair of gold earrings or a ring— were commanded by Franco.

Under the Republic many Basques and Asturians helped found the PCE, or Spanish Communist Party, and although it never flourished, the flaming oratory of one of its leaders, a woman, earned her the name La Pasionaria, the Passion Flower.

In 1936, when my wife and I came to Spain for the New York *Post,* by coincidence we met La Pasionaria. We had just returned from Paris, where she had appealed for help for the Republic and coined the immortal phrase *"Mas male morir a pie que vivir en rodillas"*—"It is better to die on your feet than live on your knees." As members of the press we sat on the stage of the Barcelona theater where La Pasionaria spoke, repeated her slogan, and concluded with the words that electrified the Republic—but did not save it: *"No pasaran"*—"They shall not pass," the words that had once saved Verdun and France.

From early February to just six days before we were scheduled to leave Madrid at the end of April 1978, I tried to make an appointment, if only for a minute or two, with Dolores Ibarruri. I had a letter from Alvah Bessie, the author of *Men in Battle,* one of the great books on the Spanish war. He had been a volunteer soldier in the Lincoln Battalion of the International Brigade. My friend Edmund Gress of CBS Radio had telephoned as many as fourteen times a week repeating my request. We knew that La Pasionaria had spent months in Yugoslavia, we knew that she now had a pacemaker planted in her heart—and we also knew that well-known persons had been commissioned by famous publications to journey to Spain for an interview, and that none had succeeded.

Finally my friend Ed said one day, "Let's just taxi over to thirty-six [Calle Castillo] and walk in and ask for Señora Falcon" [La Pasionaria's secretary for some forty years].

And so we did.

"But this is the first we have ever heard of your wanting to see Señora Dolores," said Señora Falcon in good English; "she is in her office right now—please follow me."

La Pasionaria sat in a little room only two or three times the size of her desk, white-haired now but just as recognizable as forty-two years earlier; clear-eyed, an unwrinkled face, young for a woman of eighty-two, a strong face, a Basque woman's face, a smiling face . . .

First, I presented Bessie's letter, saying the writer sent his apologies for his mistakes in Spanish. La Pasionaria glanced at it and said, "Almost none." There was a moment of silence. I presented my credentials—I recalled her *No pasaran* speech of forty-two years before—I mentioned the *Post,* our being on the stage with her, and I said the *Post* was the liberal paper, but my wife and I were not Communists. Señora Falcon translated.

Señora Ibarruri replied, "I understand," and continued speaking very slowly and clearly to me, but resumed her normal quick, energetic Spanish to Ed Gress, who replied in the same manner, so that I did not understand more than a word or two here and there.

From my folder I now took the Bulletin of the Lincoln Battalion, proofsheets of four chapters on the destruction of the Spanish Republic from a book I was writing, and also the June 1977 cover story in *Time* headlined SPAIN SAYS "SI" TO DEMOCRACY—words that needed no translation.

"But everywhere," I said, "people blame everything that now goes wrong, from the guerrilla attacks in the Basque country to the pickpockets on the Gran Via of Madrid on 'your American democracy.' Everything from children smoking to the pornography now on sale in the newspaper kiosks. And of course the high cost of living. Some may want Franco back although no one ever mentions his name. But many say to me, 'This is your American democracy,' and some even predict an uprising. What does Senora think?" Señora Falcon interpreted.

"There is great unrest at present, true," replied La Pasionaria slowly so that Ed did not have to translate; "we are passing from fascism to democracy without bloodshed. I do not foresee another fascist uprising. I do not believe the streets of our cities will again run with blood.

"I do not think it is now possible for the fascists—or for rightists—to come into power again.

"The cycles of history do not present one instance of a reactionary—a rightist—a fascist government, overthrown violently or bloodlessly by a people wanting liberty, being succeeded by another reactionary or fascist government.

"There is no future for fascist reaction in Spain."

La Pasionaria spoke these last words with the voice of 1936.

The foregoing may or may not have been the most important statements she made to us; future years will prove her right or wrong. Every day books, monthly magazines, weeklies and even the old newspapers, free after thirty-nine years of a censorship and fear, inform more than thirty million people, to most of whom it is strange news, that Franco was also a murderer, that he executed either ten thousand or twenty thousand persons a year, each year of his first ten years in power—the figure depends on which British historian you read, but the minumum is always ten thousand a year, always 100,000 executed, not only men—Republicans—but also many women, and a number of teenagers, girls. Men were tortured. The Freemasons were massacred and every member's possessions confiscated. Books were burned. The press was totally corrupted. Education somehow survived. Thirty-nine years of fascist indoctrination of two generations, the manipulation of minds by fascist teachers, did not produce a new ruling class faithful to the ideology of the dictator, as it had done in other countries.

"Fascism was not Spanish," continued La Pasionaria. "But, consider another movement—which did flourish in Spain. One of the truly important events in today's history, which seems to have escaped notice, is the downfall *verticalmente* of the anarchists." To emphasize *verticalmente* she made a grand gesture with her right hand, first raised above her head, then brought down suddenly on her desk.

When the Spanish War began, Communist strength was placed at between 25,000 and 100,000—the larger figure was the party's figure; but no one disputed the fact that the anarchists had more than a million in their unions. Both Gress and I were surprised at her statement. When I mentioned a newspaper report that the anarchists might one day form a political party, and asked whether this wasn't a historical contradiction, La Pasionaria smiled.

"Haven't you found much in Spain, now as always, a contradiction, a paradox?" she asked us.

"The anarchists are no longer the great power in Catalonia," she continued. I then mentioned the headlines of the morning papers: a reported split in the Communist Party, the Catalonians for more Leninism, the Madrileños—whose technical head is Carillo, but whose real head, and heart and soul, is La Pasionaria—opting for Eurocommunism.

"Our party is not split," she said firmly; "there are ideological differences, it would be correct to say that; but there is no split. There are serious problems. There will be mistakes made. There will be ups and downs. But there is no danger now in Spain of a failure of democracy. Everyone wants it. We will keep it." The first free vote after thirty-nine years of Franco dictatorship was more than seventy percent for democracy—everyone, the royalists, the anarchists and the Communists as well as the old Republican majority voted for a democratic state.

But six days after our conversation the *International Herald-Tribune* of Paris headlined SPANISH RED PARTY DROPS "LENINIST" FROM CHARTER and further reported "a decisive break with Soviet-style Communism, dropping the word Leninist . . . and declaring themselves simply Marxist, democratic and revolutionary." In other words, Eurocummunism, or independence from Moscow, the movement begun in 1948 by Tito, when he broke with Stalin, had finally reached the last fascist country.

My "two or three minutes" with Señora had now lengthened to exactly forty-five, and although at eighty-two La Pasionaria did not appear at all fatigued, I thanked her for talking to us and that afternoon wrote Señora Falcon a note saying "the conversation today has crowned my seventy years of interviewing the leaders of our century."

"The Revolution, like Saturn, successively devours all its children," said Pierre Vergniaud, who had himself taken a part in the greatest revolution in history.

The Spanish War was not a Civil War (despite the opinions of all the historians in the world except Claude Bowers), but it is true there were elements that attempted to make it a "people's

454

revolution." They failed. When Pasionaria came back from Moscow—it was the Russians who had sheltered her, not Spain's neighbor France, which had acted so shabbily throughout the war—she was in 1975 hailed as the greatest of the war's heroes.

But in 1979 Santiago Carillo, secretary-general of the PCE, the Spanish Communist Party, now a minor member of the ruling coalition, stated that Spain needed neither a left nor a right government, and denounced the Basque separatists. Finally, he informed the Party's central committee that its figurehead president, Dolores Ibarruri, " . . . would not run in the March 1 elections because of old age and poor health." (This was reported in the *International Herald-Tribune* on January 15.) From then on the successful revolution never again mentioned its most famous child. However, as late as February 1986 in several of the European picture papers I looked at in Baker Library at Dartmouth, I found a picture of La Pasionaria among many other notables of our time, looking as young as in the days I saw her in the extreme left seats in the Cortes.

Part XIV

And in Conclusion...

Chapter 62

~~~~~~~~

Citizen Nader

Is Dolores Ibarruri the greatest living woman—one of the greatest of all time? Eventually historians free from the passions of party politics will sit (or stand) in judgment.

Chronologically, my anecdotal history of seventy years in journalism ends with a few words about a great living American who has devoted his life to one of the main purposes for which this nation was founded: he is the number-one promoter of the general welfare of the people, and his name is Ralph Nader. He is now so well known that his picture—as a knight in shining armor—has appeared on the cover of *Newsweek*; and he has even been suggested for President of the United States. But few know that for many years Attorney Nader was hated and shunned by the press—which makes its living from advertising, the three largest advertisers being automobiles, cigarets and drugs—that he was the victim of a "non-conspiracy of silence." It was thanks mainly to a public relations stupidity that Nader was able to break through the paper curtain—which is even stronger than iron.

Neither does the public know that the first congressional investigation of automobile safety began in 1956—as Nicholas Johnson of the Federal Communications Commission has pointed out. On July 16, 1956, Representative Kenneth A. Roberts of Alabama opened the session of his committee's probe with a triple-barreled statement:

— that the number of auto deaths, from 1899, when one person was killed, up to the present, was more than 1,125,000;
— that faulty design was partly to blame for many of these deaths;
— that news of congressional hearings was largely suppressed by the newspapers and magazines, which lived on advertising.

From 1956 to 1963—seven years of silence—there were intermittent technical conferences. Doctors, engineers, specialists in crash injury, said Mr. Johnson, testified "that the industry had the faculty to design cars to make it possible for the occupants to survive or to suffer injuries of lesser severity." But "the general news media gave these hearings absolutely negligible attention."

Finally, in 1965 Senator Abraham Ribicoff (Democrat from Connecticut) held hearings which Ralph Nader, already known to many as "Public Citizen," helped initiate and again the press failed the people.

A year earlier one of the *New Republic*'s editors, James Ridgeway, wrote an article, "The Corvair Tragedy," blaming faulty construction for serious accidents, and Richard Grossman, an alert publisher, saw the possibility of a book dealing with that and other makes of cars appealing to a large public. He asked Ridgeway to investigate further and produce the book, and Ridgeway suggested Attorney Nader—who was then neither a journalist nor a book writer nor a muckraker, but nevertheless a public citizen who had studied this subject. The result was Nader's *Unsafe at Any Speed*.

Books, with rare exceptions, reach only a small audience. But when General Motors hired detectives to spy on Nader day and night and Nader spotted them and reported it, the scandal became so great that the mass-circulation newspapers had to report it. America was shocked.

The non-conspiracy of silence on automobiles having been broken, in a very short time Nader became so well known and admired that, before and following Watergate, when the general press for probably the first time was on the side of the general welfare—an almost forgotten objective for which the Founding Fathers fought—he was mentioned in public speeches and in print as a possible choice for President of the United States, although no one seemed to know to which party, if any, he belonged.

In the belief that Ralph Nader, better than any other man in public life, could best confirm (or deny) my view that the American press, despite its unbroken record of serving special interests, from colonial slave-owners to dangerous automobile makers, had had a real change for the better, of which Watergate was the best but not the only illustration, I sent Mr. Nader a sort of questionnaire:

— Has the attitude of the press toward you changed?
— Did you get a square deal in reviews of your book?
— Was the story in the newspapers on General Motors' spying on you fairly reported?
— Did the media suppress you previously? When did they begin to report you fairly?
— Were you ever red-baited?
— And finally, would you agree with me that there has been a great change in the American press—for the better?

Nader telephoned me immediately. He said the newspapers had reviewed his book "quite fairly," but just as generally the newspapers omitted names of automobiles—some referred to "small or medium-sized, rear-engined American cars"—they would not mention a highly advertised name. But by the time Detroit began recalling them by the thousands and hundreds of thousands, the press began naming names.

"Before 1965," the time of the Ribicoff investigation, Nader said, "it had been impossible to warn the public about cars via their newspapers. In 1965 the dam broke. . . . "

When I interrupted to ask why and how, Nader replied:

"Because the issues had become known to many and could no longer be ignored. The public was being informed by federal court actions, by the Senate investigation, by pro-consumer publications. The press had to cover what everyone knew or suspected or was talking about. The best treatment we got was from the big city press, national newspapers like the *Washington Post*, the *Wall Street Journal*, *The New York Times*, *The Baltimore Sun*, and the big news services, the AP and UPI."

Finally, I asked: "Do you agree with me that the crusaders today generally have a fair deal, if not support, in the press, as compared with the enmity shown the muckrakers? And that the mass media generally have changed, and mostly for the better, since the days of the muckrakers? Would you say that the press now is a much better press?"

Nader said, yes, he agreed with each of my conclusions.

We talked awhile about the first great muckraker, Lincoln Steffens, whose work antedated Nader's birth, and Upton Sinclair, and without false modesty I mentioned the ten-year job that my newsweekly *In fact* had done. Shortly after this conversation I received a letter from Nader that concluded:

> You may be interested in knowing that I completed reading your books and those of Lincoln Steffens by the time I reached fourteen years of age. How stimulating and very real they were. Then in my freshman year in high school I stumbled upon a pile of back copies of *In fact* in the closet of the school library. It was the moral equivalent of finding a lost treasure. How the printed word radiates into the future!

(If Mr. Nader is ever elected President of the United States he will be the second known to me to have been an *In fact* reader.)

Chapter 63

I Was There

From the day I reached my ninetieth birthday, the American press, which had for almost fifty years maintained a "non-conspiracy" of silence about me and my work, suddenly seemed to forgive and forget, and again treated me as a living human being.

Many leading newspapers, including those with regular book-review departments who had never acknowledged the fifteen books—most of which criticized the press—I had published in those decades or my newsletter which devoted 520 issues over ten years to printing news generally suppressed—the tobacco-cancer story for example—now began pressing me for interviews.

I cannot explain this change of heart except to say: if you can make it to the magical age of ninety, all your sins are forgiven.

Meanwhile, one by one, my book publishers had dropped me: Bobbs-Merrill, Little Brown, Harper & Row. At seventy, I could not find anyone to publish *The Great Quotations,* until my doctor, Milton Kissin, happened to mention this fact to another of his patients, the noted music writer Irving Caesar. Caesar immediately offered to risk $10,000 on the venture. Lyle Stuart, who previously had published sex books, agreed to take it. Although in time sales eclipsed one million copies, I do not recall ever seeing the book reviewed. Later, Stuart published *Never Tire of Protesting* (1968) and *Even the Gods Can't Change History* (1976) and again, the press was silent.

The big, powerful, book-selling commercial press. In contrast to its silence, I attracted notice in *The Churchmen,* an excellent monthly magazine published by the Episcopalian bishops. In the *Columbia Journalism Review,* Professor Curtis Mac-Dougall of Northwestern acknowledged me as "the first professional iconoclast to specialize in analysis of the press," and Sidney Blumenthal of *The Nation* called me one of the founders of press criticism. But it remained for a professor at the University of Paris, Claude-Jean Bertrand, to declare that my newsweekly *In fact* was the first regular publication in this country's history devoted to press criticism. Two years later, he wrote that "*In fact* was the first regular publication in the world devoted to press criticism."

Of course, there were a number of small-town but nevertheless great little newspapers such as the *Gazette & Daily* of York, Pennsylvania, and the *Capital-Times* of Salem, Oregon, which had kind words to say about my efforts. And one big and powerful magazine, *Time,* in its summary of one of the greatest scandals in American history, which resulted in an American president having to resign rather than face criminal charges in a court of law, had this to say:

> There were conflicting pressures. Restless activists reviving the charges of the old George Seldes–A. J. Liebling school, insisted that the press was far too cozy with the nation's political, industrial, and cultural leadership—even as major news organizations were accused of being too sympathetic to radicals.

When I was a mere eighty-three, Derek Shearer wrote two articles about me, one for *Ramparts,* a magazine now unfortunately defunct, and the other for *Parade,* the Sunday supplement magazine of at least a hundred major newspapers, including the *Washington Post* and *Boston Globe,* and with an estimated circulation of 50,000,000. On May 3, 1973 Colman McCarthy devoted his column in the *Washington Post* to a review of many of my books under the heading "Seeking a Free Press." In March 1973, Nat Hentoff began the first of a series of articles in *The Village Voice,* the first headlined "The Father of Some of Us All," and the last, "The Press as Carcinogen" in which he forthrightly attacks the tobacco-cancer industry. His first paragraph says:

> The first documented report in a general publication on the link between tobacco and cancer appeared in the December 14, 1942 issue of George Seldes's *In fact.*

Naturally enough, the first "At 90" articles were written by persons friendly to my efforts. For example, *Journalism History* ran a special double issue in Autumn/Winter 1980:

SELDES AT 90; THEY DON'T GIVE PULITZERS FOR THAT KIND OF CRITICISM

Followed by:

SELDES AT 91

in the March, 1982 issue of *Newsletter,* published by Sigma Delta Chi, the Society of Professional Journalists;

VERMONTER GEORGE SELDES REMEMBERS

by Lee Huntington, book reviewer for the *Rutland Herald,* Vermont's leading newspaper; and again:

MUCKRAKER HONORED AT 91

by Colman McCarthy in the *Washington Post,* April 8, 1982; and once again:

SELDES REMEMBERS

by Dianne Kearns, in the first issue of a new magazine, *In-Roads,* 1982.

This trickle continued in 1983, the most notable article being that of William Cockerham, New England correspondent of the *Hartford Courant* which was syndicated by the paper's owner, the *Los Angeles Times,* throughout the United States.

At age 94 came the deluge.

On May 3, 1985 *U.S.A. Today* began its article with the words "The 94-year-old pioneer . . ." and on the 14th Helen Dudar in *The Wall Street Journal* wrote " 'Living longer,' George Seldes muses, 'is the best revenge.' "

On June 12 Elizabeth Mehren's item in the *Los Angeles Times* was headed

GEORGE SELDES AT 94: A LIVING
PANORAMA OF WORLD HISTORY

A Forbidden Word: "Miracle"

*A*nd then occurred one of several things my first city editor warned me no longer happened (I must never use the word "miracle" because the age of miracles was long past). After a silence of exactly fifty-two years, the non-conspiracy was broken in 1984, by an excellent notice in *The New York Times* headlined THE GREAT THOUGHTS WILL APPEAR IN APRIL, quoting me as saying it was "the work of a lifetime, to be read for a lifetime," (a nice phrase invented by a clever copywriter at Ballantine Books), and mentioning previous books and *In fact,* "a newsletter of press criticism."

A few days after the publication of *The Great Thoughts,* a person with whom I had exchanged letters for years but never met, devoted the last quarter of the daily column she wrote to a letter addressed to her "Dear Readers." She urged them to go to the bookshop and buy not one but several copies of *The Great Thoughts*. [It is] "not only a great gift that will last a lifetime; it's a fine addition to your own library."

This columnist, probably the number-one columnist in journalistic history, is Abigail van Buren, known everywhere as Dear Abby. Read by 70,000,000 people every day in more than a thousand newspapers, she is, I believe, one of the most influential women in our world.

On May 26, while Dear Abby's readers were besieging the bookshops, an item appeared in *The New York Times,* with the headline: GEORGE SELDES: AUTHOR AND THOUGHT COLLECTOR, signed by the noted literary critic Herbert Mitgang. This review certainly sent out a new wave of not only *Times* readers but readers of many notable dailies throughout the country to whom the *Times* syndicates. Dennis Jensen put the syndicated Mitgang review on the front page of the *Rutland Herald,* and shortly afterward the local *Valley News,* one of the best small-town newspapers in the United States, listed the book among the ten best sellers at the Dartmouth College bookshop in Hanover, New Hampshire.

In 1985, when Democratic Senator Patrick Leahy was planning to run for reelection, he asked Dear Abby if she would consider coming to Vermont to make stump speeches in his favor. To his surprise she replied that Vermont was one of the only two states of the fifty she had never visited: yes, she would come, but on one condition, and that was that during the campaign she would have one day free to visit the only friend she had in the state, and she mentioned my name. (When later she told me this, I was very happy to have her call me friend.)

When she had made her last speech for Leahy in mid-Vermont to her usual vast crowd, Dear Abby came to my farmhouse without losing her way, thanks to Editor Jensen of the *Rutland Herald.* I was surprised by the youthfulness and the beauty of my visitor, and although I do not remember in the past seventy-five years using these old platitudes, I could not help telling her she looked at least twenty-five or thirty years younger than the age she named.

During the forenoon of the visit, several neighbors dropped in—Edna Belisle, who a few years earlier with the help of Dr. Hermann had saved my life, and to whom this book is dedicated; then a fellow writer, Mrs. Longin Ambros, who uses her maiden name Melissa Mather—"Math pronounced as in mathematics"—a direct descendant not of Increase or Cotton Mather but of the third brother, John; and finally Audrey Wolpert who operates a small inn. When noontime came and Dear Abby and I were arguing as to who should take whom to lunch, Melissa spoke up.

She said to Dear Abby: "Have you ever eaten a fresh egg in your life?"

Dear Abby made the expected reply: "Every day almost—unless my housekeeper somehow manages to cheat."

"Here in Vermont," Melissa then said, "we do not consider an egg fresh unless it was laid during the night or early this morning.

"I have a great idea: We harvested twenty eggs today; if you are willing to try a country lunch, come to my house: we can have a twenty-egg omelet with bacon or sausage and whatever else my daughter, who is a cook, can rustle up."

Dear Abby was delighted. On our arrival a little while later, there was not only a splendid steaming egg dish, but biscuits right out of the oven, and for dessert, baked apples—picked in Ambross orchard that morning.

"I shall never forget Vermont and the taste of a fresh egg," said Dear Abby when the time came for farewells. Of course, I will never forget her visit!

When Pat Leahy thanked all his helpers for his overwhelming Democratic victory in what is generally alleged to be a rockbound Republican state, he disclosed that he had had no fewer than five thousand volunteer helpers.

Questions, Questions

From the day Warren Beatty resurrected me to appear as a "witness" in his film *Reds,* the telephone in my farmhouse rang at least once a week with interviewers. When they somehow found their way, I told them a few of the stories of the preceding chapters, and at the end almost without exception the question was: "How do you remember everything, all the details, of what happened way back in 1910?" And I had to tell them.

From almost the very first day of my journalistic career, when City Editor Houston H. Eagle let me into the editorial room of the *Pittsburgh Leader* in 1909 (well before the Bryan encounter which got me my first salary), he lectured me on his favorite subject: "Train Your Memory."

"You don't realize," he said, "that the moment you put your hand into your jacket and draw out a pad of paper and a pencil from another pocket, you have ruined the interview. The man freezes. The human interest is gone. The man realizes that what he is saying will appear in print and he is scared. But if you have trained your memory, meet him, and talk to him man-to-man, he is a real human being. And you'll probably have a good human-interest story to tell . . . "

"But," I interrupted, "how do you 'train' a memory?"

"Well," replied Mr. Eagle, "take today for instance. When you get home this afternoon, write down as you remember it every word I said and the way I said it. Did I smile? Or did I laugh? Anything. You won't have much success today. But do it again tomorrow—encounters with anyone, everyone, the policeman who made the arrest, the prisoner if they'll let you talk to him, what Magistrate Kirby said, how he said it, or even what the old-timers here tell you every day. I assure you that if you have any brains at all, you will eventually notice that you have trained your memory, and that pad and paper are a thing of the past." (All of this advice came back to me that memorable day in 1924 when I interviewed my former pal, now the Duce Mussolini. The moment my interpreter Alberto Dalgas and I left the

Pallazzo Venezia we "reconstructed" the interview, from the military order "Avanti" when we knocked on the door, to the moment Mussolini called us back so he could give me an autographed photo of himself and his lion cubs.)

Invariably, journalists ask me: "who was the greatest man you ever met in your life?" and invariably I answer, "For good or evil, the man who had the greatest impact on the twentieth century was the Russian leader Lenin. He, and Trotsky, and a few others, changed the course of history of our time . . . " "Who was the greatest foreign writer you ever met?" The answer obviously is Gorki, but I was a little boy then, so it doesn't count. I always answer:

"I have known the three greatest writers of my time, two of them intimately, and one was a great friend for many years. Sinclair Lewis, the first American ever to win the Nobel Prize for Literature, was the closest friend, close enough to buy Helen and me the first house we owned in Vermont (1933). And although I cannot say that Hemingway was a friend, I did know him in Paris from 1922 on, when we were both listed as editors of *Ken* in New York, and the year and a half in Madrid during the Spanish War, 1936–37, when we stayed in the same hotel, faced death by shellfire daily, and also starvation. But the myth he created about being rejected by my brother Gilbert, editor of *The Dial* from 1920 to 1924, somehow turned him against me. So I must list him as a long-time acquaintance but never a friend. As for Dreiser, I knew him only in the 1930s and 1940s, well enough for him to contribute free to my weekly, *In fact*. It was he who proposed that he and I start a "Kept Press Week" to coincide with the Free Press Week which was then being celebrated annually, along with American Cheese Week and the like. Dreiser certainly should have been the first American to get the Nobel Prize, as Sinclair Lewis first said in his acceptance speech, and as he confirmed year after year when Helen and I visited him in Vermont, by showing us copies of the annual letters he sent to the Nobel Prize committee nominating his great rival.

I am asked frequently how many presidents I had known,

and who was the greatest. But what do they mean by "known" and "greatest"? I was with Woodrow Wilson during the making of the Versailles Treaty, and on that famous three-day trip to London to meet King George, and once I met his naval attaché and the only thing about him that impressed me was that his name was Roosevelt—Franklin Roosevelt. My answer usually was Woodrow Wilson. But what had impressed me about Woodrow Wilson? His statesmanship? His scholarship? No. His effort to talk "down" to the newspapermen that day crossing the English Channel. It was so obvious, so naïve. But it was not good manners to comment on that during his lifetime.

I also try to tell one and all how impressed I was with Calvin Coolidge when he asked Colonel McCormick to send me to Washington so he could question me about Soviet Russia. But my lone effort to debunk the myth of not only "Silent Cal" but Coolidge the Vermont hick remained intact until only the other day when an organization in his hometown, Plymouth, finally undertook a campaign which restored a leading citizen to a leading place in our history.

Perhaps the most important of all questions are those about which journalistic events of my time I consider the greatest, in a historic sense. The answer is easy. The premature disclosure and publication of the Versailles Treaty—for which, incidentally the wrong newspaperman got the credit—a matter about which I am still trying at this late date and without much success to set the historic record straight. (Spearman Lewis of the *Chicago Tribune* Paris edition, got the treaty; Frazier Hunt merely carried it into the United States. But Hunt wrote an introduction and *The New York Times* published every word of the treaty, four solid pages of it—and the rest is history.)

Most frequently, towards the conclusion of every interview there are one or more of the following questions:

— Why did you write that Lindbergh was not the first man to fly across the Atlantic in a heavier-than-air machine?
— Why did you claim that the American press supported the wrong side in the Spanish war?

471

— Why did you report that Franco's airplanes and not the
Spanish Republicans destroyed the holy city of Guernica?
— Why do you always say that Lady Astor was not the
first woman ever elected to Parliament?
— Why did you write that Pershing did not storm and
capture the town of Saint-Mihiel?

And many similar, if less important, questions.

To most of them I have a very short answer: "Because I
was there." (In fact at one time I considered writing and publishing a book entitled "I Was There"—and it is still a good
title.)

I certainly was there, in Saint-Mihiel, a good two hours
before General Pershing ever saw the town. I certainly was with
Lady Astor throughout her campaign for a Parliament seat, and
I was there in her house in Plymouth celebrating her victory.
Although I was not in Dublin in 1916 when the Countess
Markievicz (née Gore-Booth) was elected to the House of Commons by the Sinn Fein Party, I certainly interviewed her some
time later, and I certainly spent many months of 1919 in Ireland.
(The historians who want to be accurate say that Lady Astor was
the second elected, the first to sit.) I certainly was in Spain for a
year and a half of the war—and my first contention is that every
history book which refers to that time as "The Spanish Civil
War" is wrong: the Madrid garrison and its generals remained
true to the Republic; the traitor General Franco, with an army
consisting mostly of Italian infantry and the entire Nazi air force,
was on Franco's side. And nobody seems to remember that it was
two Englishmen named Alcock and Brown who first flew the
Atlantic. It is true that Alcock and Brown were two men and
that Lindbergh was the first to fly the Atlantic solo. But I will
continue to hail Alcock and Brown: they flew in 1919, in a
World War I "crate," sometimes known as a "flyin coffin,"
whereas seven years later Lindbergh flew the finest, safest, best
airplane ever built up to that time. (Can it possibly be that
Americans still hold a grudge against the English whose fore-
fathers taxed tea?)

Almost always there are questions about my favorite, and for years my only, subject: the press. And of the scores of interviewers the one I will never forget is Bill Moyers'.

We discussed the sacred cows of the press, past and present; the disappearance of the great lords of the press, Hearst, McCormick, Roy Howard, Frank Gannett, Sr., and others less well known but once formidable and each one, almost without exception, a great corrupting influence in American journalism. And when we came to the new critics—or, shall I say, the new attackers of the press of the present day—and I stated my views, Moyers suddenly straightened up and pointing a finger at me said something like: "You're not *defending* the American press now, are you; that's what it sounds like to me."

I replied: "When I read the publications and listen to the statements of persons ranging from the 'acting' President of the United States to actually crooked journalists and editors and many who are bringing libel suits—aimed not so much at getting money as trying to intimidate the press—then I want to be counted in the front rank of the defenders of the American press of the present day."

In answer to further questions, I told Bill Moyers that although I was not suggesting that journalistic Utopia had arrived—I do not think it ever will—there can be no comparison between the press of my earliest years, the famous "Muckraking Age," 1900 to 1914, the press of my middle age, and the press of today.

I then showed Moyers the 1937 report of the American Civil Liberties Union which, under the headline "Chief Offenders" (Against Civil Liberties in the Past Year) listed: The American Legion, the Catholic Church, chambers of commerce, the DAR, the Klan, and Nazi agencies. In those dark journalist days, just about fifty years ago, almost every element mentioned by the ACLU was still a powerful influence on the nation's press, or at least its regional press. As for chambers of commerce, they represent big business, and big advertising, and their influence I do not think can ever be broken. However, I do not see the hidden hand of the National Association of Manufacturers today as it existed, out in the open, during the lifetime of *In fact*.

Moyers then asked: "Are you telling me that there are no more sacred cows today?"

"Of course there are," I replied, "and probably always will be. Come to think of it, one I never mentioned, the press itself, is probably the sacred cow that will outlive all others. Let me give you an example of how bad it was in the old days. When Ambassador Dodd gave me the story of the Hearst deal with Hitler, by which Hitler practically bought the editorial policy of the Hearst's nineteen large city newspapers, for $400,000 a year and got a signed Hearst editorial immediately favoring Naziism, praising Hitler for restoring the integrity of the German people, and within a few weeks publishing full-page articles in the Sunday magazines of all Hearst papers signed by Goering and favoring a great airforce for Nazi Germany, not one big city daily newspaper, not even Hearst's bitterest rivals, printed a word about the matter. Our ambassador to Germany told me later that not one newspaper so much as telephoned him to confirm or deny the *Infact* story. Today the Hearst family can be proud of what they have made of their inheritance—and, incidentally the *Chicago Tribune* is today frequently listed on the honor roll of ten best papers in the country."

As for the Catholic Church, I told Moyers I would not point it out today; I would say that as a general rule all churches are sacred cows. No newspaper has ever and probably never will criticize any church, and if a priest, preacher, or rabbi is ever arrested for the violation of any law—will not find an account of it in your daily paper. The other sacred cows mentioned by the ACLU seem to have vanished. Department stores of course are powerful local influences, and the tobacco interests, with their billions of dollars in advertising are still influential, although in the past year it seems that they too have realized that although an end to smoking is inevitable, the American public at long last has recognized its danger and is quitting by the millions. "It is true," I told Moyers, "that when the annual Smokeout Day is celebrated, a great liberal honest newspaper such as our local *Valley News* (serves New Hampshire, notably Hanover with Dartmouth College, and Woodstock, Vermont) will run a six-

column headline across the front page saying 59 MILLION
AMERICANS OBSERVE SMOKEOUT DAY, whereas the
great New York papers may bury a little story inside under a
one-column head." Since my meeting with Bill Moyers I am
happy to report that the olympian *New York Times* has in the
past year published many big-news and feature stories all directly
aimed at ending this cause of cancer, emphysema, and heart
failure. The day may come when not only the daily papers but
the magazines, notably the women's magazine who are the worst
offenders, voluntarily omit all tobacco advertising. I hope my
readers will live to see that day.

News and Truth

Although the foregoing pages are devoted to anecdotes of personal history, they are only too obviously journalistic; the questions of freedom of the press, the making of public opinion, the
falsification of news, and—if one may defy doubting Pilate and
use the forbidden five-letter word "truth"—truth in the news,
are asked in numerous preceding chapters.

One answer, the answer I agree with and believe in, was
given me in the late 1930s, about the time of the general forgery
of the history of the Spanish War, and before the founding of *In
fact,* by one of the giants of American journalism, William Allen
White—owner, editor and publisher of the *Emporia Gazette,* a
man liberal enough to welcome rather than fight the American
Newspaper Guild, and conservative enough to be known as "Mr.
Republican"—he is, although no one has documented it, credited with proposing and making Herbert Hoover President of
the United States.

It was my good fortune to meet Mr. White three times, and
each meeting began and ended with a discussion of the status of
the American press. We spent hours, whole afternoons, and one
long pre-dinner, dinner and post-dinner evening arguing the
subject. Mr. White had never backed away from all his previous
criticisms, his most notable being his powerful address to the
Wharton Assembly of the University of Pennsylvania in May

1938, shortly before our last meeting. The entire press had either suppressed all mention of this criticism or buried a paragraph under a short story relating to something said or done after the lecture. Only the liberal weekly, *The Nation*, published the news, which included these damning paragraphs:

> The owners of newspaper investments, whether they are bankers, stockholders of a corporation, or individuals, feel a rather keen sense of financial responsibility. . . . The sense of property goes thrilling down the line. It produces a slant and a bias. . . .
>
> These advertising agencies undertake to protect their clients from what the clients and agents may regard as real dangers from inimical social, political or industrial influences. . . . There is grave danger that . . . this capacity for organized newspaper opinion by the political advisers of national advertisers may constitute a major threat to a free press.
>
> But I suppose in the end newspapers cannot be free, absolutely free in the highest and best sense, until the whole social and economic structure of American life is open to the free interplay of democratic processes.

Was this the voice of the Middle West or the voice of Eugene V. Debs? I did not ask Mr. White this question. I did ask him about the power of the advertising agencies in the future, and it was he, not I, who made the suggestion that these powerful agencies, for example the Big Four, were actually heading toward a fascist ideology. The older reader may remember that two of the three leading advertising–public relations men of the time, Ivy Lee and Bruce Barton, were either openly committed to fascism or dedicated to reaction in general. (The third, Edward L. Bernays, was a confirmed liberal.)

What, then, would Mr. White say to the Newspaper Guildsmen, to all reporters, journalists and their editors? Mr. White went back to Abraham Lincoln: the country was safe when the people knew the facts, "the real facts." White's exact words were: "the facts, fairly and honestly presented. . . . " To my obvious interruption he declared that every man and every woman who writes the news knows when he or she is slanting it, or cutting it on the bias or injecting propaganda—in short, when he is manipulating and corrupting the news. "And if he doesn't, he isn't a newspaperman and ought to be fired from the profession. And if the editor cannot detect unfair and dishonest news, he too is not much of a newspaperman and should also be driven away." As his final word, Mr. White said: "The facts, fairly and honestly presented," and I added, more in the nature of a question than a statement, the words: "and truth will take care of itself?"

White leaped at these words. "That's it" he said, "that is our formula: "The facts fairly and honestly presented; truth will take care of itself."

I have thought of these words for more than forty years. I know of no better rule for all the newspapers of the world. Of course, Mr. White could have made this a conditional statement, saying, "If ever the facts are presented fairly and honestly, truth will take care of itself." Mr. White was not afraid of the "controversial" word "truth."

Index

~~~~~